SCIENCE FRAMEWORK

*for California Public Schools
Kindergarten Through Grade Twelve*

Developed by the

Science Curricu
and Criteria Co
under the direct
Curriculum Dev
Supplemental M
Commission

Adopted by the

California State

Publishing Information

The *Science Framework for California Public Schools* was adopted by the California State Board of Education on November 9, 1989, and the members of the Board at that time were: Francis Laufenberg, President; Joseph D. Carrabino, Vice-President; Agnes Chan; Lee Manolakas; Marion McDowell; Paras Mehta; Kenneth L. Peters; David T. Romero; and Joseph Stein. The framework was developed by the Science Curriculum Framework and Criteria Committee and recommended to the State Board for adoption by the Curriculum Development and Supplemental Materials Commission. (See pages ix and x for the membership of the full committee and the names of the principal writers and others who made significant contributions to the document.)

The *Science Framework* was edited for publication by Marilyn Butts and Stephanie Prescott, working in cooperation with Bill Andrews and Thomas P. Sachse of the Mathematics, Science, and Environmental Education Unit. The document was prepared for photo-offset production by the staff of the Department of Education's Bureau of Publications, under the direction of Theodore R. Smith, Editor in Chief. Cheryl Shawver McDonald designed and prepared the layout for the framework, and Steve Yee prepared the cover, using a photo provided by the National Aeronautics and Space Administration (NASA). The typesetting was done by Merribeth Carlson, Jeannette Huff, and Carey Johnson. The framework was published by the California Department of Education, 721 Capitol Mall, Sacramento, California (mailing address: P.O. Box 944272, Sacramento, CA 94244-2720). It was printed by the Office of State Printing and distributed under the provisions of *Government Code* Section 11096 and the Library Distribution Act, which means that it is available through the public libraries in California.

Ordering Information

Copies of the *Science Framework* are available for $6.50 per copy, plus sales tax for California residents, from the Bureau of Publications, Sales Unit, California Department of Education, P.O. Box 271, Sacramento, CA 95802-0271 (phone: 916-445-1260). A partial list of other publications that are available from the Department of Education appears at the end of this document.

Cover Photo

The photo used for the cover was provided by courtesy of NASA. It was photographed through the aft flight deck of a space shuttle and shows astronauts David C. Leestma (left) and Kathryn D. Sullivan prepare for extravehicular activity (EVA), the first such feat for an American woman.

ISBN 0-8011-0870-5

Contents

List of Figures

List of Tables

State Board's Message

THE 1990 *Science Framework* deals with the convictions of modern science. More than any previous framework, this document addresses the science enterprise and the effects of this powerful force on our daily lives. Much has been written about the new "State Board of Education Policy on the Teaching of Natural Sciences." This new policy was drafted and approved by the State Board of Education because our conviction that all science should be taught nondogmatically needed clarification and amplification. As the State Board of Education, we needed to go on record in support of modern science. We wanted to ensure that the ideas of science are made clear to students and that they begin to learn and appreciate the distinctions between fact and theory, between belief and dogma. Students in today's culture must routinely be reminded that skepticism and understanding are characteristics of a scientifically literate mind.

There is much in this *Science Framework* for the State Board of Education to endorse. Beyond the Board's resolve to support modern science is the predisposition toward major reforms that can improve science education significantly. We look forward to improvements in the way science is taught and learned. Thematic teaching, coupled with active learning, is the best way to provide students with the science education they will need as voters, consumers, and parents in the future. As the State Board of Education, we join with science teachers, science specialists, and the educational community in support of science education in the 1990s that provides a lifetime of learning and living in the year 2000 and beyond.

California State Board of Education

FRANCIS LAUFENBERG, PRESIDENT

JOSEPH D. CARRABINO, VICE-PRESIDENT

AGNES CHAN

LEE MANOLAKAS

MARION MCDOWELL

PARAS MEHTA

KENNETH L. PETERS

DAVID T. ROMERO

JOSEPH STEIN

Foreword

THIS *Science Framework* calls for a new dynamic in science learning. We want our students to be actively engaged in learning about the natural and technological world in which they live. We want our students to grapple with the ideas of science as they learn the inner workings of the counterintuitive universe. We want students to enjoy learning science and to develop an interest in and responsibility for protecting the environment. The expectation that students be active learners is favored throughout the curriculum, but nowhere is it more demonstrable than in applying the five senses to the learning of science.

By active learning we mean instructional activities where students take charge of learning the major ideas in science. There are many ways in which students can be active learners. In science classes we typically think of hands-on laboratory experiences, but there are many other forms of active learning, including active reading, listening, discourse, and using new learning technologies. The important common denominator for active learning is that students regularly make new associations between new ideas and their previous conceptions of how the world works.

We are learning more each year about how students develop conceptual understanding in science. So far, we have learned that teachers must be cognizant of the conceptions students hold about how things work. And we know that students must create meaning for themselves, which means we need to feature, rather than sterilize, the context in which science is presented. We need to move beyond a simplistic dichotomy that emphasizes just content or process. Instead, we need to merge the two in ways that students see the meaning and utility of the scientific issues and ideas.

Just as we want students to be active learners, we also want an active response to the challenges posed in how science education is organized. Testing and accountability mechanisms must move toward more authentic assessment. Instructional materials must exploit electronic technologies and refined pedagogy. The high school program must be reorganized to compete with science education on an international scale. The middle school science program must reflect the unique needs of students as they move through adolescence. The elementary school program must be a well-organized effort in which teachers collaborate to offer a sound science experience at each grade level. Overall, we need to fashion science education to present students with the lively, engaging stories that science reveals.

This framework is designed to help science educators at all levels understand and appreciate the needed reforms before us. Accordingly, this is a complex and challenging manuscript. The reader is directed to the introductory materials, which emphasize the appropriate sections for each audience and purpose. I look forward to a time when every student is involved in learning science every year. California is technologically advanced because of the ways we use science. We can perform no better service than helping all students share in the science-rich heritage that defines California.

Bill Honig

State Superintendent of Public Instruction

vii

Preface

THIS new *Science Framework* arrives at a time when educators throughout California and indeed the United States are grasping for a way to help all students achieve scientific literacy. Two previous frameworks, issued in 1978 and 1984, attempted to address the definition and development of scientific literacy. Surely, those frameworks—and the experiences learned in their implementation—have had an important impact on the directions of the science reforms for the 1990s. There will likely be one additional framework before the close of the millennium, but for the students in the class of 2000, this framework represents the best chance to make the necessary improvements systemwide. Therefore, the ideas and strategies contained in this document are especially important for addressing the crisis in science education. We urge readers of this document to reflect on how the efforts made by each student, teacher, school, and school district can contribute to reforming science education in California and in the nation.

This framework is about connections. As James Burke writes, "This interdependence is typical of almost every aspect of life in the modern world. We live surrounded by objects and systems that we take for granted, but which profoundly affect the way we behave, think, work, play, and, in general, conduct our lives and those of our children."[1] The framework embodies this sense of connections: Each section draws on and contributes to those that precede and follow it.

The framework opens with a discussion of the nature of science and the need for science educators to model the attributes of scientific investigation, including objectivity, testability, and consistency. The framework also calls for the thematic presentation of science concepts so that students appreciate the connections across science disciplines and learn how science relates to other subjects.

Three chapters address the content of science. The repeated use of "sidebars" helps readers appreciate the connections among the three branches of science. Part III of the framework demonstrates how science education might be implemented in the 1990s. There are specific recommendations for the teaching of science and the restructuring of science education at the elementary, middle, and high school levels. There are also suggestions for attracting into science classes students who historically have been underrepresented in those classes. Finally, the framework closes with ideas on how other facets of the system, including staff development, assessment, and, especially, instructional materials, need to be changed to help all students achieve scientific literacy.

Ultimately, the implementation of the ideas in this framework rests with California's classroom teachers. To the extent that they make these connections manifest for their students, teachers will be modeling the spirit and practice of science in their classrooms. As we reach for scientific literacy by the year 2000, we salute California's science teachers in their quest to make science basic for all students.

JAMES R. SMITH
Deputy Superintendent
Curriculum and Instructional
Leadership Branch

FRANCIE ALEXANDER
Associate Superintendent
and Director
Curriculum, Instruction,
and Assessment Division

WALTER DENHAM
Administrator
Office of Mathematics,
Science, Health, Nutrition,
and Physical Education

THOMAS P. SACHSE
Administrator
Mathematics, Science, and
Environmental Education Unit

---

[1]James Burke, *Connections.* Boston: Little, Brown & Co., 1980.

Acknowledgments

Contributing Writers

The following individuals made significant contributions in the writing of the chapters or sections noted for each:

Kathryn E. DiRanna, Executive Director, California Science Implementation Network, University of California, Irvine (Implementation)

Peter Giddings, Meteorologist, KGO-Television, San Francisco (Meteorology)

Scott Hays, Teacher and Curriculum Coordinator, Coffee Creek Elementary School District (Physical Sciences Implementation)

Arie R. Korporaal, Science Consultant, Office of the Los Angeles County Superintendent of Schools (Science Processes, Teaching All Students)

Lawrence S. Lerner, Professor of Physics and Astronomy, California State University, Long Beach (Heat, Electricity and Magnetism, Light, Sound; Earth Sciences; The Nature of Science)

Larry Lowery, Professor of Education, University of California, Berkeley (Science Processes)

George E. Miller, Senior Lecturer in Chemistry, University of California, Irvine (Physical Sciences, Secondary School Science)

Kevin Padian, Associate Professor of Integrative Biology and Curator, Museum of Paleontology, University of California, Berkeley (The Nature of Science, Life Sciences, Earth Sciences, Instructional Materials Criteria)

Wendell Potter, Associate Professor of Physics, University of California, Davis (Physical Sciences)

Science Curriculum Framework and Criteria Committee

Danielle A. Andrews, Teacher and Elementary Science Specialist, Vacaville Unified School District

Kathryn E. DiRanna, Executive Director, California Science Implementation Network, University of California, Irvine

Thomas C. Edholm, Science Teacher, Fresno Unified School District

Gary E. Estep, Science Teacher and Department Chair, Chico Unified School District

Philip D. Gay, Science Curriculum Coordinator, San Diego Unified School District

Judith S. Gordon, Science Resource Teacher, Los Angeles Unified School District

Scott Hays, Teacher and Curriculum Coordinator, Coffee Creek Elementary School District

Helen E. Huey, Teacher, Ukiah Unified School District

Michael E. Jay, Product Analyst, Apple Computer, Inc.

Arie R. Korporaal, Science Consultant, Office of the Los Angeles County Superintendent of Schools

Lawrence S. Lerner, Professor of Physics and Astronomy, California State University, Long Beach

George E. Miller, Senior Lecturer in Chemistry, University of California, Irvine

Gary A. Nakagiri, Coordinator of Mathematics and Science Education, Office of the San Mateo County Superintendent of Schools

Kevin Padian, Associate Professor of Integrative Biology and Curator, Museum of Paleontology, University of California, Berkeley

Joe Alfonso Smith, Teacher, Ramona Unified School District

Dorothy J. T. Terman, Science Curriculum Coordinator, Irvine Unified School District

California Department of Education

Bill Andrews, Consultant, Mathematics, Science, and Environmental Education Unit

Jerry Cummings, Consultant, Curriculum Framework and Textbook Development Unit

Gayland Jordan, Consultant, Mathematics, Science, and Environmental Education Unit

Thomas P. Sachse, Administrator, Mathematics, Science, and Environmental Education Unit

Zack Taylor, Consultant, Mathematics, Science, and Environmental Education Unit

Glen Thomas, Administrator, Curriculum Framework and Textbook Development Unit

Science Subject Matter Committee of the Curriculum Development and Supplemental Materials Commission

Elizabeth K. Stage (Chair), Executive Director, California Science Project, University of California (formerly Lawrence Hall of Science, University of California, Berkeley)

Ann Chlebicki, Assistant Superintendent, Saddleback Valley Unified School District

Charles Koepke, Teacher, Upland Unified School District

Jesse Perry, Program Manager for English Language Arts, San Diego Unified School District

Roger Tom, Director of Curriculum and Staff Development, San Francisco Unified School District

Tom Vasta, Teacher and Science Resource Specialist, Elk Grove Unified School District

On January 13, 1989, the State Board of Education adopted the following policy statement on the teaching of natural sciences. This statement supersedes the Board's 1972 Antidogmatism Policy that was distributed statewide in 1981 and printed in the 1984 Science Framework Addendum. To this new policy statement are appended standard scientific dictionary definitions of several scientific terms to emphasize their meanings in scientific contexts.

State Board of Education Policy on the Teaching of Natural Sciences

- The domain of the natural sciences is the natural world. Science is limited by its tools—observable facts and testable hypotheses.

- Discussions of any scientific fact, hypothesis, or theory related to the origins of the universe, the earth, and of life (the how) are appropriate to the science curriculum. Discussions of divine creation, ultimate purposes, or ultimate causes (the why) are appropriate to the history–social science and English–language arts curricula.

- **Nothing in science or in any other field of knowledge shall be taught dogmatically. A dogma is a system of beliefs that is not subject to scientific test and refutation. Compelling belief is inconsistent with the goal of education; the goal is to encourage understanding.**

- To be fully informed citizens, students do not have to accept everything that is taught in the natural science curriculum, but they do have to understand the major strands of scientific thought, including its methods, facts, hypotheses, theories, and laws.

- A scientific fact is an understanding based on confirmable observations and is subject to test and rejection. A scientific hypothesis is an attempt to frame a question as a testable proposition. A scientific theory is a logical construct based on facts and hypotheses that organizes and explains a range of natural phenomena. Scientific theories are constantly subject to testing, modification, and refutation as new evidence and new ideas emerge. Because scientific theories have predictive capabilities, they essentially guide further investigations.

- From time to time natural science teachers are asked to teach content that does not meet the criteria of scientific fact, hypothesis, and theory as these terms are used in natural science and defined in this policy. As a matter of principle, science teachers are professionally bound to limit their teaching to science and should resist pressure to do otherwise. Administrators should support teachers in this regard.

- Philosophical and religious beliefs are based, at least in part, on faith and are not subject to scientific test and refutation. Such beliefs should be discussed in the social science and language arts curricula. The Board's position has been stated in the Board's adopted policy, *Moral and Civic Education and Teaching About Religion* (1988), and in the *History–Social Science Framework* (1988). If a student should raise a question in a natural science class that the teacher determines is outside the domain of science, the teacher should treat the question with respect. The teacher should explain why the question is outside the domain of natural science and encourage the student to discuss the question further with his or her family and clergy.

- Neither the California nor the United States Constitution requires, in order to accommodate the religious views of those who object to certain material or activities that are presented in science classes, that time be given in the curriculum to those particular religious views. It may be unconstitutional to grant time for that reason.

- Nothing in the California *Education Code* allows students (or their parents) to excuse class attendance based on disagreement with the curriculum, except as specified for certain topics dealing with reproductive biology and for laboratory dissection of animals. (See California *Education Code* sections 51550 and 32255.1 [Chapter 65, Statutes of 1988], respectively.) However, the United States Constitution guarantees the free exercise of religion, and local governing boards and districts are encouraged to develop statements like this one that recognize and respect that freedom in the teaching of science. Ultimately, students should be made aware of the difference between understanding, which is the goal of education, and subscribing to ideas, which is not.

From *Hammond Barnhart Dictionary of Science.* Maplewood, N.J.: Hammond, Inc., ©1986.

Definitions

Law, n. 1. a statement of what always occurs under certain conditions; description of a relation or sequence of phenomena invariable under the same conditions: *the laws of motion, Mendel's laws.* . . .

Hypothesis, n. 1. a proposition assumed as a basis for reasoning and often subjected to testing for its validity: . . .

Theory, n. 1. an explanation or model based on observation, experimentation, and reasoning, especially one that has been tested and confirmed as a general principle helping to explain and predict natural phenomena: *the theory of evolution.* . . .

Theory, hypothesis as terms in science mean a generalization reached by inference from observed particulars and proposed as an explanation of their cause, relations, or the like. **Theory** implies a larger body of tested evidence and a greater degree of probability: . . . **Hypothesis** designates a merely tentative explanation of the data, advanced or adopted provisionally, often as the basis of a theory or as a guide to further observation or experiment: . . .

Executive Summary

Chapter 1
The Nature of Science

Science is a field that is constantly adapting to new advances in basic knowledge, medicine, and technology. An understanding of the nature of science and an appreciation of its methods and philosophy continue to be necessary parts of education. How the natural world works is important to everyone's education. Students need to understand the way of thinking and asking questions that is the essence of science. Science is also important for its own sake. A person can carry an appreciation of science all through life and use it to learn more about the natural world.

Technology is based on fundamental science. Educators have the chance to prepare students for the technology of the future by helping them develop a deeper knowledge of basic science. We must clearly present how science works, what processes and methods expand scientific knowledge, and what science is and what it is not.

To be effective, science education should be enjoyable. Science is a source of enjoyment much as music is. The appreciation of science is likely to increase as the audience becomes more knowledgeable about the workings of the discipline. Science is concerned with all of nature, medicine, and technology; it can prepare students for decisions they must make as adults—decisions that are increasingly dependent on a clear understanding of science.

Science is guided by a particular kind of theory that can be tested in the natural world, with methods that any practitioner of science can and must follow. The scientific method aims to be testable, objective, and consistent. Science is open-ended, but scientists operate with expectations based on predictions of theory. Scientists use a preexisting body of observations, facts, inferences, hypotheses, and theories to build expectations of what will happen and to guide further inquiry. Teachers must strive to show students how expectation and openness both play important roles in science. Scientific knowledge must be presented as authoritative, not authoritarian. We can depend on scientific knowledge and theory, yet we can always learn more and must constantly revise what we know in the light of new discoveries.

Science is based on observations set in a testable framework of ideas. To observe is to use the evidence of our senses to obtain the information on which scientific work is based. Scientific inquiry is guided by theory, which is a logical construct of facts and hypotheses that attempts to explain a range of natural phenomena. Theories are sometimes replaced wholly or in part by new theories. The new theory does this by explaining everything that the old theory explained, as well as other evidence that might not have fit very well in the old theory. This is how science proceeds. But science never commits itself irrevocably to any fact or theory, no matter how firmly it appears to be established in the light of what is known. This is not a weakness of uncertainty but a strength of self-correctability. Science is not a matter of belief; rather, it is a matter of conclusive evidence that can be subjected to the tests of observation and objective reasoning. The open competition of ideas is a major part of the excitement of science. Emphasis in the classroom should be placed not on coming up with the right answers but on doing science the right way.

There are scientific issues that arouse controversy. Some of these issues are ethical, some involve clarification of scientific methods and philosophy, and some are not strictly within the realm of science. School boards, administrators, and parents must support the teaching of rigorous science, a rational application of science to scientific and technological activities. Science instruction should respect the private beliefs of students; on the other hand, the teaching of science cannot be suppressed simply because some individuals disagree with findings on religious or philosophical grounds.

Chapter 2
The Major Themes of Science

This *Science Framework* differs from previous frameworks and addenda in its emphasis on the major themes of science.

Themes are the big ideas of science, larger than facts and concepts; they link the theoretical structures of the various scientific disciplines. Themes are a way to integrate the overarching concepts of science into a curriculum, much as theories encompass and connect the basic data and evidence of science.

Six major themes are developed in this framework: (1) energy; (2) evolution; (3) patterns of change; (4) scale and structure; (5) stability; and (6) systems and interactions. Educators and developers of instructional materials are encouraged to weave these or alternative thematic strands into science curricula. These major themes occur again and again in the sciences, whether one studies ecology, plate tectonics, meteorology, or organic chemistry.

Themes are necessary in the teaching of science because they are necessary in the doing of science. In order for science to be a philosophical discipline and not merely a collection of facts, there must be a thematic connection and integration. Themes provide a framework to guide teachers in developing instructional tools. If curricula and instructors are successful in developing themes for students to use in connecting and integrating scientific concepts and facts, then this intellectual habit will carry over and enrich other fields and disciplines.

Themes should be used to integrate concepts and facts at all levels of the curriculum. Through the use of themes, such as those of scale and structure and systems and interactions, students can see how the parts fit together logically and how the information they are learning is used to describe other kinds of phenomena.

Within individual disciplines, such as physical sciences, earth sciences, and life sciences, themes need to be instituted and developed throughout a year's study and from one year to another.

Themes should be used to integrate the main subfields of scientific disciplines. The subfields of life science—genetics, evolution, and paleontology—are connected by using the themes of evolution as well as those of patterns of change and scale and structure.

Themes in science should direct the design of classroom activities. They can connect classroom activities and provide them with a logical sequence and scope of instruction.

Assessment should be thematically and conceptually based. Instead of repeating facts learned in chapters and units, explaining the connections among concepts in the light of themes represents an improvement in assessment practices.

The use of conceptual themes will not by itself solve all the problems of science education. However, the incorporation of themes in thoughtful and judicious ways should improve the integration of facts and ideas, the interrelationships of theories and disciplines, and the quality of instructional materials.

Part II The Content of Science

THE content of a science program is its heart. The thematic approach described in this framework makes connections among the scientific disciplines that have traditionally been taught as separate subjects. Here we illustrate one way that a conceptual approach can be organized within the traditional content areas of science.

It is important to distinguish between *theories*, which are conceptual and empirical entities within a discipline that unify the content of that discipline, and *themes*, which are pedagogical tools to unify ideas among different disciplines.

Some ideas, such as energy and evolution, appear as both theories and themes. Evolution, for instance, is the theory that unifies the content of biology. Evolution is also a theme that unifies the content of various disciplines by observing evolution in both geological and biological history.

Within the traditional areas of physical sciences (Chapter 3), earth sciences (Chapter 4), and life sciences (Chapter 5), we describe the underlying theories in the discipline. Then we present a set of questions central to the content area. These are followed by a narrative description of content, written from the perspective of one or more of the major themes of science, appropriate to various grade levels. The purpose of this approach is to avoid an emphasis on isolated facts and definitions that have long dominated science instruction.

The choice of questions is not definitive nor exclusive; we did, however, concentrate on areas that have been poorly represented in the past. For instance, the framework may emphasize learning the causes of weather, rather than how to read a weather map (though students will still learn this, but it is an activity already well represented in traditional materials).

The intended audience for these descriptions is not students but educators and textbook publishers.

Part III Achieving the Desired Science Curriculum

Chapter 6
Science Processes and the Teaching of Science

Students should be helped to increase their knowledge of the natural world and to understand its connection to our technologically advanced society. A student-centered science program can be created by teachers who are free to design the types of experience that best fit their students.

The content of science consists of a highly structured, complex set of facts, hypotheses, and theories in a context where many observations have meaning. Theory development is progressive; theory suggests further observations that often make possible further elaboration and testing of the theory. Scientists use their senses and extensions of their senses to see, touch, and otherwise view the world, *observing* its characteristics and behaviors as objectively as possible. Scientists describe and picture what they observe in various ways, thus *communicating* their ideas to others so that they can exchange views and interpretations and pass along information. They test what they know against what they do not yet know, *comparing* features and behaviors for similarities and differences. Scientists organize their understandings, *ordering* and *categorizing* them into broader, more general groupings and classifications. They study the interactions among objects and describe the events, *relating* factors that reveal deeper insights into causes and effects. Scientists hypothesize and predict what will happen, based on accumulated knowledge and on the events they expect to take place, *inferring* something that they have not seen because it has not yet happened or because it cannot be observed directly. And as knowledge grows through the use of these scientific thinking processes, scientists develop expertise, *applying* both knowledge and processes for useful purposes, to make still further extensions of the explanatory power of theory and to perceive fresh possibilities.

In developing science concepts, a teacher should: (1) pose questions to determine what ideas students hold about a topic before beginning instruction; (2) be sensitive to and capitalize on students' conceptions about science; (3) employ a variety of instructional techniques to help students achieve conceptual understanding; and (4) include all students in discussions and cooperative learning situations.

It is necessary to engage students in science activities by placing them in a position of responsibility for the learning task. Students should be provided with experimental problem-solving experiences where the result has direct meaning for them.

As a human endeavor, science has a profound impact on society. Values and ethics are important components of science teaching and must be considered by teachers, textbook authors, and curriculum writers. It is important to (1) identify the commonly shared values of the scientific community; (2) promote scientific values in the classroom; and (3) develop rational decision-making skills applicable to major issues of personal and public concern.

Science is directed towards a progressively greater understanding of the natural world. Technology is related to science as a human endeavor, but the direction is toward using accumulated knowledge from science and other fields in order to control and alter the way things work. Teaching a Science, Technology, and Society (STS) approach is invariably interdisciplinary, with strong connections to history–social science, mathematics, literature, and the arts. Teaching science in the context of STS helps reveal the situations in which science has meaning.

The elementary science program holds great potential for exploring natural phenomena and technological applications in science. At a time when children are most curious about the world, teachers can capitalize on this joy of learning in ways that make science enjoyable, interesting, and meaningful.

In most curricular areas, middle school programs are seen as transitions from a sound basis provided during elementary grades to the specialization of high school. For students in middle school, it is important to provide a semester of health and relevant adolescent topics as well as electives for those interested.

The high school science curriculum is less subject to mandate than that of the elementary school. Not all students take more than a minimum of science in high school, and no textbook adoption process is used beyond grade eight. In spite of strong traditions regarding what high school biology, chemistry, and physics courses should be like, many excellent options for teachers and students have been developed. The process of science as an aesthetic pursuit and an effective tool with the power to both create and solve problems must be apparent to graduates from high school.

With concerns of domestic equity and international competitiveness, science educators must help ensure that all students—including the historically underrepresented—have an equal opportunity to succeed in science-related endeavors. By all reports and analyses, females, minority groups, and persons with disabilities are underrepresented in undergraduate and graduate programs, research, industry, and other scientific enterprises. Fortunately, there are individuals and pilot programs working to help youngsters overcome barriers that keep them from succeeding.

All children in California, including those whose primary language is other than English, should have access to high-level science instruction. Students who are limited-English proficient (LEP) can have immediate entry into science via their primary language while acquiring English. The strategies described here can be used by teachers to lower the linguistic barriers that prevent access to their disciplines.

Chapter 7
Implementing a Strong Science Program

A well-formulated districtwide plan for science education provides the basic design for the establishment of an effective science program. Proof of the establishment of a good science program lies in student growth in understanding and enthusiasm for science.

Implementation entails more than the dissemination of information, materials, and programs. To ensure that an adopted science curriculum results in knowledge, experience, and understanding for students, the program must be challenging, stimulating, and useful. Students should be doing science in their classrooms, not merely reading about it.

The changes suggested by this framework build on the preceding *Science Framework* and *Science Framework Addendum* and strengthen the position that students should actively experience science rather than passively read about it. The changes in practice that are required to implement this framework faithfully involve a shift from instruction that emphasizes accumulation of knowledge to a program that develops concepts and an understanding of the connections among the disciplines of science.

Effective implementation incorporates both a districtwide plan and plans for individual schools. A whole range of people should participate throughout the implementation process—principals, governing boards, district and county personnel, and local college and university representatives.

An effective science program depends primarily on teachers who are enthusiastic, informed, and provided with adequate resources. Teachers need the opportunity to experience the kind of instruction they are being asked to provide. While generic workshops on teaching techniques and classroom management strategies are of benefit to science teachers, it is important that substantial time and resources be devoted to strategies for incorporating these techniques most effectively in the teaching of science.

If the goals of the science program are scientific literacy and the ability to make sense of the world, then tests of vocabulary and knowledge will not measure their attainment. The design of an assessment program requires as much care and consideration as the design of the instructional program itself. There is a temptation to limit assessment of teachers to what can be most easily observed: direct instruction. This is as much to be avoided as limiting student assessment to what can be most easily measured: factual recall. The assessment of instruction must meet the challenge of the wide range of instructional strategies proposed in this framework in the same way that teachers meet these challenges in making decisions about instruction.

The physical resources of the entire school plant and the community should be taken into consideration in planning the science instructional program. Equipment and materials must be made available to all teachers—elementary and secondary. Traditional equipment, such as test tubes, scales, meter sticks, and microscopes, has always had a prominent role in effective science programs. As newer products of technology, such as scientific calculators, computers, videotapes and videodisks, become less expensive and more significant as mechanisms for teaching and learning, their role should be constantly evaluated for their contribution to an effective science program.

Technology can provide conduits to new information, experiences, and an opportunity to experiment and fail in a safe environment. A likely result of the increased use of technology in the classroom is the evolution of the role of the teacher from disseminator of information to facilitator of the students' learning. Mechanisms for changing the way that teachers teach will have to incorporate this view of technology's role in instruction.

Parents and the community offer tremendous potential for supporting and enhancing the school's science program.

The California Science Implementation Network has developed a school-based model that many teachers and principals have found useful. The planning process, which involves the entire school staff, has three steps: (1) complete a matrix for program elements and one for content; (2) conduct indicated staff development; and (3) monitor individual teacher progress. (Information about this network can be obtained from the California Department of Education's Mathematics, Science and Environmental Education Unit.)

The reforms in science education that are reflected in this framework are part of an overall reform strategy to transform education for all students so that it promotes thinking and reasoning. The manifestation of this attempt to cultivate higher-order thinking takes different forms in different subject areas. In each case, the details and mechanics of the discipline are being subordinated to the goal of a meaning-centered curriculum, with the aim of increasing the thinking and reasoning in which students engage.

Chapter 8
Instructional Materials Criteria

The California State Board of Education has begun to use the adoption process as a way of supporting the curriculum reform reflected in its recent frameworks and standards. More stringent criteria place additional demands on publishers and teachers alike. We feel, however, that fine instructional materials can themselves instruct teachers while they support student learning.

The instructional materials criteria that follow differ from past criteria in a number of ways. The overall weighting is as follows: content, 50 percent; presentation, 25 percent; and pedagogy 25 percent. (See Table 9 in Chapter 8 for the full list of weighted criteria.)

Content refers to the subject matter—how well it represents what is currently known of science. Content should be treated dynamically, including a thematic approach that makes connections among ideas, and it should value depth over breadth of coverage. Standards for evaluation include whether (1) the topics discussed in Part II of this framework are treated in the instructional materials under consideration; (2) content is treated accurately and correctly; (3) instructional programs are organized around themes, not around facts; (4) instructional materials in science emphasize depth of understanding, not encyclopedic breadth of coverage; and (5) explanations embroider the accumulation of knowledge, with a detailed description of how it is that we came to know these facts and why this information is important.

Presentation means how science is described, organized, written, and illustrated. Standards for evaluation include whether (1) the prose style of instructional materials is considerate and engaging and the language and vocabulary of science are respected; (2) language is accessible to students; (3) the character of science is represented faithfully: that it is shown as open to inquiry, open to controversy, and nondogmatic by its nature; and (4) science is presented as an enterprise that does not operate in isolation from society and technology or from other fields of knowledge.

Pedagogy refers to the instructional methods that are employed. Standards for evaluation include whether (1) instructional programs are connected with experience; (2) instructional materials recognize cultural diversity and reflect strategies that research and practice have shown to be successful in meeting the needs of all students; and (3) assessment is integrative and oriented toward solving problems, not simply recall-based.

The criteria previously described will guide the Instructional Materials Evaluation Panel (IMEP), a group of approximately 40 teachers, curriculum specialists, and scientists who review the materials submitted for adoption and submit its recommendations to the Curriculum Development and Supplemental Materials Commission (CDSMC), which will in turn make recommendations to the State Board of Education. This section concludes with some ex-

amples of what is and is not desirable in science writing.

The most important points made in this section are (1) the desirability of thematic orientation in science curricula; (2) the motivation and learning that can be generated by hands-on, experience-oriented activities and curricula; (3) the importance of "considerate prose" and the elimination of readability formulas as determiners of grade-level appropriateness of curricular materials; and (4) the fundamental respect for scientific methods of inquiry and for the language and philosophy of science that is absolutely necessary to a science program.

Improvement in instructional materials must be coupled with support for more in-service training for teachers and reevaluation and change in criteria commonly used in the adoption and selection of instructional materials. These improvements are the principal means by which the current system of developing, adopting, and using instructional materials can meet the challenges of educating students about what science really is and how it matters to their lives.

Introduction

IN 1983 *A Nation at Risk* declared that American education had become victim to "a rising tide of mediocrity." The National Science Board's Commission on Precollege Education in Mathematics, Science, and Technology confirmed that the situation in science education was particularly critical. Recent studies have placed America's students last among their international counterparts in understanding science. In 1988 the National Assessment of Educational Progress of the Educational Testing Service (ETS) issued *The Science Report Card*. ETS noted that although the responses in the years since 1983 have resulted in some progress, "average science proficiency across the grades remains distressingly low."

What are the major reasons for this state of affairs, and what can be done to improve it? A first wave of educational reform, stimulated by the early reports, prompted legislatures to regulate administrative strategies. Both nationally and in California, the results were raised standards, increased graduation requirements, and a longer school day and year. The second wave of reform addressed the teaching profession and again raised standards while increasing responsibilities and roles.

By establishing a stronger and more demanding apparatus, these reforms paved the way for a third wave of reform that focuses on what and how students learn. The 1990 *Science Framework* addresses two aspects of this focus: (1) What is important to learn? and (2) How can we ensure that all students have the opportunity to learn it? It is natural to respond to these questions in terms of a common core curriculum for all students. A core curriculum is not unique to science. But in a field in which proliferation of knowledge is so extensive and the exclusion of

certain students from access to that knowledge so pervasive, it is essential to develop a core curriculum that is appropriate for *all* students.

Although it is founded on the 1978 *Science Framework for California Public Schools* and the 1984 *Science Framework Addendum*, the 1990 *Science Framework* shifts the emphasis of science education by centering on the answers to the questions raised in the preceding paragraph. In recent years tremendous progress has been made in response to those previous documents by making science instruction more experiential and engaging for students. Yet the general trend has been to reduce and compartmentalize science content and focus on isolated facts and concepts. This fragmentation is especially detrimental in the elementary grades. Rather than being encouraged to attain a global and integrated understanding of the natural world, which the disciplines and the nature of science describe and define so beautifully, students have been encouraged to memorize isolated facts and concepts.

To counteract this situation, this framework emphasizes a thematic approach to science. Its approach is derived from the most current available thinking and criticism of instructional practices. *Science for All Americans,* a report issued by Project 2061 of the American Association for the Advancement of Science in February, 1989, envisions an ideal content for future science courses. That report shows a need for a thematic approach to science instruction to demonstrate the connections that exist among the various disciplines of science and enable students to understand the rapidly changing world.

The purposes of this framework are consistent with those of the *Instructional Materials and Framework Adoption Policies and Procedures* developed by the

Office of Curriculum Framework and Textbook Development of the California Department of Education and approved by the State Board of Education in June, 1988; that is, to (1) establish guidelines and provide direction to help districts revise their curricula, evaluate their programs, assess their instruction, and develop instructional strategies; (2) serve as a resource for preservice and in-service education of teachers and administrators; (3) provide direction to publishers for the development of textbooks and instructional materials and to reviewers for selecting instructional materials and testing programs; and (4) make information on curricula available to parents and the general public.

Another primary audience for the framework includes science curriculum specialists, science supervisors, science staff developers, and those in curriculum development and leadership roles. The committee, members of which are listed on page ix, is representative of these roles, including faculty from public schools, kindergarten through grade twelve, and universities; science consultants from district and county offices; and other persons with responsibility for curriculum and staff development. This portion of the audience that the committee members had in mind was very much like themselves but was operationally defined as the teacher whom you would expect to find on a district curriculum development committee. Therefore, what follows presumes some background and interest in science. We do not expect teachers or others who have no background or particular interest in science to use this framework as their first experience in teaching science. This document is not a textbook or a curriculum guide, nor is it a substitute for extensive staff development, in-service training, or professional preparation.

Different audiences will be interested in different sections of this framework. Part I answers the question, What is science? and should be read by those interested in science and the science curriculum. In describing the nature and themes of science, it promotes the conceptual teaching of science. Part II outlines the required content of physical, earth, and life sciences programs. Part III has three chapters: Chapter 6 is intended for teachers and supervisors who are interested in the processes of teaching and the processes of science; Chapter 7 is intended for supervisors, department chairs, principals, and other administrators who have responsibility for imple-

menting the science curriculum; and Chapter 8 is intended for publishers and other developers and reviewers of instructional materials who collectively form the other primary audience for the framework.

After the approval of a framework by the State Board of Education, the Department of Education takes several steps to provide a consistent science curriculum. The Department will review and, if necessary, revise the *Quality Criteria* (for elementary, middle grades, and high schools), the *Model Curriculum Standards, Grades Nine Through Twelve*, and the *Science Model Curriculum Guide, Kindergarten Through Grade Eight*. The California Assessment Program will use this framework as the basis for designing assessment of students in grades three, six, eight, and twelve. State-supported professional development programs, such as the California Science Implementation Network (for elementary schools) and the California School Leadership Academy (for administrators), will review their curricula and bring them into alignment. The Intersegmental Committee of the Academic Senates will consider the match with its *Statement on Preparation in Natural Science Expected of Entering Freshmen*. Of course, these changes will not take place immediately, but they should assist educators in preparing for the changes embodied in this framework. And in 1992 the State Board of Education will adopt instructional materials that meet the criteria delineated here.

To achieve scientific literacy for all of our students, we hold the following expectations—which reflect the main ideas in the framework—for science programs:

1. The major themes underlying science, such as energy, evolution, patterns of change, scale and structure, stability, and systems and interactions, are developed and deepened through a thematic approach.
2. The three basic scientific fields of study—physical, earth, and life sciences—are addressed, ideally each year, and the connections among them are developed.
3. The character of science is shown to be open to inquiry and controversy and free of dogmatism; the curriculum promotes student understanding of how we come to know what we know and how we test and revise our thinking.

4. Science is presented in connection with its applications in technology and its implications for society.

5. Science is presented in connection with students' own experiences and interests, frequently using hands-on experiences that are integral to the instructional sequence.

6. Students are given opportunities to construct the important ideas of science, which are then developed in depth, through inquiry and investigation.

7. Instructional strategies and materials allow several levels and pathways of access so that all students can experience both challenge and success.

8. Printed materials are written in an interesting and engaging narrative style; in particular, vocabulary is used to facilitate understanding rather than as an end in itself.

9. Textbooks are not the sole source of the curriculum; everyday materials and laboratory equipment, videotapes and software, and other printed materials such as reference books provide a substantial part of student experience.

10. Assessment programs are aligned with the instructional program in both content and format; student performance and investigation play the same central role in assessment that they do in instruction.

The 1990 *Science Framework* builds on previous work and, much like science itself, is subject to revision. We trust that it represents a step forward for science education in California, and we hope that it helps to bring the joy and power of scientific inquiry and understanding to all of our students.

Part I

What Is Science?

The Nature of Science

THIS first chapter is about science itself: what it is, what it is not, what its philosophies and methods are, and how these differ from those of other intellectual activities. Structured closely after the State Board of Education's 1989 policy statement on the teaching of science (reproduced in the beginning of this document), it is meant to serve as a guide for teachers, administrators, and parents on the nature of science and what is and is not appropriate to teach in a science classroom. Beyond these functions, this chapter also guides teachers on how to deal with socially relevant and sensitive scientific issues and how to ensure that the views and beliefs of all students are treated with respect. This chapter is instrumental to the understanding of the rest of the framework.

Section A   Introduction

EDUCATING children for the future is one of the principal aims of any well-balanced curriculum. This is especially important in science education, a field that is constantly adapting to new advances in basic knowledge, medicine, and technology. Though it is increasingly difficult to anticipate the world that our children will face and shape, it is clear that a basic understanding of science and an appreciation of its methods and philosophy will continue to be a necessary part of education—perhaps more than ever.

With this in mind, the State Board of Education adopted in January, 1989, a new statement of policy on the teaching of the natural sciences. This policy, which supersedes previous statements, is reproduced in full in the front of this document. It delineates the responsibilities of science educators in explaining what science is and how it differs from other intellectual endeavors. Instructional materials submitted for adoption in the State of California must conform to the letter and spirit of this policy in order to be considered.

This chapter is about science itself. What are its basic operating principles and methods? What part of scientific philosophy needs to be communicated to young students? Why study science at all? How can the excitement of science be communicated? And what are the educator's responsibilities in discussing moral, ethical, and social issues on which scientific understanding has some bearing? Some basic thoughts in response to these questions follow. (For a similar point of view, see *Science for All Americans* [Project 2061, American Association for the Advancement of Science, Washington, D.C., 1989].)

How the natural world works is important to everyone's education.

The genetic code, the history of the universe and the earth and its life, the structure of the atom, the force that brings apples to the ground and moves the tides, and the logic of the periodic table of the elements are more than just the facts and ideas of science: they are an integral part of our cultural heritage. We need to understand the way of thinking and asking questions that is the essence of science.

Science is important for its own sake.

The American poet Walt Whitman characterized science as a limitless voyage of joyous exploration. A person can carry the appreciation of science all through life and use it to learn more about the natural world. There are many well-known stories of how famous scientists became captivated by science at an early age, but there are just as many stories of ordinary people—the true "amateurs" (lovers) of science—who went on to pursue other careers, but remained fascinated by the endless possibilities for discoveries in the natural world. Enjoyment is a superb motivator of understanding.

Technology is based on fundamental science.

An understanding of the principles and practice of science is essential for students to cope successfully with the world they will inherit—a world about which we can predict but little. Much of modern science is based on technological development, largely in instrumentation. Educators have the chance to prepare students for the technology of the future by helping them to develop a deeper knowledge of basic science and how science works. We cannot expect our democratic society to make intelligent decisions about science, technology, and public policy unless its citizens are scientifically literate.

As educators we face a complex and difficult task. We cannot present the entire body of scientific knowledge because there is too much to teach. We can hope for best results if we clearly present how science works and the processes and methods which expand scientific knowledge. A stimulating classroom environment can nurture natural curiosity to convey the excitement of science. But we must also foster an understanding of what science is and what it is not. Because scientific knowledge figures in so many other aspects of life and culture, we have to help students to deal with this relationship. Nature itself is morally and ethically neutral, but those who deal with science must make important moral and ethical choices. We have the responsibility of confronting students with some of the political and social issues that require an understanding of science. After all, science is universal; it engages people without regard to their sex, race, culture, or views on matters outside the realm of science, and its findings transcend cultural differences.

The remainder of this chapter is devoted to an exploration of these matters and how they can be incorporated in the daily use of any science textbook, classroom, and curriculum. This treatment should not be regarded as exhaustive but merely as a basic introduction.

Section B   The Joy of Science

To be effective, science education should be enjoyable. The enjoyment of science is open to everyone of every age: as thrilling as the experience of a five-year-old on seeing *Tyrannosaurus rex* for the first time or as cerebral as the aesthetic appreciation of a beautiful new idea set forth by a masterful physicist such as Stephen Hawking. Science is a source of enjoyment, much as music is. It is not only virtuosos who enjoy and benefit from playing a musical instrument—even those who do not play an instrument can enjoy listening to music. The appreciation of science, like the appreciation of music, is likely to increase as the audience becomes more knowledgeable about the workings of the discipline.

Science educators want their students to take this message to heart: If you like some aspect of science, you should consider pursuing science as a career. Whether your taste runs to physics instead of pharmacology does not matter any more than whether you prefer piccolos to pianos. The point is to become involved and to communicate your enthusiasm to others. Science careers are delightfully varied; you do not have to be a professor, an engineer, or a chemist to be a successful scientist. You can be a wildlife manager, a forester, a nature guide, a laboratory technician, or—best of all—a science teacher. But even if you simply increase your appreciation of science and your regard for the natural world, your life will be enriched.

"Life is not easy for any of us. But what of that? We must have perseverance and, above all, confidence in ourselves."

—Marie Curie (1867–1934)

The most personal message that a science teacher can bring to students is this: Science is concerned with all of nature, medicine, and technology. These concerns are not simply empirical; they are ethical and social. The responsibility of science educators and the function of science curricula are to prepare students for the decisions they must make as adults—decisions that daily become increasingly dependent on a clear understanding of science.

Section C   Teaching What Science Is

As an intellectual activity science shares many characteristics with other fields of knowledge, but it also has its own unique characteristics. All fields of knowledge benefit from open-minded, open-ended investigation and an honest exchange of ideas. More than any other field, however, science is guided by a particular kind of theory that can be tested in the natural world, using particular methods and principles that any practitioner of science can and must follow. This is why progress in scientific research is so consistent and so universal—and why it is so rapid. Any investigator following the universal methods and principles of science can test, verify or reject, and use previous discoveries to take scientific knowledge a step further.

In general, scientists plan investigations by working along the lines suggested by theories, which in turn are based on previous knowledge. This knowledge is formed from empirical observations; that is, observations of the natural world, which are then organized systematically into logical frameworks called hypotheses. Hypotheses must be testable by recourse to observations of the natural world if they are to qualify as scientific hypotheses. Thus, theory and observation interact: each contributes to the other.

There is an important lesson in this for students. Any new scientific knowledge must be communicated fully and openly to others if it is to be of use. This basic obligation makes even the full-time researcher a teacher of his or her colleagues and students, and this obligation binds scientists to teachers at all levels. The process of teaching science requires a precise, unambiguous use of language and a clear demarcation of the criteria, power, and limits of scientific investigation. The following points should be made clearly and integrated into science textbooks, curricula, and class discussions:

1. Science has its own character as an intellectual activity.

Science differs in several ways from other scholarly inquiries, such as literary criticism, historical writing, or the development of a philosophical or religious perspective. Science aims to be testable, objective, and consistent.

Testability. Observations and inferences about science are based in the natural world. An explanation should suggest a crucial experiment, fact, or empirical observation that can settle the controversy between it and alternative explanations. In the most theoretical fields, such experiments may be difficult or impossible at present, but it must be at least possible in practice to test them by recourse to natural phenomena. If an idea cannot (even potentially) be so tested, then it is outside the realm of science.

Objectivity. We make observations through our senses, which are necessarily subjective, and approach each problem with certain explicit and implicit ideas about what we are looking for and the possible outcomes of our investigation. We cannot change this; we are human. Nevertheless, explanations of nature must be based on natural phenomena and observations, not on opinions or subjective experiences. One good control of scientific objectivity is the repeatability of science; that is, any observation ought to be repeatable and capable of being confirmed or rejected by other scientists. This applies as much to the interpretation of the structure of a fossil plant or animal as it does to the result of an experiment in a chemistry lab.

Consistency. A scientific explanation does more than provide a plausible account; it must clearly agree with all the observable facts better than alternative explanations do, and it must show an explicit connection between cause and effect. Some observations remain puzzling for years and do not seem to fit well within established understanding. Many of these turn out to be incorrect, or the inferences based on them turn out to be erroneous in the light of other data. Some observations are highly valued because they signal a need to alter theory to accommodate them— usually with a better, more inclusive theory.

When we test forms of inquiry such as parapsychology, the study of unidentified flying objects, or astrology, we find that claims for their validity on scientific grounds fail repeatedly; thus, belief in them must be based on other, nonscientific considerations. Such realms of inquiry cause confusion in students, and scientists raise objections when their proponents attempt to set them forth as science. Teachers must be careful to separate science from pseudoscience and to explain the criteria for the distinction. Excessive time should not be spent in discussing pseudosciences; they should be treated only in passing, as examples of subjects that do not meet the criteria of science discussed here.

As educators we have a responsibility to teach students what science is and how it differs from other kinds of inquiry or knowledge, such as art history, literary criticism, or philosophy. We need to show students how to differentiate between scientific inquiry and other kinds of inquiry that do not adhere to the methods and principles discussed in this section.

2. Science is open-ended, but scientists operate with expectations based on the predictions of theory.

There are no preordained conclusions in science. However, along with the legendary open-endedness and serendipity of science goes another very important factor. Scientists build expectations of what will happen on a tremendous preexisting body of observations, facts, inferences, hypotheses, and theories. They use these expectations to guide further inquiry. If scientists did not base further inquiry on what had gone before, if there were no reasonable base for scientific prediction, scientific research would be reduced to random trial-and-error experimentation.

Because science is open-ended, those who would practice or understand it must be open-minded. To be open-minded is to use our experience. For example, it is probable that future discoveries may give us a more precise age for the earth than the currently accepted rough value of 4.54 billion years, a value that has changed by only 0.01 billion years in over three decades of research. But we know that the new value will not be 10,000 years or 100 billion years. Science builds on what has gone before and refines its conclusions. The first scientific estimates of the age of the earth were based on rates of erosion, estimates of deposition of sediments and of mountain building, and they ranged from several thousands to hundreds of millions of years. In the 1800s Lord Kelvin derived a famous estimate of 100 million years, on the basis of his assumption that all the energy radiated by the sun was gravitational. When radioactive energy was discovered, this assumption and the constraint that his calculation had put on the age of the earth proved false. As estimates of sedimentary rates and cycles were refined and as radiometric dating of isotopes in rocks became a repeatedly robust technique, the age of the earth's various rock layers was confirmed from a variety of measures. Indeed, our understanding of the age of the various geological periods has not changed markedly in 50 years.

Two examples may illustrate how experience and open-mindedness are inseparable in science. A naturalist exploring an uncharted tributary of the Amazon River would not expect to find polar bears, corals, and platypuses; it would be more logical to expect lizards, crocodiles, tapirs, and other members of the South American jungle fauna. These reasonable expectations are based on our knowledge of a host of biogeographical patterns and processes—the distribution and spread of animals and plants and their ecological relationships. This does not mean that it would be impossible for any of these exotic organisms to appear in the Amazon, only unexpected. To find them there would, of course, be of extraordinary

"We are in an age of discovery, we live in the world of the unknown. That's the only place to live."

—*Lloyd Quarterman (1918—1982)*

interest—to see how they differed from their relatives elsewhere and what historical and adaptive features might account for their unexpected presence.

Expectations in science, as this second example shows, also suggest possibilities and drive further inquiry. Most life science textbooks give accounts of the Miller-Urey experiments of the 1950s, which tried to synthesize amino acids, some of the simple molecules that are the building blocks of life. Other scientists had suggested the possibility that on the primordial earth, amino acids were first synthesized naturally from simpler compounds such as ammonia, methane, and water. Miller and Urey decided to see whether the synthesis was possible. They assembled a variety of mixtures of the simpler compounds in closed vessels. But they had clear expectations that nothing would happen if they simply mixed the compounds together. They knew from elementary chemical theory that they would need additional energy in the system, so they introduced an electrical spark through the vessel. Indeed, amino acids were produced. Miller and Urey did not know in advance exactly which compounds would form, nor in what proportions. But they knew from expectation that energy was needed in order to synthesize more complex compounds from simpler ones. This is a good example of how the open-endedness of scientific inquiry goes hand in hand with structured scientific expectations based on previous knowledge.

What do these examples mean to science teaching? Simply that teachers must strive to show students how expectation and openness both have important roles in science. The interplay between them confirms both the body of accumulated scientific knowledge and the value of its open-ended philosophy. Scientific knowledge must be presented as authoritative, not authoritarian; we can depend on scientific knowledge and theory, yet we can always learn more and must constantly revise what we know in the light of new discovery.

3. Science is based on observations set in a testable framework of ideas.

Scientific terms such as *fact* and *theory*, which were originally nonscientific words but which have reentered our everyday vocabulary with the veneer of scientific authority, are easy to misunderstand or use loosely. When these terms are used in a scientific context and in science teaching, we must preserve their proper meaning. In detective novels, the sleuth discovers the corpse and develops a "theory" as to "whodunit." At the end the murderer confesses, and the "theory" becomes a "fact." These words have different meanings to a scientist.

When we say that all science is based on observations, we mean that we use the evidence of our senses (seeing, feeling, hearing, and so forth) to obtain the information on which scientific work is based. Even when we use an instrument to detect and measure things too small to be seen with an optical microscope, the output of the instrument must feed into one of our senses before we can interpret the data that it supplies.

When our observations of a phenomenon have been confirmed or found to be repeatable, such observations become fact. However, even though there is little doubt about the observation, it cannot be accepted as an absolute certainty without experimental confirmation.

For example, suppose a child comes into a classroom with wet, shiny rubber boots. Everyone can observe these features, so they are facts. To explain *why* the boots are wet requires another level of intellectual activity called inference. An inference is reasoning based on observation and experience. In the case of the rubber boots, one could draw a rational inference that it is raining outside or that the child has recently stepped in a puddle. It is easy to think that an inference is automatically a fact, but critical thinking is required to maintain the distinction between the two. An inference can become a fact when it is confirmed by other observations.

A hypothesis is an attempt to convert an explanation into a testable prediction. If we make the hypothesis that the child's boots are wet from rain, we can test it by looking to see if it is raining. If it is clear outside, we reject the hypothesis. But even if it is raining, the rain may not have anything to do with the wet boots. Perhaps the child has not been outside at all but has been playing with the water fountain in the hall. Further inquiry might be necessary.

There is still the possibility that we did not observe with sufficient care. Perhaps the boots were not wet at all but were shiny because they were new. Observations may be mistaken and may lead to mistaken inferences. This is a weakness of human observation because humans tend to see what they expect to see:

When a child wears rain boots, it is usually because it is raining.

We cannot ever expect to be completely free of preconditioned expectations. An important part of the scientific method is to maintain an awareness of this frailty and allow for it. To do this, it is essential to keep an open mind and to test ideas systematically and thoroughly.

4. Scientific inquiry is guided by theory.

As already noted, the concept of theory is enormously important in science, but the term is often misunderstood and misused by nonscientists. A theory is a logical construct of facts and hypotheses that attempts to explain a range of natural phenomena. For example, gravitation is a fact, and it is also a theory. The principles that underlie the phenomenon of gravitational attraction are not fully understood. But no one doubts the fact of gravity; apples do not suspend themselves in midair pending the happy day when a physicist observes an apple exchanging gravitons with the earth. Moreover, if some hypothesis concerning the gravitational behavior of objects under certain conditions is tested and shown to be in error, the theory of gravitation does not become invalid. Only the part of the theory that failed the test must be modified and reevaluated.

Theories are replaced in their entirety infrequently and then only when a new theory is proposed that subsumes the old theory. The new theory does so by explaining everything that the old theory explained as well as other evidence that might not have fit very well in the old theory. In time the new theory may itself be modified or replaced; this is how science proceeds. For example, in Columbus's time the earth was generally thought to be the center of the cosmos, and the sun, moon, and planets were thought to circle the earth. But in this cosmology, it was difficult to account for the irregular motion of many heavenly bodies: planets slowed, sped up, and sometimes reversed their motion. With Copernicus's proposal that the sun, not the earth, was the center of the system, the calculations of the motions of heavenly bodies were simplified and made more sense. Heliocentric theory, which better explained the known observations, replaced the geocentric theory.

However, that was not the end of the story. The shape of the planetary orbits was assumed to be circular. Kepler proposed that the orbits were elliptical, and this further simplified calculations of their motion and improved the accuracy of such predictions. Even this advance did not solve everything; there are "hitches" in the rates at which planets move through space, partly because they exert a physical attraction on each other, as Newton showed. So the advent of Newtonian mechanics further improved our explanatory power of these natural phenomena. Newtonian theory has now been superseded and embedded in a more general theory, the theory of relativity pioneered by Einstein. But Einstein's theory is not the last word on the subject. It may one day be replaced by an even more comprehensive theory—perhaps developed by a student now sitting in a science classroom in California!

The lesson of the previous example of solar mechanics is simple. Educators must be precise in the use of scientific language because that language is crucial to its teaching. A *theory* is not a half-baked idea nor an uncertain fact but a large body of continually refined observation, inference, and testable hypotheses. Terms such as *fact* and *theory* are used differently in scientific literature than they are in supermarket tabloids or even in the normal conversation of well-educated people. For clear communication scientists, teachers, and students must communicate the definitions of scientific terms and use them with consistency.

Notice that in the preceding discussions we have avoided the word *prove*, the use of which should be limited to abstract mathematics. Most scientific work does not result in infallible propositions, such as the word *proof* seems to imply to the nonscientist. We have already explored the ways in which scientific ideas are tested, observations made, facts gathered, and theories built. But science never commits itself irrevocably to any fact or theory, no matter how firmly it appears to be established in the light of what is known. Science is never dogmatic; it is pragmatic—always subject to adjustment in the light of solid new observations like those of Joule, or new, strong explanations of nature like those of Einstein and Darwin. This is a cardinal property of science. It is not a weakness of uncertainty but a strength of self-correctability. Students should be carefully taught this intrinsic value.

A similar issue is very closely related to the use of terms. Language used to describe science must represent science accurately as an intellectual and social process. For example, in discussing a particular scientific issue, students should never be told that "many scientists" think this or that. Science is decided not by vote but by evidence. Nor should students be told that "scientists believe." Science is not a matter of belief; rather, it is a matter of evidence that can be subjected to the tests of observation and objective reasoning. A phrase such as "Many scientists believe . . ." misrepresents scientific inquiry. It also obscures for students what scientists really do and how they come to their understandings. Educators should be encouraged to stretch their pedagogical vocabularies. Say instead that scientists reach conclusions based on evidence and that all conclusions are always subject to modification based on new knowledge. Students should be told about evidence and how scientists reach their conclusions, not whether scientists believe something or how many do or do not. Scientists no more believe in their findings than a superior court judge believes in a verdict.

How certain or uncertain is science? What are its limits? And how should these issues be presented to students? Science should be presented in the spirit evoked in the previous discussions. Detractors of science deride the idea that science can be authoritative on the grounds that it cannot be omniscient. Since scientists cannot know everything, how can we depend on what they say they know now? Students can be misled into seeing a contradiction here: Science seems to know so much, yet changes its mind constantly and has more to know the more it discovers. Educators should show clearly how this unique combination of reliability and tentativeness is the central characteristic and fundamental strength of science. Show students that nothing in science is decided just because someone important says it is so (authority) or because that is the way it has always been done (tradition). In the free marketplace of

---

Science is never dogmatic; it is pragmatic—always subject to adjustment in the light of solid new observations like those of Joule, or new, strong explanations of nature like those of Einstein and Darwin. This is a cardinal property of science.

---

ideas, the better new idea supersedes or absorbs the previous ones. This open competition of ideas is a major part of the excitement of science.

Section D Scientific Practice and Ethics

SCIENTISTS have responsibilities to their colleagues and to the public. Because all observations are based on human senses and expectations, results must be reported as fully and openly as possible. Scientists also have a responsibility to limit the scope and the implications of their results, not to overgeneralize their findings. Negative results—those that do not agree with the hypothesis—must be reported along with those that do agree. (Trivial results are not normally reported, although what seems initially trivial can turn out to be important. Therefore, records must be kept carefully and made available to other qualified researchers.)

Students, especially younger ones, often feel under pressure to come up with the right answer when doing hands-on science activities. Older students sometimes falsify results, usually because they just assume that they have made an error in observing, measuring, or recording data. This conduct simply reflects human nature. To relieve this problem, teachers and writers of instructional materials should encourage students to report the results they get. They should also use open-ended experiments, not "cookbook" ones and not even good ones that have as their only aim to duplicate a known result. In a well-designed instructional activity, there is no single right answer, and students' results may reveal problems with the experiment, the apparatus, or the conclusion. Even if their data are incorrect for some reason, repeated trials and independent observations made by others will uncover error. Emphasis should be placed not on coming up with the right answer but on doing science the right way. Teachers should emphasize discussion that reveals how the errors crept in and whether and how anomalous observations reveal features of interest in the experimental design, the equipment, or the results.

For students famous cases of scientific error or fraud perpetrated on the scientific community can be confusing. Some such cases, notably the "Piltdown man" hoax, have been used to suggest that science is somehow unreliable or dishonest. Piltdown man, discovered in rural England in the early 1900s, appeared to be a very interesting but anomalous specimen of early hominid that altered the prevailing understanding of human ancestry and evolution. Eventually revealed as the altered jaw of an orangutan placed with the skull of a human, it was so cleverly done that it influenced scientific understanding about the early evolution of humans for some decades. Because the identity of the hoaxer is still not known for certain, the reason for its perpetration is a mystery. Several factors conspired to keep the hoax from being discovered sooner. One was the absence for many decades of other fossil human remains. Another was the inaccessibility of the fossil. A.S. Woodward of the British Museum kept it locked away from investigators. Indeed, an eminent paleontologist was thrown out of the museum bodily when he was discovered attempting to open the specimen case in Woodward's absence! As time went on, however, and more fossils were found, a pattern of hominid evolution in which Piltdown man was increasingly anomalous was elucidated. These findings contributed to widespread skepticism, held since its discovery, that Piltdown man was authentic. Eventually, after Woodward's retirement, and with the development of new analytic tools and investigation of the specimen, the fraud was uncovered. Again, the self-correcting process of science and the importance of consistency of scientific results were paramount in solving the problem.

How can teachers infuse the ethics of scientific practice into their curricula? They can do so by stressing laboratory-oriented, open-ended activities designed to allow students to explore and discover new ideas for themselves. Such activities are more effective than self-contained lessons in internalizing ideas for students. But even if laboratory activities are not a practicable approach to every scientific concept, the teacher may well describe the path taken by scientists in exploring these problems, including well-chosen examples of wrong turns and overlooked evidence. Students should learn that science corrects itself in many ways. They should also understand that early scientists whose work has now been superseded were not stupid, quaint, or primitive. Often false starts are necessary in order to eliminate the incorrect approaches. Simply formulating the problem is often an enormous step in the right direction.

OUR present world is so dependent on the discoveries of science and technology that progress is almost universally identified with progress in science and technology—often to the disregard for progress in other human areas such as global politics, economics, and human justice. Because science is such a large part of today's world, it is more important than ever that each student understand its workings and its material basis. The presentation of some topics in science, however, sometimes disturbs individuals who hold religious or philosophical beliefs that they feel conflict with certain findings of science.

Teachers are given the job of teaching their subjects to students, of representing the knowledge in a given area at an appropriate pedagogical level, and of helping their students make informed decisions about issues they may encounter in their future years. How can teachers meet the challenge of explaining socially sensitive issues in science to their students? Some guidelines are given as follows:

Education's goal is understanding, not belief.

Education does not compel belief; the goal is to encourage understanding. Students do not have to accept everything that is taught in school. But they do need to understand the major strands of scientific thought because this thought is the backbone of our intellectual heritage and the basis for the construction of future knowledge.

A major task of education is to explain the methodology and evidence that bears on accepted conclusions. To teach about communism in a history class, for example, is not to advocate communism and should not be construed as an attempt to undermine a student's democratic beliefs. But the students who do not learn in a history class the fundamentals of a philosophical-political-social system that governs hundreds of millions of people are missing something important about today's global politics as well as vital information that will help them make intelligent decisions in the voting booth as adults.

In the same way there are scientific issues that arouse social controversy. Science teachers are expected to present and interpret these issues for their students, but the issues must be dealt with as scientific issues and discussed in the light of accepted scientific evidence. In carrying out this obligation, the teacher does not exceed the boundaries of scientific inquiry or the role of a science teacher. The teacher must also make every effort to delineate and separate nonscientific material in reaching a scientific conclusion.

The educator's role is to promote scientific understanding.

Educators must present accepted scientific understanding in a conscientious way and should be supported in this goal by their communities. Any educator who communicates science to students is bound to encounter sensitivities to certain issues. Some of these issues are ethical, some involve clarification of scientific methods and philosophy, and some are not strictly within the realm of science. While recognizing the right of individuals to hold and practice their own beliefs, teachers must not be pressured by anyone to distort or suppress science or to go beyond what they are professionally obligated and charged to teach. Administrators especially should be sensitive to the pressures faced by teachers in communicating the philosophy, substance, technological implications, and ethical issues of science.

No one can be an expert on all scientific issues. Every teacher must feel free to say and know when to say, "I don't know; that's outside my range of expertise," and to suggest other resources to the student who wants to pursue the question further.

Furthermore, every teacher must feel free to say and know when to say, "Sorry, but that's not a question for science," and explain why. Such questions should be treated with respect and referred to family or clergy for further discussion.

At times some students may insist that certain conclusions of science cannot be true because of certain religious or philosophical beliefs that they hold. This is a difficult problem for these students and their families, and such difficulties should be acknowledged and respected. It is appropriate for a teacher to express in this regard, "I understand that you may have personal reservations about accepting this scientific evidence, but it is scientific knowledge about which there is no reasonable doubt among scientists in this field, and it is my responsibility to teach it because it is part of our common intellectual heritage."

Sometimes it is difficult to separate the science curriculum from social and ethical concerns that pertain to students or are a matter of vital public debate. In these cases, teachers are ethically bound to teach the scientific facts and the scientific perspectives on the issue. It is perfectly acceptable to acknowledge that nonscientific concerns (such as legal rights, aesthetics, and economics) bear on an issue that is not purely scientific but has scientific content. But the educator must distinguish carefully between the scientific and nonscientific components of the issue and not present the latter as though they were the former.

Socially sensitive issues have a place in the science classroom.

The following examples are meant to explore several issues that are commonly associated with social sensitivity. We do not provide solutions to the problems but only suggest perspectives that educators may use to present them to students.

Conservation. Controversies over conservation issues are not two-sided struggles between lovers of nature and the voices of industry and progress, nor do such controversies have simple solutions. But no workable solution of this issue or any other issue with scientific content can conflict with the relevant scientific evidence and principles. Students should be taught that they must evaluate public policy and choose their stances on issues, with an appreciation of the empirical constraints on the problem that science can provide. For example, one cannot achieve an intellectually defensible stance on the use of natural resources without a knowledge as to which natural resources cannot be replaced and the rates at which renewable ones can be renewed. Beyond these considerations are those of present human needs, the need to preserve natural beauty for posterity, and the need to adjust how humans now use natural resources to preserve nonrenewable ones for the future. All these considerations require scientific understanding.

Students should also understand that technology has often brought, along with its advances, some undesirable secondary effects such as pollution, acid rain, mutagenic agents, and biotic poisons. Such undesirable effects can often be reduced by further technological advances, at a cost that must be evaluated by the standards of public policy. Scientific and

Evolution is the central organizing theory of biology and has fundamental importance in other sciences as well. It is an accepted scientific explanation and therefore no more controversial in scientific circles than the theories of gravitation and electron flow.

technological knowledge is essential for intelligent judgment on these issues. Cost-benefit considerations are not merely scientific questions. Whether the issue is power generation or agricultural crop management, the educator should seize the opportunity to explore the relationship between science and other subjects and to help students develop the habit of rational, orderly thought in an area of popular misinformation, emotion, and instant solutions.

Conservation should not be taught simply as a matter of classic Malthusian population growth according to which natural resources are stripped by unchecked population control. Rather, there is now a neo-Malthusian component: Some populations use more of the available resources than others. For instance, an American may use 50 times more energy than the average resident of India; as 6 percent of the world's population, the United States uses 40 percent of the world's resources. One additional American, therefore, can have a disproportionate effect on the world's supply of resources. Students should be educated about these perspectives in order to help them make informed judgments about their habits and priorities and to help them to set policies for the next generation.

Animal experimentation. This is a very difficult, emotionally charged issue. People are very sensitive to uses of animals that are abusive or that can be portrayed in some lights as abusive. There are many legitimate feelings that certain experiments may be unnecessary to carry out or to repeat, and that the good that comes from such work does not sufficiently counterbalance the discomfort to the experimental subjects. Distress at such conditions may become dismay or disgust with the scientific community for allowing such practices to continue.

Students need to learn how important it is to scientists, too, that unnecessary experimentation be avoided. Cost-benefit analyses must be considered in carrying out research. Concerning scientific and medical issues, one thing is clear: The use of lab

animals can save lives, and not just human lives. If animal experimentation were forbidden, we could not test certain vaccines and lifesaving medicines. We could not develop new surgical techniques, nor fight epidemics of disease. And we would have to use other humans as test subjects at all stages of research. (Apart from the obvious ethical considerations, it is worth noting that we would have to wait an average of 25 years for the first results of experiments on genetic effects, as opposed to a few weeks for mice or a few months for rabbits.) We could not as effectively train new physicians, surgeons, and veterinarians.

It is sometimes difficult to conceive of how our lives would be different if animal experimentation were forbidden. One has only to look at the changes in disease and death rates of infectious childhood illnesses in our own century to realize how much we take for granted the advances that have been built on responsible experimentation with animal subjects. This observation does not mean, of course, that every animal experiment saves lives nor that laboratory animals are always kept in the best possible conditions. Public awareness of this issue should contribute both to the maintenance of strict humane standards in laboratories and to the public appreciation of what such experimentation means to public health and medicine. These goals should be important to all science educators in presenting this complex and emotional issue to students.

Evolution. Evolution is the central organizing theory of biology and has fundamental importance in other sciences as well. It is an accepted scientific explanation and therefore no more controversial in scientific circles than the theories of gravitation and electron flow. When scientists say that gravity is a fact, this is based on many observations of the attractions that objects have for each other. What causes that attraction and how these forces work forms a body of investigation that comprises the theory of gravitation. In the same way anyone can observe the workings of electricity by connecting a

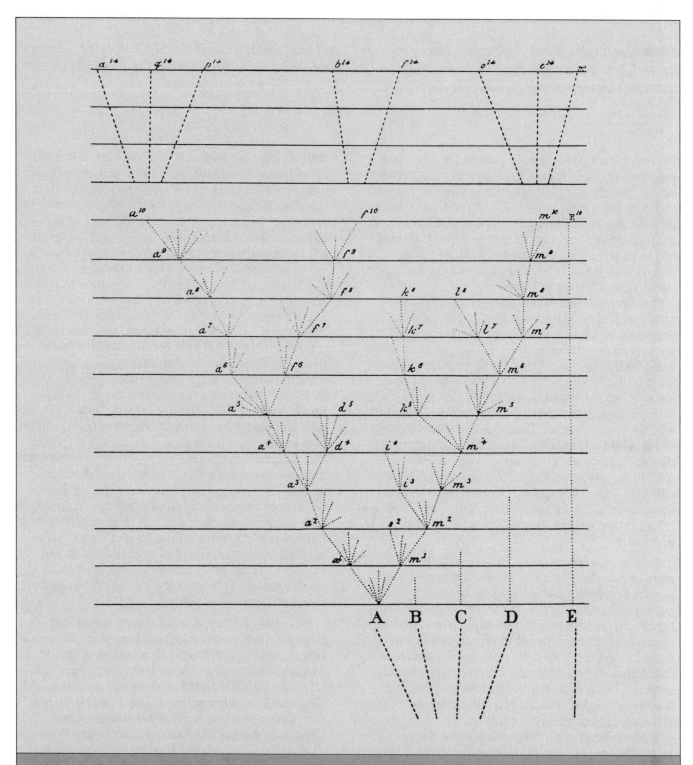

Figure 1. Darwin's conception of how lineages of organisms diversify and evolve through time.

battery to wires and a light bulb. It is a fact that the bulb lights because of electrical energy, even though the electron flow cannot be observed directly. The theory of electron flow is how we explain that fact and how electrons behave. Though we cannot see electrons—and there are probably ideas that we have about electrons that will be modified with further investigation—we are reasonably confident in saying that the motion of the electrons explains the lighting of the bulb. Saying that we understand how gravity and electricity work does not mean that we understand everything about gravitation or electron flow. Recently, for example, physicists were intrigued by reports that a previously unobserved force may act on ordinary bodies in addition to the familiar force of gravity. Current theory classifies all the forces of nature into four fundamental types, of which the force of gravity is one. If further investigation and testing substantiate the new reports, the theory of fundamental forces will have to be modified to include a theory of the new *fifth force*.

And so it is with evolution. Just as scientists observe the fact that apples fall and devised the theory of gravitation to explain the fall, scientists observe the fact that animals and plants change over time. They constructed the theory of evolution to explain how these changes occurred. Scientists base the theory of evolution on observances of the sequences of appearance, change, diversification, and disappearance of forms through the fossil record. Scientists breed wild and cultured plants and animals and note how inherited characteristics are modified and passed on to offspring. They observe how characteristics are also modified by genetic mutations, which contribute natural variations on which natural selection acts. Scientists also observe the detailed correspondence of genetic and biochemical sequences among closely related organisms that have been inferred from evidence of fossils and anatomy. As was predicted, there is a higher degree of correspondence in the genetic and biochemical composition of closer relatives than of more distant relatives. Scientists also compare the gradual differentiation of embryonic stages from nearly identical beginnings. To establish relationships, they identify unique characteristics of development, such as going through the metamorphosis of a butterfly or the veliger stage of a larval mollusk.

These observations constitute some of the evidence that evolution has occurred; evolution is the most

Some students may be concerned about evolution and its bearing on their religious beliefs. Teachers—and textbooks—should make it very clear that from a scientific perspective, evolution, like other scientific topics, does not bear on an individual's religious beliefs. Science is not theistic, nor is it atheistic; it does not presuppose religious explanations.

consistent and accountable explanation of these observations. The theory of evolution, like other theories, is more than the sum of the facts from which it is derived. It is the best explanation for the facts, and it has predictive value. How evolution has worked—its patterns, processes, mechanisms, and history—composes the theory of evolution, which is constantly being modified as new evidence emerges. Like the idea of a fifth force in physics, new mechanisms of evolutionary theory, such as punctuated equilibria, species selection, and periodicity of mass extinction, are current subjects of debate which, if they turn out to be well supported by all the available evidence, will modify current evolutionary theory. Regardless of the existence of a fifth force, apples still fall. And, regardless of whether the changes in plants and animals are gradual or sporadic, the evidence remains that plants and animals have evolved over time. Thus, the theory of evolution is the accepted scientific explanation of how these changes occurred.

It is very important for students to understand the observed facts and evidence that contribute to and form the basis for potential modification of the overarching theories by which science operates and advances. It is equally important for students to understand theories, because theories give meaning to the facts and guide further gathering of facts and evidence. Without theory, facts have little meaning; and without facts, theories are empty structures.

Occasionally, allegedly scientific evidence that appears to falsify or contravene the theories of evolution, geologic dating, the fossil record, or other related knowledge may be brought to the attention of the teacher. Criticisms of scientific evidence and theory on scientific grounds are part of science; teachers should treat the scientific challenges to the understanding of evolution in the same manner that they treat challenges to other well-established scientific theories. If teachers have the background and resources to investigate the claims, they should do so thoroughly and scientifically. If they do not have the background and resources to do so, they should indicate that they are not prepared to deal with the particular claim and that they have confidence that every effort has been made to make their curriculum as scientifically accurate as possible.

Teachers should be aware that the theory of evolution has been tested and refined for over a hundred years and that the majority of criticisms that find their way into popularly circulated publications have not been validated scientifically; usually, the criticisms have been evaluated and rejected by the scientific community. Teachers should consider the validity of such criticisms carefully before accepting them or deciding whether they are worth consideration. The particular case of "creation science" (or "scientific creationism") has been thoroughly studied by the leading scientific societies and rejected as not qualifying as a scientific explanation.

Some students may be concerned about evolution and its bearing on their religious beliefs. Teachers—and textbooks—should make it very clear that from a scientific perspective, evolution, like other scientific topics, does not bear on an individual's religious beliefs. Science is not theistic, nor is it atheistic; it does not presuppose religious explanations. Science is concerned with the mechanics, processes, patterns, and history of nature; it is neutral with respect to divinity, the supernatural, or ultimate causes. In fact, many of the scientists who have made important contributions to evolutionary biology, genetics, and geology have been deeply religious persons from many different faiths who did not find a conflict between their religious beliefs and their scientific understandings. Some people however, reject the theory of evolution purely on the basis of religious faith. Consistent with the State Board of Education's policy, concepts in the science curriculum should not be suppressed or voided on the grounds that they may be contrary to an individual's beliefs; personal beliefs should be respected and not demeaned. The way in which scientific understanding is related to religion is a matter for each individual to resolve; thus, the State Board's policy is that there should be a clear separation between science and religion.

Human reproduction. To make responsible decisions about their own lives, students must have knowledge of and respect for their own bodies. They must understand not only the heart, liver, and lungs but also the reproductive organs. Dangers facing our citizens and others throughout the world because of sexually transmitted diseases, birth defects, and the condition of young women who experience pregnancy and motherhood long before they are ready persist as everyday images in our technologically advanced world. With scientific and technological advances comes a responsibility to educate students about these dangers.

All students should understand the reproductive system, the causes of birth defects and advances in overcoming them, the ecological problems posed by overpopulation, and the means by which humans regulate their reproductive rate. Particularly in the past decade, which has seen the rise and rapid spread of the acquired immunodeficiency syndrome (AIDS) virus and the herpes viruses through a substantial part of the American and global population, education on these issues is more important than ever. We cannot hope to stem the flood of sexually transmitted diseases through our society without fundamental education about their etiologies and prevention.

Overpopulation is a biological issue with distinct human ramifications. It is well known that an ecosystem can support only a limited number of organisms. As populations grow, they strain natural ecosystems by overusing limited resources and by degrading the environment. This strain has an adverse effect on the quality of life and frequently opens the door for other maladies such as contaminated resources and disease. Students must appreciate, therefore, that environmental planning and research must include an analysis of how different population levels will affect the environment. Such populations include the plants and animals that humans use for food, shelter, clothing, and other purposes; and they also include humans themselves. Technology may not find answers fast enough to counter the impact of expanding human populations; therefore, people will have to make difficult but well-informed decisions about planning families and planning their use of environmental resources to the best advantage.

On the issue of human reproduction itself, many studies have shown that students have received a considerable amount of misinformation about sexual-

Technology may not find answers fast enough to counter the impact of expanding human populations; therefore, people will have to make difficult but well-informed decisions about planning families and planning their use of environmental resources to the best advantage.

ity from their peers, and as a population they are not sufficiently educated about this topic in their homes. Public education must include reliable, scientifically based, candid information on the anatomy and physiology of the human reproductive system, menstruation, pregnancy, birth, and birth control methods, including abstinence. Public education should include a discussion of the causes and transmission of sexually transmitted diseases. These topics should be treated professionally and openly. Students should be encouraged to ask questions. (See the State Board policy statement in the front of this document concerning excusing students from the discussion of certain subjects.) If a teacher feels uncomfortable with the subject, students should be referred to other personnel in the school system or to outside agencies.

These and other scientific or scientifically related issues may raise controversy in the science classroom. But controversy should not be a stranger in the classroom. The task of the science teacher is to guide students in the development of their abilities to approach controversial subjects coolly and rationally, with clear and critical understanding of what is understood in science, what is uncertain and to what degree, what is scientific and what is not, and how the scientific and technological factors bear on the controversy. The teacher is ethically and professionally bound to confine science instruction to the facts, hypotheses, and theories of science.

School boards, administrators, and parents must support the teaching of rigorous science, a rational application of science to broader issues in which science plays a part, and a careful study of the ethical issues raised by scientific and technological activities themselves. Teachers can stress that science as a system of knowledge is based on empirical evidence rather than on belief. While every student ought to feel comfortable in class, a teacher must not make accommodation at the expense of sound science or sound pedagogy. Science instruction should respect the private beliefs of students; on the other hand, the teaching of science cannot be suppressed merely because individuals disagree with it on religious or philosophical grounds.

Chapter 2

The Major Themes of Science

THE themes of science are ideas that integrate the concepts of different scientific disciplines in ways that are useful to the presentation and teaching of scientific content. As opposed to theories, which unify and make sense of facts and hypotheses related to a particular natural phenomenon, themes are pedagogical tools that cut across disciplines. The incorporation of themes into science curricula is a major goal of this framework. They are meant to integrate concepts and facts, to provide a context through which to present content matter, and to encourage better writing in science instructional materials.

The major themes of science are explained in this chapter. In Part II, the content portion of this framework, each paragraph ends with a bracketed reference to themes that may suggest ways the material can be presented. We stress that many thematic organizations are possible and present here some criteria and possibilities for developing themes in science curricula.

Section A   Introduction

THIS *Science Framework* differs from previous frameworks and addenda in its emphasis on themes of science. This section discusses (1) why themes are essential; (2) what some of the major themes in science are; and (3) how instructional materials and curricula can incorporate themes in their presentations of science.

As Project 2061 of the American Association for the Advancement of Science (AAAS) has noted in its book, *Science for All Americans,* themes should be a major emphasis of science curricula in order to reinforce the importance of understanding ideas rather than the memorization of seemingly isolated facts. Ideas connect facts, just as the framework of a house connects its building blocks. This vital framework is missing from much of what is taught as science today, and it must be restored. Along with the emphasis on the concepts and practices presented in Chapter 1, incorporation of major themes in the science curriculum is the principal focus of this framework.

What are themes? They could also be called big ideas, overarching concepts, unifying constructs, or underlying assumptions. They are distinct from facts and concepts. A fact is a statement based on confirmed observation and inference, such as the number of electrons in an atom of iron, the date of the discovery of helium, or the descent of birds from dinosaurs. A concept often involves several facts; for example, the concept of continental drift, the need for repeatable observations in constructing science, or how magnets work. Themes are larger ideas; they link the theoretical structures of the various scientific disciplines and show how they are logically parallel and cohesive. Scientific literacy lies not only in knowing facts and concepts but also in understanding the connections that make such information manageable and useful.

What are the major themes of science? Science can be organized in many ways; those presented here should be regarded as only one way to integrate the overarching concepts of science into a curriculum that spans scientific disciplines. The suggested arrangement of themes is designed to encompass and connect a great deal of the basic data and evidence of science. No doubt there are alternative arrangements that would work equally well. The important point is that at least some thematic structure will improve the recitation of disunited scientific facts and examples that has come to pass for science in many current curricula and instructional materials.

Six themes, explained in the following pages, are developed in this framework. They are:

1. Energy
2. Evolution
3. Patterns of Change
4. Scale and Structure
5. Stability
6. Systems and Interactions

The presentation of science could be organized along other thematic lines; possibilities include actions, reactions, interactions, matter, diversity and unity, hierarchy, energy and matter, and many others. While the particular configuration and number of themes is not crucial, the organization of content along thematic lines is.

Educators and developers of instructional materials are encouraged to weave these or alternative thematic strands into science curricula. The main criterion of a good theme is its ability to integrate facts and concepts into overarching constructs; thus, diversity and unity would make a good theme; conservation, applied to biology or physics, might also. Dinosaurs or apples, no matter how diversely or inventively used, are not themes in the sense described here.

Themes are also not the same as theories, which were discussed at length in the preceding chapter. Theories are organized around content in particular disciplines of science, such as the theories of gravitation in physics, evolution in biology, or continental drift in geology. Themes, such as energy or patterns of change, cut across specific content matter. By showing the interrelationships of different facts and ideas, themes serve primarily as pedagogical tools for the presentation of science.

With themes as a major emphasis, science curricula align with similar advances in other fields of education. These major themes—evolution, energy, patterns of change, and so forth—occur again and again in the sciences, whether one studies ecology, plate tectonics, meteorology, or organic chemistry. This is not surprising; unifying constructs are a part of any philosophically united discipline. Themes also appear in the arts, for example. In the study of painting,

Science can be organized in many ways; those presented here should be regarded as only one way to integrate the overarching concepts of science into a curriculum that spans scientific disciplines. The suggested arrangement of themes is designed to encompass and connect a great deal of the basic data and evidence of science. No doubt there are alternative arrangements that would work equally well.

"Science is constructed of facts, as a house is of stones. But a collection of facts is no more a science than a heap of stones is a house."

—Henri Poincaré (1860–1934), Science and Hypothesis

music, or drama, there are essential elements of aesthetics, such as balance and symmetry, direction, form and proportion, and tension and release, that permeate human expression and give meaning and purpose to our understanding of how art affects us. A theme in science might be compared to a theme in a symphony or a novel. In a symphony, a theme is a repeated musical idea that gives structure and unity to the music. In a novel, a theme such as success, war and peace, love, or duty provides a conceptual basis for the unfolding of the plot. In science a theme is more like the theme of a novel, whereas the content or subject matter of science might be similar to the plot of a novel. A theme represents a recurring idea that provides a context for explaining facts and events.

Section B   Why Themes Are Essential

THEMES are necessary in the teaching of science because they are necessary in the doing of science. A scholar does not merely collect facts and categorize them. Facts are useful only when tied to the larger theoretical questions of the natural world—how it works and how its parts fit together. Charles Darwin understood this truth perfectly well and expressed it eloquently in a letter to Fawcett:

About 20 years ago there was much talk that geologists ought only to observe and not theorize. . . . And I well remember someone saying at the time that at this rate a man may as well go out to a gravel pit and count the pebbles and describe the colours. . . . How odd that anyone should not see that all observation must be for or against some view, if it is to be of any service.

Darwin's message is that discrete pebbles of particulate knowledge build nothing. They must build an overarching structure. There must be some thematic connection and theoretical integration in order for science to be a philosophical discipline and not merely a collecting and dissecting activity. A thematic basis to a science curriculum reflects what scientists really do and what science really is.

Recent critics of science education have been dismayed by the lack of progress in students' understanding of the major concepts and issues in science. They cite the historical (and current) fragmentation of the major disciplines of science and complain that trivia seem to be the stock-in-trade of science lessons. Paul Hurd, Professor Emeritus at Stanford University, has observed that science is often taught "as a foreign language" in which isolated terms and apparently meaningless facts are arrayed for students' reading and regurgitation. Instead, themes should connect the realms of science; they should be stressed as students learn science; and they should also provide a framework to guide teachers in developing instructional tools.

Science and technology are expanding so rapidly that a thematic approach for students to use in learning science is more than just helpful. It is essential. Each branch of science has accumulated an enormous amount of detailed information. If the basic concepts of one field can be transferred by connection or analogy to another field, students will understand that there is a purpose and a logic to the system. If curricula and instructors are successful in developing themes for students to use in connecting and integrating science facts, then this intellectual habit will carry over and enrich other fields and disciplines. In this way an integrative, thematic approach to learning will help students not only to develop a meaningful framework for understanding science but also to approach problems in other disciplines as well as in their daily lives as citizens, consumers, and workers.

As noted before, this selection of themes is not the only possible configuration nor even the optimal number. These themes are emphatically *not* intended to be the titles of textbook chapters, units, or instructional programs. They are suggested as means of linking facts and ideas within and among scientific disciplines. They are not intended to be buzzwords. Indeed, the purpose of including thematic strands in science curricula would be defeated if the focus of science education now shifted to constant iteration of these isolated terms. Rather, themes should be integrated in their appropriate philosophical and empirical forms into existing curricula, to make the curricula more unified and more logically developed for students. In other words, it does not matter whether or not publishers and teachers use these exact themes in teaching science as long as they communicate explicitly the interconnections of facts through major ideas of science.

1

Energy

Energy is a central concept of the physical sciences that pervades biological and geological sciences because it underlies any system of interactions. Energy can be taught as a bond linking various scientific disciplines. Defined in physical terms, energy is the capacity to do work or the ability to make things move; in chemical terms, it provides the basis for reactions between compounds; and in biological terms it provides living systems with the ability to maintain their systems, to grow, and to reproduce.

In the physical sciences, energy can be explored in various manifestations (heat, light, sound, electricity, and so forth), in conversions from one form to another. Energy is perhaps the most important theme to the physical sciences because all physical phenomena and interactions involve energy. Whether one discusses the energy of heat, light, sound, magnetism, or electricity; the conversions of energy from kinetic to potential or from electrical to heat or sound; or even the products formed by the combination of an acid and base, energy is involved.

In the earth sciences the flow of the earth's energy comes from two sources. First, there are forces within the earth, fueled by nuclear reactions within the mantle and core, that translate through the crust and are responsible for the processes that drive mountain building, continental drift, volcanic eruptions, and earthquakes. Second, there are the forces on the surface of the earth, such as wind, precipitation, physical and chemical reactions, and the activities of living organisms (mostly driven by the sun's energy), that alter the face of the earth and are responsible for many geological processes.

In the biological sciences the flow of energy through individuals drives metabolism, growth, and development. The flow of energy through ecosystems determines how organisms interact through the trophic levels of communities. Because all life requires energy, biochemistry is really the study of how energy facilitates biochemical reactions that allow the body to synthesize biochemical molecules —the basis of growth.

The theme of energy is important to considerations of ethical behavior and the relationships of science and technology to society. Sources of energy on earth include solar, wind, and water power; geothermal energy; nuclear energy; and fossil fuels. Some sources of energy are virtually inexhaustible, such as solar, wind, water, and nuclear. Renewable sources, such as water power, can be recycled and replaced, while nonrenewable sources, such as fossil fuels, cannot be replaced. Students should appreciate these distinctions, the limitations of some sources of energy, and the need to conserve them or avoid their use.

2

Evolution

Evolution in a general sense can be described as change through time, and virtually all natural entities and systems change through time. But evolution is not just the history of natural things; it is also the study of patterns and processes that shape these histories. These patterns and processes may be astrophysical, geological, biological, or biochemical,

and all contribute to the evolution of the universe as we know it.

Evolution is more than simple change because it is change with a direction: that direction is time. Through time, life has evolved from simple forms into the present array of organisms on earth. Through time, the earth has also evolved from its original formation: oceans have formed; mountains have risen and have been leveled; continents and oceans have been formed, sundered, and re-formed; and the histories of past oceans and terranes (sections of land buffeted by tectonic plate action) have left their records in the geologic column. Evolution is not confined to the earth and its systems but extends to the entire universe. The progression of time has seen galaxies flung across space, interactions among celestial bodies influenced by their relative positions and gravitational attractions, solar systems flourish and die, and the universe expand at a changing rate. It is literally true that "even the stars have histories," and these histories are known in considerable detail.

Evolution embodies history and therefore is a part of every discipline in which history has a role. Current evidence indicates that the universe is at least 16 billion years old and that the present solar system condensed in more or less its present form about 5 billion years ago. The earth is about 4.6 billion years old, the oldest known rocks are nearly 4 billion years old, the first oceans are known from about 3.8 billion years ago, and the first forms of life from about 3.5 billion years ago. In order to teach life science, earth science, or astronomy, evolution should be a fundamental, central concept of the curriculum.

Evolution, which Darwin described as "descent with modification," is the central organizing principle in life science. Theodosius Dobzhansky said that nothing in biology makes sense without it. Evolution explains both the inherited similarities and the diversification inherent in all forms of life. While providing a comparative basis for studies of anatomy, structure, adaptation, biochemistry, and ecology, evolution is the basis for classifying living things and the operating principle on which biomedical research is founded.

History illuminates the study of all events and patterns in nature because these events leave their marks on their products. Light spectra emanating from distant stars can tell astronomers how old the star system is and where it stands in its life cycle. The sediments of natural geological features, such as the Grand Canyon, are traces of the past that can be read like a history book, telling what kinds of environments existed through time in a particular place, and how that place has changed. Fossils, of course, are the signature of life's history and evolution. Living things also show the marks of history, by retaining characteristics, however modified, that have been inherited from their ancestors. (An example is the bones of the mammalian middle ear, inherited and modified from the ancestors of the first mammals, in which they were bones of the lower jaw.) Using evidence of inherited characteristics, scientists classify living things into natural evolutionary groups.

Within evolution there are some recurring subthemes that can be woven into instructional curricula. One such subtheme is direction, and, as noted earlier in the treatment of evolution, time provides the direction to evolution. In most natural systems, what happens next depends to a large extent on what has happened before. In ecosystems, succession of a biome is more likely to have a predictable direction based on previous successional stages of the biome than it is to be random, because one successional community sets the stage for the next. The evolution of life on earth has been facilitated by the evolution of the atmosphere, which the organisms on earth have changed substantially through time. This has been an interactive process (see a related discussion under the theme of systems and interactions).

A related subtheme is that of constraints because, as just noted, what happens next is frequently constrained by what has happened before. Other kinds of constraints are physicochemical; they place limits on the future potential of systems. (If bones and shells were made of silicates instead of calcium phosphate and calcium carbonate, how would the architecture of life differ?) Some constraints are historical in the sense of descent: Organisms, as they evolve, have to work with the genetic tools they have inherited to modify their structures into new adaptations. (Vertebrates, for example, are built on a four-limbed pattern; in the course of vertebrate evolution, wings for flying have had to be fashioned from existing limb systems and have not sprung full-blown as new structures from the vertebral columns.) So there are strong constraints on evolution. There are constraints on physical phenomena, too. The sun affects and constrains planetary conditions of climate, geophysical processes, and rates of rotation and revolution.

A third subtheme is that of chance. The randomness of Brownian movement, genetic mutations, the Heisenberg uncertainty principle, and the toss of coins are familiar concepts in science curricula. Chance has played an important role in the development of molecules, structures, and societies because it presents natural variation in what is possible. Of course, each case is determined by specific factors and is anything but random. However, we use the term chance to describe what may happen in any given case, given the possibilities. For example, the chance impact of a giant asteroid with the earth billions of years ago appears to have thrown into space a chunk of earth that eventually became the moon. The chance colonization of a new continent by a small group of mammals triggered the adaptive radiation of horses in the New World; such chance events through the history of the Tertiary period, back and forth between America and Europe, fostered the evolution of horses. Random mutations are typical chance events; yet such mutations need the right combination of a genetic and physiological environment, to say nothing of the adaptive and physical environment of an organism, to be successful in their effects.

Chance factors important in the history of life include the unpredictable effects of genetic recombination, the restructuring of the genome, and the migration of new individuals in and out of a population and of populations into new areas. On a larger scale the introduction of predators or competitors, long-term and short-term changes in climate, and environmental catastrophes are all chance factors that shape the history of the earth and its life.

3

Patterns of Change

Change through time, of course, is one pattern of change, but there are other kinds. Rates and patterns of change are essential features of the natural world. Analyses of changes help us to describe and understand what is happening in a natural system and, to some extent, control changes (particularly in technological applications). Understanding different kinds of changes helps us to predict what will happen next. Knowing about different patterns of change helps us to identify patterns of nature as we encounter them and to look for underlying mechanisms and connections. Patterns of change can be usefully divided into three types: (1) trends; (2) cycles; and (3) irregular changes. Some systems or processes show more than one kind of pattern of change.

Changes that occur in steady trends are not necessarily all steady in the same sense, but they do progress in one direction and have fairly simple mathematical descriptions. Examples include the velocity of falling objects in acceleration, the decay of radioactive material, and the colonization of offshore islands by continental plants and animals.

Cyclical changes can be defined as an interval of time during which a sequence or recurring sequences of events or phenomena are completed; they are characterized by the range in variation from a maximum to minimum, by qualitative distinctions that appear and reappear, and so forth. Cyclical changes are often found in systems containing feedback mechanisms or where a system depends on the periodicity of another system (such as the life cycles of annual plants and animals, which are dependent on the earth's annual revolution). Cyclical changes are common to living systems: They include life cycles, seasonal cycles, biochemical cycles of nutrients, water, gases, and so forth; and the flow of energy and matter through food webs and food chains. In earth science cyclical changes include the various planetary cycles and their effects on seasons, tides, and weather; the rock cycle; the cycles of natural compounds such as water, minerals, and so forth; and the great geophysical tectonic cycles of mountain building, plate movement, and subduction, coupled with cycles of deposition, lithification, and erosion. In the physical sciences, cyclical phenomena include sound waves and ocean waves, feedback in electronic systems, and the action/reaction systems of chemistry, particularly cell chemistry.

Irregular changes are those that manifest the natural unpredictability of systems. These were discussed in a related way under the theme of evolution. Random changes may occur in reaction to small changes in stable conditions; some, for example, may appear cyclical but actually are never repeated in exactly the same way. These include the motions and periodicities of planetary bodies, the predator-prey cycles of ecosystems, population cycles and the dynamic equilibrium of populations, and plant succession cycles. Some random patterns of change may be unpredictable in details but in a larger sense are very predictable, and these include the examples just mentioned. The percentage of heads in a long series of coin tosses is expected to approximate 50 percent, but in a short series the fluctuation from this figure may be great. The toss of a single coin is considered such a randomly governed event that we use it, for instance, as an arbiter of fairness to assign the kickoff at the start of football games.

4

Scale and Structure

The kinds of structures that can be described in the natural world are many. The diversity of life, of geological forms and microstructures, of chemical and physical structures, configurations, combinations, and interactions appears to be almost endless. And it can be endlessly described in instructional programs, often to the exclusion of other important themes in science. The point is to show how different kinds of structures are related, how they explain and illuminate each other, and how structure at different hierarchical levels (a phenomenon of scaling) shows unique properties at each level.

The structure of the natural world requires language to explain it, but there are many ways to describe natural phenomena. Customarily, we recognize a phenomenon and give it a name that describes the phenomenon in the terms that make the most sense to us. Sometimes in science curricula, remembering the names and their definitions seems to become an end in itself. This is partly because scientific terminology is complex. A name, however, should not become more important than the phenomenon being described or than its empirical or logical relationships with other phenomena. Pure description, as Darwin's quotation in the preceding section points out, is not of much use until it is employed in the service of an idea.

The structure of matter—whether molecules, mountain ranges, or ecosystems—can generally be approached in several ways. One way is *reductionist*, a continuing search for the minutest levels of operation of natural phenomena. Research in the genetic code, the microstructure of cells, the lattice of a crystal, and the properties of neutrinos are all intended to explore the finest-scale workings of the natural universe. The complementary way to study the same natural phenomena is *synthetic*, in which all the levels of phenomena in a system are examined to see what roles they play in the overall behavior of the system. In a description of the structure of any system, both approaches are useful. One can reduce the study of an ecosystem to observations on individual organisms, their interactions with other organisms, and their own internal metabolic workings. Conversely, a vast body of knowledge can be synthesized about an ecosystem, including its interactions of predation, competition, and coevolution and its diversity and richness of species; these patterns and processes can be compared to those of other ecosystems.

There are component levels to the structures of most natural systems—whether one considers the hierarchy from atoms to molecules to compounds in chemistry, or the hierarchy from organelles to cells to tissues to organs to individuals to populations, species, and so on in biological organisms. What is usually striking about the structure of any natural system is that each level of its hierarchy has what are called emergent properties; that is, the phenomena at one level of the hierarchy cannot always be predicted from knowledge of another level. Some properties, of course, are readily predictable from other levels—such as the properties of diamond from knowledge of the tetrahedral arrangement of carbon atoms. Others are less readily determined; for example, one could scarcely predict the behavior of a deer simply by knowing the structure of its liver. The behavior of the deer is an emergent property of the level of its structure that interacts with its environment and cannot be easily reduced to lower levels of its structure.

The theme of scale and structure is intimately tied with that of systems and interactions because most systems are studied at some scale. As noted above, one could study a deer in several ways: as a part of an ecosystem; as a natural system of its own with circulatory, respiratory, and other functions; or as a host for many living systems of bacteria, parasites, and other organisms. The importance of any structural level in a hierarchy depends on the scale being studied.

The interplay of structure and function is another important component of scale and structure because it shows how parts function and how their actions work to support the whole system. The function of the deer's legs in running, for example, is an important part of its survival, and its locomotory adaptations can be contrasted with those of a crocodile or an elephant. The deer's digestive system, with its adaptations to digest plant material efficiently, also contributes to its overall survival. In a steel building, the function of each beam and the walls connecting them extends the microstructure and strength imparted by the arrangements of the atoms in the steel.

5

Stability

Stability refers to constancy; that is, the ways in which systems do not change and why. The ultimate fate of many systems is to settle into a balanced steady state or a state of equilibrium. In such states all forces are balanced. It is important to distinguish between the state of equilibrium and the steady state. The former is typified by a person sitting on a step of a stopped escalator, the latter by a person walking down a moving escalator just as fast as the escalator moves upward. Equilibrium is rare in living systems because living systems are inherently dynamic. (What physicists call steady state is what chemists and biologists call dynamic equilibrium.)

There are several kinds of equilibrium. A system can be in static equilibrium, as when a rock rests at the foot of a cliff, or in dynamic equilibrium, where the surface appearance is steady but much action is occurring at underlying levels. An example is a dish of water and carbon dioxide in equilibrium. Equal numbers of water and carbon dioxide molecules are always escaping into the atmosphere and returning to the solution, yet observable concentrations and pressures remain in a steady state. Other examples are the cellular and metabolic homeostasis of an individual organism and species and populational densities in an ecosystem.

Stability is related to the idea that nature is predictable. Given a set of initial experimental conditions, results are expected to be replicable. Indeed, failure to obtain reproducibility begins an immediate search for uncontrolled variables. Science is based on observations and set in a testable framework of ideas. Scientific theories and laws usually remain fairly stable because they are based on consistent evidence.

There is only an apparent contradiction between the theme of stability and those of evolution and patterns of change. The different themes may be applied to different situations or to different parts of the same natural situation. For example, the apparent stability in the composition of a lush tropical forest may mask constant change in its plant and animal populations. Students will learn to recognize these concepts, differentiate between them, and appreciate when it is appropriate to describe natural systems in these terms.

6

Systems and Interactions

Natural systems may include solar systems, ecosystems, individual organisms, and chemical and physical systems. By defining the boundaries of a system, a study of the system and its parts and interactions is possible.

There are many kinds of interactions in systems. The components of an ecosystem (individual species) may interact through predation, competition, commensalism, mutualism, parasitism, or any number of other patterns. At any time, a single component of a system can be interacting in various ways. A deer in an ecosystem can be a herbivore, an item of prey for a carnivore, and a living system itself with many subsystems of life functions (circulation, respiration, digestion, and so forth). To study systems, we generally focus on one or a few aspects of interactions at a time to avoid an overload of information. These interactions are commonly described in simplified terms as models. Models almost never simulate all the factors that are interacting, nor all the ways in which the factors interact, but they do provide a way of describing natural phenomena that are organized in systems.

Some aspects of systems can be studied in the language of technology: input and output. Air and fuel go into an engine, and mechanical energy, exhaust, and heat come out. Carbon dioxide, solar energy, and water react in a chloroplast to produce sugars, oxygen, energy, and heat in the photosynthetic system. The fruit, seeds, and oxygen that are the products of flowering plants are input for animals in the same ecosystem.

Feedback is an important feature of interactions in many systems. We are all familiar with the squeal from a loudspeaker as a microphone is placed too close to it, but some forms of feedback are not so immediate. If a deer population increases in an area one year it may overgraze its habitat. As a result the starvation rate may increase the next year, and the population may be reduced to its original carrying capacity. In turn, the abundance or condition of other organisms that depend on the deer for part of their biotic interactions as well as the entire system and its interactions are affected. (Obviously, there is a lesson here for human intervention and interaction with other living things.)

Section D   Incorporating Themes

THE role that themes play in science programs will ultimately depend on the knowledge base of classroom teachers and the techniques they employ. Incorporating themes into the science curriculum is most likely to happen when there is close and continual dialogue between teachers, science specialists, university faculty, and curriculum developers. Connecting the important science concepts with science themes will improve students' ability to make more meaningful the relationships between science concepts and other related disciplines.

This section develops a number of ways that themes can be used to enhance the science curriculum.

1

Themes should be used to integrate concepts and facts at all levels of the curriculum.

Science is too often presented as an endless and detailed description of natural phenomena, a parade of seemingly unconnected experiments and activities. Themes can integrate these separate pieces of information into broad and logically cohesive structures in which relationships among pieces of information are shown to illuminate the phenomena that are being described.

For example, when describing natural phenomena, instructional materials frequently present a series of boldfaced terms that are then defined, often using other terms that also require definition. Science instruction thus becomes little more than an exercise in the memorization of terms. Through the use of themes, such as those of scale and structure and systems and interactions, students can see how the parts fit together logically and how the information they are learning is used to describe other kinds of phenomena. A flower's parts can be named, described, and detailed, but this information is more useful and more vivid to a student if these parts are described in terms of how they facilitate reproduction or how their great diversity evolved from a basic floral plan or how they compare with reproductive systems in other kinds of plants and animals.

The integration of themes into science curricula does not mean that the usual curricular divisions of physical, earth, and life sciences need be discarded; in fact, they should not be. Within the individual disciplines, themes need to be instituted and developed throughout a year's study and from one year to another. In a general science curriculum, there is even more opportunity to show how individual disciplines are connected by thematic strands. Rather than being reorganized around themes, science curricula should be permeated by themes.

Consider an example of the theme of energy. In the physical sciences, energy can be explained in the context of basic chemical reactions and physical phenomena. Energy is required for or is a product of most chemical reactions. The physical forms of energy—kinetic and potential—are basic concepts of physics. In the earth sciences, energy drives geophysical processes of mountain building and continental drift, erosion and deposition of sediments, weather, and the expansion of the universe. In the life sciences, energy is the basis of growth and development of all living things: Each must gain energy in some way. Metabolism is based on deriving energy from biochemical processes. If a general science teacher discusses all of these topics in the course of a year, the theme of energy will surface again and again, and students will see it as a major, overarching idea of science. This is what might be called a horizontal use of the theme of energy to cut across disciplinary lines.

Now consider a more vertical concept: how themes can be developed through grade levels, continuing with the theme of energy. An elementary teacher can explain to students that energy is needed to make things move or work. Experimenting with different kinds of levers, the students can learn that some tasks require more energy than others. A simple pinwheel can be used to illustrate that there are many different forms of energy. You can make the pinwheel move by blowing on it, or you can hold it in the wind, or you can place it in front of a jet of steam from a kettle, or you can attach it to a small electric motor. In the upper elementary grades, such an activity can also be used to demonstrate the conversion of energy, a very important concept. In the higher grades the forms of energy can be classified as light, heat, electrical, nuclear, and so on. The flow of energy in living organisms and through ecosystems can be studied, modeled, and measured. Complex social and ethical issues involving scientific information about sources of energy for humans can be discussed and evaluated in light of this information.

It is possible that educators and providers of educational materials may wish to use themes creatively in the organization of one or more disciplines and at various grade levels. *Energy* is frequently found in curricula in these contexts, especially in physical or general science programs. This device is encouraged as a way to show the interconnectedness of scientific knowledge. But it is not mandatory or even recommended to reorganize the entire curriculum to do so, as long as thematic strands permeate curricula to provide depth of meaning and integration of information.

Of course, not all themes are for all teachers. The theme of stability, for example, may be difficult to bring to kindergartners in any context. The theme of evolution may be equally inappropriate for a chemistry teacher trying to convey molecular structure and chemical reactions. This should not be of concern. The same material can be presented in the context of energy or scale and structure. In teaching the primary grades, teachers can best build the foundations for science education by (1) instilling in students the joy of science through enjoyable, expanding activities and experiences; and (2) beginning to teach the processes of science, showing how they form the basis of all scientific activity.

2

Themes should be used to integrate the main subfields of scientific disciplines.

By using themes to integrate the principal subfields of scientific disciplines, teachers can help students to see the logical and material interrelationships of all sciences. For example, the subfields of life science such as genetics, evolution, and paleontology must be clearly connected. Genetics provides the understanding for the raw material of evolutionary change as seen in the fossil record. These connections are the principal ideas by which the facts of the subfields are explained.

The theme of evolution, in particular, as well as those of patterns of change and scale and structure, are unifying strands in the biological science curriculum. In a similar way the understanding of plate tectonics must be shown to proceed from lines of evidence coming from many different fields of science, including reversals of the earth's magnetic field, the geophysical data of matching mountain ranges, the technological monitoring of crustal "hot spots," the development of sonar, and the paleontological evidence of ancient distributions of plants and animals. Instructional materials must explain and emphasize these thematic connections in order to be acceptable.

3

Themes in science should direct the design of classroom activities.

Themes can be used to connect classroom activities and to provide them with a logical sequence and scope of instruction. For example, in a study of how energy flows through biological systems, students can initially monitor the flow of nutrients through a few easily kept organisms, such as houseplants, paramecia, flour beetles, or hamsters. Later, they can apply this knowledge to a consideration of the energy flow through ecosystems via food chains and food webs. Using the theme of energy to connect these two activities fosters a spiraling effect of the concept rather than the treatment of the two activities as

isolated. Activities should be used to explain terms and concepts in the service of themes because active learning better promotes the internalization of ideas and processes.

4

The emphasis on themes in science requires a reconsideration of how much detailed material should be included in science curricula.

Explaining the connections created by the use of themes in a curriculum takes time and space. To some extent omission of various traditional terms and concepts that are not well integrated in current instructional materials will be required. In evaluating what should be included, teachers and curriculum planners should give weight to those terms and concepts that support and develop the basic ideas of a field and the overarching themes that connect these ideas.

Current science textbooks are plagued by "the mentioning problem." This is what happens when an instructional program tries to include too many terms and concepts. They end up being mentioned instead of being explained. There is no optimal number of terms that should be covered and defined in a curriculum at a given grade level. If a term serves no further use in a chapter or unit than to define itself, its utility must be questioned. More than likely, this term is covered but not really explained or integrated in any useful way.

Some traditions of science education, including time-honored ones, may be found faulty if examined with the above considerations. For example, students traditionally learn in earth science classes that there are three kinds of rocks: igneous, metamorphic, and sedimentary. This taxonomy is a false one. Igneous rocks are extruded from within the earth, but they can be laid down just like sedimentary layers, which form through the action of wind, water, and ice. Both igneous and sedimentary rocks are subject to metamorphism by the pressure of overlying rocks through long spans of time. These kinds of rocks are not mutually exclusive. Furthermore, their explication as different kinds obscures the processes of sedimentation, metamorphism, and extrusion from within the earth's mantle that are only three of many important geological mechanisms. These processes of geology could better be explained through the themes of systems and interactions, patterns of change, evolution, and energy.

The emphasis on themes in science curricula provides a focus around which the terms and concepts given in an instructional program may be evaluated. One danger, however, is to take too literally the limited number of themes that are suggested in this framework. Other formulations are possible: Diversity, matter, hierarchy, motion, and conservation are examples of other themes around which curricula might be organized, and there are certainly many more. Other sets of themes are also possible; Project 2061, for example, uses systems, models, constancy, patterns of change, evolution, and scale. The point is for educators to ask of curricula and instructional programs, Why is this material being included here? What larger purpose does it serve in explaining this discipline or concept of science? Themes provide some guidelines for this kind of evaluation.

5

Using themes in curricula can improve the quality of prose.

When logical and structural relationships are emphasized in instructional materials, the writing is often improved. To explain relationships and themes adequately, writers will probably have to abandon typical readability formulas. (This idea is considered at greater length in Chapter 8, "Instructional Materials Criteria.")

6

Assessment should be thematically based.

The use of themes not only encourages better logical connections in science textbooks but also encourages such connections in review and assessment materials and in activities. The strict repetition of facts learned in chapters and units can be replaced by activities that encourage students to discover and construct connections between the important ideas of science in a thematic context. How do these facts and concepts, for example, form cyclical patterns, show the hierarchical scale in the system, demonstrate the role of evolution in producing this pattern, underscore the importance of energy flow? This is more interesting than the typical chapter review heading "What Have We Learned?"

7

Themes can be used to lay out basic principles of science that will operate in many subfields and other disciplines of science.

For example, the understanding of scale and structure is applicable whether one studies geological structures, biological structures, chemical structures, or what physicists call the structure of matter. The student who expects to find systems in which given interactions will be encountered and in which emergent properties of each level in the structural hierarchy will be explained and related is a student who is really being trained to understand science. Students can learn to expect that history leaves its mark on many details of structure, whether one studies life science or earth science.

Learning how to construct and apply conceptual models, one of the tools of advanced science, depends on the ability to see patterns, interactions, scale in structure, and the flow of energy in a variety of ways. These are all manifestations of the basic themes elucidated here. Furthermore, the understanding of themes such as evolution and patterns of change can help a student to anticipate concepts not only in science but also in history–social science, English–language arts, and other disciplines.

The use of conceptual themes will not by itself solve all the problems of science education, and educators should not be tempted to view themes as a new panacea. However, the incorporation of themes in thoughtful and judicious ways should improve the integration of facts and ideas, the interrelationships of theories and of disciplines, and the quality of instructional materials. It is clear that science education will not begin to reflect more closely on what science is all about until the overarching themes and ideas of science become the most important feature of science education at all instructional levels.

Part II

The Content
of Science

Overview

THE content of a science program is its heart. To take the thematic approach described in this framework, educators must make connections among scientific disciplines that have traditionally been taught as separate subjects. This can be accomplished in a great many ways. What follows should be interpreted as an illustration of one way that a conceptual approach might be organized within the traditional content areas of science. The themes that annotate the content detailed here are only one set that encompasses the important ideas of science; other sets are not only acceptable but also encouraged. Because this organizational scheme is somewhat different from previous ones, a few words of explanation are necessary.

Most sections begin with a paragraph about the unifying theories in the discipline. These paragraphs are meant to guide teachers in making the connections among the ideas within the discipline. There is a difference between *theories*, which are conceptual and empirical entities within the disciplines, and *themes*, which are pedagogical tools that cut across disciplines. The theoretical summary is followed by a set of questions that are central to the content area. The descriptions of content appropriate to various grade levels are then developed in the form of narrative responses to these questions. The purposes of this technique are to eliminate the emphasis on *factoids*—the isolated facts and definitions that have long dominated science instruction—and to provide a sense of discourse for instructional purposes. The choice and sequence of the questions are not definitive nor exclusive; another set of questions could portray the content equally well.

The questions are content-oriented, not theme-oriented. The narrative responses, however, are written from the perspective of one or more of the major themes of science, which are identified at the conclusion of the paragraph. They could often, just as appropriately, be written from other perspectives and address different themes. To illustrate this point, consider the first set of questions in Chapter 3, Section G, Energy: Light, which are: "How does light enable us to see? What are the sources of light? What is light?" A narrative written for the kindergarten through grade three response to those questions from the perspective of the themes of *energy*, *scale and structure*, and *systems and interactions* might be expressed as follows:

> When we see something, our eyes and brains are responding to the light that comes from objects we are looking at. Light itself is not something that we see or touch. Light comes from objects and enters our eyes, the organ of the body that is sensitive to light. A picture of what we are looking at is formed in our eyes and brain. Light is not like other things; it is not ordinary matter. The eye can see both very dim and very bright light, but there are limits. Because the sun is so bright a source of light, too much light enters our eyes if we look at it directly, and serious damage to our eyes occurs. Most objects do not emit their own light but reflect light from other sources. We can see them by means of this reflected light. The sun is our primary source of light. Other sources include electric lights of all sorts and objects that are burning. We can classify the light we see according to its brightness and its color.

In contrast, a narrative focusing on the themes of *patterns of change* and *systems and interactions* might read as follows:

> Light is given off by a variety of familiar sources, most importantly the sun. We seldom should look

directly at or into a light source because our eyes, the organs that receive light, are very sensitive. We can observe and discuss patterns in the intensity of light that allow us to see best because the human eye is sensitive to only a certain range of light—if the light is dimmer or brighter than the light in this range, the more difficulty we have with our vision. We also can note patterns in the amount of light that objects reflect, because different objects reflect different amounts of light. It is this reflected light that allows us to see.

To take a second example, in Chapter 5, Section C, Ecosystems, the first question is: What are ecosystems, and how do organisms interact in ecosystems? Part of the response for grades three through six is the following paragraph, written from the perspective of *systems and interactions*:

All organisms have roles in their environments. They eat some species and serve as food for others. Some organisms, like trees, shelter other species. Others, like fungi, decompose them. Some organisms fill more than one role.

An alternative passage, from the view of *scale and structure*:

All organisms have roles in their environments. Both the role they play and the ecosystem itself depend on the scale at which we investigate them. Under a rock, for example, we might find organisms and microorganisms that eat other species and their own kind, serve as food for other species, or decompose dead organic material. We would not expect to find a large range of diversity in kind or number of organisms. If we expand our scale of observation to include the entire forest in which the rock is located, we will find a range of organisms much wider in terms of numbers, types, and sizes, but they would all fill the same roles of producer, consumer, and decomposer.

Here is an example, from Chapter 4, Section C, Oceanography, of how the saltiness of the ocean might be explained to junior high school students from the standpoint of *scale and structure* and *patterns of change*:

Salts in the ocean have come largely from the earth's interior, mainly by volcanic activity. These salts (containing mainly chlorine, sodium, magnesium, sulfur, calcium, and potassium) contribute to the

shells of marine animals and are recycled into the waters and ocean sediments when these animals die.

The same concept can be written from the standpoint of *evolution*:

Originally, salts in the oceans came from dissolved minerals that were extruded from inside the earth. New material, brought up at spreading zones, has increased the dissolved mineral content in the oceans' waters even as these salts have been lost through deposition and subduction of oceanic crust. Freshwater runoff from continental surfaces has also contributed to the oceans' salt content through time. Although the oceans have always been salty, it is diffficult to determine precisely how the dissolved salt content has fluctuated through time.

These illustrations are given to demonstrate that different themes can be used to frame the same content. This framework insists that science prose be enjoyable to read, and this is a goal that we have also tried to achieve in its writing. When the prose flows more naturally, the connections among themes are clear; a mere checklist of isolated facts is more difficult to create or defend. Finally, it should be noted that vocabulary, though present in the narratives, is not a dominant force. Indeed, vocabulary should be used in an appropriate context and not introduced for its own sake.

The intended audience of these narrative descriptions is not students, but educators and textbook publishers. Essential vocabulary has been included for these readers, but it is not necessarily appropriate for the students of the grade spans indicated. For example, in life sciences, emphasis is given to the comparative structures of plants and animals, and the word *stomate* is used. Kindergartners can and should understand that plants have structures that perform specific functions, and their teacher may well use the word stomate in context, but the objective of the lesson should not be the students' ability to spell or define the word stomate. Appropriate vocabulary should be used at all levels; vocabulary should not dominate the curriculum or be an end in itself.

At the high school level, the use of mathematics has sometimes assumed a role similar to vocabulary at the elementary level—as a barrier and an end in itself. In the text of Part II, we sometimes have used a formula as shorthand for a concept or relationship. Students need not memorize the formula for the acceleration due to gravity with time, or to know how to calculate pH. It is important for everyone to understand acceleration as it relates to riding a bicycle or driving a car and to understand pH as it relates to chemical properties or to acid rain. Proficiency in mathematics should not be a prerequisite to learning science. Many students will be motivated to learn more mathematics when they see it applied in the context of a scientific problem. The content that is delineated here is for all students, not only those who plan to attend college but also those who need to acquire scientific literacy for their lives as informed citizens.

In certain cases, content that has caused confusion or misconceptions in the past is presented at a greater level of detail than is warranted for most readers. These comments, primarily intended for authors and editors, are often presented as sidebars.

The presentation by grade spans is intended to be cumulative. Each grade span after kindergarten through grade three presupposes not only the material in the prior levels but also its review and elaboration at higher levels. The effort in this presentation, and in the curricula that we hope it inspires, is to deepen concepts when they are revisited, rather than to repeat ideas at the same level of understanding.

Chapter 3

Physical Sciences

Section A — Matter

IN the study of matter and its interactions under familiar conditions, the central organizing principle is that the amount of matter stays constant. It is neither created nor destroyed; only its form is changed. In general, the number of atoms, the basic building blocks of matter, remains constant. Mass is an excellent measure of the amount of matter, so we express the constancy of matter as the principle of conservation of mass. Strictly speaking, mass and energy are interrelated in such a way that the true principle is one of mass-energy conservation. The conversion of mass to energy is observable only when very large energy changes occur, as in nuclear transformations. The focus in kindergarten through grade twelve is on the study of matter under familiar conditions, when energy changes are not large.

A-1 **What is matter, and what are its properties?**

A-2 **What are the basic units of matter, and where did matter come from?**

A-3 **What principles govern the interactions of matter? How does chemical structure determine the physical properties of matter?**

A-1

What is matter, and what are its properties?

Kindergarten Through Grade Three

Matter is the name we give to all the stuff in our physical world. From stars to dust, from elephants to fleas, everything is made of the same basic building blocks. Although the scale of our universe ranges from the very large to the very small, all of it is matter. [Scale and Structure, Stability]

All matter has properties that can be observed, defined, and recorded. Matter occupies space, it has substance, and we can measure its weight. Depending on the particular form of matter of which they are made, some solid objects float in water while others sink. Many forms of matter are identifiable by their color, texture, or shape; by their hardness or flexibility; by their taste and odor; by the sound or light that they emit and that we can perceive. [Scale and Structure, Systems and Interactions]

All things that we can sense directly are constructed of progressively smaller things. We use tools like microscopes, telescopes, or thermometers to perceive things for which our senses are poorly adapted or which exist beyond the range of our senses. To measure and talk about our observations of matter with others, we use standardized tools like rulers, scales, and clocks. The more we know about the properties of matter, the better able we are to describe

Careful observation is needed to distinguish superficially similar objects, such as an orange from an orange-shaped candle, or a glass of hot water from a glass of cold water.

Young students need practice in using their senses to observe and to gain confidence in their own observational skills. They need to observe and report and judge for their own benefit, not to meet an adult standard of what is right or wrong.

its structure, and the better we can apply our intellects to constructing an understanding of the world. [Scale and Structure]

Most things we see are mixtures of several pure substances. We make a mixture when we dissolve sugar in water. The taste of sugar is found throughout the mixture, which looks like water. The water and sugar can be separated again by evaporating the water to leave the sugar. [Systems and Interactions]

The matter around us exists in three forms or states: solid, liquid, and gas. Water, for example, is ice as a solid, water as a liquid, and steam as a gas. The state of water can be changed by heating or cooling it. Each of the states of matter has distinguishing characteristics. [Energy, Patterns of Change, Scale and Structure]

A-1   What is matter, and what are its properties?

Grades Three Through Six

The basic building blocks of ordinary matter are very small particles called atoms. Atoms are much too small to be seen with ordinary microscopes, but they can be seen with recently invented devices called atomic force microscopes. There are about 100 different kinds of atoms. The smallest particle of a pure substance that retains the properties of the substance is usually a molecule. A molecule is a group of atoms tightly bound together. Because there are so many ways to put atoms together, there are an almost unlimited number of different kinds of molecules and different kinds of pure substances. Substances that are made of only one kind of atom are called elements. [Scale and Structure]

The properties of matter depend very much on the scale at which we look. For example, sand flows through your hands almost like a liquid. But an ant carries a single grain of sand very much as you might carry a rock. Very often, however, the properties of matter at larger scales depend on its properties at smaller scales. Solid objects and liquids are made of particles that stick together; gases are made of particles that do not stick together. This accounts for many of the differences in properties between gases on the one hand and liquids and solids on the other. For example, gases are compressible or springy—see what happens if you strike the handle of a plugged bicycle pump—because the particles in gases do not touch. Liquids and solids are not very compressible, because their molecules do touch. [Scale and Structure]

To get a better understanding of matter at a basic level, it is useful to study the properties of pure substances. Some properties, such as the amount of space an object occupies, simply depend on how much matter is present and do not help us understand the substance itself. Other properties, such as color or hardness, do not generally depend on how much substance is present. Studying such properties can give us clues about how the substance is organized at a more basic level. [Patterns of Change, Scale and Structure]

This very fundamental principle—that the amount of matter (mass) remains constant—can sometimes be difficult to demonstrate successfully in practice by determining the mass before and after an interaction. This is particularly true if the interaction causes a gas to be produced, due either to a change of state or a chemical change. However, it is important to include gases to help students extend their understanding of this principle.

Because many properties of matter depend on the fact that atom-size building blocks exist, but not on the distinction of whether these are atoms or molecules, it is convenient to simply use the generic term particle whenever the distinction is not important.

The properties of most things around us, because they are mixtures, are very different from the properties of the substances that constitute the mixture. The strength of a fiberglass fishing rod, for example, is many times greater than the strength of either the plastic or the glass that, together, make up the solid mixture that we call fiberglass. Mixtures and their properties are very important to people who design and build things.

The amount of matter in an object is referred to as its *mass*. Mass is measured indirectly with a balance, which compares one mass with another according to the effect of gravity. If the effect is equal, then the masses are the same. [Scale and Structure, Systems and Interactions]

When matter interacts with other matter under ordinary circumstances, it changes in various ways, but it does not disappear nor is it created. The amount of matter (mass) remains constant. [Stability]

A-1   What is matter, and what are its properties?

Grades Six Through Nine

It is useful to make a distinction between those properties of matter that can be measured without changing the substance into another substance—physical properties—and those properties that are observed when the substance changes to another substance, known as chemical properties. Examples of physical properties include the boiling and freezing temperature of a substance and its color. [Stability, Scale and Structure]

Mixtures of elements or compounds can be separated using physical processes such as flotation, filtration, distillation, chromatography, and magnetic separation. All of these processes depend on differences in the physical properties of the substances. [Systems and Interactions]

Density is a property of substances that describes the amount of the substance that is packed into the volume which it occupies. Some substances are denser than others; the densest solids are about a hundred times denser than the least dense ones under normal conditions. A substance sinks in a liquid if it is denser than the liquid; it floats in the liquid if it is less dense than the liquid. Oil floats on water because it is less dense than water. [Scale and Structure, Patterns of Change]

The density of a substance depends on both the mass of the atoms of which it is made and the way in which they are arranged or packed together. The density of nearly all solids and liquids lies in the range between 0.2 g/cm^3 and 20 g/cm^3. The density of gases, however, depends greatly on their temperature and pressure. At atmospheric pressure, the density of most gases is roughly 1/1000 that of the corresponding liquids and solids. That is why it is not so easy to recognize the fact that gases do possess mass and can be weighed. Scientists did not understand this point clearly until the eighteenth century. [Scale and Structure, Systems and Interactions]

The individual particles that make up matter are in constant, random motion. In a solid, neighboring atoms are bound together strongly and vibrate back and forth. In a liquid, the particles are not so strongly held together. In addition to vibrating, they can slide past one another. However, they are still bound together and cannot easily move apart from one another. In a gas, the particles are independent of each other. They can move as far from one another as the container space allows. These differences are reflected in the density of matter. The fact that a gas consists of particles in rapid motion can easily be observed by studying the way in which a perfume can be detected rapidly at a distance. [Energy, Patterns of Change]

A-1   What is matter, and what are its properties?

Grades Nine Through Twelve

How the things of the universe look depends very much on the scale at which one is looking. When we use the tools of science to help us perceive the properties of matter at the atomic or subatomic levels, we learn new things because we see things in a new way. Chemistry is the branch of science concerned with the behavior of matter at the molecular and atomic levels. Over the past two centuries, chemists have developed an elaborate theory that explains and predicts the chemical behavior of matter very successfully and in great detail. Atomic physics is concerned with the behavior of individual atoms. Nuclear physics studies the structure of the nucleus, and elementary-particle physics (sometimes called high-energy physics) is concerned with the very smallest building blocks of which nuclear particles and all other matter are made. [Scale and Structure, Patterns of Change]

Atoms consist of electrons, which occupy most of the space in the atom, and very tiny nuclei consisting of protons and neutrons. Protons and neutrons have approximately the same mass, which is about 2,000 times greater than the mass of an electron. (Though the nucleus contains almost all the mass of an atom, it occupies a smaller proportion of the volume of the atom than the sun occupies of the solar system.)

The periodic table was originally developed in the latter half of the nineteenth century as a way to rationalize a seemingly limitless body of information about the chemical properties of the elements. Precise description of the properties and behavior of atoms requires a model more elaborate than the simple planetary picture furnished by the Bohr model. The precise description is not pictorial, but mathematical. This description, pioneered during the period 1925–1935, was the first major triumph of the then new field of quantum mechanics on which modern chemistry and physics are firmly based. Students should be helped to understand how periodic relationships can be used systematically to predict chemical behavior at least roughly, and so be led away from dependence on memorization. [Systems and Interactions, Stability, Patterns of Change]

Chemistry is concerned primarily with the arrangements of the electrons in the atom, since the spatial arrangement and energy of the outermost electrons determines the chemical properties of the atom. While it is difficult to observe the shapes of atoms directly, we can readily measure the energies of the electrons within them.

Models of atomic structure help us think about how chemical reactions take place. The simplest model, the Bohr atom, depicts the atom as a miniature solar system with the electrons orbiting the central nucleus. The Bohr model can explain some (though not all) features of the behavior of atoms. For instance, atoms in which the outermost one or two electrons are weakly bound to the atom easily lose these electrons. Consequently, such atoms exhibit metallic behavior. In solution the atoms can release electrons to form positive ions; in solid metals the atoms release some of their electrons to the solid as a whole, and the solid can conduct electricity because the electrons move freely through the solid. [Scale and Structure, Patterns of Change]

The way in which the properties of elements depend on the number of electrons contained in their atoms is exhibited clearly in the periodic table of the elements. [Scale and Structure]

Mass is a property of matter that directly affects the size of the gravitational attraction to other matter and the response of matter to unbalanced forces. Under ordinary circumstances, mass is an expression of the amount of matter, determined, for example, by counting all of the atoms in the sample of matter. In these circumstances, conservation of mass implies conservation of matter, and vice versa. [Stability, Scale and Structure]

A-2

What are the basic units of matter, and where did matter come from?

Kindergarten Through Grade Three

What we consider to be the building blocks of matter depends on how closely we look at matter. The building blocks of a house might be considered to be wood, brick, stone, and so forth. The building blocks of wood are different kinds of cells that are observable with a microscope. There are some things, however, that continue to appear the same as we look closer and closer, even with a microscope. Examples of these kinds of things are water, iron, plastic, and glass. The basic unit of a pure substance is smaller than a piece or amount that we can see or touch. [Patterns of Change, Stability, Scale and Structure]

A-2   What are the basic units of matter, and where did matter come from?

Grades Three Through Six

A pure substance, such as salt, is composed of very small particles which are all the same and which all have the properties of that substance, salt. These particles can get so small that we can no longer touch or see them, even with a microscope; they are still salt. However, if we dissolve the salt in water, we break the particles into even smaller units that no longer have the properties of salt. These basic units, of which salt as well as all ordinary matter is composed, are called atoms. When the salt dissolves, the atoms are separated and rearranged. All ordinary matter is made up of different combinations of atoms. [Patterns of Change, Scale and Structure]

Atoms are much too small to be seen, even with an ordinary microscope. (A penny contains more than ten thousand million billion billion atoms.) Atoms can be detected, both directly and indirectly, in many different ways. The properties of the things we see depend both on the particular atoms of which they are made and on the way in which the atoms are arranged. When ice melts into water, the arrangement of the atoms is changed. A very important special case of such change is chemical change. In many substances, atoms are strongly held together in tight clusters called molecules. In chemical reactions, there is rearrangement of the atoms within molecules. The burning of a match involves chemical reactions. In the burning process, the atoms of the match and the atoms of the surrounding air change their arrangement, regrouping into molecules different from those originally present. But the atoms themselves are unchanged. Atoms last much longer than the things made of them. All of the atoms of which you are made were once part of something else. Most atoms themselves were constructed from simpler atoms billions of years ago inside a star. [Scale and Structure, Stability, Patterns of Change]

A-2   What are the basic units of matter, and where did matter come from?

Grades Six Through Nine

Substances containing only one kind of atom are pure elements. Ninety-one different elements occur naturally, and about 14 more can be made artificially in the laboratory. A universally accepted chemical symbol is used for each element. Atoms of some elements can link together very weakly (as in solid neon at very low temperatures); others link strongly (as in the diamond form of carbon). In some elements, strongly bound molecular units are formed. For example, two nitrogen atoms form a tightly bound molecule which is given the symbol N_2, and oxygen atoms form O_2 molecules. [Systems and Interactions, Stability, Patterns of Change]

Atoms of different elements can react to form stable, homogeneous compounds. Energy is often released in such reactions, but in others, energy must be added. Compounds have properties quite different from those of the elements of which they are composed. [Systems and Interactions, Patterns of Change]

Atoms are made up of three kinds of particles, called electrons, protons, and neutrons. While an atom is itself tiny, the protons and neutrons are confined in a much tinier nucleus, and the electrons surround the nucleus in a "cloud." The electron cloud is 100,000 times bigger across than the nucleus. Each electron has a fixed amount of negative electric charge. Each proton has an equal amount of positive charge. Neutrons have no electric charge. The number of electrons and protons in an atom are equal, so the atom itself is electrically neutral. The properties of an atom are determined by the numbers of electrons, protons, and neutrons it contains. [Scale and Structure, Stability]

The properties of a molecule are determined by the number and types of atoms it contains and how they are arranged. The oxygen molecules we breathe consist of two oxygen atoms each; each of the carbon dioxide molecules we exhale has one carbon atom situated between a pair of oxygen atoms. In the quartz crystals that are the major component of ordinary sand, there are two oxygen atoms for every silicon atom. The silicon and oxygen atoms form a regular array, with each silicon atom surrounded by four oxygen atoms; each oxygen atom is connected to two silicon atoms. [Scale and Structure]

Sticking, linking, and bonding are all words used to indicate the existence of attractive forces between atoms or molecules. These forces are deduced from the observed properties of substances. Strong forces between atoms result in the formation of strongly bound groups called molecules. The origin of these attractive forces is the attraction between the positively charged nuclei and the negatively charged electron *clouds*. [Energy, Systems and Interactions, Stability]

A-2 What are the basic units of matter, and where did matter come from?

Grades Nine Through Twelve

The known properties of matter at the atomic and subatomic levels make it possible to reconstruct the history of the universe. The energy of stars is derived from a process called nuclear fusion in which light nuclei (nuclei comprising small numbers of protons and neutrons) combine to form heavy nuclei (nuclei comprising larger numbers of protons and neutrons). In this way, chemical elements more complex than hydrogen and helium (the two simplest) are formed. In all stars, fusion produces some of the elements. But processes called *supernova events*, which take place only in the violent explosion of large stars (much bigger than our sun), are required for the formation of others of the elements. The explosion spews these newly formed elements into space, where they later help to form other new stars. Two successive supernova processes are required to form all of the naturally occurring elements. We thus know that our solar system centers on a sun that is at least a third-generation star, formed about 4.6 billion years ago. The material constituting our earth, as well as the rest of the solar system, has come in part from supernovae which exploded and died at an earlier time in the approximately 20-billion-year history of the universe. [Evolution, Patterns of Change, Energy]

The chemical properties of an element are determined almost entirely by the number of electrons its atoms contain, which is equal to the number of protons in the nucleus. Most chemical elements have two or more isotopes. The isotopes of an element differ only in the number of neutrons in the nucleus. For example, an atom of the most common isotope of carbon, carbon 12, contains six electrons, six protons, and six neutrons. The isotope carbon 14 contains six electrons, six protons, and eight neutrons. The nuclei of carbon 12 are stable; under ordinary conditions they remain unchanged indefinitely. Like many isotopes, carbon 14 has an unstable nucleus that decays radioactively. Measurement of the ratio of carbon 14 atoms to carbon 12 atoms present in a sample of once-living matter is the basis of a powerful tool for measuring the ages of such samples. For determining the ages of rocks, meteorites, and many other types of samples, other radioactive isotopes are used. Radioactive isotopes are valuable tools for studying chemical and biological processes. [Evolution, Patterns of Change, Stability]

A-3

What principles govern the interactions of matter? How does chemical structure determine the physical properties of matter?

Kindergarten Through Grade Three

Substances behave differently when they interact. For example, solutions are formed when some substances are added to water, but others do not dissolve. This principle can be used to separate a mixture of sugar and sand. The amount of substance dissolved affects the properties of the solution, such as color or taste. [Systems and Interactions, Stability]

A-3 What principles govern the interactions of matter? How does chemical structure determine the physical properties of matter?

Grades Three Through Six

We observe objects behaving in many different ways, depending on their structure and their surroundings. Living organisms, for example, grow and change their shapes. Crystals also grow, but in a much simpler way. Some things float in water while others do not; some things dissolve in water while others do not. Many substances can undergo changes that do not involve alteration of their material composition. Water, for example, can freeze, melt, or evaporate, but it remains water in all three states. The components of mixtures of solid substances, such as salt and sand, can be separated from one another. So can mixtures of liquid substances, such as alcohol and

Many students at the grade three-through-six level will prepare their own foods and use household equipment and chemicals. They should learn to examine and respect these. All substances should be treated as potentially hazardous, especially when inappropriately used or handled. Substances can be categorized as hazardous in relation to their properties, such as flammability, corrosive nature (acid, base), or toxicity.

Students should understand the importance of radioisotopes in biochemistry, medicine, and industry. They should be aware that there are many natural sources of radioactivity to which the biosphere has been exposed since earliest times and that nuclear reactors are known to have existed in nature.

water. Substances can be distinguished by the ways in which they interact with one another. Oily substances, for example, tend to mix with other oily substances but not with water. Other familiar substances, such as vinegar, antifreeze, and household ammonia, mix readily with water. Some substances have special properties that allow them to interact with both groups. Soap is such a substance: When added to oil and water, soap allows the two to mix.

A-3 What principles govern the interactions of matter? How does chemical structure determine the physical properties of matter?

Grades Six Through Nine

The basic building blocks of large-scale matter, atoms and molecules, can combine in many ways. The field of science that deals with these combinations is called chemistry. Chemistry is devoted to understanding the properties and interactions of groups of atoms and how these affect the properties of substances. We use chemical theory to understand how compounds can be formed, naturally or artificially. Many interactions and changes are possible, from simple phase changes induced by heating or cooling to synthetic fabrication of new materials (e.g., polymers). Many common substances mix with water; some also react with it and create what are called acids or bases. An acid substance can be neutralized by adding a proper amount of a basic substance. [Systems and Interactions, Scale and Structure]

Chemical reactions either absorb or give off energy, often in the form of heat energy but also in other forms such as light energy or electrical energy. [Systems and Interactions, Scale and Structure]

Chemists continually create new atomic arrangements to fill human needs. For example, compounds are being synthesized to replace the commercially important Freons that do damage to the ozone layer of the upper atmosphere. It is important to know as much as possible about substances because, among other reasons, many forms are dangerous if not used knowledgeably. They may be dangerous in themselves, they may combine to form dangerous substances, or their beneficial applications may have undesirable long-term effects. It requires good judgment, based on an understanding of chemical and biochemical principles, to make wise decisions about substances that, though useful, may be hazardous if not properly controlled. [Systems and Interactions]

The interactions of matter can be detected in many substances, including most household chemicals, by using colored indicators. The idea that a given quantity of a substance will react with a fixed quantity of a second substance should be introduced early in the study of science. Students can titrate clear ammonia with white vinegar using red cabbage indicator, or they can compare antacid tablets quantitatively. Such experiments should be used to reinforce the distinction between absolute quantities and concentrations.

A-3 What principles govern the interactions of matter? How does chemical structure determine the physical properties of matter?

Grades Nine Through Twelve

The number and arrangement of electrically charged particles within atoms or molecules govern the predictable arrangements and rearrangements of the atoms in new substances. In these chemical reactions, matter is neither created nor destroyed but merely rearranged; mass is conserved and the atoms themselves remain unchanged. The electrical forces of attraction and repulsion between the particles determine how the atoms are bonded, or connected, to one another and how the connections will change. [Systems and Interactions, Patterns of Change]

The study of chemical reactions has led, over a long history starting with iron, bronze, and glass manufacture, to the creation of a vast complex of industries that produce materials essential to modern life. Among these materials are plastics, fuels, metals, and medicines. An understanding of chemistry is essential to understanding agriculture, health, geology, and the use of natural resources. Chemical reactions of direct significance to society are also involved in the manufacture of fertilizers, in the burning of fuels, in cooking, photography, medicine, and pollution control, among many other fields. [Systems and Interactions, Energy]

In many circumstances, atoms and molecules are present in the form of *ions*—atoms or molecules that have lost one or more of their outermost electrons or gained one or more extra electrons. Because they can carry electrical charge from one place to another as they move, ions are of central importance in many solutions (such as the liquid in automobile batteries), in living systems (ionic balance is essential to proper function and metabolism), and in many crystals (such as table salt). [Systems and Interactions, Scale and Structure, Energy]

The complex interactions among the atomic or molecular units of a substance determine the large-scale behavior of the substance. If the forces between atoms or molecules are very weak, the substance is likely to be a gas at normal temperatures. If stronger attractions exist, the substance may be a liquid. Still stronger forces lead to the formation of solids of various types. In metals, the atoms are organized with a minimum of space between them, and some elec-trons can move relatively freely throughout the solid. This property underlies the familiar properties of metals: electrical conduction, malleability, luster, and the ability to take a high polish.

Intermediate between metals, which conduct electricity well, and nonmetals, which conduct electricity very poorly because all the electrons are tightly bound to the atoms, is the class of materials called semiconductors. In semiconductors, the number of electrons that are free to move can be controlled precisely over a wide range by means of tiny amounts of deliberately added impurities. By exploiting this property, it becomes possible to fabricate many different kinds of electrical switches and amplifiers and to build a wide range of devices that include miniature radios, computers, and information transmission systems. [Systems and Interactions]

Modern chemical and physical techniques have advanced to the point that materials with certain properties can be "custom built" in very small amounts. Such materials include liquid crystals used in watches and other custom-built materials used in superconducting magnets, radiation detection devices, and chips for advanced miniature computer networks. As more is understood about the relationships between structure and properties and about ways to control chemical reactions (see Section B), it will be possible to manufacture larger quantities of such materials and create new applications and new industries. [Scale and Structure]

Many substances, both natural and artificial, are toxic to human life, as are radioactive products. For each such substance, it is important to establish safe tolerance levels and to devise procedures to ensure that these levels are not exceeded. Waste disposal and food preservation and production problems have important social, political, economic, and scientific aspects. Satisfactory solutions of these problems require a substantial public understanding of all of these aspects. [Systems and Interactions]

Section B   Reactions and Interactions

IN the study of the changes in the properties of substances as they interact, chemists observe the changes in internal organization and in energy content as a function of time, temperature, concentration of substances, type of solvent, and so forth. The science of chemistry aims to understand the detailed principles governing how such changes take place so that new substances are governed by a principle of minimization of the energy, provided that a suitable pathway for change is available. A molecular collision model is successful in explaining most features of substances undergoing change. Molecules react to form different molecules when they collide with sufficient kinetic energy and in the appropriate orientation. In kindergarten through grade twelve, the focus is on establishing an understanding of the main features of chemical change and the roles of energy and time. Students should gain considerable experience in observation of substances and change and in making inferences about what is happening on the microscopic level after constructing physical and mental models of the structure of matter at the molecular level.

B-1 What happens when substances change?

B-2 What controls how substances change?

B-1

What happens when substances change?

Kindergarten Through Grade Three

Two substances can interact to form new substances with different observable properties. Such changes can occur instantly, such as when vinegar or lemon juice is added to milk, or take much time, as when an iron nail rusts in water. In some reactions, a solid plus a liquid will produce a gas, as when vinegar is added to baking soda. In other cases, a solid may be formed from a gas, such as when carbon dioxide is blown through a limewater solution. In every case, careful observation is needed to see that new substances are formed. [Systems and Interactions, Patterns of Change]

Chemical change can be helped by adding heat and can be useful, as when a cookie is baked from raw ingredients. Chemical reactions are useful in other ways, as when soap is made to foam better in water which has been treated with washing soda to precipitate salts as carbonates. [Energy]

B-1   What happens when substances change?

Grades Three Through Six

The amount of matter present before and after reactions remains the same when measured as mass with a balance.

Compounds result when true chemical reaction has occurred. It is sometimes difficult to distinguish between the formation of a new compound from the interaction of substances and the formation of a mixture. The latter can generally be separated by physical methods such as filtration, chromatography, or distillation; the former defy reseparation by simple means into the original components. Even in the formation of mixtures, energy changes, observed as temperature changes, may occur. [Scale and Structure, Energy]

Compounds have well-defined compositions involving new molecular combinations of whole numbers of atoms with new linkages. In mixtures, no linkages are broken or formed, but existing units are intermingled. Thus, in the formation of water molecules, linkages in hydrogen and oxygen molecules must be broken so that new arrangements in H_2O can be made, whereas to mix NH_3 molecules with H_2O molecules, no linkages need be broken. Compounds also have well-defined geometric arrangements of atoms. Some are in a straight line, others are triangular, or pyramidal. Simple rules govern the great majority of possible atomic arrangements. It is important to establish that drawings of molecules on

The reaction of vinegar with baking soda can be performed in a two-liter plastic bottle to demonstrate that the amount of matter remains the same after reaction. Other methods may be subject to buoyancy corrections.

Students at the grade three-through-six level benefit from continual practice in careful observation and in making inferences from such experiments as the lighting and subsequent burning of a candle. Hot packs and cold packs, familiar to sports enthusiasts, are ideal subjects for observation and inference.

Students should be introduced to the concept of the use of models in science by such exercises as constructing molecules from toothpicks and candies or bolts with nuts and washers following certain valency rules for allowed combinations. The HONC rule (H=1, O=2, N=3, C=4) can be used to construct correct models of large numbers of real molecules. Change of one molecule to another can be accomplished only by pulling apart the appropriate stick or connection. Class-constructed molecules can be intermingled without breakage to simulate a mixture.

paper or the chalkboard are a poor representation of the real shapes of three-dimensional atoms and molecules. [Scale and Structure, Patterns of Change]

Many substances that seem quite different react in similar ways. For example, acids present in many household chemicals or foodstuffs will change the color of plant extracts in a similar way. Those which are bases will have an opposite effect. [Patterns of Change]

Heat energy assists many chemical reactions; on the other hand, reactions can also result in continuous production of heat. [Energy]

B-1   What happens when substances change?

Grades Six Through Nine

In chemical reactions, atoms are neither created nor destroyed. By using familiar symbols for atoms, the science student can convert this conservation principle to a useful bookkeeping method for atoms. Such chemical equations are useful in keeping track of the quantities of substances involved by using mass as a measure of quantity. Just as in a bank, where weighing is used to count large numbers of coins of defined mass, atoms have defined masses, and so total masses must balance, even though the organization of units may change. Amounts of chemicals needed for complete reaction, product yields, and leftover unreacted quantities can thus be predicted and/or measured.

In some reactions, the changes in linkages result in a reorganization of electrons within substances, so that electrons can be transferred between substances. Such reactions can be used to form useful devices called batteries and to create coatings of metals through electroplating.

Certain reactions can be classified as *displacements*, in which one atom or group in a substance is exchanged with that from another substance. This concept explains why precipitates form when two solutions are mixed.

Even in the complex chemical systems found in living organisms, chemical reactions follow the same basic principles: conservation, accountability, reaction type. For example, the process of photosynthesis in plants requires the presence of all the ingredients (light, carbon dioxide, water, chlorophyll) in the proper amounts in order that a certain amount of product starch and oxygen can be produced. The human body needs a balanced diet to carry out the proper chemical reactions needed for healthful living. [Scale and Structure, Patterns of Change, Systems and Interactions]

B-1   What happens when substances change?

Grades Nine Through Twelve

When atoms are rearranged in a chemical reaction, there is a very small change in mass, but it is far too small to be significant. The total electric charge of the system of atoms also remains constant as they recombine under the influence of the electric forces that underlie all chemical interactions. The total energy of the system also remains constant in a reaction, but energy is converted from the electrical form involved

In explaining nuclear processes, nuclear theory plays a role at the subatomic level that is analogous to the role played by atomic theory on the atomic level. Neutrons and protons in nuclei occupy energy states analogous to the energy states of electrons in atoms. Conservation of mass-energy is important as measurable mass-energy interconversion occurs. Other more complex conservation rules also exist.

in atomic bonding to other forms, or vice versa. [Energy]

Conservation (constancy) of mass, electric charge, and energy are extremely important theoretical considerations in the study of chemical reactions and make it possible to account for everything occurring in reactions. Balanced quantitative equations such as:

$$2H_2 + O_2 \rightleftarrows 2H_2O + 3.92 \times 10^{-19} \text{ joules of energy}$$
per molecule of H_2O produced

describe the arrangements and numbers of atoms in both the reactants and the products in the reaction of hydrogen gas and oxygen gas to form water. The plus sign before the quantity of joules of energy indicates that this is released to the surroundings when this reaction takes place. This energy must have come from reorganization of the electrical forces as the hydrogen and oxygen atoms are bonded in the water molecule.

In practical situations, scientists usually work with much larger numbers than one molecule. A common unit is the *mole*, which refers to 6.02×10^{23} molecules. The energy released when hydrogen and oxygen react to produce 1 mole of water is 3.92×10^{-19} joules/molecule $\times$ 6.02×10^{23} molecules $= 2.36 \times 10^5$ joules. This is a large amount of energy and indicates that if hydrogen is readily available, reacting it (burning) with oxygen from the air can be a useful source of heat. [Scale and Structure, Energy]

Charge balance can also be accounted for by use of quantitative equations, such as:

$$HCO_3^- + Ca^{2+} \longrightarrow CaCO_3 + H^+,$$

which represents what happens when baking soda is added to hard water containing calcium ions. The equation predicts that the solution will become more acid because more hydrogen atoms are added.

In many chemical reactions, energy must be added from external sources to accomplish a desired reorganization of electrical forces. Such energy is commonly added as heat or as electrical energy. This is especially important in the manufacture of very

important simple chemicals—frequently elements—from naturally occurring ores. Obvious examples are the production of iron and aluminum carried out on a very large scale. The energy per mole needed to melt and reuse materials such as aluminum cans is much less than that needed to free aluminum from its ores. Thus, recycling must gain in importance as energy costs increase.

The nuclei of atoms are unaffected by chemical processes; however, they can be altered by nuclear processes. Since the amount of energy involved in forces within the nucleus is much larger than that involved in chemical reactions, much more energy may be released per nuclear event. Such processes involve about a million times more energy than the typical chemical reaction and can result in the transmutation of an atom of one element to an atom of another.

Understanding nuclear reactions enables us to construct electrical power plants that do not produce carbon dioxide or smog-producing substances. It also enables the construction of extremely destructive weapons and the production of radioisotopes of great

The mole unit is historically based on the number of hydrogen atoms in 1 gram of hydrogen atoms. Today it is more precisely the number of atoms in exactly 12 grams of atoms of an isotope of carbon—carbon 12. Students need help in realizing that this awkward-sounding number is a useful concept in helping do bookkeeping of atoms and enables us to use convenient mass quantities as a substitute for actual counting. It is no more complicated than handling eggs in dozens and keeping track of the differing masses of small, large, or extra-large eggs by using a balance.

importance to medicine, industry, and research in biology and chemistry. Radioisotopes also occur in nature, and the study of these natural radioisotopes has enabled scientists to determine the age of samples of inorganic and organic matter. Such knowledge is important to history and archeology as well as to geochemistry. For example, with the use of samples from the earth, the moon, and meteorites, scientists have been able to develop dating techniques that are used to build up a consistent set of ages for the earth and the various portions of the solar system.

B-2

What controls how substances change?

Kindergarten Through Grade Three

Change is affected by surroundings. On a hot day, an ice cube melts more rapidly, while it will survive for a long time in a freezer. If a cup of water is sealed in a plastic bag, condensation on the plastic demonstrates that the liquid has changed to a gas and then back to a liquid. If the cup is left in the open, change to a gas occurs, but the evidence is different.

Change often must be initiated by providing energy; for example, a match is needed to light a fire. [Patterns of Change, Energy]

B-2   What controls how substances change?

Grades Three Through Six

Measurements can be used to explore the effects of changing conditions on the way change occurs. For example, the time a seltzer tablet takes to dissolve can be measured as a function of the temperature of the water. Food preparation involves relationships between temperature and time.

The kinetic-molecular theory of matter explains how chemical interactions can take time and depend on temperature. Molecules must meet and collide with enough impact for successful change. [Energy, Patterns of Change]

B-2   What controls how substances change?

Grades Six Through Nine

The ease with which chemical substances gain or lose electrons in forming compounds or in forming ions in water solution is related to the basic electrical structure of the substance. For the chemical elements, this property is related to their position in the periodic table. Many other properties of elements and families of elements can be related to their location in this table.

In forming linkages with each other, atoms are in contest for attraction of the electrons farthest away from the nuclei. This contest is often unequal and results in linkages in which the electrical charge is not symmetrically distributed. Such linkages are called *polar bonds*. Molecules containing polar bonds are frequently unsymmetrical and are called *polar molecules*. These molecules with unsymmetrical charge shapes attract each other. Thus, substances with polar molecules tend to mix well with other substances with polar molecules but not with substances consisting of nonpolar molecules, and vice versa. This principle explains why wax dissolves in oil but not in water, why gasoline and water do not mix, and why many other observed phenomena occur. [Scale and Structure, Patterns of Change]

A certain energy is released or used by each molecule changed in a chemical reaction. Since a mole is a fixed number of molecules and has a determined mass for each substance, the reaction energy is proportional to the mass of the reacting substance. Approximate reaction energy can be determined by measuring the temperature change and mass of the reacting substances in water solutions. However, heat energy is easily lost, so insulated equipment and careful control are needed. (See Section E, Energy: Heat.) [Energy, Scale and Structure]

Certain reactions are aided by the presence of substances called catalysts or enzymes. The amount of these substances present is not important, and they

Here is one way to demonstrate equilibrium in a chemical reaction system: Prepare a tube containing pure alcohol (ethanol), a few cobalt chloride crystals to color it, and a few drops of water. This system is very sensitive to temperature, changing color from pink to blue and back again as the temperature is raised and lowered.

Chemical reactions appear to be difficult to understand, but various demonstrations can be used to initiate discussion. For instance, two oil drops on a thin film of water will not coalesce unless they actually touch and are pushed together, but if a small amount of detergent is added, they coalesce readily. This set of observations is analogous to what happens when two atoms combine chemically in the absence or presence of a catalyst.

are not changed in the reaction. They are especially important to the function of living systems, which must carry out complicated chemical reactions within a very small range of temperature. [Systems and Interactions, Energy]

Closed systems often reach an equilibrium situation. For example, water in a clear, sealed container can be seen not to evaporate completely. However, the amount of liquid varies with the temperature. [Stability]

B-2   What controls how substances change?

Grades Nine Through Twelve

The collision model for chemical reactions explains the observable features. The more molecules that are present, the greater the chance of interaction. The more rapidly molecules are moving, the greater is the chance that they will collide with sufficient energy to undergo the desired changes in structural organization. A catalyst assists this organizational step by helping to hold the molecules together in a more suitable orientation for successful reaction. Thus, less energy is needed, and the reaction can proceed at a lower temperature. [Patterns of Change, Energy, Systems and Interactions]

Elements that are metals can be compared in terms of ability to transfer electrons by means of cell voltage measurements or comparative displacement reaction observations. Metals that are widely dissimilar in this series can be used in a battery or electrical energy source. Many similar reactions are involved in corrosion of commonly used metals. Protection methods can be devised once the chemical reactions occurring are understood. Electron transfer reactions are important in living systems in vital cell processes. [Systems and Interactions, Stability]

Section C   Force and Motion

THE central organizing principle of classical mechanics is the set of three laws called Newton's laws of motion. These laws can be applied to specific situations; most notable are those in which the force is either gravitational or electromagnetic. In light of the more general laws of relativistic mechanics pioneered by Einstein and of the laws of quantum mechanics, Newton's laws become a special case. However, for most cases involving familiar scales of size and speed, classical mechanics is completely satisfactory.

C-1   **What is motion? What are some basic kinds of motion? How is motion described?**

C-2   **What is force? What are the characteristics of forces? What is the relationship of force to motion?**

C-3   **What are machines, and what do they do? What principles govern their action?**

C-1

What is motion? What are some basic kinds of motion? How is motion described?

Kindergarten Through Grade Three

The location of stationary objects can be specified with reference to other stationary objects. Distances between objects can be measured. The motion of moving objects can be described and categorized (straight, circular, crooked, and so forth), and speed can be described as fast, slow, the same, and so forth. [Patterns of Change]

C-1   What is motion? What are some basic kinds of motion? How is motion described?

Grades Three Through Six

A moving object is one that changes position as time passes. Speed is a measure of the distance traveled (change in position) by the object during a certain time interval; it is, for example, the distance moved in one second or in one hour. The units of speed will be determined by the units used to measure distance and time. For example, a speedometer provides a quick reading of the speed of a car in miles per hour. The motion of an object at a certain speed also has a direction. Direction can be specified in various ways: up/down, left/right, compass directions, and so forth. [Patterns of Change, Systems and Interactions]

C-1   What is motion? What are some basic kinds of motion? How is motion described?

Grades Six Through Nine

Speed (v) is expressed quantitatively by the relation $v = d/t$, in which d is the distance moved during a time interval t. The units of speed depend on the units chosen for distance and time. If the speed is not constant over the distance d, v should be interpreted as the average speed. Speed in a particular direction is given the name *velocity*. Thus, to specify the velocity of an object, it is necessary to give the speed and the direction in which the object is moving. Measurements of both position and speed depend on which reference system is chosen. [Patterns of Change]

Various kinds of motion are characterized by the behavior of an object's velocity. Three common and important kinds of motion are constant velocity (constant speed in a straight line), uniform circular motion (speed is constant, direction continuously changes), and oscillatory motion (speed continuously changes and direction reverses periodically). [Patterns of Change]

C-1   What is motion? What are some basic kinds of motion? How is motion described?

Grades Nine Through Twelve

When the velocity of an object is changing, we say the object is accelerating. The concept of acceleration is difficult for students and therefore should be presented with many real examples. Acceleration (a) is defined as the change in velocity (Δv) divided by the change in time (Δt); i.e., $a \equiv \Delta v/\Delta t$. Acceleration is the quantity that tells us the rate at which the velocity is changing.

Like velocity, acceleration has a direction. Many important physical situations occur in which acceleration is constant or nearly so. The ability to represent and analyze motion in one dimension both quantitatively and graphically when either the velocity or the acceleration is constant is important. A much deeper understanding of the concepts of displacement, velocity, and acceleration is obtained by the use of multiple representations and repeated practice relating them to the motion of real objects. [Patterns of Change]

Science concepts should be related to the everyday experience of students and introduced in language with which the students are familiar. Therefore, customary (common or everyday) units such as feet and inches would be used initially when discussing concepts such as position and speed. Metric units should be introduced early and continually reinforced, but when new concepts are being learned, the units with which students are most familiar should be used. However, teachers should be aware that some students will be more familiar with metric units than others. This applies from kindergarten through grade twelve.

The extension of the concept of speed to include direction is important, because the relation of force to motion involves both speed and its direction. Velocity should be introduced when the relation of force to motion is discussed.

Another important motion is uniform circular motion, such as that of a ball on the end of a string, the rotation of a centrifuge, or the nearly circular motion of the earth around the sun. For this type of motion, the speed is constant, but the direction of the velocity is changing, so the object is accelerating. The acceleration is toward the center of the circle. [Patterns of Change]

Wave motion is another common and important type of motion. A mechanical wave is a repetitive disturbance that propagates (moves) through a continuous medium. Ripples on the surface of water and sound waves are typical mechanical waves. When a wave propagates through a medium, the individual particles move back and forth. The disturbance itself propagates through the medium by setting new parts of the medium into oscillation. Although no particle actually moves very far, the wave moves and carries energy through the medium from one location to another. (See Section H, Energy: Sound.) [Systems and Interactions, Energy]

Waves fall into two general categories. The first is transverse waves, in which the particles of the medium oscillate perpendicular to the direction of propagation of the wave. The second is longitudinal waves, in which the particles oscillate parallel to the direction of propagation. Sound waves in air and liquids are longitudinal. Sound waves in solids can be both longitudinal and transverse. Some more complicated waves, like surface water waves, are combinations of the two. [Systems and Interactions]

A wave is characterized by its wavelength (λ), its frequency (f), and its propagation speed (v). The relationship of these quantities is given by the expression $v = f\lambda$. Waves conform to the principle of superposition: Any number of waves can pass through the same part of the medium simultaneously, and their effects are cumulative. The phenomena of standing waves and interference are results of the principle of superposition. [Systems and Interactions]

C-2

What is force? What are the characteristics of forces? What is the relationship of force to motion?

Kindergarten Through Grade Three

Force is the name given to pushes and pulls. Objects (both inanimate and animate) exert forces on other objects. [Systems and Interactions]

Gravity is the name given to the pull of the earth on other objects. The weight of an object can be measured with a scale. [Systems and Interactions]

A particular object can be acted on by multiple forces. The effect of the forces on the object depends on whether the forces balance (cancel each other out). [Systems and Interactions]

If the several forces acting on an object (including gravity) do not cancel out, they cause a change in the motion of the object. The change can be speeding up, slowing down, starting, stopping, or turning. [Systems and Interactions]

If an object is at rest, then the several forces acting on an object totally balance each other (cancel each other out). [Systems and Interactions]

C-2   What is force? What are the characteristics of forces? What is the relationship of force to motion?

Grades Three Through Six

Forces are often measured with a spring scale. The customary units of force are pounds (lb.) and ounces

---

Light waves are not mechanical waves and do not require a medium for propagation. However, they have many properties in common with mechanical waves and are described by the same mathematical language used to describe mechanical waves. (See Section G, Energy: Light.)

(oz.). The SI metric unit of force is the newton (*N*). A force of one pound is equal to a force of 4.5 newtons. [Systems and Interactions]

The direction in which a force is exerted is important in determining its effect. The effect of two forces acting in the same direction is the same as if there were one force equal to the sum of the separate

---

A person riding in a jet airliner cruising at 450 miles per hour 3,500 feet above the surface of the earth might describe the position and speed of a person walking down the aisle this way, "She is 25 feet from the rear exit moving towards it at 2 miles per hour." A person on the ground looking up at the plane might say, "She is 2 miles south and 3,500 feet above me moving north at 448 miles per hour." From this example, we see the importance of specifying the reference system. Students need practice using both informal and formal reference and coordinate systems. The property of velocity, that there is no inherent difference between being at rest and moving at constant velocity, is difficult for students to understand. Because of its importance in developing an understanding of the relation of force to motion, it should receive considerable attention throughout grades six through twelve.

Even students intending to major in science in college have considerable difficulty in fully understanding the difference between velocity and acceleration, even in the simplest case of one-dimensional motion. However, it is necessary to introduce acceleration if Newton's second law is to be introduced. When acceleration is introduced, it should first be approached conceptually and related to students' intuitive notions of speeding up and slowing down before defining it mathematically. Students familiar with drag racing will have no problems here.

forces. If two forces have opposite directions, the effect is the same as a single force in the direction of the larger and equal to the difference of the two forces. If the two equal forces have opposite directions, they balance each other out and there is no net force. If two forces act at an angle with respect to each other, then the effect is the same as that of a single force acting at an intermediate angle. Unless two forces point in exactly opposite directions, they can never cancel each other out, regardless of their magnitude. [Systems and Interactions]

In ordinary situations, moving objects slow down and come to rest. Under these circumstances, most objects collide with or rub against other objects or surfaces and experience "backward" forces—forces that act in the direction opposite to the direction of motion. These forces, which exist in several varieties, are broadly labeled *frictional forces*. Frictional forces always act to oppose motion. They can be used to control motion, as is done with automobile brakes. Friction with air slows the space shuttle so that it can land at a conveniently low speed.

Objects do not have to touch in order to exert forces on each other. Gravity is an attractive force between any two masses and acts even when the objects are far apart. Objects fall to earth and the moon orbits the earth because of this force. Forces between magnets and forces between electrically charged objects also act over a distance without the objects being in contact. [Systems and Interactions]

If one object exerts a force on another object, the second object exerts an equal force in the opposite direction on the first. For example, in order to start to walk or run, a girl must push with her foot against the floor in the direction opposite to that in which she intends to move. The floor pushes back against her foot. This unbalanced force (floor pushing on girl) is the direct cause of the change in her forward motion. [Systems and Interactions]

The intuitive notion that there exists something inside or associated with an object that keeps it in motion corresponds to the scientific concept called *momentum*. Consider expressions such as "If an object has a lot of momentum, it is hard to stop it or to change its direction"; or "A large truck has a lot more momentum than a small car going the same speed"; or "The faster you go the more momentum you have." These statements make sense to many students before they have formally studied momen-

Newton's third law focuses on an important property of forces. As with Newton's first and second laws, the concept behind Newton's third law should be taught first, and then it can be given a name. It is not important that students remember a memorized definition of Newton's third law using words that do not make any sense to them. What is important is that they have a conceptual understanding of its content.

The fundamental properties of force are not intuitive for most students. Consequently, they need to be reintroduced and reinforced at all levels—kindergarten through grade twelve. Because it is difficult to change misconceptions that have been held for several years, appropriate and useful conceptions of forces should be established as early as possible. At the kindergarten through grade three level, students should be given many opportunities to identify forces and explore the difference between instances when they balance and when they do not. These should be experiences in which they directly feel and sense the forces. [Systems and Interactions]

tum. Momentum depends both on how much matter there is (its mass) and on the velocity of the mass. Momentum has the same direction as the velocity of the object. Like velocity, the actual value of momentum depends on the reference frame in which the velocity is measured. [Patterns of Change]

Net forces cause the momentum of an object to change. Conversely, if the net force acting on an object is zero, its momentum will remain constant. For example, air friction exerts a force opposite to the direction of motion on an object thrown horizontally. This force causes the forward momentum to decrease (the object slows down). At the same time, gravity exerts a force in the downward direction, which causes the object to start moving downward (if it was initially moving horizontally). [Systems and Interactions]

C-2   What is force? What are the characteristics of forces? What is the relationship of force to motion?

Grades Six Through Nine

If a net force acts on an object, its momentum will change, and the longer the net force acts, the more the momentum will change. When the net force acting on an object is zero, the object's momentum will not change. It means that an object in motion will continue to move in a straight line at constant speed, or if it is not moving, it will not start to move if there is no net force acting on it. [Patterns of Change, Systems and Interactions]

Particular attention needs to be devoted to the common experience of objects on earth always coming to a stop once the cause of the motion has been removed (a box sliding on the floor, a car coasting to a stop, and so forth). In all these cases, the object's forward momentum is changed (reduced) by the unbalanced force of friction; the greater the frictional force, the less time it takes for the object to stop. Conversely, if an object's forward momentum remains constant in the presence of friction, there must be another force acting on the object to balance the frictional force. [Systems and Interactions]

Near the surface of the earth, the force of gravity exerted by the earth on an object does not change appreciably with changes in elevation of the object. When an object falls toward the earth, the speed it has when it hits the ground increases as the height from which it is dropped increases. This is not due to the fact that the force is greater when it is higher (a commonly held misconception), but is readily explained by the concepts of forces and acceleration. The constant force of gravity produces a constant acceleration. The higher the point from which the object falls, the longer it accelerates, producing higher velocity and momentum. [Systems and Interactions]

Mass and *force of gravity* have exact meanings in science, but the term *weight*, as used popularly, can have several meanings. Usually, the term is related to gravity and refers to a force whose magnitude is proportional to mass. When the term is used in

Only very simple and straightforward examples similar to those mentioned should be studied at this level. Their purpose is to provide a lot of everyday applications in which the concepts of force and momentum can be distinguished and clarified. [Systems and Interactions]

science, it must be distinguished from mass and should be defined carefully.

The magnitude of weight can be thought of as that quantity measured by a bathroom scale. Normally, you are not moving when you weigh yourself, so the upward force of the scale on you exactly balances the force of gravity. In this case your weight equals the force of gravity. However, if you weigh yourself in an elevator, you will find that your weight changes as the elevator starts up or comes to a stop. The force of gravity does not change, but additional forces which cause the change in speed also cause the change in weight. An astronaut in free-fall, floating around the cabin of a spacecraft in low earth orbit, would register zero weight on the scale and so could be said to be "weightless," even though the force of gravity is only slightly reduced. The focus in science should be on the relationship between force and mass, not on the meaning of the term *weight*. [Systems and Interactions]

The implications of Newton's second law are far-ranging and affect practically everything we do in our daily lives. In those instances for which the forces are easily identified (exerted by animate objects, for example), it is easier for students to determine whether an unbalanced force exists. For example, in a tug-of-war the players exert forces on the rope. If they balance, the rope does not move. Another class of examples that is fairly straightforward involves objects subjected only to the force of gravity (for example, a ball in flight after it has left the thrower's hand). If air friction is negligible, there is only one force acting on the object; it can not be balanced, and the object's momentum will change in response to the unbalanced force.

C-2   What is force? What are the characteristics of forces? What is the relationship of force to motion?

Grades Nine Through Twelve

The force of gravity acting on an object near the surface of the earth in newtons is numerically equal to the product of the object's mass in kilograms and the "acceleration of gravity" ($g = 9.8 \ m/s^2$, $F_g = mg$.) [Systems and Interactions]

The force of gravity acts between all pairs of objects, not just between the earth and other objects. The size of the force increases with the mass of each object. However, unless at least one of the objects is very massive (like the earth), the force of attraction between the objects is usually negligible compared to other forces. The force of gravity decreases as the distance between the objects increases. It is necessary, however, to go very far from a planet or the sun before its gravity is reduced substantially. The force of the earth's gravity at an elevation typical of most earth satellites is reduced by only 5 to 10 percent from that at the surface of the earth. [Systems and Interactions]

At a fundamental level there are four basic forces: the attractive force of gravitation that acts between all matter, the electric force that acts between charged matter and can be either attractive or repulsive, and two kinds of nuclear forces that act to hold atomic nuclei together. The first two act over large distances, while the two nuclear forces decrease to zero just outside the nucleus. The forces we experience in our everyday lives are the result of either gravitation or electric force. Forces of friction and other contact forces are due to the electric force acting at the atomic and molecular level. [Systems and Interactions]

The particles of fluids (gases or liquids) exert forces on each other and on surfaces with which they are in contact. Pressure is the amount of force acting on one unit of area. Particles are free to move in a fluid. In equilibrium the particles will be distributed so that pressure at any point is the same in all directions. [Systems and Interactions]

There is some ambiguity attached to the concepts of weight and weightlessness because they can be defined in slightly different ways. Any of these definitions is acceptable, provided it is used consistently. Textbook authors should take care to do so. For a clear, complete discussion of this point, together with a set of recommendations, see Robert A. Nelson, SI: The International System of Units, *(Second edition). Stony Brook, N.Y.: American Association of Physics Teachers, 1982, pp. 47–57.*

Pressure in a fluid increases with the depth of the fluid. This can be understood in terms of the pressure required to support the fluid above that location. [Systems and Interactions]

Fluids exert forces on objects immersed in them, just as they exert forces on other parts of the fluid. Whether an object sinks or floats depends on whether its weight is greater than or less than the weight of a volume of fluid equal to the volume of the object. This can be understood by considering the forces acting on an equal volume of fluid. Since this volume of fluid does not move, the net force must be zero. Further, since the force of gravity acts down, there must be an equal force acting in the up direction. When the volume of fluid is replaced with the actual object, the same force acts on the actual object. That is, the upward force exerted by a fluid on a submerged object (buoyant force) is equal to the weight of an equal volume of fluid (volume of fluid displaced). This is Archimedes's principle. [Systems and Interactions]

Newton's second law relates acceleration to force and mass and can be stated: Acceleration is directly proportional to the net force, is inversely proportional to the mass of the object, and is in the direction of the net force. In symbols, $a = F/m$. [Systems and Interactions]

When a drag racer accelerates along a straight track, the acceleration is parallel to the direction of motion and to the velocity. When the racer brakes to a stop, the acceleration is opposite to the direction of motion and the velocity. In this case, acceleration affects the speed but not the direction of motion. When a train goes around a circular curve at constant speed, the acceleration is directed inward along the radius of the circle, perpendicular to the direction of motion and the velocity. Now, the acceleration affects the direction of motion, but not the speed. In oscillatory motion, the acceleration is always directed opposite to the displacement from the equilibrium point. [Systems and Interactions]

A net force *(F)* acting for a time *(Δt)* causes a change in the momentum of an object: $(\Delta(mv)\ F\ \Delta t = \Delta(mv))$. The direction of the change is in the direction of the net force. If the force is not constant during the time interval, then average force can be used in the formula. If there is no net force, there will be no change in momentum. This fact is stated as the principle of conservation of momentum and applies to groups of objects as well as to single objects. A single object without external forces or a group of objects that interact with each other but have no effect on other objects constitutes a *system*. The principle can be stated: If there is no external net force acting on a system, then the momentum of the system remains constant, regardless of the interactions among the parts of the system. [Systems and Interactions]

"Isaac Newton formulated his First Law of Motion in the eighteenth century. It stated that 'every body continues in its state of rest, or of uniform motion in a right line, unless it is compelled to change that state by forces impressed upon it.'

"(Joseph) Needham's researches have now established that this law was stated in China in the fourth or third century BC. We read in the Mo Ching: *'The cessation of motion is due to the opposing force . . . If there is no opposing force . . . the motion will never stop. This is as true as that an ox is not a horse.'"*

—*Robert Temple*, The Genius of China

C-3

What are machines, and what do they do? What principles govern their action?

Kindergarten Through Grade Three

Machines are made of parts that move, such as a lever. Simple machines, such as soft drink bottle openers, contain only one part. More complicated machines, such as a can opener, contain several parts connected together in various ways. The purpose of all machines is the same: to change the effect of an applied force. The change might be the direction of the force, the magnitude of the force, or both. For example, a crowbar can be used to increase the magnitude of force applied by the user. [Systems and Interactions]

C-3　What are machines, and what do they do? What principles govern their action?

Grades Three Through Six

There are several kinds of simple machines. Among them are levers, inclined planes, wedges, and screws. If a certain force is applied to a machine through a certain distance, a machine's output can be either a larger force acting over a smaller distance or a smaller force acting over a greater distance. A

Students should reexamine the operation of various machines using the concepts of "work" and energy. They should identify the system that loses energy and the system that gains energy and verify that the work output of a machine is no greater than the work put in. [Energy, Systems and Interactions]

machine can either increase the magnitude of an applied force or it can increase the distance through which the force acts. It cannot do both at the same time. All machines can be analyzed and understood on this basis. [Systems and Interactions, Energy]

C-3　What are machines, and what do they do? What principles govern their action?

Grades Six Through Nine

The product of the force and the distance through which it acts (force × distance) is given the name *work*. [Energy, Systems and Interactions]

The basic principle governing all machines is simply stated in terms of the concept of work: The work output of a machine can be no greater than the work put into it. In any real machine, the work output is less than the work input because there is friction between the moving parts. [Energy, Systems and Interactions]

C-3　What are machines, and what do they do? What principles govern their action?

Grades Nine Through Twelve

Work *(W)* is equal to the product of force *(F)* and distance *(x)* moved in the direction of the force. If the direction of the applied force is the same as the direction of motion, $W = Fx$. If F is not constant, then the average value of F must be used. The unit of work is the newton-meter *(Nm)*, called the joule *(J)*. [Energy, Systems and Interactions]

The rate at which work is done is called *power*: $P = W/t$. The unit of power is the joule per second *(J/s)*, and is given the name watt *(W)*. An obsolete (but still frequently used) unit of power is the horsepower *(hp)*, equal to 745.7 *W*. [Energy, Systems and Interactions]

The efficiency of a machine is the ratio of the output of the machine to the input. Careful design can improve the efficiency of a machine (for example, by minimizing friction).

The definition of work in the preceding section can be confusing to students because in everyday language we use the word "work" to mean more than is implied by this restrictive definition. For example, if you hold a heavy book in your outstretched stationary hand, you do not do any work on the book in the scientific sense. It is certainly true, however, that your arm gets tired. You are likely to say, "This sure is hard work!" Students can appreciate the usefulness of the restrictive scientific definition, however, when it is used in the context of energy transfers by mechanical means. In this example, no energy was transferred mechanically from the person to the book, so no work was done on the book. [Energy, Systems and Interactions]

Section D   Energy: Sources and Transformations

THE idea that separate systems can separately gain or lose energy, but that the total energy of all interacting systems remains constant, is known as conservation of energy. It is one of the great conservation principles around which science is organized. Mass is one form of energy that must be taken into account in cases involving atoms and their components. In such cases, a unified principle of conservation of mass-energy replaces the separate principles of conservation of mass and conservation of energy.

D-1   What is energy? What are its characteristics?

D-2   What do we do with energy? What changes occur as we use it?

D-1

What is energy? What are its characteristics?

Kindergarten Through Grade Three

Forms of energy can be classified in several ways, depending on our purposes. Energy is manifested when we drop a ball, strike a match, make waves in a bathtub, clap our hands or rub them briskly together, or turn on a flashlight. Each form of energy has its own characteristics. For example, a given material will transmit some forms of energy and absorb or

reflect others. A sheet of thick paper transmits sound but not light. A stretched sheet of plastic wrap transmits light but not water waves. Heat is a form of energy often produced by conversion from other forms, as can easily be demonstrated by the warming of a dark object exposed to sunlight. The capacity of waves to carry energy can be demonstrated by observing how water waves (for example, in wave tanks) set floating objects into motion. Energy is required when work is done on a system or when matter changes its form. [Energy, Systems and Interactions, Patterns of Change]

D-1   What is energy? What are its characteristics?

Grades Three Through Six

Energy passes through ecosystems in food chains mainly in the form of the chemical energy supplied to each organism by the nourishment it consumes. All organisms convert some of this energy into heat. Animals also convert some of it into mechanical energy. Green plants convert light energy into chemical energy by means of the photochemical process called photosynthesis. (See Chapter 5, Section A. Living Things.) [Systems and Interactions, Energy]

D-1   What is energy? What are its characteristics?

Grades Six Through Nine

When systems interact, energy is often transferred from one system to another. When energy conversion takes place, the total energy is conserved. Sometimes conversion processes involve conversion of part of the energy to undesired forms, typically to heat energy. In terms of systems, we say that part of the energy is transferred to a third system, the environment, in the form of heat energy. [Systems and Interactions, Energy]

Under nuclear conditions, when the energy of a substance is changed, its mass does not change. Under certain conditions, such as when nuclear fusion or fission occurs, mass and energy are interconverted, and measurable mass changes occur.

The unit of energy is the joule, named after the English physicist James Prescott Joule in recognition of his key contributions to our understanding of the principle of energy conservation. When energy is transported from one place to another (e.g., by an electric transmission line), we measure the rate at which it is transported. When a device transforms energy from one form to another (as an electric motor does), we measure the rate at which it does so. The rate at which energy is transmitted or transformed is called power. The basic unit of power is the watt (W), named after the Scottish engineer James Watt, who made crucial improvements to the steam engine and thereby contributed to the industrial revolution. [Energy, Patterns of Change]

Conversion of energy from one form to another usually has some effect on the surroundings. This is especially true of conversion of heat energy into mechanical energy, which is accomplished by heat engines. Heat engines (such as gasoline engines and steam turbines) inevitably produce a certain amount of waste heat. Sometimes the waste heat is useful, as when steam from power plants is used for heating buildings. Sometimes it is an environmental pollutant, as when river water used for cooling is warmed so much that it affects the ecological balance of the river. [Energy, Systems and Interactions]

Because there are two fundamental ways in which a system can change, there are two basic types of energy. A system can change when the distance between the parts of a system change or the parts are rearranged. Energy associated with these kinds of changes is traditionally called *potential* energy. The second way the parts of a system can change is by going faster or slower. The energy that things have because they are in motion is called *kinetic* energy. Other forms of energy are really manifestations of these two basic types. For example, chemical energy is the electrical potential energy of a system of atoms and molecules capable of being rearranged. Heat

energy is the total kinetic and potential energy of the random motions of the particles of a substance. [Energy]

The use of electrical energy is pervasive in our technological society. Electrical energy can be obtained by the conversion of gravitational potential energy (hydroelectric plants do this), chemical energy (fossil fuel plants do this), or potential energy of atomic nuclei (nuclear plants do this). Other conversion processes furnish small amounts of electrical energy as well. [Energy, Systems and Interactions]

Electromagnetic waves transfer energy from their source to where they are absorbed at the speed of light. Electromagnetic energy has many forms, some of which are familiar. Among these familiar forms are light, infrared radiation, radio waves, and X rays. The forms differ because their wavelengths vary widely. For example, X rays will penetrate objects that are opaque to light; we can feel infrared radiation as heat energy is absorbed by our skin. Nevertheless, all of these forms of energy transfer share many properties in common. [Energy, Systems and Interactions]

D-1   What is energy? What are its characteristics?

Grades Nine Through Twelve

Chemical energy is the electrical potential energy associated with the configuration of electrons in molecules. Each molecule has a specific spatial configuration and therefore a specific electronic potential energy. In chemical reactions, the configurations change and, therefore, the electrical potential energy changes as well. In exothermic reactions, energy is released to the environment as the electric potential energy of the molecules decreases. An example of such a reaction is the main reaction in the burning of coal:

$$C + O_2 \longrightarrow CO_2 + 6.54 \times 10^{-19} \text{ joules per molecule of } CO_2 \text{ produced.}$$

(See Section B, Reactions and Interactions.) The release is usually in the form of heat energy, but sometimes in the form of electrical or electromagnetic energy. In endothermic reactions, energy must be supplied from outside to make the reaction proceed. In such reactions, the electric potential energy of the molecules increases. An example of an endothermic reaction is the production of mercury from the ore cinnabar:

$$2HgO + 1.51 \times 10^{-19} \text{ joules per molecule of}$$
$$HgO \longrightarrow 2Hg + O_2.$$

Photosynthetic reactions are endothermic; the energy input comes from light. The reactions are well understood but complex. Roughly speaking, however, the overall reaction is:

water + carbon dioxide + light energy—> sugar.

(See Chapter 5, Section A, Living Things.) [Energy, Systems and Interactions]

D-2

What do we do with energy? What changes occur as we use it?

Kindergarten Through Grade Three

Energy is used to do mechanical work. Most of this energy is provided by using fuel to produce heat energy and then using the heat energy to run a heat engine. The heat engine does either the desired mechanical work directly (as when a gasoline engine drives an automobile) or indirectly through conversion to electrical energy, which then drives an electric motor that does the work (as in a trolley car or a vacuum cleaner). (See Section C, Force and Motion.) Heat engines inevitably produce waste heat. (See Section E, Energy: Heat.) [Energy, Systems and Interactions]

The ultimate source of most of the energy we use is the sun. We call the sun a renewable resource because its energy is available forever for practical purposes. Coal and petroleum have, ultimately, solar origins: They are the remains of green plants that lived and died millions of years ago. But we use coal and oil far faster than they are produced. We therefore call them *nonrenewable resources*. (See Chapter 4, Section B, Geology and Natural Resources.) [Energy, Systems and Interactions, Patterns of Change]

D-2   What do we do with energy? What changes occur as we use it?

Grades Three Through Six

The transfer of energy is necessary for change to occur in matter. Energy transfers are essential to all living organisms. [Energy, Systems and Interactions]

Humans use energy in many ways, including forms not available to other living things. Electric energy is used for heating, lighting, mechanical motion, and information transport and processing. Nuclear energy and the energy of fuels are used for a vast variety of purposes. [Energy]

D-2   What do we do with energy? What changes occur as we use it?

Grades Six Through Nine

All energy conversion processes have undesirable side effects. We try to minimize these effects both directly, by careful design, and indirectly, by balancing various resources in building an energy network. For example, hydroelectricity is a renewable resource because rain and snow fall in the mountains every year. However, reservoirs flood valuable property that has other possible uses, and dams occasionally break disastrously. Coal is nonrenewable, dangerous to mine, and contains potential pollutants which are difficult to remove; in addition, burning coal produces carbon dioxide, which may have undesirable

---

In dealing with energy and power quantitatively or semiquantitatively, give preference to SI metric units: the joule, the watt, and their multiples. Students who have familiarity with U.S. customary units (e.g., the foot-pound, Btu, and horsepower) should be encouraged to learn how to convert to SI metric. Other units of energy sometimes used are the kilowatt-hour and the kilocalorie. The use of these units is discouraged by international convention and is slowly dying out.

It is unfortunate that the term "potential energy" is used to descibe a type of energy because of position. Kinetic energy has just as much ability to be converted into another form as does potential energy. Many persons have developed misconceptions regarding energy because of the use of this term. This needs to be clarified with students.

climatic effects. Nuclear power does not exhaust desirable resources and does not produce carbon dioxide, but the waste products are difficult and expensive to store reliably. Energy conservation is very useful, but there are limits beyond which energy use cannot be reduced. The search for the optimum balance is one having many scientific, technical, political, economic, and social aspects. [Energy, Patterns of Change]

Technological applications of energy conversion are numerous. Heating, cooling, and cooking devices use energy, either in the form of the chemical energy of fuel or in the form of electrical energy. Undesirable heat transfer is minimized by means of insulating materials. Electricity is useful for energy transmission and communication because of the convenience and speed of transmission. Information can be processed in very elaborate ways by means of tiny, often inexpensive, devices using electronic techniques. [Energy, Systems and Interactions]

D-2　What do we do with energy? What changes occur as we use it?

Grades Nine Through Twelve

Electromagnetic energy is used in many ways. Infrared photography and detection, microwave ovens, and X-ray technologies are but a few examples. Information is processed rapidly in the form of electric pulses, as is done in computers. Most information is transmitted electromagnetically, either by cable, by light pipe, or by radio transmission. Much of the electric energy consumed by people is generated using heat engines of various types. The most common of these is the steam plant, which transforms the energy stored in fossil fuels or in uranium into the disordered energy of heat and, thence, by means of a steam turbine, into ordered mechanical energy. The mechanical energy is then used to drive an electric generator. Electric energy is difficult to store at present and must usually be transformed into some other form of energy for storage. However, the advent of a new generation of superconductors may make it possible to store the energy directly and efficiently in the form of the magnetic field of a superconducting coil. [Energy, Systems and Interactions]

Section E　Energy: Heat

Heat and temperature are words commonly used in our everyday language. The concepts of heat, temperature, and other thermal properties of matter are intimately related to the concepts of force and motion. The concepts of force and motion are useful to describe the interaction of a few objects. The concepts of heat and temperature are useful for describing the large-scale effects of the interactions of the vast numbers of atoms or molecules of which a substance is composed. Because there are such large numbers of particles interacting, new principles arise that are based simply on statistical concepts that supplement the principle of energy conservation.

E-1　What is heat energy? Where does it come from, and what are its properties?

E-2　How do we use heat energy?

E-1

What is heat energy? Where does it come from, and what are its properties?

Kindergarten Through Grade Three

The form of energy called heat energy can be produced in many ways. Heat energy is produced in an object when it is exposed to the sun, to other light sources, or to fire. It can also be produced by rubbing two objects together. Heat flows from a hotter region or object to a cooler one. We say that the region from which the heat flows has a higher temperature than the region to which it flows. If an object is not too hot or too cold, we can tell its approximate temperature by feeling it. (See Section D. Energy: Sources and Transformations.) [Energy, Systems and Interaction]

E-1　What is heat energy? Where does it come from, and what are its properties?

Grades Three Through Six

Heat and temperature are not the same thing but are related to one another. Temperature can be measured with a thermometer. Most materials expand with

Organelles in the cells of green plants have the ability to convert light energy into chemical energy, which can be stored, transported, and used by the plant in a variety of ways. The ability of animals to see is based on the conversion of light energy into electrical energy in sensitive cells in their eyes. The ability of animals to hear is based on the conversion of sound energy into electrical energy by sensitive cells in their ears. Electric eels, sharks, many fishes, and duck-billed platypuses are among the animals that have organs sensitive to electrical energy, which they use to detect their prey. (See Chapter 5, Section A, Living Things.) [Energy, Evolution, Systems and Interactions]

increasing temperature and contract with decreasing temperature. That is how familiar thermometers work. Heat cannot be measured directly. However, an increase of the temperature of an object can mean that heat is flowing into it; a decrease of the temperature can mean that heat is flowing out of it. Heat affects matter in many ways. Chemical reactions require an input or output of heat energy in predictable amounts, as do phase changes—melting or freezing, boiling or condensation. [Energy, Patterns of Change]

E-1 What is heat energy? Where does it come from, and what are its properties?

Grades Six Through Nine

Heat and temperature are not the same thing but are related to one another. Heat affects matter in many ways. A thermometer is a device for predicting which way heat energy will flow from any object to any other one; that is, which of the two objects has the higher temperature. [Energy]

The molecules of any substance are in constant disordered, random motion. Heat energy is the total kinetic and potential energy of the disordered motion of the molecules of the substance. The temperature of a substance is a measure of the average random motional energy of the molecules (or other particles) composing the substance. Temperature is usually not measured directly, by measuring this average kinetic energy, but indirectly, by using a device whose macroscopic properties are affected by temperature. A mercury-in-glass thermometer is such a device in which the volume of a fixed quantity of mercury varies with temperature. [Systems and Interactions, Energy]

Phase changes always involve the flow of heat into or out of an object. But this heat flow does not result in a temperature change. (For example, the temperature of a kettle of pure water always remains at the boiling temperature of water, $100°C$, no matter how hard it boils.) For this reason, the amount of heat energy required to produce a phase change in a certain mass of substance is called its latent (hidden) heat. [Energy, Patterns of Change]

In order to change the phase of a substance—for example, to boil a liquid—its molecules must be rearranged. This requires a change in the potential energy of the bonds holding the particles together, rather than a change in the random disordered motional energy of the molecules. For this reason, the heat added does not result in a temperature change. [Patterns of Change, Energy]

Heat energy can be transferred from one place to another by processes called conduction, convection, and radiation. Heat energy flows quickly by conduction through substances called heat conductors and slowly through substances called heat insulators. Insulators are important in reducing the cost of home heating and cooling, as well as making homes more comfortable. In convection, heat is transferred by warm matter (for example, air) moving into a cooler region. Good insulation prevents large-scale motion of air. Wool is a good insulator because it traps air in tiny cells so that convection cannot take place. In radiation, a body at high temperature emits electromagnetic radiation which is absorbed by a cooler body. Highly reflecting surfaces are effective at reducing heat transfer by radiation. That is why a Thermos bottle is silvered and thermal or solar curtains are aluminized. [Energy, Systems and Interactions]

E-1 What is heat energy? Where does it come from, and what are its properties?

Grades Nine Through Twelve

As heat energy is removed from a sample, its temperature decreases. In principle, a point is reached at which no further energy can be removed because all of the molecules have the minimum possible energy. This is the lowest temperature possible and is called absolute zero. On the absolute or Kelvin temperature scale, absolute zero is assigned the temperature value $T = 0\ K$. The size of the kelvin (the degree of the absolute scale) is defined by fixing the temperature of the so-called triple point of water at $273.16\ K$, exactly. Absolute temperatures, expressed in kelvin, must be used in the ideal gas law, and use of the absolute temperature scale makes many other physical and chemical calculations simple. The Celsius scale is often convenient for everyday use. The zero of the Celsius scale ($0°C$) is set by the definition $0°C = 273.15\ K$. The Celsius degree is of the same "size" as the kelvin. [Energy]

Because heat is a form of energy, it can be produced only by conversion from other forms of energy and can never be created from nothing. This statement is one form of the first law of thermodynamics. [Energy]

Disordered heat energy can be converted to ordered macroscopic motion (mechanical energy) by a heat engine. The statement that the mechanical energy is converted from heat energy and not created from nothing is one form of the first law of thermodynamics. However, the conversion can never be complete. A heat engine always takes heat energy in from a source at a relatively high temperature and ejects a smaller amount of heat energy to something at a lower temperature. The amount of ejected heat can never be zero. Thus, some of the heat energy taken in by the engine at high temperature must always be ejected to the environment at a lower temperature and is lost to the engine. This is the meaning of the second law of thermodynamics. The second law limits the maximum possible efficiency (work output divided by heat energy input) of any heat engine to a value less than 100 percent. [Energy, Systems and Interactions]

Because some heat energy is always rejected to the environment when a heat engine operates, the temperature of the environment is raised. Sometimes this so-called waste heat can be used (e.g., for steam heating), but usually it is not desired and is called thermal pollution. (For example, the summer temperature of the Connecticut River, whose waters are used to cool many electric generating plants, often exceeds $100°F$, to the detriment of the fish and other aquatic life.) Measures must be taken to minimize these undesirable effects; sometimes this involves considerable cost. [Energy, Systems and Interactions]

Entropy is a measure of the disorder of the energy contained in a system. If a system is isolated, its entropy can only remain the same or increase. (This is an alternative statement of the second law of thermodynamics.) But if two systems interact, the entropy of one system can be reduced at the expense of the other, provided the total entropy of both systems increases or remains the same. Living organisms constantly decrease their own entropy at the expense of the entropy of their surroundings. So do heat engines, crystals (as they grow out of solution), and other systems as well. [Energy, Systems and Interactions, Patterns of Change]

E-2

How do we use heat energy?

Kindergarten Through Grade Three

Heat is essential to all living organisms. We produce heat energy ourselves by metabolizing food. We also produce heat energy by burning fuel to warm our houses. By adding heat to our environment, we

Many effects operate to convert ordered, large-scale motion to disordered, small-scale motion. Friction is one of these effects. When an object rubs against another, the molecules on the surface are disturbed and set in motion. They then set their neighbors in motion. The ordered motion of the entire object is converted into disordered motion of its molecules. The spreading of the motion through the body is the flow of heat energy. [Energy] can raise its temperature to a comfortable level. We use cooling devices to remove heat from our environment and thus to lower the temperature to a comfortable level. We use heat energy also to drive heat engines (such as automobile engines) and thus to do mechanical work. [Energy, Systems and Interactions]

E-2   How do we use heat energy?

Grades Three Through Six

Heat flows by itself only from an object at a higher temperature to another object at a lower temperature. Thermometers can be used to predict which way heat will flow when two substances are placed in contact. As heat flows, the warmer body cools and the cooler one warms until the two achieve the same temperature. This final temperature lies somewhere between the initial temperatures of the two bodies. [Energy, Systems and Interactions]

E-2   How do we use heat energy?

Grades Six Through Nine

It is possible to make heat energy flow from a cooler object to a warmer one, but only at the cost of other energy. Any device that does this is called a refrigerator. Household refrigerators, air conditioners, ice-making machines, and the space-heating devices called heat pumps are examples of refrigerators. [Energy, Systems and Interactions]

E-2   How do we use heat energy?

Grades Nine Through Twelve

Heat engines include steam engines, steam turbines, gas turbines (such as jet engines), and internal combustion engines. A heat engine designed to operate in reverse uses mechanical energy to take in heat energy at a low temperature and reject it at a higher temperature. Such a device is called a refrigerator or a heat pump. [Energy, Systems and Interactions]

The efficiency of a heat engine depends on many factors, some of which can be optimized by careful engineering. But there is an upper limit set on the efficiency of a heat engine by the second law of thermodynamics. If the engine takes in heat at temperature T_{in} and rejects waste heat at temperature T_{out}, its efficiency can never exceed the Carnot

As an example of entropy, consider ten pennies on a tray, all heads up. The tray is shaken; the pennies will probably settle with some heads up and some tails up. The ordered, low-entropy state (ten heads) has been transformed into a disordered, high-entropy state (some heads, some tails). Further shaking is very unlikely to produce the reverse process. But you can always produce the ten-heads state by turning over all the pennies with tails up. Doing this requires energy. [Energy, Patterns of Change]

efficiency, $e = (T_{in} - T_{out})/T_{in}$. It follows from this relationship that an efficient heat engine should take heat in at the highest practicable temperature and exhaust heat at the lowest practicable temperature in order to have the highest efficiency. [Energy, Systems and Interactions]

Section F   Energy: Electricity and Magnetism

AT a fundamental level, electricity and magnetism are manifestations of the same basic phenomenon called *electromagnetism*. In our everyday lives we sometimes experience them separately and at other times as the combined phenomenon. For example, static electricity can be understood simply as an electrical phenomenon. Similarly, at a certain level of understanding, it is useful to consider the attraction and repulsion of permanent magnets as simply a magnetic phenomenon. However, radio and TV signals and electric motors can be understood only as electromagnetic phenomena. The complete theory of electromagnetism, called *quantum electrodynamics* (which includes the effects of quantum mechanics), is at present our most precise and best tested physical theory.

F-1   **What are electricity and magnetism? What are they like, and what are their basic properties? How do they interact?**

F-2 How do we use electricity and magnetism?

What are electricity and magnetism? What are they like, and what are their basic properties? How do they interact?

Kindergarten Through Grade Three

When you walk across a rug on a dry day, you may get a shock when you touch a doorknob. Clothes coming out of a dryer stick together. When it is stormy, you sometimes see lightning. These phenomena are seen because matter can be electrically charged by friction. The large sparks that are lightning bolts and the tiny sparks you feel when you touch the doorknob result from the flow of electrically charged matter from one place to another. Electric forces can act over a distance without the objects having to touch. This is seen when a balloon which has been electrically charged by friction attracts hair on a person's arm or head without actually touching it. [Systems and Interactions]

Electric charge can be made to flow through wires connected to batteries or electric generators. The moving electric charge can be used to light lamps, run motors, and power radios and cassette players. We use this kind of electricity continually in our everyday lives. [Systems and Interactions, Energy]

Electricity used to power battery-driven toys, radios, and flashlights is safe and will not produce dangerous electric shocks. The electricity from wall sockets used to run household appliances is very dangerous if it is used improperly. Students should be warned never to experiment with household electric circuits and should be taught about the dangers of frayed wiring, of touching the metal prongs of electric plugs, and of inserting any kind of object into electric outlets. [Systems and Interactions]

Magnets attract and repel one another and attract common materials made from iron or steel. Magnets can attract steel paper clips at a distance, and this effect can be transmitted through a series of several clips in contact with one another. Magnets do not attract common materials other than iron and steel. [Systems and Interactions]

F-1 What are electricity and magnetism? What are they like, and what are their basic properties? How do they interact?

Grades Three Through Six

Electric charge comes in two kinds, arbitrarily named positive (+) and negative (-). Particles having like charges exert repulsive forces on one another. Particles having opposite charges exert attractive forces on one another. (See Section A, Matter.) This effect can be seen using charged plastic balls suspended from threads. [Systems and Interactions, Scale and Structure, Patterns of Change]

Electricity is most familiarly encountered in the form of electric current. When electric charge flows, it is called a current. Some materials carry electric charge from place to place better than others; these are called conductors. Metals and salt solutions are conductors. The flow of charge requires a complete circuit of conducting material through which charge can pass easily. A battery, a generator, or other device is needed to pump the charge through the circuit. Materials that do not carry electric charge well are called insulators. Clean glass and most plastics are insulators. [Systems and Interactions, Patterns of Change, Energy]

The magnetic force is readily observed in permanent magnets. Magnets affect only certain materials, notably steel and other materials made from iron, cobalt, and nickel. Magnets can be used to separate objects made of such magnetic materials from other, nonmagnetic materials. Objects made of magnetic materials can be magnetized—made into magnets—by placing them near strong permanent magnets. [Systems and Interactions]

Magnetism and electricity are related, but they are not the same thing. Electrical attraction and repulsion arise from electric charges, but there are no such things as magnetic charges. Magnetism arises from electric current—that is, moving electric charge. Whenever there is an electric current, any magnetic material in the neighborhood will experience a force. The material becomes magnetized and remains so as long as the electric current persists. Electromagnets are a direct application of this principle. The earth is a huge magnet, and this property of the earth arises from the large electric currents that exist in the earth's metallic core. [Systems and Interactions, Scale and Structure, Energy]

Most students have difficulty understanding the concept of complete circuit. It is helpful to distinguish carefully between charge and energy. Energy is transferred from a battery to a light bulb by the circulating charge. The complete circuit is necessary to provide a path for the charge to get back to the battery. When the battery has run down, it has not run out of charge; rather, it has run out of the ability to change chemically any further. Since it cannot change further, it can no longer transfer energy by pushing the charge around the circuit. [Patterns of Change, Systems and Interactions, Energy]

F-1   What are electricity and magnetism? What are they like, and what are their basic properties? How do they interact?

Grades Six Through Nine

Just as an electric current can produce magnetic forces, magnets can in turn cause electric currents. An electric current can be produced in a conducting loop (a circuit) by moving it in the vicinity of a magnet. The mechanical energy of motion is thus converted into electrical energy. This is how most electric generators work; by turning a coiled conductor in the space between the poles of a magnet, a generator converts mechanical energy into electrical energy. [Energy, Systems and Interactions]

In addition to the attractive and repulsive forces exerted by charged objects on one another, an electrically charged object can attract an uncharged object. This attraction is due to the induced polarization of the charges. In the uncharged object, the + and - charges are present in equal numbers, and the system has zero net charge. Suppose the charged object possesses more positive than negative charges, so it has a net positive charge. Due to the forces exerted by this net positive charge, the charges on the uncharged object separate, the negative charges moving as close as possible to the charged object and the positive charges moving as far away as possible. The net result is an attractive force, because the unlike charges are closer together than the like charges. A plastic comb run through your hair will attract little bits of uncharged paper, which will then stick to the comb. After a while, they are sometimes repelled. This happens when enough of the charge on the comb has leaked onto a bit of paper to result in a net repulsive force. [Systems and Interactions]

Electrical resistance is the opposition offered by matter to the flow of electric charge. Most conductors offer some resistance to the flow of electric charge. As a result, some electrical energy is converted to heat energy. Current will not continue to exist in a circuit with resistance without something to drive it, such as a generator or a battery. The driving influence is expressed quantitatively as a voltage, and the unit is called the volt (V). Most common battery-powered devices are low voltage, 1-1/2 to 12 volts. This is normally not a high enough voltage to cause perceptible electric shocks. Common household lights and appliances, however, normally operate at 110 to 120 V. This is sufficient voltage to cause dangerous or fatal shocks. [Energy, Systems and Interactions]

Superconducting materials are an important exception to the rule that even good conductors offer some resistance to the flow of charge. At sufficiently low temperature, a superconductor loses all of its resistance to current. [Systems and Interactions, Scale and Structure, Energy]

All matter is made up of elementary particles. Among these elementary particles, electrons and protons contain an equal amount of negative and positive electric charge, respectively. (See Section A. Matter.) In most metals, electric currents are the result of the flow of electrons, while the positive charges remain in place. (This is not true in all conductors.) In insulators, few electric charges are free to move. [Scale and Structure]

Commercial electric energy is almost always transmitted in the form of alternating current (AC). In AC systems, the current switches direction (oscillates) many times a second. In the U.S., the frequency is 60 Hz; in many other countries it is 50 Hz. Although the electrons flow back and forth rather than moving in one direction like the water in a river, the electrons nevertheless transfer energy to the various devices plugged into the circuit. [Systems and Interactions]

The operation of the magnetic compass depends on the fact that the earth is a huge electromagnet. The compass, consisting of a small magnet suspended on a low-friction axis, is free to swing in a horizontal plane. The end of the compass needle that points north is called the north pole (short for north-seeking pole) of the magnet. The end that points south is called the south pole (short for south-seeking pole). As unlike magnetic poles attract one another, the north magnetic pole of the earth—located near the geographic North Pole—is actually a magnetic south pole. [Systems and Interactions]

The voltage (the driving pressure) of commercial electric systems is also carefully controlled. In the United States, the standard voltage is 110 *V* to 120 *V*; in many other countries 220 *V* is standard. [Energy, Systems and Interactions]

F-1 What are electricity and magnetism? What are they like, and what are their basic properties? How do they interact?

Grades Nine Through Twelve

Electric charge never disappears or suddenly appears in ordinary chemical or physical processes, because the electrons and protons that carry the charge cannot disappear or suddenly appear. This is expressed by saying electric charge is conserved. [Stability]

Electric and magnetic fields are theoretical concepts that emphasize the effect of electric and magnetic forces on charged particles. They do not describe the original charges and currents that produce the forces. These are very useful concepts, because it is much easier in most cases to understand the effects by knowing the fields rather than by knowing the configuration of charges and currents that produce the fields. For example, specifying that the magnetic field in the gap of a permanent magnet is a particular strength enables an electrical engineer to readily calculate the effect the magnet will have on an electron that passes through its gap. Specifying the field, however, tells the engineer little about the magnetic details of the material of which the magnet is made. [Systems and Interactions]

Radio waves, microwaves, infrared radiation, visible light, ultraviolet radiation, X rays, and gamma rays all transmit energy from one location to another. In order to understand how this energy is transmitted, it is useful to develop a model that considers all of these as waves. They are given the name *electromagnetic waves*. These waves are fundamentally different from sound waves or other waves that occur in matter, aside from having a much higher speed. (The speed of light in vacuum (*c*) is 300 million meters per second *(m/s)*, compared with about 300 *m/s* for sound in air. There is nothing material that vibrates as the wave passes, as the air particles do with sound waves, for example. Instead, a mathematical description can be given that involves the periodic variation of electric and magnetic fields. The electromagnetic waves mentioned in this paragraph all have the same speed but differ in frequency and wavelength. Radio waves have the longest wavelength and lowest frequency, while gamma rays have the shortest wavelength and highest frequency. The frequencies of standard AM and FM radio signals range from about one million to 100 million *Hz* (cycles per second). [Energy, Systems and Interactions]

The work required to drive electric charge through a conductor against electrical resistance can be measured in terms of electric potential difference (*V*), often called voltage. The current driven through a given conductor that is part of a circuit depends on the potential difference between the ends of the conductor. For metals and some other kinds of conductors, the relation between potential difference and current (*i*), is given by Ohm's law,

$$V = iR$$

In this relation, the proportionality constant *R* is called the electrical resistance. *V* is measured in volts, *i* in amperes, and *R* in ohms.

Some electrical energy is converted to heat when charges flow through a part of a circuit with resistance. The rate at which electrical energy in a circuit is transferred from the source to other parts of the circuit is power *P*. Power is measured in watts (*W*). Electrical appliances are often marked with a voltage rating, a current rating, and a power rating. For example, light bulbs are specified by their voltage rating and power rating. [Energy, Systems and Interactions]

The concept of field is difficult to understand and requires significant mathematical sophistication to appreciate fully. It is introduced because the terms "electric field" and "magnetic field" are part of our everyday language. It is possible for students at this level to understand that they describe the effect of charges and currents and that larger fields produce larger effects. [Systems and Interactions]

When a potential difference V exists between two points in a circuit, the electrical power P that is converted into other kinds of energy when a current i passes through the circuit is given by Joule's (pronounced Jowell's) law,

$$P = Vi$$

If the conductor between the two points in the circuit conforms to Ohm's law, Joule's law can be written in either of the following two forms:

$$P = i^2R \quad or \quad P = V^2/R$$

[Energy, Systems and Interactions]

Power companies sell energy to their customers. At the customer's location, this electrical energy is converted to other kinds of energy. The usual unit of electric energy is the kilowatt-hour (*kWh*). One 1000 *W* light bulb burning for one hour will transform 1 *kWh* of electrical energy to heat and light. In many places in the United States, the charge for a kilowatt-hour is ten cents at the present time. [Energy, Systems and Interactions]

Electrons can be extracted from conductors and made to move at high speeds through vacuum through the use of sufficiently high voltages. Using this basic technique, X rays, television images, and fluorescent lighting can be produced. [Systems and Interactions, Energy]

F-2

How do we use electricity and magnetism?

Kindergarten Through Grade Three

Electricity is used to make motors run, light lamps, operate telephones and television sets, heat homes, and do many other things. [Patterns of Change, Systems and Interactions]

Magnetism can be used to separate materials containing iron from those that do not. Permanent magnets are frequently used to hold notes and messages to vertical metal surfaces (refrigerator doors, for example). [Systems and Interactions]

F-2   How do we use electricity and magnetism?
Grades Three Through Six

Current electricity is used to transport energy. Electrical energy, carried from one place to another by conductors, is the most versatile form of energy available. Most conductors offer some resistance to electric current, causing some of the electric energy to be converted to heat in the conductor. This conversion is often undesirable, as in electric transmission lines. But it can be desirable as well, as in the operation of electric heaters and incandescent light bulbs. (See Section D, Energy: Sources and Transformations.) [Energy, Scale and Structure, Systems and Interactions]

F-2   How do we use electricity and magnetism?
Grades Six Through Nine

Electromagnets are important components in electric motors and generators. But they are also used by themselves to attract, separate, and carry magnetic materials, such as iron. In ore processing, electromagnets are sometimes used to separate magnetic particles from nonmagnetic particles in crushed ore. [Systems and Interactions]

Cassette tape recorders and VCRs store magnetic patterns on a plastic tape coated with a material that can be magnetized. These patterns are electronically converted to electric currents that produce the picture on the video tube and drive the speakers. The speakers convert the electric energy to sound energy. [Energy, Systems and Interactions]

F-2   How do we use electricity and magnetism?
Grades Nine Through Twelve

Superconductors are beginning to make important contributions to technology. The absence of resis-

tance makes possible more efficient electric generators. Very powerful electromagnets are made out of
superconductors and are used in many branches of
science, technology, and medicine. Superconducting
magnets may make possible high-speed, almost
frictionless, magnetically levitated trains that ride
above their tracks. The recently developed high-
temperature superconductors will likely expand the
use of superconductors into new areas over the next
several years. [Systems and Interactions]

The very strong magnetic fields produced by
superconducting magnets offer possiblities of improved transportation systems and better medical
diagnostic methods, but they also pose unknown risks
to the human body. Scientists and medical professionals must be continually alert to the possibility of damage to the human body. [Systems and Interactions]

Electrostatic copying machines make use of the
attractive electric force. A large drum is coated with a
thin film of a photoconductor, a material which is an
insulator in the dark but a conductor in the light. The
drum is electrically charged. Then a camera lens
projects an image of a document onto the drum.
Where the image is dark, the charge is not disturbed.
Where the image is light, the charge flows through
the photoconducting film and leaks away. Thus the
drum holds an electrostatic image of the original
document. A fine, black, waxy powder sticks to the
charged (dark) regions only, thus forming an image in
powder. The powder is subsequently "ironed" onto a
sheet of paper. [Systems and Interactions]

The use of miniaturized electronics is pervasive in
our modern technological world. Tens of millions of
electronic parts can be put on on microchip smaller
than the nail of your little finger at a cost of only a
few dollars. This has made possible very sophisticated desktop computers for both home and industry.
These are more powerful than even the largest
computers of only a few decades ago. [Patterns of
Change, Evolution, Scale and Structure]

Section G   Energy: Light

LIGHT enables us to see; sight is considered by many
to be the most important of our senses. Younger
students in particular have difficulty understanding
the properties of light simply because it is so closely
connected with vision. Even after the distinction
between light and vision has been made, it is not easy
to understand what light really is. We can certainly
understand and describe many properties of light at a
fairly elementary level. But to get at what light really
is requires the use of a highly mathematical theory.
For physicists and other scientists who study and use
light, this theory, called quantum electrodynamics,
provides one of the most precise and exact understandings of all physical phenomena.

**G-1 How does light enable us to see? What
are the sources of light? What is light?**

G-2 What are the properties of light?

G-3 How do we use light?

G-1

How does light enable us to see? What are the
sources of light? What is light?

Kindergarten Through Grade Three

When we see something, our eyes and brains are
responding to the light that comes from the objects
we are looking at. Light itself is not something that
we see or touch. Light comes from objects and enters
our eyes; the eye is the organ of the body that is
sensitive to light. A picture of what we are looking at
is formed in our eyes and brain. Light is not like other
things; it is not ordinary matter. The eye can see in
both very dim and very bright light, but there are
limits. Because the sun is so bright a source of light,
too much light enters our eyes if we look at it directly, and serious damage to our eyes occurs. Most
objects do not emit their own light, but reflect light
from other sources. We can see them by means of this
reflected light. The sun is our primary source of light.
Other sources include electric lights of all sorts and
objects that are burning. We can classify the light we

see according to its brightness and its color. [Energy, Scale and Structure, Systems and Interactions]

G-1   How does light enable us to see? What are the sources of light? What is light?

Grades Three Through Six

Light radiates outward in all directions from the sun and from other hot objects. Some things can emit light without being hot (glow-in-the-dark paint and fireflies, for example). Light travels at great speed. If not interrupted, light travels in straight lines. [Systems and Interactions]

Light is a way that energy is transferred from the source that emits the light to the object or substance that absorbs it. [Systems and Interactions]

All surfaces reflect some of the light that strikes them. We are able to see objects that reflect light as well as objects that emit their own light. When light reaches the eye, the cornea and lens of the eye focus the light on the retina where it is absorbed. The retina contains nerve cells that respond to light and transmit electrical impulses to the brain via the optic nerve. The brain further interprets these signals to produce the visual images of objects we see. [Systems and Interactions]

G-1   How does light enable us to see? What are the sources of light? What is light?

Grades Six Through Nine

Light, infrared radiation, and ultraviolet radiation are forms of electromagnetic radiation. (See Section F, Energy: Electricity and Magnetism.) Visible light is distinguished from other forms by its particular range of wavelengths, to which our eyes are sensitive. Many insects and some birds (such as hummingbirds) can see using a wider range of wavelengths, including a part of the ultraviolet region of the electromagnetic spectrum. [Energy, Scale and Structure, Systems and Interactions]

G-1   How does light enable us to see? What are the sources of light? What is light?

Grades Nine Through Twelve

Different models for light are useful in helping us understand it. To best understand how light is emitted and absorbed, we use the model that considers light as particles, called photons. The energy of individual photons increases as the wavelength of light decreases. Light's behavior is best understood in terms of waves when we study the propagation of light. [Scale and Structure, Systems and Interactions]

G-2

What are the properties of light?

Kindergarten Through Grade Three

We observe and classify light in terms of its intensity (brightness) and color. We cannot see when the light is too faint; when light is too bright, it can be harmful to our eyes. We give names to different colors. Light passes more readily through some materials than through others. [Systems and Interactions]

Shadows result when an object blocks the light coming from a bright source. The object that casts the shadow is located between the light source and the surface that is lit by the light on which the shadow is seen. If the object moves closer to the light source, the shadow gets bigger because the object blocks more of the light. [Systems and Interactions]

The direction of light going out from an object is changed when it hits a mirror. Our eyes cannot tell if the direction of the light has been changed. That is why our eyes and brain form a picture which seems to tell us that the object is on the other side of the mirror. [Systems and Interactions]

G-2   What are the properties of light?

Grades Three Through Six

Lenses bend light that passes through them. When we look at an object through a lens, our eyes do not know that the lens has bent the light. Depending on exactly how far the lens is from the object and our eyes, the object seems larger or smaller than it really is. [Systems and Interactions]

Most substances (even mirrors) absorb some of the light that strikes them. The absorbed light is converted into heat energy. Substances like clear glass that absorb very little light are said to be transparent. [Energy, Systems and Interactions]

The cornea (front part of the eye) is mainly responsible for focusing the light that enters the eye. The lens (located behind the cornea) provides the fine adjustment that lets us focus on objects close up as well as far away. A prevalent misconception is that the lens is primarily responsible for focusing the light that enters our eyes.

Most surfaces reflect some of the light that strikes them, some more than others. Objects like clear plastic and glass (contact lenses, for example) are sometimes hard to see because they reflect so little light. [Systems and Interactions]

G-2   What are the properties of light?

Grades Six Through Nine

The speed of light is very much greater than the speeds of other familiar things. It takes light only about eight minutes to reach the earth from the sun, which is approximately 150 million kilometers away. A light-year is the distance that light travels in one year, almost 10 trillion kilometers. [Scale and Structure]

G-2   What are the properties of light?

Grades Nine Through Twelve

The speed of light can be measured in several different ways. Formerly, it was determined experimentally in terms of a standard meter and standard second. Today, the speed of light (c) can be measured so precisely that the unit of length, the meter, is defined in terms of c, as is the unit of time, the second. [Scale and Structure]

The speed of light in vacuum is exactly the same for all observers. This statement is one of the fundamental principles of the theory of relativity. [Scale and Structure] The speed of light is related to its frequency (f) and its wavelength (λ); the relation is $f = c\lambda$. (See Section C, Force and Motion.) For visible light, the range of wavelengths runs from 400 *nm* (nanometers) to 700 *nm*. [Scale and Structure]

Like all waves, light waves conform to the principle of superposition. When waves superpose—pass through the same space—in such a way that their crests correspond and their troughs correspond, the result is a larger wave; this is called *constructive interference*. When the waves superpose so that the crest on one corresponds to the trough of the other, and vice versa, the result is a smaller wave or no wave at all. This is called *destructive interference*. Interference can be demonstrated by letting light from the same source pass through two narrow, parallel slits and then fall on a screen. [Systems and Interactions]

G-3

How do we use light?

Kindergarten Through Grade Three

We can see only if there is light present. Devices to reflect light can be used to see ourselves or around corners. If the light is coming from all directions, as in fog, it is difficult to see objects. [Systems and Interactions]

G-3   How do we use light?

Grades Three Through Six

What we see as white light consists of light of many colors mixed together. Sometimes white light is seen to separate into colors, as in the rainbow, or in light patterns reflected by a soap bubble, or in light passing through a prism. The light is separated into separate colors because light of different colors is bent differently when it passes from air into water or glass, or vice versa. [Systems and Interactions, Scale and Structure]

When a surface appears colored, it is because it reflects more light of some colors than of other colors. The light that is not reflected is absorbed. Thus a red flower is red because it is a good absorber of blue and green light, reflecting only red light to our eyes. If we try to observe a red flower in pure blue light, it appears black because the blue light is absorbed. If we go into a store to buy a red shirt, we must be careful not to look at it in colored light. Outside the store, in the sunlight, the shirt may appear to be a very different color. When red, yellow, and blue paint are mixed together, the mixture appears dark brown or black. This is because each of the colored paints absorbs some of the white light falling on it. With the proper mixture, all colors are absorbed equally, and little or no reflected light is seen. [Energy, Scale and Structure, Systems and Interactions]

Many technologies and devices use or manipulate light. Among them are cameras, camcorders, computer monitors, VCRs and videodisk players, telescopes, microscopes, and the light-pipe endoscopes used by surgeons for such procedures as arthroscopic surgery. [Systems and Interactions]

G-3   How do we use light?

Grades Six Through Nine

Energy is transferred from the source of light to the substance that absorbs the light. This energy can then be converted to other forms. It can provide the energy for certain chemical reactions; it can be converted into heat energy; or, by means of photovoltaic devices, it can be converted directly into electric energy. [Energy, Systems and Interactions]

Some light is absorbed by fluorescent substances, the energy stored temporarily and then emitted, usually as a different color. If blue light shines on a glow-in-the-dark toy, it glows brightly yellow or green for a few minutes after the light is turned off. If red light is used, there is no afterglow because red light does not have enough energy to activate the fluorescent substance. Manufacturers of washing machine detergents add fluorescent materials to make clothing look "whiter than white." When the washed clothing is put in sunlight, some of the ultraviolet light in the sunlight is absorbed by the substance in the clothing and then reemitted as blue or violet light, making the clothing look whiter. A similar effect is often used in amusement park fun houses to produce startling images. [Energy, Scale and Structure, Systems and Interactions]

G-3   How do we use light?

Grades Nine Through Twelve

A beam of light can carry a great amount of information. For this reason, many telephone transmission cables are being replaced by fiber-optic lines. [Systems and Interactions, Scale and Structure]

When light of a sufficiently short wavelength (high enough energy) falls on a metal surface, the surface can emit electrons. This emission is called the photoelectric effect. The photoelectric effect has many useful applications. Equally important, a study of the effect leads to a better understanding of the interaction between light and matter. [Energy, Scale and Structure, Systems and Interaction]

Lasers are devices that produce light of precisely one wavelength. The beam of light that emerges from the laser does not diverge, as do light beams from other sources. When the laser beam strikes a surface, this concentrated energy is absorbed into a very small area. The amount of heat energy transferred in this way, even from low-power lasers, can easily damage unprotected eyes. From high-power lasers, the heat can be sufficient to cut through thick layers of steel. In medicine, lasers have become invaluable for depositing precise amounts of heat energy to cut away unwanted substances. A serious social issue that must be debated and discussed is the use of very high power lasers in satellite-based military weapon systems. [Energy, Systems and Interactions]

Section H   Energy: Sound

THE science of sound, called *acoustics*, is interdisciplinary. It involves the physical aspects of the creation and transmission of energy in the form of sound waves to the eardrum as well as the interpretation by the auditory nerve and brain of the electrical nerve impulses generated in the middle ear by the vibrating eardrum. *Physical acoustics*, the process up to the eardrum, is considered in this section. The remainder of the process is in the domain of *physiological* and *psychological acoustics*.

H-1   Where does sound come from? What are its sources? How can sound be described?

H-2   How does sound enable us to hear? How do we produce sounds?

H-3   How do we use sound?

H-1

Where does sound come from? What are its sources? How can sound be described?

Kindergarten Through Grade Three

Sound comes from many sources. Sound can be produced by making an object vibrate (move back and forth). All sounds can ultimately be traced to a vibration of some material object, whether it be the strings of a guitar or violin, the membrane of a drum, the reed in a clarinet, the speaker cone of a loudspeaker, the vocal cords in our throats, or two spoons being hit together. The vibration is transmitted to anything the vibrating object touches, including the air that surrounds it. [Systems and Interactions]

The range of loudness of sound is very wide; it runs from the threshold of hearing to very loud sounds that can cause pain and ear damage. It is important to avoid excessively loud sounds. [Scale and Structure]

H-1   Where does sound come from? What are its sources? How can sound be described?

Grades Three Through Six

We are most familiar with sound that travels from its source to our ears through air, but sound can travel through other substances as well. Whales communicate over great distances by means of sound that travels through seawater. [Systems and Interactions]

Sound can be reflected or absorbed by walls and other surfaces. Echoes are the reflection of sound we hear from large surfaces. Because some surfaces absorb sound well, they are used to soften or reduce the loudness of sounds generated in a room. Carpets and acoustical tile are used to reduce the noise level in a classroom, for example. [Energy, Systems and Interactions]

Higher or lower tones of sound are produced, depending on how fast the sound source vibrates; the difference between high and low is known as *pitch*. The faster the vibration, the higher the pitch. [Energy, Scale and Structure, Systems and Interactions]

H-1   Where does sound come from? What are its sources? How can sound be described?

Grades Six Through Nine

Sound is a mechanical wave in matter. Like all waves, sound transfers energy when it travels through a medium from one place to another. The energy exists in the form of rapid back-and-forth motion of the particles composing the medium. [Energy, Systems and Interactions]

The sensation of musical pitch is determined by the frequency of the sound that produces the sensation. A sound of a particular frequency traveling through air has a particular wavelength. (See Section C, Force and Motion.) The pitch can be changed by changing the frequency of the vibrating source. The pitch of a stringed instrument, for example, can be changed by increasing or reducing the length of the string or by changing its tension. The pitch of a wind instrument can be changed by changing the effective length of the vibrating column of air inside the instrument. A musical sound of a given frequency, traveling through air, has a particular wavelength. The intensity of sound vibrations is perceived as loudness and can be varied by changing the amplitude of the vibrating source. [Energy, Systems and Interactions, Scale and Structure]

Earthquake waves are sound waves that travel through the earth. (See Chapter 4, Section B, Geology and Natural Resources.) Their frequency is too low to hear. However, they transfer great amounts of vibrational energy and can shake objects, such as buildings, hard enough to do a great deal of damage. So-called sonic booms, produced by airplanes moving faster than the speed of sound, sometimes also carry enough sound energy to do damage. [Energy, Scale and Structure, Systems and Interactions]

H-1   Where does sound come from? What are its sources? How can sound be described?

Grades Nine Through Twelve

Sound waves consist of rapid vibrations of molecules in solids, liquids, and gases. For example, the vibrating surface of a bell starts a sound wave in the surrounding air by pushing against the adjacent air molecules back and forth. One back-and-forth vibration composes one cycle of the sound. The disturbed molecules in turn push against neighboring molecules and disturb them, and so forth. The disturbed molecules do not move very far. What travels away from the bell at the speed of sound is the collision process itself. [Energy, Systems and Interactions]

The speed of sound through air is about 340 metres per second, the exact value depending on the temperature and humidity. (This is roughly one and a half times as fast as the speed of a commercial jet plane.) Sound travels faster through liquids and solids than through gases. Sound cannot travel through a vacuum because there is nothing in a vacuum that can vibrate. [Scale and Structure]

The frequency of a sound is perceived by an observer to be the same as the frequency of the source only if the observer and the source are at rest with respect to the intervening medium. If either the source or the observer is moving with respect to the medium, the source frequency and the observed frequency can be different. This is called the Doppler effect. Relative motion that brings the source and the observer closer together increases the perceived frequency; relative motion that separates the source and the observer decreases the perceived frequency. (See Chapter 4, Section A, Astronomy.) [Energy, Scale and Structure, Patterns of Change]

The propagation of a sound wave depends on the springiness of the medium through which it propagates. If you hit a steel bar with a hammer, you distort the bar, and it springs back to its undisturbed shape. But in doing so, the disturbed material distorts neighboring material. Solids are springy, both in compression (back-and-forth squeezing) and in shear (side-to-side twisting). [Systems and Interactions]

Waves, including sound waves, interact strongly with structures whose size is roughly comparable to their wavelength. Some objects have resonant frequencies at which they tend to vibrate. These frequencies can be measured. [Energy, Scale and Structure]

H-2

How does sound enable us to hear? How do we produce sounds?

Kindergarten Through Grade Three

The ear is the organ of the body that receives sound. In humans, the ear is sensitive to a wide range of sounds, both soft and loud in intensity and high and low in pitch. Loud sounds can cause damage to the ear and should be avoided. Some sounds are too high-pitched for humans to hear, but some animals, including dogs and deer, demonstrate ability to hear them. [Systems and Interactions]

H-2   How does sound enable us to hear? How do we produce sounds?

Grades Three Through Six

When sound reaches our ears, the vibrating air next to the eardrum sets the eardrum to vibration. The vibrating eardrum stimulates nerve cells, which transmit electrical impulses through the auditory

nerve to the brain, producing the sensation of sound. The energy carried by normal sound waves is small, and the ear can hear such sounds because it is very sensitive. Like most other mammals, humans can produce sound by passing air across the vocal cords, causing them to vibrate. The sound thus produced can be modified by shaping the mouth, lips, and tongue to produce speech. Speech is the primary mode of communication among humans. Many other animals communicate with the sounds they make, though the information they communicate is much more restricted than that of human speech. [Scale and Structure, Systems and Interactions]

H-2   How does sound enable us to hear? How do we produce sounds?

Grades Six Through Nine

It is important to distinguish clearly between the physical vibration that is one of the factors composing sound waves and the physiological sensation of sound. Sound waves stimulate the sensory process, but that process is electromechanical and involves complex interpretation on the part of the brain. Even though both processes are called *sound*, confusing them can result in unanswerable questions; for example, "If a tree falls in the forest and there is no one there to hear it, is there any sound?" [Scale and Structure, Systems and Interactions]

H-3

How do we use sound?

Kindergarten Through Grade Three

Sound arises from a great variety of sources. Recognizing the source and understanding the meaning of sounds from our environment is very important in our interaction with the environment. We use sounds to communicate with one another by speaking, singing, and listening. [Evolution, Systems and Interaction]

H-3   How do we use sound?

Grades Three Through Six

Two ears are better than one for locating a sound source. Stereo sound systems represent a technological application of this fact. Some animals are much better adapted than humans for sound source location. In the predator-prey relationship, for example, many predators can orient their external ears to focus on the sounds they hear to locate their prey. In a similar fashion, many prey animals can focus their hearing to locate and thus avoid predators. [Evolution, Systems and Interactions]

Sound frequencies beyond the range of human perception are used by some animals adapted to do so. Bats and dolphins, for example, make sounds with frequencies higher than those that humans can hear and use the echoes for navigation and hunting. [Evolution, Systems and Interactions]

H-3   How do we use sound?

Grades Six Through Nine

Musical tones are sounds having a fundamental frequency component, together with a set of higher frequency components called harmonics. Tuning forks are designed to produce predominantly the fundamental frequency, but musical instruments are carefully designed to produce a typical harmonic spectrum. The production of music represents a highly developed technological application having a long history. [Scale and Structure]

In persons who have impaired hearing, the ear loses sensitivity to a range of sound. In older persons, the loss is usually at the high-frequency end of the range of human hearing. Nearly all elderly persons have

some degree of hearing loss. In persons whose ears have been damaged by exposure to loud sounds, like rock musicians and persons who work in loud environments without proper ear protection, the loss is typically in the midrange of frequency. Hearing aids are carefully tailored so that they selectively amplify sound at the frequencies where the hearing loss has occurred. Present-day hearing aids are an imperfect substitute for normal hearing, but they are extremely helpful to many persons. Hearing-aid technology is currently improving rapidly. [Patterns of Change, Systems and Interactions]

H-3   How do we use sound?

Grades Nine Through Twelve

In sonar, a pulse of sound is used to determine the distance to the object that reflected it. This requires a knowledge of the speed of sound and the elapsed time from transmission of the pulse to detection of the echo. Sonars are used to find fish and measure water depth. Sophisticated sonars can apply the Doppler effect, using the frequency of the reflected sound to determine the speed of the object producing the echo. Bats use sonar (also called echolocation) to avoid obstacles and to catch their prey as they fly in the dark. The frequency used by bats is well beyond the upper limit of human ears. Other animals use similar but less well-developed sonar techniques. [Evolution, Systems and Interactions]

Very high frequency sound (ultrasound) has a variety of applications in medicine and industry. Medical ultrasonic imaging is used for a variety of noninvasive examination and diagnostic techniques, notably in obstetrics and cancer diagnosis. The technique depends on differential reflection or absorption of sound by various body structures. The short wavelength of high-frequency sound makes possible high resolution of detail in the image obtained. High-energy, focused sound pulses are used in lithotripsy to break up kidney stones, making surgery unnecessary in many cases. [Systems and Interactions, Energy]

Chapter 4

Earth Sciences

BEFORE Galileo's invention of the telescope in 1609, stargazers relied on their unaided sight. The lenses used by Galileo enabled him to see roughly ten times more stars than could be seen earlier with the unaided eye. Today, scientists use such modern-day instruments as reflector telescopes, radio telescopes, and spectroscopes to expand their "vision" of the universe far beyond the imaginations of early astronomers. These and other tools of astronomy have led scientists closer to understanding the evolution of our universe.

A-1   **What kinds of objects does the universe contain, and how do these objects relate to one another?**

A-2   **How has the universe evolved?**

A-3   **How do we learn about the contents and structure of the universe?**

A-1

What kinds of objects does the universe contain, and how do these objects relate to one another?

Kindergarten Through Grade Three

When the sun is up, it is daytime; daylight comes from the sun. When the sun is down, it is nighttime, and the stars can be seen. The sun provides heat as well as light; it is usually warmer during the day than at night. The moon may be visible in the daytime or the nighttime. [Patterns of Change]

Every day, the sun rises in the east, moves higher until about noon, and then moves lower until it sets in the west. In autumn the daylight period grows gradually shorter, becoming shortest about the time of winter vacation. Then it grows longer, becoming longest about the time that summer vacation starts.

The sun does not always rise and set in exactly the same places. In summer the sun rises to the north of east and sets to the north of west. At noon it is high in the sky. In winter the sun rises to the south of east and sets to the south of west, and does not rise very high in the sky at noon. Days are longer in summer than in winter because the sun travels a longer path above the horizon. This variation is the main cause of the climatic changes of the seasons. [Patterns of Change]

The moon also rises and sets. The moon appears to change shape over the course of a month. First, it waxes (increases) from a crescent to a full disk, then wanes back to a crescent before waxing again. If we observe and record the shape of the moon every two or three days for about a month, we can see the entire cycle of the moon. [Patterns of Change]

The earth we live on is a gigantic sphere, or globe, made mostly of rock. It only appears to be flat because we see just a tiny part of it. People live all around the globe. There is no top and no bottom; people do not fall off the earth because they are held to it by a force called gravity. Wherever we are on the surface of the earth, down is toward the center of the earth.

The apparent daily motions of the sun, the moon, the planets, and the stars are due to the rotation of the earth about its axis. If we observe the sun and the moon every two or three days, we can see that the moon grows fuller (waxes) as it moves farther away from the sun in the sky and becomes thinner (wanes) as it returns toward the sun. The phases of the moon depend on the angle between the sun and the moon, as we see them from the earth. When the moon is full, it always rises about the same time the sun sets. The reason is that we on earth must be between the sun and the moon in order to see the entire illuminated face of the moon. When the moon is new, it rises and sets at about the same time as the sun. This is because we see the sun and the moon in approximately the same direction, and most of the lighted side of the moon is facing away from us. [Patterns of Change]

Eclipses occur when the earth, sun, and moon come into alignment so that the earth's shadow falls on the moon (lunar eclipse) or the moon's shadow falls on the earth (solar eclipse). Eclipses do not occur every month because usually the sun, earth, and moon are not exactly in line.

The universe is rich and varied. Among other things it contains rocky spheres like earth; globes largely made of liquid and gas like Jupiter; bigger and hotter globes of gas like the sun; huge numbers of other stars much like the sun—some smaller and longer-lived, some bigger and shorter-lived; and groups of stars. The universe also contains clouds of gas and dust. There is much other material in the universe as well; but we have not yet observed it, and we know very little about it. Most objects we see are separated from one another by vast, seemingly empty space. [Scale and Structure, Systems and Interactions]

A-1 What kinds of objects does the universe contain, and how do these objects relate to one another?

Grades Three Through Six

When we look at the stars at night, we see them moving westward in the sky. Some stars rise in the east and set in the west. But some stars never set at all; they revolve in counterclockwise circles around the pole star, never passing below the horizon. We learn to identify stars by their positions with respect to their neighbors; these patterns are called constellations. [Patterns of Change]

Some of the brightest objects in the nighttime sky (aside from the moon) do not stay in the same place relative to the neighboring stars. Instead, they move slowly against the stellar background. These objects are called planets. [Patterns of Change]

Although some planets are considerably brighter than most stars, planets are easily mistaken for stars when they are observed only once. By observing the same planet every few nights for several weeks, we can see that it wanders among the constellations. Like the moon, the planets shine by reflected sunlight. All planets, including earth, orbit about the sun. It is very

Because a year is a very long time in the life of a child, many students find it difficult to grasp some of the motions, such as the motion of the planets relative to the stellar background. A visit to a planetarium will give vivid pictures of both the gross structure of the universe and of the directly observable consequences of rotation in the solar system.

The sun, moon, and stars are fascinating to children in the primary grades. They are naturally curious about the moon's changing appearance and the sun's progress across the sky. Although most young children cannot grasp these phenomena, they can observe the sky in a systematic way and observe patterns. Helping students discover these patterns of change through their own observations encourages their curiosity about the world as they acquire basic knowledge about astronomy.

The relative sizes of objects are not easy for students to grasp. It is important to make clear which objects (or systems of objects) are parts of which others. A visit to a planetarium or use of the small planetariums that many school districts own can be of great help in clarification as well as in conveying a sense of excitement. [Scale and Structure]

Traditionally, the teaching of astronomy in the primary grades has been largely restricted to studies of the solar system. This a good start; but with the rapid increase in knowledge about the rest of the universe, it is important to introduce broader concepts, even at the grades three-through-six level. Our solar system is an example of systems all through the universe, but there are many other astronomical objects and phenomena in the universe. Students in the later primary grades can come to appreciate that the universe is a dynamic place at all scales of size and acquire some basic ideas about such central matters as stellar evolution, the history of the universe, and the place of the earth and of humankind in a much larger environment. This approach avoids the artificial division of the study of astronomy into "the solar system" and "everything else."

likely that other stars also have systems of planets, but these have not yet been observed directly. [Patterns of Change]

Our solar system is only a tiny part of the universe, but it is the part we know the best because it is the part closest to us. Besides the planets, other objects orbit the sun. These include asteroids, which are small rocky or metallic objects ranging in size from a kilometer or less to almost a thousand kilometers; meteoroids, which are chunks of matter ranging in size from tiny specks to many tons; and comets, which contain large amounts of ice and other materials that vaporize into long tails when the comets come near the sun. [Systems and Interactions]

Meteoroids that enter the earth's atmosphere get very hot and glow as they fall; that is why they are called shooting stars. Only a very few of the largest meteoroids actually reach the earth's surface; these rocky or metallic objects from space are called meteorites. [Scale and Structure, Patterns of Change]

A-1   What kinds of objects does the universe contain, and how do these objects relate to one another?

Grades Six Through Nine

As far as we can tell, every object in the universe rotates. These rotations are most directly visible in the apparent motions of the sun, the moon, the planets, and the stars through the sky. The most marked apparent motion—the diurnal (daily) motion—is a direct consequence of the rotation of the earth about its own axis. [Stability, Patterns of Change]

The seasonal variations in the path of the sun through the sky are a consequence of the revolution of the earth around the sun. The axis of the earth is inclined at an angle of 23-1/2 degrees with respect to the poles of the solar system, and the orientation of the axis remains constant as the earth revolves around the sun. Consequently, if we start at a given place on earth, we see the daily path of the sun vary through the seasons. The variation is greater at high latitudes and smaller at low latitudes. [Patterns of Change]

Astronomers have already discovered many kinds of fascinating objects. Astronomical objects come in many different sizes, and some are parts of others. Globes of rock and of gas orbit around the sun (and very likely around other stars) and around one another under the action of gravity. We call some orbiting objects planets and others moons or satellites; these terms tell how objects move, rather than what they are made of. Our sun is a medium-sized star among many, many stars. Stars are often found in groups called clusters (containing a dozen to a million stars). Galaxies contain a billion to a trillion stars, as well as huge gas-and-dust clouds. Our own galaxy, the Milky Way, is a member of a cluster of a few dozen galaxies called the Local Group. Among other components of the universe are gas-and-dust clouds and unseen matter. At every step in scale—clusters, groups of clusters, galaxies, and groups of galaxies—there exists a variety of structures. A collection of objects at a given scale of size is called a system (e.g., solar system). Study of the structure of a system can yield information about the history of the system. [Systems and Interactions, Scale and Structure]

Among the objects composing the universe, astronomers know the most about our own solar system because all its parts are relatively close to us and therefore relatively easy to observe in detail. Planets and other components of the solar system are so close to us that we have already sent space probes to many of them. Objects in the solar system are often classified according to the way they move: planets orbit directly around the sun, whereas satellites orbit around planets. The earth is a planet; the moon is a satellite of the earth. Asteroids, comets, and meteoroids all orbit around the sun, much as planets do. But they are much smaller than planets and may have orbits that cross planetary orbits.

The solar system is bound together by gravitation, the force of attraction that every body in the universe exerts on every other body. (See Chapter 3, Section C, Force and Motion.) Larger astronomical systems—stars, clusters of stars, galaxies, and clusters of galaxies—are also bound by gravitation. Many stars are members of pairs called binary systems and orbit around a common center under the influence of gravity. Because the strength of the gravitational force can be calculated, it is possible to predict the orbits of planets and of their satellites with exquisite accuracy. [Stability]

Objects in the solar system may also be classified and studied in terms of what they are made of and how they were formed. This tells more about their roles in the solar system than their motion alone does. [Scale and Structure, Evolution]

It takes a substantial amount of scientific thinking and observation, which often takes time, before scientists understand new discoveries thoroughly. In all probability most of the types of objects that the universe contains have not yet been discovered. New objects and new categories of objects are constantly being discovered. The past few decades have been particularly fruitful for such discoveries, and they continue at a pace that appears to be increasing. [Patterns of Change]

A-1 What kinds of objects does the universe contain, and how do these objects relate to one another?

Grades Nine Through Twelve

At every step in the scale of size, astronomical objects rotate about their own axes and revolve in orbits. Everything in the universe is made of the same kinds of matter—fundamental particles, chemical elements, and compounds—known on earth, and all obey the same laws of nature that apply on earth. (See Chapter 3.) [Stability, Energy, Systems and Interactions]

From our vantage point on earth, we try to learn more and more about how the universe works, yet there are still many important processes about which we know little or nothing. But we have built a theoretical structure that provides a good working understanding of the behavior of vast numbers of objects and the relationships among them, and we have come to understand many of the principles that underlie the workings of the universe. [Evolution]

Star clusters, nebulae, galaxies, and clusters of galaxies are bound by gravity, the same force that holds our solar system together. Because the strength of the gravitational force can be calculated, it is possible to predict how the stars in a galaxy will move with respect to each other. Such calculations have shown that there is much more matter than we can observe. Thus, 90 percent of the matter in the universe is of an unknown nature. The task of detecting the as yet unseen matter by means other than gravity, and thus learning more about it, is a major problem of modern astronomy. [Systems and Interactions, Stability]

The most pervasive force on the astronomical scale is gravitation. Symmetry and regularity, so often found in astronomical objects, usually arise from the action of gravity and other forces, notably the electromagnetic force. (See Chapter 3, Section C, Force and Motion; and Section F, Energy: Electricity and Magnetism.) [Scale and Structure, Stability]

Meteoroids (and occasionally asteroids and comets) can come close to planets much larger than they are, so that the gravitational force exerted on them by the planets deflects them greatly. As a result, these smaller bodies often have orbits that are less stable than the orbits of planets. When a meteoroid comes close to the earth, it can be captured by the earth's gravity and fall to the earth as a meteor, visible in the sky. Most meteors are quite small (typically the size of sand grains) and are vaporized under the action of atmospheric friction long before they reach the earth's surface. Only the very largest meteors reach the surface, and their remains are called meteorites. [Stability, Systems and Interactions]

Astronomers not only discover new objects but also

High school astronomy has traditionally been taught as an elective or as part of other science courses, but this practice is changing. New astronomy curricula for secondary students are becoming available. Many of these curricula present astronomy in the context of the history of science, the understanding of planetary geology, and the development of mathematics and physics.

When a body is not too far from a much more massive body, it orbits around the more massive body, which is called its primary. The less massive body is called the secondary. Planets orbit the sun in this way, and satellites (moons) and rings orbit the planets. The motions are governed by the gravitational force. Newton showed that, because the gravitational force conforms to an inverse–square behavior, the orbit of every secondary around its primary conforms to Kepler's laws:

1. The orbit is an ellipse, with the primary at one focus.

2. The line joining the primary and the secondary sweeps out equal areas in equal times.

3. When several secondaries orbit the same primary, the squares of their orbit periods (T) are proportional to the cubes of their average distances (a) from the primary:

$$\frac{a_1^3}{a_2^3} = \frac{T_1^2}{T_1^2}$$

In this equation the subscripts 1 and 2 refer to any two secondaries about the same primary. With a little extension, Kepler's laws also describe the motion of stars in their local clusters, of clusters in their galaxies, and of galaxies with respect to one another.

Studies show that a great majority of students at the high school level retain misconceptions about phenomena that are often taught at the elementary and middle school levels. For example, asking students to explain why we have seasons often evokes unusual ideas about the way the earth orbits the sun and how light is absorbed by the earth and other bodies. Thus, before the teacher begins a unit on stars or any other topic in astronomy, he or she should ask questions to find out what students think about the elementary concepts that underlie the unit.

create new theories and models. For example, it has long been known that comets eventually "die" as their ices evaporate in the warmth of the sun. Where does a new supply of comets come from? Jan Oort proposed that they come from a huge swarm of ice and dust, called the Oort cloud, beyond the outermost planets of the solar system. This theory is now widely accepted, even though no one has directly observed the Oort cloud. This is because Oort's theory is currently the best explanation for why we see comets today.

Beyond the solar system are stars of many types. The appearance of a star—the amount and color of the light it emits—depends mainly on two factors: its mass and its age. Among the important types of stars are main-sequence stars with their many subtypes, red and blue giants, white dwarfs, neutron stars (among them pulsars), and stellar black holes. Closely related are the proto-stellar and post-stellar nebulae. Many stars are most readily seen by the visible light they emit; others emit mainly radio waves or X rays. Groupings of stars also have typical appearances. Among the types are open clusters, globular clusters, galaxies of many types including quasars, and galaxy clusters. Each system has a typical history. [Energy, Evolution, Stability, Systems and Interactions, Patterns of Change]

Because the nearest objects are the easiest to observe, we know the most about them. More distant objects may turn out to be more important in gaining a deeper understanding of the structure and history of the universe, but we cannot as yet observe many of

them well enough to evaluate their importance. The unseen-mass problem exemplifies how much we still have to learn.

A-2

How has the universe evolved?

Kindergarten Through Grade Three

When we look at the sky, we can see many types of objects. All of them are far away, but some of them are much farther away than others. The object that looks very much the brightest is the sun, which is the star closest to earth. The sun gives us so much light that we cannot see anything else in the sky during the daytime, except sometimes the moon. The sun is in the center of a system that includes the earth and eight other planets, satellites (moons and rings), asteroids, comets, and so forth.

There are many stars other than the sun. They are very far away, but we can see many of them when we look up at the clear night sky. Many of these stars may have planets as the sun does, but they are so hard to see at such great distance that we have not yet seen any such planets. When the sky is clear and dark, we can trace arrangements of stars (constellations and asterisms). [Scale and Structure, Systems and Interactions]

A-2   How has the universe evolved?

Grades Three Through Six

The setting point of the sun can be recorded each day to find long-term patterns or change. These patterns can help us to devise a calendar to mark the seasons.

We can make models to explain why the sun, moon, and stars seem to rise in the east and set in the west; why the moon goes through phases; and why we have seasons.

Telescopes may be thought of as funnels that collect and concentrate light. Because the amount of light that a telescope can collect depends mainly on how big its main lens or mirror is, astronomers keep trying to build bigger and bigger telescopes.

We have sent space probes to the earth's moon, several comets, and all but one of the planets. Wonderful photographs, videotapes, laser disks, and planetarium programs are available that describe these space probes and richly illustrate what we have learned about them.

A-2   How has the universe evolved?

Grades Six Through Nine

We learn about how the universe evolved by studying astronomical bodies. With telescopes and other devices, astronomers measure where objects are, how they move, what they are made of, and how they change. This helps us to reconstruct the early history of the universe. [Scale and Structure, Patterns of Change]

The universe is very old. Estimates based on the information currently available yield an age somewhere between 18 and 21 billion years, though that estimate may yet be revised to a greater age. There is strong evidence that the universe "began" with a colossal explosion called the "big bang." (See Chapter 3, Section A, Matter.)

In the first million years or so, matter and energy evolved from forms now unfamiliar into forms we know today. Prominent were the simplest gases, hydrogen and helium. The earliest stars condensed from this mixture. In condensing to form a star, the matter heats up until the nuclear fusion process can start. Hydrogen nuclei fuse to form helium nuclei, and energy is released in the process.

When a star having roughly the mass of the sun or less has fused most of its hydrogen—a process that takes billions of years—it expands greatly and becomes a red giant. It then quickly fuses nearly all of the remaining hydrogen over a much shorter period and ends up as a white dwarf. While it is not certain, it appears that white dwarfs eventually cool down and become brown dwarfs; if this process occurs, it takes a long time. But stars more massive than the sun (roughly, more than two and a half times more massive) die by exploding violently, producing the spectacular displays called supernovas. A supernova spews much of its matter into the surrounding space, where it mixes with interstellar hydrogen and helium. Later generations of stars start with this enriched mixture of hydrogen, helium, and more complex elements. Our own solar system condensed in this way about 4.6 billion years ago. Most of the hydrogen and helium ended up in the sun and in the gas-giant planets (Jupiter, Saturn, Uranus, and Neptune).

The earth and similar objects nearer the sun—Mercury, Venus, Mars, and the moon—condensed at temperatures too high for hydrogen and other light gases to condense. The matter accreting onto the earth transferred its energy of motion into heat energy. This accretionary heat was the initial heat of

Most students are familiar with three states of matter: solid, liquid, and gas. Plasmas are a fourth state of matter in which the atoms are broken up into positively and negatively charged particles. A common example of a plasma is the glowing matter inside a neon light. Plasmas of a wide range of densities exist in the universe— from thin interstellar clouds to the interiors of stars. The Crab Nebula is a dramatic example of a plasma. Electromagnetic forces are very important in governing the behavior of plasmas.

The distances to a few hundred of the nearest stars can be measured by the parallax method. When we observe a nearby star twice at six months apart, we see it from viewpoints that are about 300 million km apart, because the earth moves around the sun. As a result, we see a slight shift in the position of the nearby star relative to stars much farther away. By measuring the shift, we can calculate the distance to the nearby star. Measurement of greater distances depends on a variety of other methods, which can be cross-checked.

One method, devised about 1910 by Henrietta Leavitt, uses the so-called Cepheid variables. The absolute brightness of a Cepheid variable determines its period, which can be readily observed. By measuring its apparent brightness, we can determine its distance and thus the distance of its neighbors. Still greater distances can be measured by other methods, notably by means of the red shift.

A visit to a planetarium is very useful in giving students a feeling for the scale, number, and variety of astronomical objects and distances.

the earth. During this period the matter differentiated into core, mantle, crust, atmosphere, and hydrosphere according to density. Dense material sank, and less dense material rose, forming layers. The cores of earthlike planets are formed largely of metals, the mantles are formed largely of matter less dense than the metals, and the crusts are formed largely of less dense rocks. We live on the crust in the thin zone where the crust and its waters meet the bottom of the atmosphere, and our deepest wells have not yet dug all the way to the mantle. [Evolution, Scale and Structure]

Is there life elsewhere in the universe? At present any discussion must be highly speculative. Neither living organisms nor the traces of extinct living organisms have been found to date on any of the planets and moons we have visited with space probes. However, one can argue plausibly that life is possible elsewhere. Although no planets have been definitely detected around other stars, there are vast numbers of sunlike stars in the universe. Among the many planets they may have, there may be many having conditions much like those on earth. On at least some of those, some kind of life may have evolved; the laws of nature are the same everywhere in the universe. At present, however, we know very little. If life exists outside our solar system, we could probably not detect it in the foreseeable future unless it included intelligent beings who transmitted electromagnetic signals. There has been much discussion about whether we could detect such signals. Searches for them by NASA have been unsuccessful to date, but more extensive efforts can be expected in the future. In any case we cannot at present expect to have direct contact with any intelligent beings that may exist because of the vast distances involved.

A-2   How has the universe evolved?

Grades Nine Through Twelve

The universe contains an immense quantity of the simplest element, hydrogen, and a lesser but still immense quantity of the next simplest element, helium. Because the universe is so large, the atoms of these elements are mostly spread out as extremely thin gases. However, there are places where the gases are thick enough—though still very thin—to appear to us as clouds. When such clouds condense under the influence of gravitation, fusion begins and stars form. Stars contain very concentrated matter, and most stars are very hot—much hotter than familiar flames. Stars come in a wide range of masses, from 1 percent or 2 percent of the sun's mass (that is, a hundred times bigger than Jupiter) to 40 or more times the sun's mass. [Evolution, Energy]

In the interiors of the stars, hydrogen fuses into helium, and large amounts of energy are released. More massive stars fuse helium into many still more complex elements, releasing more energy. These processes are called nuclear fusion processes. The energy works its way to the surface of the star where it radiates outward into space. This is how stars shine. In massive stars, fusion takes place much faster than in less massive stars. Even though the massive stars begin with more fuel, they run out of fuel much faster than the less massive ones. [Energy, Evolution, Stability]

The evolution of the galaxies is an important area of study. When we look at the most distant parts of the universe that we can see with instruments, we see a part of the universe that looks rather different from the part nearer to us. The reason is that the light from distant parts of the universe has taken so long to reach us—10 billion years or more—that we see a sample of what the universe was like a long time ago when it was much younger than it is today. That is, looking at distant objects is like looking back in time. A striking feature of the young universe is the very energetic galaxies called quasars. Although the relationship between quasars and the less distant galaxies that we see by the light they have emitted relatively recently is not fully understood, the study of quasars has contributed much to our understanding of the evolution of the universe and is expected to contribute much more as we learn more about them. [Evolution, Scale and Structure, Patterns of Change]

It has been known since the 1920s that the universe is expanding at a measurable rate. The major evidence supporting this understanding is the so-called red shift. When we use spectrographs to look at distant galaxies, we find that their spectra are shifted toward longer wavelengths. The more distant the galaxy, the greater the shift. This observation can be understood by an analogy. Imagine a balloon with small spots painted all over its surface. If the balloon is inflated, the spots will separate. The farther apart any two spots are, the faster they will separate. We can project the expansion backward, with proper corrections for gravitational and other effects. When we do so, we find that the universe must have been very small about 20 billion years ago.

Will the universe continue to expand indefinitely, or will it reach a maximum size and begin to collapse? The answer depends on the total mass of the universe, which we do not yet know precisely enough to make an answer. We do know, however, that the universe will continue to expand for a very long time, at least much longer than the time since the beginning of the universe.

The evidence supporting the big bang picture arises from a variety of sources, but the most compelling is the so-called 3 K background radiation. All models of the very early universe agree that during the first three minutes or so, light and other forms of electromagnetic radiation could not travel very far without colliding with matter that absorbed it. After about three minutes, the universe had expanded and cooled to the point where it became transparent, and much of the light emitted by matter at that time has continued to propagate without further collision with matter. For this reason the spectrum of the radiation preserves a record of the temperature of the universe at the outset of transparency. Because the universe continues to expand, the radiation has been Doppler shifted (see Chapter 3, Section G, Energy: Sound) to the low temperature of about 3 K, which it displays today.

The rate of expansion, which has been known since about 1930, makes possible a reconstruction of the situation that existed at the onset of transparency. Many properties of the background radiation cannot be explained by any plausible model other than the big bang picture. Many versions of the big bang model have been proposed to explain the very earliest epochs—back to 10^{-43} seconds after the big bang. Explanations of the very earliest epochs of the universe are also explanations of the structure of matter at its most fundamental level. However, much work remains to be done. Many aspects are highly uncertain. And as with all science, the focus of these models is on the mechanics, not on any notion of final cause. [Evolution, Energy, Scale and Structure, Systems and Interactions]

A-3

How do we learn about the contents and structure of the universe?

Kindergarten Through Grade Three

Most astronomical objects are so far away that we cannot visit them; all we can do is observe them from afar. We can tell that the sun is far away, for example, by noting that it is sometimes hidden from view by clouds, so it must be farther away than the clouds.

A-3 How do we learn about the contents and structure of the universe?

Grades Three Through Six

Astronomers use telescopes to gather light from distant objects. Some telescopes are large spyglasses; others look quite different. Some telescopes measure kinds of light not detected by our eyes, such as radio waves or X rays. Such telescopes look very different from the more familiar ones that are designed to work with visible light. For example, radio telescopes look like large television dish antennas. They collect radio waves from stars and other astronomical objects (these are naturally generated electromagnetic waves

The daily movement of the sun can be observed and recorded by marking the shadow of a wooden post set in the ground from time to time during the day. Each day that we can see the moon, we can record its shape by drawing a picture of it. Both of these activities are astronomical observations from which more sophisticated conclusions can be drawn as the student grows older.

Many astronomical observations are accessible to students at this level through the use of simple equipment. For example, the setting of the sun can be observed every clear day, the time being noted with a clock or watch and a protractor being used to estimate the angle between the setting point and some convenient fixed object, such as a building. Long-term patterns can be discerned and models constructed to explain the observations. Many photographs, videotapes, laser disks, and planetarium programs are available to extend and enrich the observations and inferences the students have made by themselves.

analogous to light, and not artificial radio signals). Analysis of these radio waves is analogous to analysis of visible light collected by optical telescopes, and the information gathered complements the information gathered by optical astronomy.

Astronomers put their observing instruments where they can see best. Most telescopes are far from interfering city lights, on top of tall mountains, where the air is clear and stable. Many instruments are put in spacecraft and launched into space, entirely above the air, to get the clearest possible view.

The first step in studying an astronomical object is to establish its location in the sky so that it can be located again. When that task is done, it is possible to study how the object moves, allowing us to find out about its distance and its relation to other objects. Most astronomers work at learning as much as possible about the objects they are studying—their size, mass, shape, composition, temperature, and other conditions. This information can then be used to determine how the objects must have evolved to become as we see them now. [Evolution, Scale and Structure]

A-3   How do we learn about the contents and structure of the universe?

Grades Six Through Nine

Because astronomical objects are so far away, it takes fine technology to extract as much information as possible from the tiny amount of light that reaches us from them. Much ingenuity goes into designing equipment for catching, magnifying, and analyzing the light. With the advent of spacecraft, it has become possible to detect light waves coming from the objects that do not penetrate our atmosphere and could not previously be observed. [Scale and Structure]

Galileo first used a telescope to look at the sky in 1609. There have been great improvements in telescopes since Galileo's earliest instruments. Through the nineteenth century, telescopes were improved through the use of larger and better lenses. In the twentieth century the most powerful telescopes are based on large mirrors rather than lenses. Because it is not practical to make good mirrors much larger than those currently in use, the telescopes of the 1990s use many relatively small mirrors, which are electronically controlled to act together as one very large mirror.

Astronomers rarely search the sky at random. They almost always try to obtain specific types of information and carefully design their observing instruments with that specific information in mind. That is why astronomers use so many different kinds of instruments. [Systems and Interactions]

Visible light is only one kind of electromagnetic radiation. Other kinds, which have different wavelengths, cannot be detected by our eyes. (See Chapter 3, Section G, Energy: Light.) Astronomers use devices to collect and analyze radiation of these wavelengths, too, because information can be obtained that is not present in visible light. From the longest to the shortest wavelength, the electromagnetic wavelengths useful to astronomers are called radio waves, microwaves, infrared radiation, visible light, ultraviolet radiation, X rays, and gamma rays. Some of these forms of radiation penetrate the atmosphere poorly or not at all, and the observing instruments must be launched into space. [Energy]

When an object is first discovered, very little usually is known about it beyond its position in the sky and its brightness. A spectroscope attached to a telescope can be used to break the light (or other radiation) into its component wavelength and analyze it. The resulting information can be used to determine the size of the object, its temperature, chemical composition, pressure, linear and rotational speeds, amount of magnetization, and several other characteristics. When many related objects have been studied, it is often possible to compare their similarities and differences. Such comparisons can reveal how the objects evolve and how they relate to other categories of objects. [Stability, Scale and Structure, Systems and Interactions, Energy]

A-3   How do we learn about the contents and structure of the universe?

Grades Nine Through Twelve

Astronomers are rarely able to manipulate the objects they study, as is possible in other experimental sciences. However, they can sometimes simulate the conditions on those objects in the laboratory, or they can use their observations to make predictions about further observations on the same objects or different ones. The process of planned observation, theory building, prediction on the basis of theory, and further observation characterizes the scientific practice of astronomy. In particular, astronomers draw heavily on the theoretical structures and observations of physics to carry on their work. Astronomers and physicists who carry out this type of work are called astrophysicists. [Systems and Interactions]

Spacecraft can carry instruments designed to make measurements and observations not possible within the atmosphere. Studying a few space missions can teach much about devices and methods, accomplishments and limitations. Some missions on which spacecraft have carried astronomical instrumentation have been Apollo, Viking, Voyager 2, Giotto, Venera, and various space shuttles.

A wide variety of observational data, obtained from many objects at many different times and places, can be used to build theoretical models of the structure of the universe or some part of it. It is possible to infer how the universe (or parts of it) has evolved over time spans that are vastly longer than the time over which human observation has taken place. Computer modeling has made possible much more detailed studies than were previously possible. [Systems and Interactions]

Astronomy is an interdisciplinary field. High-energy particle physics, chemistry, geology, biology,

Capable of predicting solar and lunar eclipses with remarkable accuracy, Mayan astronomers, like many around the globe, attained a high level of astronomical knowledge. They could calculate the average period of Venus's synodic revolution as well as determine the length of the year, the length of seasons, and the length of a lunar month. Remnants of what appears to be a Mayan observatory can still be seen in the stone ruins of Caracol, in Chichen Itza on the Yucatan peninsula.

Maria Mitchell (1818–1889)

This American astronomer distinguished herself internationally by discovering a comet in 1847. Her discovery was officially recognized throughout Europe, and she was awarded a gold medal by the King of Denmark. Following this discovery she was elected the first female member of the American Academy of Arts and Sciences.

After an early teaching career, which began at the age of sixteen, Maria Mitchell accepted a librarianship at the Nantucket Atheneum that allowed her time to carry out mathematical computations on celestial observations made through her father's telescope mounted on a rooftop. Appointed professor of astronomy and director of the observatory at Vassar College in 1865, she became a strong advocate for equal educational opportunities for women and later served as president of the American Association for the Advancement of Women.

electronics, optics, mathematics, computer science, space science, and a wide range of other technical fields are applied to questions that astronomers ask about the composition, structure, and evolution of our universe.

Astronomer is a general term that applies to scientists who focus their efforts on learning about the universe and objects in it. More specific terms that apply to scientists in fields within or related to astronomy include astrophysicists, radio astronomers, cosmologists, planetologists, and exobiologists.

Section B   Geology and Natural Resources

PLATE tectonics is the unifying theory of geology today. But only 40 years ago, this theory had not taken shape. Some elements of it then proposed, such as continental drift, were strongly disputed because no known mechanism could move the continents. Since about 1960, new evidence about tectonics has accumulated that has explained continental drift, as well as the origins of mountain belts, earthquakes, volcanic activity, and deep oceanic trenches.

The earth's early evolution, perhaps even before the crustal plates formed, set the stage for the earth's unique ability to support life. In that formative period, outgassing from the cooling earth released most of the water and gases that became the oceans and the atmosphere; later plate movements and their resulting volcanic activity undoubtedly added more of each. The free oxygen in the atmosphere, upon which much life depends, was produced by photosynthesizing green plants in the early seas.

There are still many questions about how life first evolved, about how mountain belts in continental interiors can be explained by plate tectonics, and why some volcanoes occur well within the crustal plates, to mention just a few.

Two other very important building blocks of a student's geological education are the concept of deep time (the ancient age of the earth) and the principle of uniformitarianism. Small children, of course, cannot grasp the vastness of time, and even older children may feel disoriented by the vast abyss of time through which the earth and its life have passed. But deep time really is the backdrop against which geological and biological evolution have occurred. Uniformitarianism simply means that the laws of nature have always been in operation as they are now. It is a primary working assumption of science as we approach questions of time and the past; it is an affirmation of method and of empirical reality that is necessary in order to draw any scientific conclusions at all.

B-1 How has plate tectonics shaped the evolution of the earth?

B-2 How are rocks and minerals formed, how are they distinguished, and how are they classified?

B-3 What is the history of the earth, and how have geomorphic processes shaped the earth's present features?

B-4 What are the responsibilities of humans toward natural resources?

B-1

How has plate tectonics shaped the evolution of the earth?

Kindergarten Through Grade Three

The earth's surface has not always had its present form; it has changed over time. We can see that moving water, wind, and ice change the features of the earth, while beneath the surface more changes are constantly occurring. Stress in the earth's crust, caused by the movement of the earth, is released through earthquakes and volcanoes. [Energy; Systems and Interactions; Evolution]

B-1   How has plate tectonics shaped the evolution of the earth?

Grades Three Through Six

The earth is broadly differentiated into a crust, mantle, and core. Each is different in its composition, structure, and temperature. One result of these differences is that the crust, which makes up the continents and ocean bottoms, floats on the molten mantle and moves slowly on it. Because we have not yet drilled into the mantle and core, we learn about the interior of the earth by recording and charting energy waves from earthquakes and other evidence.

As the earth moves through space, pressure builds up inside the earth and is released. Earthquakes occur along fault lines, which reflect the patterns of energy released from beneath the earth's surface. Earthquakes often occur along a line that can be drawn on a map; this line helps us to recognize the edges of crustal plates and places where the crust is being stretched.

Both the continents and ocean bottoms are divided into plates. Where different plates lie next to each other, the plates may be slipping past each other in different directions, or one may be moving below or above the other, or the two may be moving apart as new material comes up from beneath the surface. [Energy, Systems and Interactions]

B-1   How has plate tectonics shaped the evolution of the earth?

Grades Six Through Nine

Plate tectonics is a name for crustal processes that are driven by heat within the earth, where forces are continually shifting and releasing energy. Over geologic time, tectonic forces have been responsible for all the major features of the earth's crust, from mountains and valleys to ocean floors and trenches. Tectonic processes such as plate movements and mountain building are the chief source of construction and elevation of geologic features. These processes counter the constant destructive effects of erosion and weathering, which wear down surface features over time. [Energy, Patterns of Change, Evolution]

There are several lines of evidence by which we understand plate tectonics. First, there is structural evidence: physical features that show us that processes took place (e.g., mountain ranges, volcanoes,

faults, uplifted plateaus, and so forth). Second, there is geophysical evidence: measurements and records of stress, strain, and forces that cause movements within the earth (e.g., earthquakes and earthquake waves, records of magnetic reversals in rocks with iron-bearing minerals). Third, there is paleontological evidence that indicates that the floras and faunas of now widely separated, climatically different continents were once identical or nearly so; records of marine fossils from ancient ocean basins now separated by dry land provide us with similar conclusions about plate movements through time (continental drift, openings and closings of ocean basins, and so forth). [Energy, Evolution, Patterns of Change]

B-1   How has plate tectonics shaped the evolution of the earth?

Grades Nine Through Twelve

Plate tectonics is a unifying theory that explains a wealth of evidence for large-scale geological change through time. The principal mechanisms of tectonics

The history of the development of the theory of continental drift is a classic example of how science works. Since the 1500s explorers had noticed the match of the continental edges of South America and Africa and had wondered about whether they had once fit together.

Alfred Wegener, the German meteorologist, is well known for proposing in the early 1900s three lines of evidence that supported drifting continents: (1) the similarity of fossil records; (2) the continuity of mountain ranges; and (3) the identical surface features from ancient glaciations, all on what are now widely separated continents. But although Wegener's ideas were well accepted among scientists on the southern continents, geophysicists rejected the idea because there was no known mechanism to move the continents, plowing solid through solid.

Following World War II, with the wartime development of echo sounding, the sea floor was charted and its topography detailed. In the 1960s magnetic stripes, records of magnetic reversals, were discovered in association with oceanic sea floor ridges. These stripes make symmetrical patterns on either side of the ridges; the stripes away from the ridges were found to be older. It thus became apparent that a new sea floor was being thrust up along the ridges and that the ocean floors were spreading away from these great sutures. This discovery, perhaps more than anything else, was the evidence needed to support the reality of continental drift. With other concurrent discoveries, it led to the development of what we now know as plate tectonic theory.

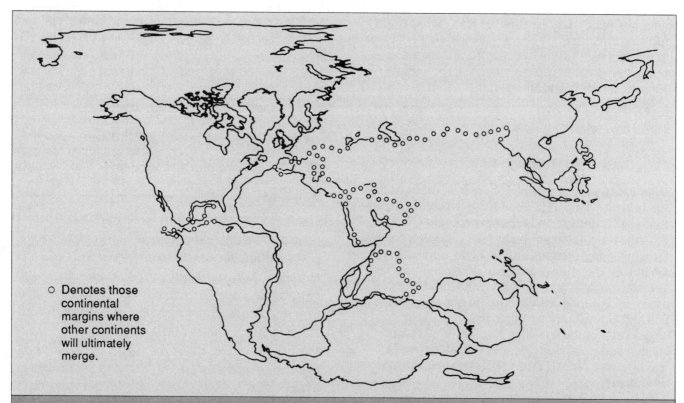

○ Denotes those continental margins where other continents will ultimately merge.

Figure 2. Reconstruction of the relative positions of current continents 200 million years ago at the beginning of the "Age of Dinosaurs" (Triassic-Jurassic boundary).

(thermoconvection) come from within the earth, whose interior is constantly changing and shifting as convection currents within the interior move and heat is transferred from inside the earth to the crust. This builds up and releases energy. Convection motion in the upper mantle of the earth appears to drive the movement of crustal plates on the surface, and together they create mountain belts, earthquake zones, and volcanic belts. As a result, the surface of the earth is in constant change, both from causes that lie within the earth and from the effects of solar energy that drive the wind and ocean-current patterns. The direction that these winds and ocean currents follow is, in turn, governed by Coriolis force. [Energy, Patterns of Change, Systems and Interactions]

Surface features and processes that are manifestations of tectonics include earthquakes, volcanoes, mountain building and plate collision, and seafloor spreading. [Patterns of Change, Evolution]

Continental and oceanic plates are distinguished by their densities (continental material is less dense) and their ages (older rocks are usually confined to continental plates because the older oceanic rocks, which are denser than continental rocks, have all been subducted). For this reason, as far as we know, no oceanic plates are older than about 200 million years (Jurassic period). [Evolution, Patterns of Change]

In addition to spreading centers (divergent plate boundaries; e.g., mid-oceanic ridges) and subduction zones (convergent plate boundaries; e.g., the Peru–Chile trench or the Himalayas), there are other kinds of plate boundaries. Some former plate boundaries are seismically inactive at present, yet at one time were very active. In other boundaries, notably transform boundaries such as the San Andreas Fault, plates slide past each other with no significant loss of land mass from either plate to the lower crust. Sometimes, however, these boundaries are characterized by occasional large earthquakes. [Patterns of Change, Energy]

The past positions of the continents can be reconstructed by analyzing the magnetic orientation of iron-bearing minerals in their rocks. When these rocks were laid down, their iron minerals assumed positions marking the magnetic declination at the time (that is, they pointed toward the magnetic poles of the earth, as fossil compasses). A magnetic needle will point straight down over a magnetic pole and occupy a horizontal position at the magnetic equator;

in between these points it will show varying degrees of inclination. As a result the vertical component of this inclination (magnetic dip) can be used to determine the latitude (but not the longitude) at the time the magnetic minerals were formed or deposited. Such minerals also indicate that the earth's magnetic field has reversed many times through geologic history. (The reasons for this are not entirely clear, but processes within the earth are the most likely causes.) Data from these investigations have been used to reconstruct the ancient positions of the continents. [Evolution, Patterns of Change, Systems and Interactions]

B-2

How are rocks and minerals formed, how are they distinguished, and how are they classified?

Kindergarten Through Grade Three

Rocks are made of minerals. Minerals are made from pure elements in the earth that combine to form a great array of substances. Minerals are identified by key characteristics, including hardness, color, and other features. [Scale and Structure]

Most rocks are combinations of several different minerals, and they are formed in many different environments. Some are formed under heat and pressure inside the earth. Some are laid down in wet and cool environments by water, wind, and ice. Some rocks are melted within the earth and cooled into rock again. [Scale and Structure, Patterns of Change]

B-2   How are rocks and minerals formed, how are they distinguished, and how are they classified?

Grades Three Through Six

Minerals vary in their hardness, crystal form, and color because they have different chemical makeups

Crystals have no power to heal, enhance energy, or reduce your electric bill; neither does water witching have any demonstrable scientific value; nor can animals predict earthquakes, though some are more sensitive to the precursor waves of earthquakes than humans are.

Students should not be taught that there are three kinds of rocks. Instead, they should be taught the processes that explain the origin of rocks and the changes that rocks frequently experience after being laid down. Igneous and sedimentary rocks have different sources and environments of formation, but both of these are subject to metamorphism; metamorphism is a process that results from increased temperature and pressure within the earth.

and because they form under different conditions within the earth. The internal crystal structure of a mineral is unique, even though the shape and color of a mineral can vary, depending on the conditions under which it was formed. [Scale and Structure, Patterns of Change]

Rocks are classified by how they are formed within the rock cycle fluid, which is the cycle of deposition, formation, and erosion of rocks. Rocks that were once fluid within the earth (igneous) can be brought to the surface and cooled (volcanic) or hardened within the earth (plutonic). Rocks that are formed on the earth's surface are laid down by water, wind, and ice into sediments. Both igneous and sedimentary rocks can be buried and affected by high temperatures, pressure, and hot fluids within the earth so that their physical structure and their chemical arrangement are changed (metamorphism). [Scale and Structure, Energy, Patterns of Change]

B-2 How are rocks and minerals formed, how are they distinguished, and how are they classified?

Grades Six Through Nine

Minerals are further classified by criteria of luster, crystal structure, cleavage, and their reaction to certain chemicals. Minerals have many uses, from jewelry to precision instruments, and are the source of all our metals. Rocks are used in paving, building, farming, and other industries. [Scale and Structure]

In addition to being classified by how they were formed, rocks are classified by their mineral contents. Igneous rocks and sedimentary rocks generally have different mineral contents. Igneous rocks are further classified by their cooling histories—whether they cooled within the earth or on its surface, how quickly, and so on. Sedimentary rocks are largely made up of particles of other rocks. They are also composed of organic remains and chemical precipitates. Sedimen-

tary rocks are further classified by these components. [Scale and Structure, Energy]

Sediments become rocks mostly by compression and cementation of their particles. Some rocks, such as mudstones, are more consolidated by pressure than cemented; other rocks, such as sandstones, are cemented. The cement comes mostly from silicates, sulfates, carbonates, or iron oxides that are dissolved in water and fill spaces between the particles of the sediments. Pressure squeezes out most of the water. [Scale and Structure, Patterns of Change]

B-2 How are rocks and minerals formed, how are they distinguished, and how are they classified?

Grades Nine Through Twelve

Because igneous rocks cool and solidify at different rates, they are classified in part according to the conditions under which they were formed. This gives evidence of their sources and of the processes beneath the earth's surface that extrude them. Sedimentary rocks are further classified by the sizes of their particles. When rocks have undergone metamorphism, whether they are igneous or sedimentary in origin, they are studied and classified according to their metamorphic structure, which relates to the conditions and degree of alteration. Thus, important information about metamorphic rocks includes their mineral content and texture. [Energy, Scale and Structure]

The properties that separate different forms of minerals should be taught as manifestations of chemical composition and energy bonds and the conditions under which such minerals were formed in the earth.

Gravity causes all sedimentary rocks to be laid down as nearly horizontal beds (except in structures such as talus slopes), conforming to the surface on which they rest. Through tectonic processes and metamorphism, these layers may become compressed, warped, folded, fractured, or overturned. Their original depositional structures can be obscured because the structure of the rock has been physically and chemically transformed. Erosion may remove some layers completely in some areas. [Energy, Scale and Structure, Patterns of Change]

Almost all fossils are found in sedimentary rocks. Sedimentary rocks also provide evidence of past environments through analysis of their fossil, mineral, and organic content; their depositional structures (such as ripple marks); and their larger features (such as cross-bedding). [Systems and Interactions, Evolution]

Minerals have physical and chemical properties by which they are analyzed and classified. Bonds of chemical energy give mineral crystals their physical structure, which can be altered by the energy of heat and pressure. The chemical and physical structure of each mineral is diagnostic; when these are altered, a different mineral is frequently formed. [Scale and Structure, Energy]

B-3

What is the history of the earth, and how have geomorphic processes shaped the earth's present features?

Kindergarten Through Grade Three

The earth is very old. Through time, many changes have occurred in its features. Mountains have been elevated, worn, and washed away. Rivers have arisen, changed their course, and disappeared. Lakes and ponds and continental arms of the seas have expanded and dried up. The earth's surface is constantly changing. Through time, many different kinds of plants and animals have lived on the face of the earth, and most of these are now extinct. [Evolution, Patterns of Change]

Geologists say, "The present is the key to the past." This means that we can observe the earth and its life today to give us clues about how it was in the past. It does not mean that things have always been as they are today. Many things about the earth and its life

have changed through time. (See Chapter 5, Section B, Cells, Genetics, and Evolution.) [Evolution]

Mountains, valleys, plains, deserts, rivers, lakes, and oceans are all features of the surface of the earth. They are formed by the construction and uplift of land by forces within the earth and by the processes of wind, water, and ice that wear down surface features over time. [Scale and Structure, Patterns of Change, Evolution, Systems and Interactions]

B-3   What is the history of the earth, and how have geomorphic processes shaped the earth's present features?

Grades Three Through Six

In an undisturbed sequence of rock strata, the oldest rocks are on the bottom, and the upper ones are successively younger. Similar rock strata in different areas can be compared and matched to demonstrate that they were laid down at the same time. Both the composition of rocks and their fossils can be used to match strata. [Evolution, Scale and Structure]

Through time many landforms have risen and subsided, as the processes of uplift and erosion have continued to work. Different features of the earth have different ages: the high, craggy Himalayas are younger than the low, rounded Adirondacks; parts of the Pacific Ocean seafloor are older than the Atlantic Ocean seafloor. Many groups of living things have evolved and become extinct. This sequence of change in living things, a result of the process of evolution, can be seen in the fossil record. Because different living things evolved at specific times in the past and then became extinct, the presence of their fossils in rocks can tell us the age in which the rocks were deposited. (See Chapter 5, Section B, Cells, Genetics, and Evolution.) [Evolution, Patterns of Change]

B-3   What is the history of the earth, and how have geomorphic processes shaped the earth's present features?

Grades Six Through Nine

Uniformitarianism is the assumption that the chemical and physical laws of nature as we know them now have always been in operation. Through this assumption scientists are able to study patterns and rates of changes in the earth through geologic time and to see how they have differed. Uniformitarianism does not imply that rates and processes have always been the same as they are today. [Patterns of Change, Stability]

The age of rocks can be measured by absolute means (radioactive decay of isotopes of various elements; each calibration is independent and useful for different ranges of time) and by relative means (comparisons of rock sequences, fossil assemblages, and so on). These methods provide the means to place geologic events in a time sequence called the geologic time scale. [Evolution, Scale and Structure]

The history of the earth is marked by changes in sea level and the uplift and subsidence of landforms, the formation and breakup of continents, and the openings and closings of ocean basins. The principal driving force of these changes is slow convection in the earth's upper mantle. With these changes have come changes in the flora and fauna that reflect different environments in an area over time. [Systems and Interactions, Patterns of Change, Evolution]

Soils are formed from the weathering of rocks and the decomposition of organisms. Soils can be characterized according to their chemical composition and physical structure. Different kinds of soils are peculiar to different areas and owe their compositions to the rocks that are in an area, the climate, and the organisms in the area. The extent to which societies can farm and develop agricultural resources depends on the properties of their local soils. [Scale and Structure, Evolution, Systems and Interactions]

Soils are part of the rock cycle because they are formed from the breakdown of rock (and organic material) and later may become lithified themselves. Soils in a region reflect their local geology and determine in part what kinds of plants can grow in a region. [Patterns of Change]

Geographic features of the earth's surface are manifestations of its geology. The topography of a region; the content and mineral resources of its rocks and soils; its economic resources, transportation routes, water sources, and potential for agriculture, fishing, and support of domesticated animals all ultimately depend on geology. (See *History–Social Science Framework*.) [Scale and Structure, Systems and Interactions]

B-3   What is the history of the earth, and how have geomorphic processes shaped the earth's present features?

Grades Nine Through Twelve

Uniformitarianism is the basic operating principle of historical geology. It affirms that the laws of the universe have always been in operation as they are now, although natural rates and processes (such as erosional rates, which were surely altered by the evolution of land plants) may have differed in the past. [Evolution, Patterns of Change, Stability]

The age of rocks and formations can be compared by relative means (the comparison of rock sequences and fossil assemblages, called stratigraphy) or by absolute means (radioactive decay, which can be calculated independently of the strata in which the elements are found and which depend only on chemistry and physics). Isotopes of different elements are useful for calibrating different ranges of time. Carbon dating is useful only to about 50,000 to 70,000 years in the past, even with enhanced techniques. By contrast, rubidium-strontium dating is useful up to almost 50 billion years in the past, although at a scale so vast that it can be calibrated only to the nearest several billion years. For events in the more recent past, carbon, potassium-argon, or uranium-lead isotopes are more useful. [Scale and Structure, Evolution, Stability]

The ancient environments of the earth can be studied through sedimentologic analysis and through paleoecology. Through time, the movements of plates and changes in the configurations of bodies of water have had tremendous effects on the evolution of life on earth, the geography of plants and animals, and the

Uniformitarianism should not be called "the law of uniformity" or "the law of uniform change."
It implies neither uniformity nor uniform change, and it is not a law but a principle.

The age of the earth and the growth of the geologic time scale are good examples of how scientific understanding evolves and is refined through time. It is instructive to show how Lord Kelvin's original calculations of the maximum possible age of the earth were too low because he assumed that the earth had cooled uniformly from an originally molten state. He did not know that radioactivity inside the earth provided an important source of energy that invalidated his calculations. When nuclear energy was understood, Kelvin's arguments were no longer valid. Isotopic radiometric dating, based on the uniformitarian principles of physics and chemistry, provides a set of independent time scales for the geologic record. This is the source of absolute dates, which are complemented by the relative dates provided by fossils and stratigraphy.

vast changes in climates of marine and continental areas. (See Chapter 5, Section B, Cells, Genetics, and Evolution.) [Evolution, Stability]

All of the biological processes of earth's life depend on the rock cycle, the water cycle, and the nutrient cycle of soils. Together, these cycles determine the character and resources of earth's dynamic environment. [Patterns of Change, Evolution]

B-4

What are the responsibilities of humans toward natural resources?

Kindergarten Through Grade Three

All resources used by humans, including fuels, metals, and building materials, ultimately come from the earth. Many of these resources are not in endless supply. They have taken many thousands and millions of years to develop and accumulate. They must be used with care, conserved, and recycled. [Energy, Systems and Interactions]

B-4   What are the responsibilities of humans toward natural resources?

Grades Three Through Six

Humans use air, fresh water, soil, minerals, fossil fuels, and other sources of energy that come from the earth. Some of these materials are nonrenewable; they cannot be replaced or can be replaced only at such slow rates and under such rare conditions (e.g., fossil fuels) that they are for all practical purposes not

renewable at all. Therefore, their use must be seen as ephemeral, and they must be conserved judiciously. [Energy, Systems and Interactions]

B-4   What are the responsibilities of humans toward natural resources?

Grades Six Through Nine

Energy is often required to convert matter from a less useful into a more useful form for human needs; e.g., ore into metal, seawater into fresh water, and the retrieval and refinement of fossil fuels. (See Chapter 3, Section D, Energy: Sources and Transformations.) Conservation and management of resources are ethical and practical concerns involving public policy and individual responsibility. [Energy, Systems and Interactions]

Geological phenomena such as earthquakes and landslides affect how people must plan their cities and their uses of resources. Buildings, dams, and bridges must be constructed to resist earthquakes and should not be situated on unstable soil or near active fault zones. This is also true for areas subject to landslides. Public landfills must be planned responsibly to allow maximal use of the land once it is reclaimed. Toxic wastes buried in landfills adversely affect the groundwater supply and thus affect public water and public health. Improperly graded and settled landfills are unsuitable for building. Aqueducts that run across fault zones should be designed to accommodate movement because earthquakes may break them and cause great waste of water. [Systems and Interactions, Patterns of Change]

B-4 What are the responsibilities of humans toward natural resources?

Grades Nine Through Twelve

Nonrenewable resources can be conserved through careful use, recycling, and application of energy. If the energy applied in recycling and conserving comes from another nonrenewable source, then the effect is to trade one nonrenewable resource for another. If the energy is taken from a renewable source or inexhaustible for all practical purposes, such as the wind, sun, waterpower, or from nuclear energy, then a net gain in resources is generally made. [Energy, Systems and Interactions]

In addition to the potential dangers of earthquakes and landslides, soil types must be considered when planning houses and other buildings. Sedimentary structures such as talus slopes and the "toes" of hills are not suitable for buildings and should not be removed. The angle of repose of beds is important to consider. [Patterns of Change]

Environmental reclamation involves the need to restore mining sites, clean up oil spills, and dispose of toxic wastes properly. These responsibilities always accompany the exploitation of natural resources. [Energy, Systems and Interactions]

The water cycle provides not only water in the form of precipitation (rain and snow); it is also the source of the earth's groundwater resources. Much of the United States depends on groundwater as its water source for humans and agriculture. There is a finite amount of fresh water on earth, and many groundwater sources are renewed at a slower rate than they are used, because their ultimate source is precipitation. The permeability and porosity of rocks under the surface determines groundwater movement and resources. The composition of these rocks also affects the mineral composition and the quality of the water for human use. [Energy, Systems and Interactions]

Section C   Oceanography

IN the earth sciences, the disciplines of geology, oceanography, and meteorology are interconnected, and one should not be studied in isolation from the others. The water cycle should be taught as a vital part of oceanography, as well as of geology and meteorology. The water cycle integrates the earth, air, and water components of the earth's surface environments. Ocean water evaporates, condenses, and precipitates over land and water. Movement of water through rivers, lakes, and oceans recycles nutrients, nourishes living things, and sculpts the earth's surface features. Water is the single most important determinant of how life persists on earth. We have water on earth because of tectonic processes that released and combined hydrogen and oxygen within the earth to form the original oceans and atmosphere. Gravity holds the atmosphere on earth, which in turn allows the water cycle to occur. This in turn controls the climate and weather on the earth's surface. Therefore, meteorology is best presented as an extension of oceanography and geology.

It is important for students to understand that solar energy and forces within the earth and the earth's rotation are the basis for the circulation of ocean waters and the water cycle. Much of earth's secondary atmosphere has come from outgassing, released by tectonic processes. Astronomers are interested in other planets that show signs of tectonic processes. The planets may have once had molten interiors and thus could have held atmospheres and oceans capable of supporting life.

Other vital areas in oceanography are the structures and environments of the ocean bottoms and their histories through time, the habitats and life that the oceans have sustained through time, and the composition of the oceans' waters. There are many divisions of oceanography, including biological, chemical, and physical, but the study of oceans is interwoven with the theory of tectonics and its ramifications for the structure and evolution of the oceans.

C-1 What is the water cycle? How does the water cycle affect the climate, weather, and life of the earth? How does water affect surface features of the land and the ocean floor?

C-2 What are the oceans? What are the environments and topography of the ocean bottoms? How do the oceans support life, and how have the oceans and their marine life changed through time?

C-3 How do waters circulate in the ocean, and how does this circulation affect weather and climate?

C-4 How do humans interact with the oceans? What may be some long-term effects of human interactions with the oceanic environments?

C-1

What is the water cycle? How does the water cycle affect the climate, weather, and life of the earth? How does water affect surface features of the land and the ocean floor?

Kindergarten Through Grade Three

Rain, snow, hail, and sleet all come from clouds, which are made of water. This water comes mainly from the oceans and rises into the air as water vapor when the sun evaporates water on the ocean's surface. (Often, water can evaporate from the surface simply when the air is cooler or warmer than the water, as when fog rises from a river, or when warm and cold air masses meet.) Most rain falls directly back into the ocean. Much of the water that falls to the earth's surface runs into rivers and streams that return it to the oceans, where the cycle starts again. The fresh water provided by the water cycle is necessary to all terrestrial life on earth. [Systems and Interactions, Patterns of Change]

C-1   What is the water cycle? How does the water cycle affect the climate, weather, and life of the earth? How does water affect surface features of the land and the ocean floor?

Grades Three Through Six

Precipitation comes from water vapor that condenses in clouds when weather conditions are appropriate. It provides the continental land areas with their source of fresh water, which plants and animals need to live. Water may be collected in natural waterways and reservoirs or tapped by wells from below ground surface; but it all comes from precipitation. This water may sink below ground, and it may also drain into streams and rivers that carry it to the sea. [Systems and Interactions, Patterns of Change]

C-1   What is the water cycle? How does the water cycle affect the climate, weather, and life of the earth? How does water affect surface features of the land and the ocean floor?

Grades Six Through Nine

Evaporation of water from the surfaces of the oceans is the principal source of the clouds that form precipitation. Because the earth constantly rotates, these clouds circulate over the land surfaces in patterns that are affected by the topography of local regions. The oceans also affect climate because they retain heat energy better than the air or the land surfaces do. Differences in the water, air, and land temperatures cause the condensation of water vapor that creates precipitation for the water cycle. Precipitation gradually erodes rocky surface features of the land, washes away soil, and redistributes it in rivers, lakes, and oceans, thereby creating new geological features by erosion and deposition. (See Section B, Geology and Natural Resources.) [Systems and Interactions, Patterns of Change]

Water evaporating from the oceans leaves most salts and particulate matter behind, and the evaporated water condenses into clouds. Precipitation from these clouds falls over land and water surfaces. Much of the rain and snow that falls on continental surfaces collects in rivers and is returned to the oceans enriched with nutrients. [Systems and Interactions]

C-1   What is the water cycle? How does the water cycle affect the climate, weather, and life of the earth? How does water affect surface features of the land and the ocean floor?

Grades Nine Through Twelve

The water cycle sustains the earth's land life, which is in constant need of new supplies of fresh water. This cycle can continue because the earth's gravitational field holds the atmosphere on the planet. As the earth constantly rotates and the sun warms a portion of the earth's surface, differential conditions of temperature and moisture are created and changed in the atmosphere, causing ocean currents, winds, and evaporation, condensation, and precipitation of water.

Water vapor reacts chemically with gases and particles dissolved in the atmosphere, and these are precipitated along with water. (Acid rain is a harmful by-product of such chemical reactions.) As precipitation falls, its physical and chemical action on the earth's surface features causes rock to erode and dissolve and soil to wash away. These effects are usually gradual, but catastrophic rates and events can also occur during episodes of especially high precipitation. (See Section B, Geology and Natural Resources.) Eroded material is transported to other land and water surfaces, and also to the oceans, where it enriches the mineral and nutrient content of nearshore waters. It can also form deltas, undersea fans, and other submarine geomorphic features.

The water cycle describes the flow of water through evaporation, condensation into clouds, and precipitation over water and land, returning most water to the oceans. Additional water comes from melting of polar ice caps. Enough water is stored in the ice caps to produce large variations in ocean volume and sea level through time; this has happened repeatedly in the past. [Patterns of Change]

C-2

What are the oceans? What are the environments and topography of the ocean bottoms? How do the oceans support life, and how have the oceans and their marine life changed through time?

Kindergarten Through Grade Three

The oceans are vast bodies of salt water that cover almost three-fourths of the earth's surface. Their

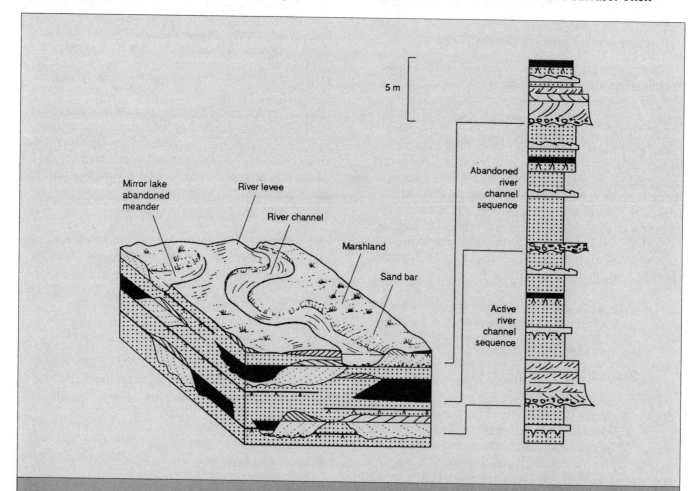

Figure 3. Geologists use rock strata to reconstruct ancient environments, observing how different kinds of beds were laid down, composed, and affected by wind and water.

deepest parts are deeper than the highest mountains. [Scale and Structure]

The oceans are salty, unlike freshwater lakes and streams. Many forms of life live in the oceans, mostly near the shores. (See Chapter 5, Section A, Living Things, and Section C, Ecosystems.) [Scale and Structure, Systems and Interactions]

Through time, many different kinds of life have lived in the oceans. Most of these forms are now extinct. [Evolution]

C-2 What are the oceans? What are the environments and topography of the ocean bottoms? How do the oceans support life, and how have the oceans and their marine life changed through time?

Grades Three Through Six

Oceans cover three-fourths of the earth's surface, but compared with the mass and volume of the whole earth, they are really only thin films on parts of the outer surface. The four largest oceans (Atlantic, Pacific, Indian, and Arctic) are connected, though each has its own features of water circulation, climate, and marine life. The ocean bottoms are punctuated by mountain ranges, active and extinct volcanoes, and deep trenches. [Scale and Structure]

The oceans are salty because of the salts that are dissolved in ocean waters. Some dissolved components (such as nitrogen, silicon, calcium, and phosphorus) and other minerals are used by marine life as nutrients and to build their skeletons. Marine organisms take in oxygen and carbon dioxide that are dissolved in sea water. (See Chapter 5, Section A, Living Things, and Section C, Ecosystems.) Water is cycled through the earth's environments. Because the oceans contain most of the water on earth, there are many forms of life that depend on the oceans. The oceans have a profound effect on local weather patterns and general climatic conditions. (See Section D, Meteorology.) [Systems and Interactions]

The oceans provide many different habitats for marine life, ranging from shallow shores and tide pools to abyssal depths. Characteristics of these physical environments, such as light, temperature, and proximity to upwelling areas, are primary determinants of the living communities that they support. (See Chapter 5, Section C, Ecosystems.) [Scale and Structure]

Over geologic time, the continents have moved with respect to each other and to the poles. (See

Section B, Geology and Natural Resources.) For some time until about 200 million years ago, a giant supercontinent (Pangea) was composed of nearly all of the present continents and was surrounded by one world ocean. Today, the world oceans are connected, but continental drift has separated the supercontinent Pangea into several continents. As the continents have drifted, new oceans have formed, and new species of marine life have evolved and filled them. Marine life has evolved through time as the oceans have changed. (See Section B, Geology and Natural Resources, and Chapter 5, Section B, Cells, Genetics, and Evolution.) [Evolution]

C-2 What are the oceans? What are the environments and topography of the ocean bottoms? How do the oceans support life, and how have the oceans and their marine life changed through time?

Grades Six Through Nine

The surfaces of continents and the bottoms of oceans compose great pieces of the earth's outer crust called plates. Ocean waters cover the oceanic crust and parts of the continental margins. Along the continental margins are shallow waters rich with nutrients. Where ocean plates meet continental plates, trenches form on active margins where subduction is occurring. Mountain ranges (e.g., the Andes) can arise from this interaction. The ocean bottoms are streaked by mountain ranges, trenches, and fault zones where plates meet. Like continents, the oceanic plates have been continually moving through time. Active and extinct volcanoes mark undersea "hot spots" where molten material from the earth's interior escapes to the surface. (See Section B, Geology and Natural Resources.) [Scale and Structure, Systems and Interactions]

Oceans are large masses of salt water that retain heat much longer than air or smaller bodies of fresh water do. They tend to moisten air that passes over them and moderate the air temperature. This air in turn moderates the temperature of continental margins. (See Chapter 3, Section A, Matter.) [Scale and Structure, Systems and Interactions]

Chemical components in the oceans have come largely from the earth's crust and upper mantle, mainly by volcanic activity. Some of these components (containing mainly chlorine, sodium, magnesium, sulfur, calcium, and potassium) contribute to the shells of marine organisms and are recycled into

The oceans have always been salty, because salts and other minerals and compounds were part of the crust of the earth when the primordial ocean was formed. As water goes through the water cycle, these compounds are left in the sea and not carried in the evaporation of ocean water. Therefore, the question is not "Why are the oceans salty?" but rather "Why aren't snow, rain, rivers, and streams salty?" The answer is that evaporation leaves the salts behind.

the waters and ocean sediments when these organisms die. [Scale and Structure, Patterns of Change]

Within the oceans are many kinds of environments that support ecosystems of marine organisms. These ecosystems can be classified according to the depth of the environment (tidal, subtidal, abyssal, and so forth). Like terrestrial ecosystems, they have their own food chains and webs. The primary producers of the ocean are microscopic plants in the plankton; these form the base of food chains of planktonic herbivores and carnivores, as well as larger invertebrates and vertebrates. The flow of nutrients and energy in the ocean is concentrated around continental margins and near the surface of the ocean. Some organisms also live at the deep ocean bottom, where most of them gain energy from the constant rain of fecal matter and decaying plankton from the surface. Much of the ocean is nutrient poor and sparse of life. (See Chapter 5, Section A, Living Things, and Section C, Ecosystems.) [Scale and Structure, Systems and Interactions, Energy, Patterns of Change]

The ocean floor, like the continents, is made up of crustal plates, but the oceanic crust is slightly denser than continental crust. Through time, these plates have been moved as new material has been pushed up from the upper mantle. As the surface plates have moved, some ocean basins (e.g., the Atlantic) have been opened. The shapes and positions of the continents and oceans have changed remarkably through time. (See Section B, Geology and Natural Resources.) [Evolution, Patterns of Change]

The sea level and the volume of ocean water have risen and fallen frequently through geologic time, and tectonic processes and glaciations have controlled these patterns. These changes have had great effects on marine life and on land climates. Many different kinds of marine animals that used to be very numerous and diverse, such as the ammonites and trilobites, are now extinct. Their ecological roles have been

taken up by other kinds of animals. [Evolution, Systems and Interactions]

C-2   What are the oceans? What are the environments and topography of the ocean bottoms? How do the oceans support life, and how have the oceans and their marine life changed through time?

Grades Nine Through Twelve

Sea levels have fluctuated through time. (See Section B, Geology and Natural Resources.) Because current sea levels are relatively high, the continental margins are covered with ocean water. Beneath the waters are various kinds of geomorphic features. Where rivers empty into oceans and seas, submarine fans may form that are similar to or extensions of deltaic fans. These environments are generally rich with nutrients. In the deep sea, submarine canyons, abyssal plains, and oceanic islands are among the features composing the topography of the ocean floor. [Scale and Structure]

Ocean waters are rich in minerals and salts. These substances have always been present in the oceans, and new material is constantly but slowly added by extrusion of additional material from the earth's interior at rifting zones and from runoff of material from the earth's land surfaces. [Systems and Interactions, Patterns of Change]

Various chemical elements are cycled through the skeletons of marine animals and plants, and these in turn produce biological nutrients that are cycled through marine ecosystems. Additional minerals and nutrients reach the oceans through runoff from land as water returns to the oceans through rivers. [Scale and Structure, Systems and Interactions, Energy, Patterns of Change]

Ocean environments are of two general types: coastal and open water. Environments in coastal waters are generally characterized by their depth and distance from the shore (tidal, subtidal, littoral, and so forth). Depending on local topography, wave energy, and nutrient richness, ecosystems may host reef communities, burrowing communities, and a variety of epifaunal invertebrates. Open-water ecosystems are generally limited by their organisms' need for light: phytoplankton need light to manufacture energy, and other organisms feed on them and continue the food chains and webs of the open ocean. Below about 200 meters, productivity declines considerably. The ocean floor supports communities that are fueled by the detritus that rains constantly from above. Other abyssal communities live near deep-sea vents and are supported by geothermal rather than solar energy. [Systems and Interactions, Energy]

At the end of the Paleozoic era, all the continents were merged into the supercontinent Pangaea. Near the end of the Triassic period, about 200 million years ago, the Atlantic Ocean began to form by the rifting of continental plates; this rifting is still occurring, and the Mid-Atlantic ridge remains an active source of seafloor extension. The Tethys Sea, separating the northern and southern continents, began to develop shortly thereafter. The Red Sea is an example of a young ocean in an early stage of extension. The Pacific, Indian, and Arctic oceans are similarly scored with the records of ancient movements and faults. It is difficult to reconstruct the histories of the oceans before 200 million years ago because the ocean bottom from earlier times has been subducted. (See Section B, Geology and Natural Resources.) [Evolution]

Marine communities, like their individual organisms, have evolved through time. (For example, clams have replaced brachiopods as the main epifau-

nal filter feeders; corals have replaced sponges and rudistid clams as the principal reef builders.) Vertebrates evolved in the oceans, probably in the Cambrian period; in the Devonian period, they first invaded the land. Some fishes, such as sharks, have changed little since the Paleozoic era. Others, like the ray-finned fishes, have diversified remarkably. Many invertebrate groups, including clams, snails, corals, and arthropods, have also diversified in many ways. The invertebrate marine life of the past is the best represented sector of the fossil record. (See Chapter 5, Section B, Cells, Genetics, and Evolution.) [Evolution]

C-3

How do waters circulate in the ocean, and how does this circulation affect weather and climate?

Kindergarten Through Grade Three

Water in the oceans moves because the motion is powered by the sun's energy; the earth rotates and receives solar energy that drives the winds. Waves are one kind of movement we can see in the oceans. Water in the oceans is always moving; and as its cold and warm layers move, their temperatures affect the temperature and moisture of the air that passes over the oceans and onto the land. As the atmosphere moves, different air masses collide or mix. This in turn causes patterns of climate and weather on land. The temperature difference also causes wind. (See Section D, Meteorology.) [Systems and Interactions, Patterns of Change]

C-3 How do waters circulate in the ocean, and how does this circulation affect weather and climate?

Grades Three Through Six

Cold water, like cold air, sinks because it is denser than when it is warm. As it sinks, warmer water rises to the surface. Water also circulates because the earth rotates, and the force of this rotation causes movement of surface waters. The earth receives more solar energy in tropical areas and less at the poles; this warming differential causes ocean water circulation. Tides are caused by the gravitational pull of the moon and sun on the earth.

During the Mesozoic era, shallow seas covered much of Europe and North America. Ichthyosaurs, plesiosaurs, and mosasaurs were among the top predators, but these now-extinct forms have been replaced in their ecological adaptive zones by large fishes, porpoises and dolphins, sharks, and whales. Many such examples illuminate the history of marine life.

The oxygen isotope ratio in marine shells can be used to construct a record of the variation of oceanic temperatures through time.

As ocean water circulates, its temperature affects the temperature of the air above it. This creates patterns of climate and weather when this air moves over land. Movement of the atmosphere causes different air masses to collide or mix. This, in turn, causes weather on land. Places near the ocean often have more moderate climates than places slightly inland. But such areas are often prone to hurricanes and other oceanic storms. (See Section D, Meteorology.) [Systems and Interactions, Patterns of Change]

C-3   How do waters circulate in the ocean, and how does this circulation affect weather and climate?

Grades Six Through Nine

Waters circulate primarily because of winds and solar heating. The direction that these currents follow is caused by the earth's rotation. Solar heat also causes cycles of water convection. As the earth rotates, its ocean waters circulate past the continents in patterns that determine global climatic conditions because air that passes over oceans often is warmer or cooler than air that passes over continental surfaces. (For example, the Atlantic Gulf Stream gives London a milder climate than Buffalo, New York, even though London is farther north. In the same way, San Francisco's waters are usually colder than those outside New York City because the California current moves from north to south, whereas the eastern Gulf Stream runs from south to north.) (See Section D, Meteorology.)

Ocean tides are caused mainly by the gravitational pull of the moon on the earth. The gravitational attraction of the sun also affects tides; this varies with gravitational attraction over the span of a year and is especially strong when the sun, moon, and earth are aligned in one plane. The sun-earth and earth-moon revolutions are not synchronized, but each is regular in its timing; consequently, especially high and low tides can be predicted by calculating the times at which the sun and moon together will exert the strongest and weakest effects on the earth. [Systems and Interactions, Patterns of Change]

C-3   How do waters circulate in the ocean, and how does this circulation affect weather and climate?

Grades Nine Through Twelve

Waves are phenomena of water movement generally caused by wind; they may also be produced by earthquakes, undersea landslides, volcanoes, or other geological activity. Tides are predictable, periodic fluctuations of ocean waters caused by the gravitational attraction of the sun and the moon on the earth. The surface circulation of the oceans is primarily caused by Coriolis processes, whereas deep ocean circulation is caused mainly by the difference in density between warmer and colder waters. Because the earth rotates, surface currents flow in closed loops (gyres) that move clockwise in the Northern Hemisphere and counterclockwise in the Southern Hemisphere. [Systems and Interactions, Energy, Patterns of Change]

The oceans moderate climates on land. The reasons for this effect include (1) the high heat capacity of water, which can warm or cool air that then passes over land; (2) the mixing of surface waters by waves and currents; and (3) the evaporation of water from the ocean's surface. Long-term weather patterns can be caused by oceanic disturbances, such as the Pacific oscillation and the associated El Niño phenomena. [Systems and Interactions, Energy, Patterns of Change]

C-4

How do humans interact with the oceans? What may be some long-term effects of human interaction with the oceanic environment?

Kindergarten Through Grade Three

People use the oceans for fishing and collecting food, swimming and boating, transporting people and products, drilling for petroleum, and collecting minerals. They also dump waste materials into the oceans.

C-4   How do humans interact with the oceans? What
       may be some long-term effects of human
       interaction with the oceanic environment?

Grades Three Through Six

Water is essential to all forms of life. Humans use
the oceans for food, energy, minerals, and medicine,
and disposal of waste.

C-4   How do humans interact with the oceans? What
       may be some long-term effects of human
       interaction with the oceanic environment?

Grades Six Through Nine

The oceans are frequently used as a dumping
ground for waste materials. Disposal of toxic wastes
have caused environmental problems and, unless
carefully regulated, can threaten the future of much
marine life. Pollutants carried into oceans and lakes
affect living things and need to be controlled by
individual behavior and public policy.

The ocean basins are also a source of fossil fuels
(petroleum), which can be retrieved from deposits
beneath the continental shelves. The benefits of these
fuels may be offset by the cost of retrieving them and
by the hazards to coastlines, shipping, and marine life
posed by oil spills and other accidents. Like other
fossil fuels, submarine resources are nonrenewable.

C-4   How do humans interact with the oceans? What
       may be some long-term effects of human
       interaction with the oceanic environment?

Grades Nine Through Twelve

If humans are to continue using the oceans as
repositories of waste material, they must have a
thorough understanding of ocean currents, conditions,
marine ecology, and marine geology. Marine resource
management includes an understanding not only of
science but also of sociology, economics, ethics, and
government.

As in freshwater ecosystems, marine eutrophication
occurs when the natural nutrients that contain nitrates
and phosphates become concentrated, encouraging
algal blooms. (In current usage, eutrophication refers
to the inadvertent nourishing of algae in lakes to the
detriment of other living things.) Some algal blooms
are toxic to marine animals. Eutrophication is often

*Energy consumption in America is on the rise,
according to the U. S. Department of Energy
(DOE). In order to keep domestic petroleum
production at its current levels, we will need 32
billion barrels of new oil reserves by 1995.
Throughout the 1980s, California legislators
fought off numerous attempts to open offshore
leases for oil exploration along environmentally
sensitive areas. The DOE estimates that as much
as 60 percent of the crude oil still to be discovered in America will come from public lands, and
56 percent of that amount is likely to be from
offshore drilling. Because oil reserves have both
domestic and strategic value, future voters will be
faced with the important task of weighing the environmental consequences of their energy decisions. These informed decisions will require
voters to have a deep knowledge of all forms of
energy supplies and to examine thoroughly the
environmental impacts associated with the
development and use of each energy source.*

caused by sewage outfalls and runoff from fertilized
lawns and fields that deposit high concentrations of
nutrients into waterways.

Occasionally, heavy metals (e.g., mercury) accumulate to abnormally high levels in the tissues of shellfish living in coastal waters polluted by industrial
waste. These minerals become concentrated in the
higher levels of food chains and have at times poi-
soned humans who have consumed contaminated fish
and shellfish.

Fishing for marine invertebrates, fishes, and
mammals in international waters requires international cooperation and agreement. Cultural differences in the use and harvesting of these resources has
been a frequent source of misunderstanding and
dispute. International agreements should be guided by
a thorough understanding of marine ecology and
ecosystems and by realistic biological predictions of
how such populations should be managed, used, and

prevented from becoming extinct. (See the Department's *History–Social Science Framework.*) [Systems and Interactions, Patterns of Change]

METEOROLOGY is the study of our atmosphere and weather. Although meteorologists have long collected data on the earth's surface to predict weather patterns, the advent of weather satellites vastly increased their ability to monitor the earth's atmosphere and alert the public not only of impending dangers (e.g., hurricanes) but also of long-term atmospheric perturbations such as ozone depletions and increases in carbon dioxide. Further systems analysis of the complex interactions between earth's masses of air, water, and land may yield insight into the kinds of efforts that must be undertaken to mitigate disturbing global trends (e.g., atmospheric warming and pollution).

D-1 **What are the physical bases of the earth's climate and weather?**

D-2 **What are the major phenomena of climate and weather? What are the large- and small-scale causes of climate and weather?**

D-3 **How are we affected by weather? How do we predict it? How can we alter it?**

D-1

What are the physical bases of the earth's climate and weather?

Kindergarten Through Grade Three

We live on the surface of the earth, surrounded by a blanket of air called the atmosphere, which we need to live. We breathe the air of the atmosphere; we depend on the atmosphere for rain. Rain falls from clouds, which consist of tiny particles of water or ice. Clouds are made to move by the wind. Sometimes we can see a cloud grow bigger or smaller. [Patterns of Change]

The earth is warmed by heat from the sun. It is usually warmer in the daytime than at night. It is usually warmer in summer than in winter. The earth is not so close to the sun that we boil, nor so far from the sun that we freeze. [Patterns of Change]

Most of the earth is covered by the water of the oceans. The sun heats the water, which is continuously evaporated into the atmosphere to form clouds. Clouds may move a long distance before producing precipitation. Water falling on the ground may soak into the ground or flow immediately into streams and rivers. Eventually, the water finds its way back to the ocean. [Systems and Interactions]

D-1 What are the physical bases of the earth's climate and weather?

Grades Three Through Six

The sun heats the water near the surface of the oceans. The water holds the heat a long time, releasing it very slowly. Colder air moving over the water is warmed by the water. Warm air is less dense than cold air and cold air moves in, pushing the warm air upward. As the air rises, it cools and descends again. This cycle is the "engine" that drives the winds. Warm winds passing over cold regions tend to warm them. In many places, the wind blows from the same direction much of the time (prevailing winds). [Patterns of Change, Systems and Interactions]

Warming of the atmosphere results, among other things, in formation of regions of nonhomogeneous pressure. The variation of atmospheric pressure can be measured with a barometer. Meteorologists depend on a network of thousands of stations at which the the atmospheric pressure is measured at regular intervals. The results are displayed on weather

The discovery and careful charting of jet stream winds is an achievement of the past half century. Airplanes make much use of jet stream winds, riding them downstream and avoiding them upstream. Taking advantage of jet stream winds can be worth a considerable detour.

maps. Air tends to move from high- to low-pressure regions. [Systems and Interactions]

Because the earth is round, sunlight falls on parts of it near the equator more intensely than on parts near the poles. Generally speaking, the equatorial regions are warmer than the polar regions. [Stability]

The earth's axis is inclined with respect to the plane of its orbit. As a result, the region of most intense sunlight moves northward and southward over the year. At the same time, the length of the day varies. Taken together, these effects determine the seasons. When it is summer in the Northern Hemisphere, it is winter in the Southern Hemisphere. (See Section A, Astronomy) [Patterns of Change]

Climate is the daily and seasonal weather that a particular region experiences over a period of time. Climate is described as the average conditions and the extremes that have been experienced by the region. [Scale and Structure]

The earth's atmosphere consists of a mixture of gases. About four-fifths is nitrogen, and most of the rest is oxygen, which has an essential role in life processes. The atmosphere also contains small but significant amounts of other gases. Carbon dioxide and water vapor are the most important, both for climate and for life. Nearly all of the atmosphere lies within about 50 kilometers of the earth's surface. [Scale and Structure, Stability]

Water constantly evaporates from the earth's surface, the bulk of it from the oceans. The water is transported as vapor by the winds, often over long distances. The vapor forms clouds that release precipitation as rain, snow, and other forms. Most of the precipitation falls back into the ocean, but some falls on land. Some of the water falling on land soaks in to form groundwater. Depending on geological formations, groundwater may stay where it is for long periods, or it may percolate quickly over considerable distances, or it may reappear at lower points on the surface as springs that feed streams and lakes. Much groundwater is returned to the atmosphere as vapor through the process of transpiration in plants. This process is especially important in rain forests and affects weather and climate. Runoff water goes directly to streams, which coalesce into larger streams and rivers. Most rivers flow into the oceans; some flow into deserts and are completely evaporated. [Patterns of Change]

When water evaporates, it changes from the liquid to the gaseous state, and we cannot see it. When air

Change in temperature is both an important weather effect and an important cause of weather changes. Systematic temperature measurement is vital to understanding weather. Galileo was the first person to measure temperature quantitatively, about 1592, but the first reliable thermometers were made early in the eighteenth century by Gabriel Daniel Fahrenheit. He took 0° to be the lowest temperature he could achieve with an ice-salt mixture and 100° to be his wife's body temperature. Because there are 100 degrees between these two fixed points, Fahrenheit's scale is a centigrade (100-degree) scale. Fahrenheit soon found that his fixed points were not readily reproducible and shifted to the freezing and boiling points of water. In order to keep the new scale compatible with his old one, he assigned the value 32° to the freezing point and 212° to the boiling point. The modern Celsius scale is also a centigrade scale, but the chosen fixed points are more reproducible.

containing water vapor cools, the vapor condenses back into the liquid state. (See Chapter 3, Section A, Matter.) This liquid water forms tiny droplets or ice crystals that make the air opaque. When this occurs on the ground, we call the effect fog. When it occurs above us in the air, we see the result as clouds. [Patterns of Change, Systems and Interactions]

D-1   What are the physical bases of the earth's climate and weather?

Grades Six Through Nine

The overall temperature of the earth is determined largely by two factors: its distance from the sun and the properties of the atmosphere. If it were too close to or too far from the sun, the earth would be too hot or too cold to support life, regardless of other conditions. But within these broad limits, the properties of the atmosphere are very important in determining how much of the heat of the sun is retained by the earth and how much is reflected. [Stability]

Success in agriculture depends heavily on close understanding and exploitation of microclimates. Farmers have known for millenia, for example, that frost will damage crops in a hollow when crops grown on the hillside above escape frost, or that fruit will mature on trees on hills facing south while it does not ripen on neighboring, northward-facing hillsides. The California grape-growing industry has benefited greatly from new and more detailed understanding of microclimates all over the state.

Most students are aware of the dramatic climatic differences between the California coast, the Central Valley, the mountains, and the high and low deserts. California students may not be aware that these wide variations over relatively small distances are atypical and result largely from the prevailing westerlies blowing from the ocean over a series of mountain barriers. Study of weather maps will reveal that Midwestern climate, for example, varies significantly only over much larger distances.

The hottest part of the summer usually comes after the day when the sunlight is most intense and the day is longest. This is because it takes time to warm the earth and the sea. Similarly, the coldest part of the winter usually comes after the day when the sunlight is least intense and the day is shortest. Because water is heated so slowly, the delay is longest on parts of the land near the ocean; these parts have a coastal climate. In the middle of the continents, far from the ocean, the delay is shorter, and the extremes of temperature are greater; these parts have a continental climate. The range of coastal climates depends very much on the direction of the prevailing winds and the presence of mountains. [Scale and Structure]

The atmosphere is divided roughly into several layers. The lowest layer, the troposphere, is the region where most weather phenomena take place. The stratosphere (above the troposphere) is less turbulent but has some effect on weather. [Scale and Structure]

Most clouds form in the troposphere. Clouds consist of tiny water droplets, or ice crystals, or a combination of both. Water vapor condenses around tiny particles in the air into these forms. Such particles can be made of dust, or sea salt, or other substances. [Patterns of Change, Scale and Structure]

Differences in temperature between regions lead to differences in barometric pressure. These pressure differences cause air to flow from high- to low-pressure areas. We call this flow wind. The greater the pressure difference, the stronger the wind. However, air masses do not flow in straight lines from high to low pressure. Because the earth rotates, force is exerted on the moving air in a direction perpendicular to its motion (Coriolis force). As a result, moving air masses follow a curved path. In the Northern Hemisphere, air masses circulate clockwise around high-pressure areas and counterclockwise around low-pressure areas. The opposite is the case in the Southern Hemisphere. These circulating air masses interact with one another in a complicated way that can be seen on a weather map. Weather—the short-term variation of temperature, humidity, winds, and barometric pressure, among other things, in any given place—is a result of the details of these interactions. [Systems and Interactions]

Winds can be influenced by many things. Near the surface, trees and buildings cause winds to break up into a complex of irregular, twisting eddies. These eddies can cause the wind speed and direction to fluctuate rapidly. [Patterns of Change, Systems and Interactions]

Land breezes and sea breezes occur because the land warms up faster than the sea in the daytime and cools faster at night. In the daytime, for example, air rises over the warmer land, and cooler air rushes in from the sea. Valley winds and mountain winds are caused by a similar temperature difference. Down-slope winds flow down mountains, warming due to compression as they sink. [Energy, Systems and Interactions]

On a larger scale, winds constitute the general circulation of the atmosphere. Prevailing winds are the westerlies of the temperate zones, the trade winds of the tropics, and the polar easterlies. Between the westerlies and the adjacent trade winds lies a region of variable and frequently weak winds called the horse latitudes. Between the Northern and Southern hemisphere trade winds are the doldrums, where sailing ships have often spent weeks in stifling heat waiting for wind. Prevailing winds arise from the large-scale warming of air near the equator and cooling near the poles. [Scale and Structure, Systems and Interactions]

Cold air is generally associated with high pressure; and warm air, with low pressure. The equatorial "low" and the polar "high" are fairly stable and do not move much; they influence the earth's weather in a fairly predictable way. The same is true of other important highs and lows. [Stability, Systems and Interactions]

When large air masses migrate, the leading edges can produce very strong winds. At an altitude of about 9 km, jet streams can form, and jet stream winds can travel over 100 knots and occasionally over 250 knots. [Patterns of Change]

Description of climate depends on the size of the area whose climate is to be described (global climate, mesoclimate, microclimate). [Scale and Structure]

Global climate is governed by the intensity and variation of sunshine with latitude, by the distribution of land and water, by ocean currents, by prevailing winds, by areas of high and low atmospheric pressure, by mountain barriers, and by altitude. [Stability, Energy, Systems and Interactions]

The earth's atmosphere has not always been the same as it is today. The earth was formed more than four billion years ago from interstellar matter consisting largely of hydrogen and helium. During the formation of the earth, most of these light gases escaped, leaving the earth with little atmosphere. Gases trapped in the interior at the earth's formation or produced by chemical reactions within the earth were probably expelled at the surface. This process, called outgassing, resulted in a second atmosphere from which today's atmosphere evolved. It is probable that the composition of these gases was similar to that emerging from volcanoes today: water vapor, 85 percent; carbon dioxide, 10 percent; the rest, mostly nitrogen with a variety of other more complex gases such as ammonia and methane.

Much of the carbon dioxide in the second atmosphere dissolved in rainwater and was transported to the oceans. Through various chemical (and later biological) processes, this carbon was locked up in sedimentary rocks such as limestone, which is a form

of calcium carbonate. With much of the original water and carbon dioxide removed, nitrogen became the main constituent of the atmosphere.

Ultraviolet light from the sun, acting on water vapor, produced oxygen and hydrogen by a process called photodissociation. Most of the hydrogen escaped to space, leaving the oxygen behind. However, the preponderance of the evidence indicates that the bulk of the oxygen in the modern atmosphere arose from photosynthesis by primitive green algae and similar photosynthesizing organisms. Photosynthesis consumes carbon dioxide and releases oxygen; the presence of photosynthesizing plants thus changed the composition of the atmosphere in a dramatic way. The present-day atmosphere consists of about 78 percent nitrogen, 21 percent oxygen, and about 1 percent of argon, carbon dioxide, other trace gases, and water vapor. [Evolution, Systems and Interactions, Patterns of Change]

D-1   What are the physical bases of the earth's climate and weather?

Grades Nine Through Twelve

Most of the light energy from the sun arrives at the earth in a range of wavelengths to which the clear atmosphere is fairly transparent. However, clouds are effective in reflecting a large amount of energy back into space. The overall temperature of the earth is influenced greatly by this proportion. Snow can reflect as much as 95 percent of the solar radiation that strikes it; clouds, on the average, about 65 per-

Analysis of global warming trends is extremely important, but it may be necessary to take significant action before the final results of scientific study are in. The risk lies in the possibility that it may be too late to avoid serious consequences if action is delayed and it turns out that the current projections are confirmed. This is an excellent example of a problem having scientific content that must be decided on the basis of a variety of social, economic, and political as well as scientific considerations.

cent; forests, from 3 percent to 10 percent. The overall average for the earth is about 30 percent. The earth's heat balance is crucial; because the amount of radiation from the sun is closely constant, any reduction in energy radiated back to space increases the average temperature of the earth. Over a year the average temperature varies by only about $0.1°C$. Any effect that substantially exceeds this variation can result in major climatic changes over the earth. [Energy, Systems and Interactions]

Sunlight that reaches the surface is absorbed by the land and the water. When the land and water are warmed, they reradiate energy upward at infrared wavelengths, longer on the average than the wavelengths of incident light. The atmosphere is somewhat opaque to the reradiated energy and retains much of this radiation. The more that is retained, the warmer the earth is, on the average. The opacity of the atmosphere is affected by the presence of water vapor, carbon dioxide, ozone, methane, and other gases present in smaller amounts. The process of heat retention is called the greenhouse effect because the glass of a greenhouse acts in very much the same way as the atmosphere in keeping the interior warm. [Energy, Systems and Interactions]

Considerable energy is required to evaporate water. Conversely, energy is released when water vapor condenses; thus, transfer of water from the sea via the air to someplace where precipitation occurs involves considerable transfer of energy as well as water. This energy transfer is very important in weather processes. The chinook phenomenon is a dramatic

example of release of energy stored in water vapor. Rising over the upwind slope of a mountain range, the air expands as the pressure decreases. Its temperature does not decrease because heat is supplied to the air as condensation of water vapor occurs, usually with precipitation. Descending the downwind side of the mountain range, the air compresses and warms, ending with a temperature considerably higher than its temperature when it began to ascend the upwind slope. [Energy, Systems and Interactions]

Water vapor also affects the movement of air. Because the molecular weight of water is less than that of dry air, humid air tends to rise when surrounded by dry air at the same temperature. [Systems and Interactions]

Climate has been observed and recorded at least since the time of the ancient Greeks, who recorded the number of days of sunshine per year more than 2,000 years ago. Humans create their own climate modifications by building cities. Urban heat islands have been known and studied for more than a century. There is evidence that air pollution can influence the precipitation pattern over an area. [Systems and Interactions, Stability]

Even the global climate may be changing as a result of human activities. The observed increase in average temperatures over the past decades may be due to increased quantities of greenhouse gases in the atmosphere. However, confirmation and quantitative analyses are very difficult because other important effects not under human control are present. Among these effects the most notable is the sequence of ice ages dating back at least as far as the Pleistocene, or about a million years, whose traces have been carefully analyzed. Nevertheless, there is a need for more study to evaluate the threat of current human activities. [Systems and Interactions, Patterns of Change]

D-2

What are the major phenomena of climate and weather? What are the large- and small-scale causes of climate and weather?

Kindergarten Through Grade Three

The surface of the earth has cold and hot places. The land and water masses near the North and South poles are cold almost all the time because they receive little sunlight. The air is warmed or cooled by the land or water it is near. There are places on the earth that are too hot and dry for people to live without water, or too cold for people to live there without shelter. Different places are warm and wet, warm and dry, cold and wet, and cold and dry. [Scale and Structure]

Weather changes all the time. We see clear skies, clouds, rain, and snow; hot and cold days and nights; and calm and windy days and nights. Short-term weather changes are superimposed on more general seasonal changes. In California, it rains more in the winter than in the summer, but this is not true everywhere. [Systems and Interaction, Stability, Patterns of Change]

D-2   What are the major phenomena of climate and weather? What are the large- and small-scale causes of climate and weather?

Grades Three Through Six

When air is warmed and rises, it is replaced by neighboring air that rushes in. The resulting horizontal flow is called wind. There are winds that affect large parts of the earth (like the westerlies), and there are winds that affect only small regions (like sea breezes). The rotation of the earth and friction between the air and the surface affect the way in which the air flows. [Patterns of Change, Systems and Interactions]

When a mass of warm air moves into a cooler area, the leading edge is called a warm front. When a mass of cold air moves into a warmer area, the leading edge is called a cold front. [Scale and Structure]

Clouds are classified according to a standard scheme. To begin with, there are high, middle, and low clouds; these terms refer to altitude above the surface. The quantitative distinction among these terms depends to some extent on the latitude. In middle and low latitudes, high clouds generally form above 6000 metres. Because the air is always very cold and dry at this altitude, high clouds are almost always thin and almost always made of ice crystals. Middle clouds have their bases between about 2000 and 7000 metres; they usually consist of water droplets, sometimes with some ice. Low clouds have their bases below 2000 metres. They are almost always composed of water droplets, except in cold weather, when they may contain ice and snow. [Scale and Structure]

Clouds are divided according to form into three main classes: cirrus, cumulus, and stratus. Further distinctions are made by means of such prefixes as alto- (high) and nimbo- (rainbearing). Types of clouds have strong associations with types of weather. [Scale and Structure]

D-2   What are the major phenomena of climate and weather? What are the large- and small-scale causes of climate and weather?

Grades Six Through Nine

In summer, the warm water of tropical seas warms the air strongly, transferring much energy to the air. The result is a weather pattern involving very strong winds and much rain (a tropical storm, a hurricane, or a typhoon). On a smaller scale, there are thunderstorms, caused when warm air is pushed up forcefully by neighboring cold air. The strong turbulence and rapid cooling result in heavy rain. The strong friction produces electric charge and results in lightning. Lightning is dangerous, and there are safety rules to follow when lightning is near. Thunder is produced when a lightning flash quickly heats a small amount of air to a very high temperature. The air expands

---

Students should be encouraged to study the weather map in the daily newspaper on a regular basis and to view videotapes of a good television weather-map sequence, with frames frozen as necessary. By studying a series of maps on a daily basis, students can see the short-term changes in weather; by comparing different geographic areas, they can understand climatic differences; by comparing maps in different seasons, they can learn about the effect of seasonal changes on weather. However, weather is a three-dimensional phenomenon that cannot be completely represented on a weather map.

suddenly. After the flash the hot air quickly cools and contracts. The two rapid movements are the source of loud sound called thunder. You can tell how far away a lightning flash is by counting the seconds between the flash and the thunder. Each three seconds correspond roughly to one kilometer. [Energy, Systems and Interactions]

Some regions of the earth, called source regions, are consistent producers of large masses of warm or cold, dry or humid air. Major source regions at high latitudes are arctic ice and the snow-covered plains in winter. At low latitudes there are subtropical oceans and hot desert regions. Air masses originating in these source regions migrate and interact in middle altitudes. The boundary between two air masses of different barometric pressure is called a front. Because the pressure difference is due to temperature difference, the temperature usually varies considerably across a front. The humidity often varies as well. [Scale and Structure, Stability, Systems and Interactions]

Even though fronts appear as lines on weather maps, they are boundaries that extend vertically as well as horizontally. They are of four types:

1. A *stationary front*, which moves very little.
2. A *cold front*, which brings a considerable temperature change over a short horizontal distance and is accompanied by changes in relative and absolute humidity, shifts in wind direction, pressure changes, and clouds, often with precipitation.
3. A *warm front*, in which the warmer, less dense air rises over the cold air, producing clouds and precipitation well in advance of the surface boundary of the front. The vertical slope of a warm front is much gentler than that of a cold front. Precipitation is usually cold or moderate and covers a wide area.
4. An *occluded front*, which results when a cold front overtakes a warm front. The oncoming cold air mass may push the warm air upward, producing drastic temperature changes and often violent weather, or the oncoming air mass may not be much colder than the warm air and may ride over the warm air. This results in extended unsettled weather. [Scale and Structure, Systems and Interactions]

Hurricanes are storms with winds exceeding 64 knots that form over the tropical waters of the world.

The temperature in a hurricane is usually above 26°C. Hurricanes are seasonal, occurring mainly in summer through autumn and usually from between 5° and 20° latitude. At higher latitudes not enough energy is available; at lower latitudes, the Coriolis force is not great enough to confer the characteristic powerful spin on the storm. Friction between air and sea is an important factor in the organization of hurricanes. [Energy, Patterns of Change]

Ocean currents arise from warming of seawater by the sun and from frictional drag of the surface water by the prevailing winds. Ocean currents are much slower than winds but carry much more heat. The temperate climate of northern Europe, for example, is due to the warming effect of tropical water carried across the Atlantic Ocean from the Gulf of Mexico by the Gulf Stream. The California coast is cooled by the southward-flowing cold water of the Japan current. [Energy, Scale and Structure, Stability]

Long-term variations in ocean currents have important economic effects. In the case of the southern oscillation or El Niño, the prevailing cold current off the coast of South America is deflected. The resulting warming of the water has disastrous effects on the important fishing industry, and the warming of the air suppresses rainfall, with equally disastrous effects on agriculture. It is becoming evident that the El Niño phenomenon is only one part of a much larger pattern involving the entire Pacific Ocean. A similar phenomenon of smaller magnitude is only now coming to light in the smaller Atlantic Ocean. [Scale and Structure]

D-2 What are the major phenomena of climate and weather? What are the large- and small-scale causes of climate and weather?

Grades Nine Through Twelve

Energy from the sun drives atmospheric circulation, whose pattern is very complex. In general, however, the winds in the upper atmosphere are westerly because of the rotation of the earth. However, the flow is not constant; it breaks up into eddies (cyclones and anticyclones) that transfer heat and momentum from equatorial to polar regions. [Energy, Patterns of Change]

Jet streams of various types arise from strong, large-scale temperature differences. The tropical easterly jet stream arises from the summer heating of land masses to temperatures that are higher than the neighboring oceanic temperatures toward the equator. Strong polar westerly jet streams, called the stratospheric polar night jet streams, arise in winter from the normal temperature difference between lower and higher latitudes. [Scale and Structure]

Jet streams have an important influence on the motion of fronts because air masses tend to be deflected by jet streams, which themselves curve under the action of the Coriolis force. Highs are deflected generally southeastward; and lows, generally northeastward. [Systems and Interactions]

When the jet stream bends, a wave develops in the form of a trough of relatively low pressure at lower elevations and ridges of relatively high pressure at higher elevations. When an upper-level trough is located to the west of an area of low pressure at the surface, horizontal and vertical air movements result in the formation of storms at the surface, driven by the rising of warm and the descent of cool air. [Patterns of Change]

The amount of water vapor contained in air is described in terms of the specific humidity and the relative humidity. The specific humidity is the ratio of the mass of water vapor contained in a quantity of air to the total mass of the quantity of air. Relative humidity is the quantity most frequently used in meteorology and is often misunderstood. The maximum amount of water vapor that can be contained in a given quantity of air depends very sensitively on temperature. A small increase in temperature leads to a considerable increase in this maximum. Relative humidity is the ratio of the amount of water vapor in a quantity of air to the maximum amount of water vapor that the air can contain at the same temperature. As the temperature of a mass of air increases, its relative humidity rises rapidly. When the relative humidity reaches 100 percent, further removal of heat leads to condensation of some water. For this reason the temperature at which a given sample of air attains 100 percent relative humidity is called the dew point if its value exceeds 0° C and the frost point if its value is lower than 0° C. [Patterns of Change, Energy]

When warm unstable air rises in an unstable environment, a thunderstorm is born. The immediate source of the instability may be uneven surface heating, or the effects of topography, or the lifting of

Relative humidity is measured with an instrument called a hygrometer. Several varieties of hygrometers exist, including the convenient but not very accurate hair hygrometer, the wet-dry bulb thermometer, and its variant, the sling psychrometer. [Systems and Interactions]

Clouds form when water condenses from air that is cooled below its dew point. The condensation almost always occurs on tiny airborne particles called condensation nuclei, whose sizes range from about 0.2 micrometer to 1 micrometer. Although the air may look clean, it almost always contains plenty of condensation nuclei; typically there are 100 to 1,000 per cubic centimeter. Even when the air is dry, these particles often show up as dry haze. [Scale and Structure]

warm air along a frontal boundary. [Energy, Systems and Interactions]

More severe thunderstorms form along fronts. There may be numerous storms in a line, and they may produce high winds, large damaging hail, heavy rains that can cause flash flooding, and even tornadoes. [Patterns of Change, Systems and Interactions]

Major ocean currents do not follow the winds precisely, though they are affected by the winds and by the Coriolis force that affects the winds as well. Currents flow in semiclosed circular whirls called gyres. [Stability, Scale and Structure]

In the North Atlantic, the prevailing winds blow clockwise and outward from the subtropical high, while the ocean currents flow in a more or less circular clockwise direction. As the water moves beneath the wind, the Coriolis force deflects the water to the right in the northern hemisphere. As a result, the surface water moves generally at right angles to the wind. [Systems and Interactions]

As ocean currents transport warm water away from its source, there is upwelling of cold water from below. The interaction of this cold water with the air has profound effects on weather and climate. [Energy, Systems and Interactions]

D-3

How are we affected by weather? How do we predict it? How can we alter it?

Kindergarten Through Grade Three

Weather forecasting is difficult. Meteorologists are quite accurate in their predictions about two days into the future. Over longer times, forecasting rapidly becomes less reliable. [Patterns of Change]

Scientists have experimented with various ways of changing the weather, especially to make it rain. [Systems and Interactions]

Severe weather can produce great damage by means of winds and floods. [Systems and Interactions]

D-3   How are we affected by weather? How do we predict it? How can we alter it?

Grades Three Through Six

Forecasting weather is very important because much of what people do is determined by the weather. Forecasting beyond a few days is very uncertain, but with sophisticated computer technology and better data-gathering networks, meteorologists will probably be able to do a better job of forecasting for a longer time in the future. However, it is doubtful that meteorologists will ever be able to predict in advance the weather patterns for an entire season. [Patterns of Change]

Severe weather can produce great damage. In some parts of the world, hurricanes are frequent. Hurricanes do damage mostly through their very strong winds and by means of the surges of seawater they push into coastal areas. Tornadoes, though very local, have even more powerful winds than hurricanes and produce severe, though localized, damage. Heavy rainstorms do damage largely through flash flooding. Lightning-caused fires sometimes do great damage, especially in forests. [Systems and Interactions]

Because particular types of clouds are strongly associated with types of weather, clouds are useful in short-term weather forecasting. Puffy white cumulus clouds are associated with fair weather. Sometimes, cumulus clouds that are small in the morning grow into towering cumulus in the afternoon and produce

Because water condenses on airborne particles, scientists have tried to induce rain by seeding clouds with fine particles. One method involves seeding cold clouds, which already contain water droplets at temperatures below—but not too far below—0° C. The water is supercooled; that is, it does not freeze. Freezing can be induced by introducing tiny crystals, such as silver nitrate crystals, which resemble ice crystals. As this freezing process progresses, crystals are formed that are large enough to fall. To date, the results of seeding are uncertain, although some countries have successfully sued others for "stealing" their rain through the seeding process. [Systems and Interactions]

rain showers. Further growth into cumulonimbus may result in thundershowers. [Scale and Structure]

D-3   How are we affected by weather? How do we predict it? How can we alter it?

Grades Six Through Nine

Clouds can indicate whether the local atmosphere is stable or unstable. When the atmosphere is stable, a volume of air that is raised or lowered tends to return to its original position. When the atmosphere is unstable, a volume of air that is raised or lowered tends to continue in the same direction. Unstable atmospheres are associated with updrafts, downdrafts, turbulence, and precipitation. [Scale and Structure, Stability]

D-3   How are we affected by weather? How do we predict it? How can we alter it?

Grades Nine Through Twelve

When a mass of air rises to regions of lower pressure, it expands. If (as often happens) it does not exchange significant heat with neighboring air, it cools. Similarly, descending air warms. As long as rising air does not cool to its dew point (reach saturation), its temperature drops at about $10°C$ for every kilometer of rise. If the rising air cools to its dew point, water vapor condenses and clouds form. [Energy, Scale and Structure, Stability]

The droplets of water or ice crystals in clouds are so small that friction with air limits the speed of their fall to negligible values. In order to fall as rain, the droplets must grow to much larger sizes; the typical raindrop is 0.5 mm in diameter and contains as much water as a million cloud droplets. Under proper conditions, the droplets can coalesce as they collide, or they can collide with ice crystals and contribute to the growth of the crystals. Once a raindrop of ice crystal is big enough to fall, it collides with smaller raindrops in its path and continues to grow. [Scale and Structure, Systems and Interactions]

Chapter 5

Life Sciences

In previous frameworks the topic Living Things was divided into separate sections on plants, protists, animals, and human beings. Although it is feasible to separate curricula into these component parts (and many teachers prefer instructional materials that do so), the present framework is designed to emphasize the continuity and comparability of living systems, their components, needs, and histories. In this way the concepts of integrative themes are stressed. Whichever format is used, it is essential to show that classification of living things is based on evolution, because evolution explains both the similarities among living things and the diverse paths taken by different groups through geologic time.

A-1 **What are the characteristics of living things?**

A-2 **How do the structures of living things perform their functions, interact with each other, and contribute to the maintenance and growth of the organism?**

A-3 **What are the relationships of living organisms, and how are living things classified?**

A-4 **How do humans interact with other living things?**

A-1

What are the characteristics of living things?

Kindergarten Through Grade Three

Living things have characteristics by which they can be described and distinguished from nonliving things (e.g., they take in nutrients, give off wastes, grow, reproduce, and respond to stimuli from their environments). They are all made of smaller structures that can be observed and studied (birds, for example, have beaks, wings, feet, and feathers). The structures themselves are composed of smaller, observable features (bird wings, for example, have feathers, skin, and bones). All living things need certain resources to grow, such as food, water, and gases to breathe. If any of these things are lacking, the organism will die. [Energy, Systems and Interactions, Scale and Structure]

A-1   What are the characteristics of living things?

Grades Three Through Six

Living things are all composed of cells, or if they are too small to have individual cells (i.e., are noncellular or one-celled), they still perform all the functions that specialized cells do in a larger body. Living things grow, metabolize food, reproduce, and interact with their environments. All living things have basic requirements of nutrition and growth, needing food, water, and gas exchange for respiration. Plants, as well as some one-celled organisms that can photosynthesize, are able to make food out of air and water,

Evidence of Molecular Evolution in the Amino Acid Sequences of Cytochrome C Molecules from 14 Organisms

	Rhodospirillum rubrum C_2	Wheat	Silkworm Moth	Dogfish	Carp	Bullfrog	Snapping Turtle	Chicken, Turkey	Kangaroo	Rabbit	Horse	Pig, Bovine, Sheep	Rhesus Monkey	Humans
Rhodospirillum rubrum C_2	0	66	65	65	84	65	64	64	66	64	64	64	64	65
Wheat	66	0	40	44	42	43	41	41	42	39	41	40	38	38
Silkworm Moth	65	40	0	30	25	27	26	26	26	24	27	25	28	29
Dogfish	65	44	30	0	14	19	18	18	19	16	16	15	22	23
Carp	64	42	25	14	0	13	13	14	13	13	13	11	17	17
Bullfrog	65	43	27	19	13	0	10	12	13	11	13	11	16	17
Snapping Turtle	64	41	26	18	13	10	0	8	11	9	11	9	13	14
Chicken, Turkey	69	41	26	18	14	11	8	0	12	5	11	9	12	13
Kangaroo	66	42	26	19	13	13	11	12	0	6	7	6	11	10
Rabbit	64	39	24	16	13	11	4	8	6	0	6	4	8	9
Horse	64	41	27	16	13	13	11	11	7	6	0	3	11	12
Pig, Bovine, Sheep	64	40	25	15	11	11	9	9	6	4	3	0	9	10
Rhesus Monkey	64	38	28	22	17	15	13	12	11	8	11	9	0	1
Humans	65	38	29	23	17	17	14	13	10	9	12	10	1	0

Figure 4. Amino acid sequences in the cytochrome C molecules of a wide variety of organisms show an increasing number of differences that correlates with evolutionary distance of relationship. For example, the bacterium *Rhodospirillum* shows an astonishingly consistent number of amino acid differences from all other organisms; this reflects its ancient split from the others and how long it has continued to evolve in isolation. More closely related organisms show fewer differences, reflecting their shorter times as separate evolutionary lineages. This chart also shows how regular has been the rate of molecular evolution in these amino acid sequence changes. Its results are exactly what would be expected and predicted by evolutionary theory.

Young students should appreciate that they are growing individuals and know what their needs are for growth and health. They should be aware of the basic body systems that enable growth to occur. Energy, derived from food, is necessary for all living things. Nutrition is based on good food habits. Humans have a responsibility to conserve life and resources and not to overuse or threaten sources of energy.

using the energy from sunlight and nutrients from soil or water. All other organisms depend on obtaining food from other sources of energy, usually by feeding on other organisms or biochemical compounds. Living things depend on other living things in many ways. [Energy, Systems and Interactions, Scale and Structure]

A-1   What are the characteristics of living things?

Grades Six Through Nine

All living things have DNA and RNA, the genetic material that determines the growth and development of each organism. Because all organisms have this genetic material, they must have evolved from a single ancestor that also had DNA and RNA. (See Section B, Cells, Genetics, and Evolution.) Digestion, respiration, metabolism, water regulation, and reproduction are functions common to all organisms; all but the simplest organisms have specialized tissues, organs, and organ systems to perform these functions.

Living things use nonliving materials to build their structures and to enable them to perform certain necessary functions of life (e.g., calcium and phosphate in bones and teeth; carbon, nitrogen, and other minerals in animals and plants; copper and iron in the blood). Cycles, such as those of carbon, nitrogen, oxygen, carbon dioxide, and other nutrients, are processes and patterns by which living things convert external materials to grow and maintain themselves. [Scale and Structure, Systems and Interactions, Energy, Patterns of Change]

A-1   What are the characteristics of living things?

Grades Nine Through Twelve

All living things have a homologous genetic material, represented by RNA and DNA (in some viruses, only RNA or DNA is present). This feature demonstrates the unity of living things and their evolution from a common source. The complex structures, cycles, and processes that characterize living things require energy to grow and to maintain them. [Energy, Evolution, Systems and Interactions]

A-2

How do the structures of living things perform their functions, interact with each other, and contribute to the maintenance and growth of the organism?

Kindergarten Through Grade Three

Living things have structures that do specific things to help the organism live and grow and meet their needs as they interact with their environments. [Scale and Structure, Systems and Interactions]

Humans, like other animals, gain information about the world around them through their senses. They need fresh air, good food, rest, and exercise to stay healthy.

A-2   How do the structures of living things perform their functions, interact with each other, and contribute to the maintenance and growth of the organism?

Grades Three Through Six

Multicelled organisms have particular tissues (e.g., bones, muscles, wood), organs (e.g., livers, lungs, hearts, stems, roots, leaves), and organ systems (e.g., circulatory, respiratory, reproductive) that perform specific life functions (structural support, water regulation, digestion, circulation of nutrients, and so forth). One-celled organisms perform all these functions within their cell membranes, using specialized organelles for each function. Organisms can tolerate some variations in the things they need in order to survive (light, temperature, water, nutrients), but they do best under certain conditions. [Scale and Structure, Systems and Interactions]

Variations in an organism's structure (e.g., flower color, bristle number in flies, sex) are passed to the next generation through reproduction. Living things have structures that allow them to reproduce sexually or asexually, depending on their adaptations and evolutionary histories. Organisms progress through life cycles of birth, growth, reproduction, and death. (See Section B, Cells, Genetics, and Evolution.) These cycles include the growth and development of the young. There is variation in the rate of growth of most species (e.g., adolescence in mammals). [Patterns of Change]

Structures of organisms show their adaptations to their environments and ways of life. (For example, tooth differences between herbivores and carnivores; warm-blooded and cold-blooded adaptations; plant adaptations to pollination by insects, birds, and mammals.) Information about the environment is collected by all organisms. This information helps them to adapt to local or temporary conditions, to obtain food, and to resist predation and death. Plants have tissues and organs that react to light, water, and other stimuli; animals have nervous systems that process and store information from the environment. [Systems and Interactions]

A-2 How do the structures of living things perform their functions, interact with each other, and contribute to the maintenance and growth of the organism?

Grades Six Through Nine

Organisms need energy to help them perform functions necessary to life. They obtain energy through various means, either from sunlight or by digesting complex molecules and producing simpler ones. [Energy, Systems and Interactions]

The digestive, osmoregulatory, circulatory, respiratory, and reproductive systems have comparable functions in different groups of organisms, even though the organ systems that perform them are often quite different. Within large groups of organisms, such as animals or plants, tissues and organ systems are homologous because they have been inherited from a common ancestor. For example, the intestines of vertebrates and most invertebrates are homologous; however, these are not homologous to the

---

Science has recently entered the great age of molecular biology, which is marked by discoveries and use of recombinant DNA. Molecules of DNA, containing genetic information, can be moved in the laboratory from one species to another. This opens seemingly endless possibilities for developing new types of living organisms, for repairing genetic defects, and for discovering new improvements in agriculture, such as "engineered" food crop plants. The laboratory techniques for working with DNA are ultramodern, and new procedures are continually being discovered and introduced.

One of the biggest scientific studies ever started, certainly the biggest single undertaking ever proposed in biology, is the Human Genome Project, which is designed to identify and characterize all the genes in human DNA. There are about three or four billion pairs of nucleotides (abbreviated as A, C, G, and T) in the DNA of a human cell. The project will attempt to map all the genes in each of the 23 human chromosomes. The total number of human genes is probably between 50,000 and 100,000, and a gene contains about 1,000 pairs of nucleotides. Hereditary diseases usually result from mutations or other changes in genes. Several countries are starting work on this project, which will take at least 20 years to complete. Molecular biology will provide careers for many scientists in genetic engineering and biotechnology.

The body systems of humans (support, respiration, circulation, and so forth) can be used as examples of animal systems necessary for the growth and maintenance of life.

organelles in unicellular organisms that perform the intestine's functions, nor to analogous digestive structures in plants. (See Section B, Cells, Genetics, and Evolution.) [Systems and Interactions, Scale and Structure, Evolution]

There is a hierarchy to the structure of biological systems. Cells are organized into tissues, tissues into organs, and organs into organ systems that perform particular functions in an individual. Individuals themselves are organized into reproductive groups (such as populations and species) that are part of larger taxonomic units (species and higher categories) changing and evolving through time. Cells are composed of organelles that perform cellular functions, including reproduction. These functional systems are different at each hierarchical level (cells, tissues, organs, and so forth). Although separate, they contribute to processes and patterns at other levels. [Scale and Structure, Systems and Interactions, Evolution]

Humans vary in their characteristics, most of which are inherited from their parents. Individuals of the same age can vary in growth, abilities, and development. During adolescence, growth is rapid and often uneven, and sexual maturation occurs at this time. [Note: Instruction in human reproduction and sexuality is subject to *Education Code* Section 51550. Special care should be taken that these concepts, including reproductive anatomy, menstrual cycle, sexual intercourse, conception, pregnancy, and birth, are introduced at the appropriate level according to local district policy. See Appendix B. For related material, consult the *Health Instruction Framework*.]

The genetic diversity of populations of organisms is greatly increased by sexual reproduction, because new combinations of characters appear. Asexual reproduction does not allow such recombination. This limits potential variation and adaptation in asexual organisms, but it also limits the spread of disadvantageous characters through a species. Some combinations of characters are better suited to some environments than others.

A-2   How do the structures of living things perform their functions, interact with each other, and contribute to the maintenance and growth of the organism?

Grades Nine Through Twelve

Metabolic energy is obtained in different ways by different organisms. Energy is stored and released as chemical bonds and structures are formed or broken down. (See Chapter 3, Section A, Matter; and Section D, Energy: Sources and Transformations.) Plants and unicellular organisms, such as algae, can photosynthesize and use this energy to convert carbon dioxide, water, and minerals into sugars and amino acids. Fungi obtain food and energy from plants, animals, or other organic matter. Viruses require host cells to obtain the energy they need in order to grow and reproduce. Animals obtain proteins and other nutrients from the plant or animal material that they digest. [Energy, Scale and Structure, Systems and Interactions]

In similar ways the systems of circulation, respiration, support, osmoregulation, reproduction, and so forth can be directly compared among different groups of organisms. Some tissues and organ systems, as well as biochemical molecules, are homologous within large groups because they are inherited from a common ancestor. Other functions are performed by completely different, nonhomologous (but analogous) structures in different organisms. These structures and functions are directly comparable at the anatomical, histological, and biochemical levels.

All basic activities of organisms are biochemical and are mediated by enzymes that regulate the rate at which chemical reactions occur. This regulating system allows the organisms to maintain the steady state of biochemical conditions known as homeostasis. The organism's health, well-being, and effectiveness in its environment depend on the ability to maintain homeostasis. The basic biochemical processes of all organisms share fundamental similarities because the conditions necessary for such biochemical reactions to occur, and for enzymes to carry out

Organ and tissue systems are often presented in life science curricula as if they were systems peculiar to mammals (e.g., "The liver is an organ in a mammal that . . ."). This approach is incorrect and misleading. Such systems should be explained in terms of their general structures and functions in living things. As necessary, variations on these structures and functions can be explained for different groups. It is important to show where in the evolutionary sequence particular organs, tissues, and functions appeared, so students can grasp the concept of homology and the evidence by which scientists unite organisms into evolutionary groups.

their functions, are based on chemical and physical processes that are universal. [Energy, Stability]

The human reproductive system, like the reproductive systems of many other animals, is adapted for the conception and development of a relatively small number of offspring (in contrast to insects or plants, for example). Some kinds of birds and mammals, including humans, have a longer developmental time and are more dependent on parental care than other animals are. Unlike other animals, human beings are capable of controlling their own reproductive rates through the control of their behavior and the use of a variety of techniques to prevent conception. (See note in the section for the grades six-through-nine level.)

Because of its size and complexity, the structure of the animal nervous system makes a variety of responses and behaviors possible. In general, as the size and complexity of the nervous system increase, so does the potential for learned behavior beyond simple innate responses. Human behavior, like that of most mammals and birds, is both innate and learned. Humans can control their behavior in many ways. Behavior can be altered by biochemical means, such as the use of drugs or alcohol. Good nutrition contributes to the well-being of both the body and the mind. (See *Health Instruction Framework.*) [Scale and Structure, Systems and Interactions]

A-3

What are the relationships of living organisms, and how are living things classified?

Kindergarten Through Grade Three

All living organisms are known to be related, because they have the characteristics of life (they breathe, take in food, reproduce, and so forth). Life has been on the earth for a long time. Many plants and animals, such as dinosaurs, trilobites, mammoths, giant tree ferns, and horsetail trees, lived long ago but have become extinct. [Evolution]

A-3   What are the relationships of living organisms, and how are living things classified?

Grades Three Through Six

Groups of organisms are known to be related because they share essential features common to them but not to other organisms. Examples are feathers, which all birds have but no other organisms have; fur,

Just as humans are mammals, they are also primates, and they retain characteristics of other primates seen in the hands, eyes, brains, and genetic and biochemical systems. Within the primates, humans are classified with the other anthropoid apes because they lack tails and have an unusual erect or semierect stance and semibrachiating forelimbs. Anatomical, genetic, and biochemical data indicate that chimpanzees and gorillas are the closest living apes to humans. The first hominids (animals on the evolutionary line from the other apes to living humans) appeared over two million years ago; human evolution since then has been marked by important changes, including upright posture, larger brains, toolmaking, speech, art, and other cultural aspects.

which is unique to mammals; and flowers, unique to flowering plants. Most groups of organisms have long histories that are known from the fossil record. The early members of groups have some, but not all, of the characteristics shared by later forms. Many forms have become extinct, while other new forms have evolved from preexisting ones.

Humans are mammals, with the basic characteristics of mammals (hair, milk-giving, sets of teeth replaced only once, and so forth). Humans also have the basic functions of mammals and other animals, including respiration, digestion, circulation, sensing the environment, movement, and so forth. [Evolution, Scale and Structure, Systems and Interactions]

The major groups of living things are plants, animals, and a variety of one-celled forms. Living things are classified according to their common ancestry. At each level of classification, distinct characters are used to identify the organisms within each group. Living things are divided into three kingdoms of multicellular organisms called fungi, plants, and animals, as well as a vast number of one-celled forms.

A-3 What are the relationships of living organisms, and how are living things classified?

Grades Six Through Nine

Groups of organisms are recognized because they share derived characteristics (evolutionary novelties) that appeared in their common ancestor and have been passed on. (For example, the first bird had feathers, and its offspring inherited them.) Many of these characteristics are adaptive, but the functions of some are not known. These characteristics serve as the basis for diagnosing and classifying groups of organisms. Within each of these groups are other groups that are distinguished by their own unique characteristics. (For example, within mammals there are hoofed animals, further divided into even-toed and odd-toed groups, and carnivores, which have unique shearing teeth.) By identifying these unique characteristics, we discover the evolutionary pattern, which is the basis for classification. [Systems and Interactions, Evolution]

Living things are conventionally divided into five kingdoms, but only fungi, plants, and animals are

Usually, organisms are divided into five kingdoms (plants, animals, fungi, Protista, and Monera) in the traditional Linnean system of classification. But Linnaeus's system (which originally had only two kingdoms) was developed when far fewer organisms, both living and extinct, were known. Besides, his taxonomic ranks (order, family, and so forth) are too few to accommodate and reflect the descent of life. (How can reptiles and their descendants, the birds, both be legitimately ranked as classes?) Accordingly, the five-kingdom arrangement needs revision. Plants, animals, and fungi are all legitimate groupings, because each has unique characteristics. Monera and Protista do not; some of their members are closer to the other three groups and share some characteristics with them, and so cannot be easily classified.

While it is still acceptable to call Protista, plants, animals, and fungi eukaryotes (comprising eubacteria and archaebacteria) and the others prokaryotes (in reference to their cell types, with or without nuclei), or Monera (cells which lack a membrane-bound nucleus), these five groups should not be treated as of equivalent rank. This situation arises because what we know goes beyond our ability to express it. What we now know of the evolutionary relationships of organisms cannot easily fit into the relatively few categories of the Linnean system of classification. We can explain the unique characteristics that unite the members of each group of eukaryotes and then show how the members of each evolved as well as how each eukaryotic group is related to specific prokaryotes.

well-unified evolutionary groups. (The one-celled forms are often divided into Monera and Protista, but the distinction is arbitrary.) Within these kingdoms, there is a hierarchical arrangement of groups within groups. Classification is founded on evolutionary relationships. The Linnean system of classification was established before evolution was understood, but in general it can be modified to accommodate new information and theory because it is a simple, workable system. [Scale and Structure, Evolution]

Viruses are not placed in any kingdom of living things because they lack cells and either RNA or DNA and are uniquely tied to their hosts for growth and reproduction. It is likely that viruses evolved from host cells and are most closely related to the groups that host them.

The fossil histories of groups show that the simplest organisms appeared first, then multicellular ones, which diversified into plants and animals. Within plants, photosynthesizing green algae were the precursors of multicellular plants, and the nonvascular mosses and liverworts appeared before the vascular plants; the most recent vascular plants to appear are the angiosperms or flowering plants. This sequence of appearance is supported independently by the patterns of shared derived characteristics from which phylogenics of living and fossil organisms are constructed. (See Section B, Cells, Genetics, and Evolution.)

A-3   What are the relationships of living organisms, and how are living things classified?

Grades Nine Through Twelve

The purpose of studying organic diversity is to discover the relationships of living and extinct organisms by linking groups into evolutionary trees, based on shared derived characteristics. Life is considered to have had a single origin (to be a "natural" evolutionary group) because all living things have the same genetic material (RNA or DNA). The kingdoms of living things, plus viruses, are united in these characteristics and within kingdoms are broken down into subgroups using successively less inclusive characteristics.

Discovering evolutionary relationships is less a search for ancestors than for groups that are most closely related to each other. We recognize these relationships on the basis of shared derived characteristics, inherited from a common ancestor. Groups

Evolutionary relationships are best understood if we use criteria of group membership, basing our classifications on shared characteristics. In this way, we can diagram a pattern of characteristics that shows us the relationships of groups within groups. (For example, the first birds evolved from small carnivorous dinosaurs, so birds are properly considered members of the dinosauria, regardless of how they are traditionally classified. Similarly, humans evolved from other apes—tailless primates—and are, in turn, apes, primates, mammals, amniotes, vertebrates, and so forth.) Group memberships must be employed fully and consistently in evolutionary classification. Shared derived characteristics, diagrammed according to how widely they are distributed among organisms, are the basis for understanding evolutionary relationships. (See the discussion of homology under Section B, Cells, Genetics, and Evolution.) [Scale and Structure, Evolution]

within groups are recognized by the characteristics that they share. (For example, all mammals have fur, but not all mammals give birth to live young. Those that do, the marsupials and placentals, are more closely related to each other than either is to monotremes, which like other amniotes retain the habit of egg laying. But monotremes, which have fur and give milk, are closer to the other mammals than are the other amniotes, such as birds and reptiles, which do not have fur and do not give milk.) [Scale and Structure, Evolution]

Organisms are classified by shared derived characteristics, and their relationships are mapped by the use of cladograms (diagrams of derived characteristics shared by successively inclusive groups of taxa; see Section B, Cells, Genetics, and Evolution). The evolutionary trees that result from cladograms can be used to test many kinds of hypotheses about evolutionary history, including how species relate, how evolutionary adaptations have been assembled, and how species and adaptations have changed through time.

A simple cladogram demonstrates how shared derived characteristics are mapped according to how they are distributed among organisms. This shows us the relationships of these organisms. In this example, note that marsupial and placental mammals are united by the shared derived characteristic of giving live birth, which monotreme mammals and other vertebrates lack. All mammals are united by having fur and giving milk, as well as by the unique mammalian jaw joint.

Mammals are united with the birds and other reptiles by having an amniote egg; amphibians are united with amniotes (and separated from fishes) by having four walking limbs; and so on. For any such diagram of evolutionary relationship, many more characteristics than the ones used in this simple cladogram are needed in order for it to be considered a robust hypothesis. Students can use these and additional characteristics to identify the correct evolutionary placement of other organisms. (For example, lions would be placed at a branch from point A, because like elephants they have well-developed placentas; lizards and snakes would branch off point B, because, like all other reptiles, they have color vision [only primates have this among mammals] and they secrete uric acid; and so on.) It is important for students to see the evidence and reasoning on which these methods are based in order to establish evolutionary relationships. They should not be told that organisms are classified based on some vague, undefined notion of similarity.

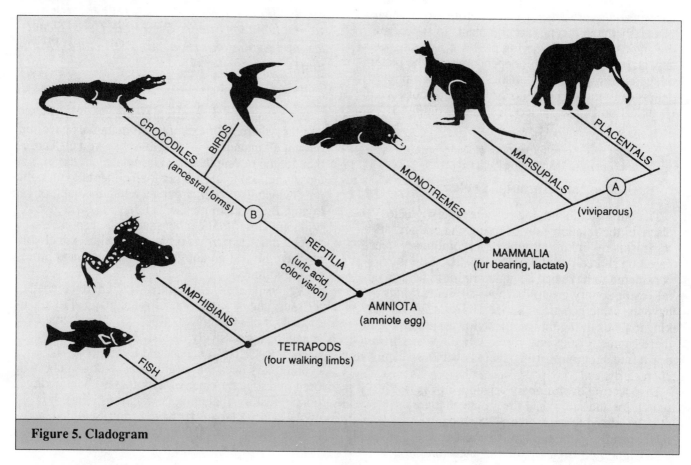

Figure 5. Cladogram

Evolutionary relationships are established by arranging shared derived characteristics on diagrams of the distributions of these characteristics (cladograms; see insert on page 121 and Figure 5). Shared derived characteristics, such as feathers for birds or fur for mammals, are evolutionary novelties that appear in an organism and are passed on to its descendants, including descendant species. Shared derived characteristics can be taken from many different kinds of information, including bones, leaves, reproductive parts, soft tissues, genetic and molecular compositions, and behavioral traits. By mapping how different characteristics are distributed among organisms, we can plot the sequence in which these characters appeared and so establish the relationships of the organisms. (See Figure 5.)

A-4

How do humans interact with other living things?

Kindergarten Through Grade Three

Humans use plants and animals for food and clothing. They farm the soil, mine resources from the earth, and get energy by burning fuels, including wood, which is also used to make paper and to build. People can become sick from infection by some tiny organisms, but human systems can also fight such diseases. Other tiny organisms produce foods, such as yogurt from cow's milk. Living things and essential resources need to be respected. [Systems and Interactions]

A-4   How do humans interact with other living things?

Grades Three Through Six

Humans are part of the biosphere and are dependent on it. Humans rely on a great variety of living things for many reasons. They need to exercise judgment, care, and planning in their use of natural resources, including plants, animals, soil, and water, and in their practices of disposing of wastewater and materials. Human-caused extinctions continue at a rapid pace. Hundreds of species of plants and animals become extinct each year as humans destroy the natural habitat in tropical rain forests and other ecosystems to plant crops and raise animals, harvest firewood, dam rivers, and drain estuaries. [Systems and Interactions]

A-4   How do humans interact with other living things?

Grades Six Through Nine

Humans first domesticated animals and plants thousands of years ago. Humans have learned to selectively breed animals and plants to obtain desirable characteristics (artificial selection), much as natural selection has operated in evolutionary time. (See Section B, Cells, Genetics, and Evolution.) By managing crops and animals and by judiciously tilling and developing the earth, farmers have increased agricultural productivity and efficiency, particularly with new breeding and genetic technologies. [Evolution, Systems and Interactions]

A-4   How do humans interact with other living things?

Grades Nine Through Twelve

Agricultural and biomedical advances have greatly improved the health of humans and the hardiness of domesticated plants and animals. The spread of disease caused by microorganisms has been drastically reduced because of advances in microbiology and epidemiology, coupled with improved public health laws and practices. These advances have resulted in rapid human population growth, especially during the last century. As a consequence, humans must be increasingly conscious of the effects of population growth and take steps to plan safe, healthy, and spacious communities that nurture the best physical and psychological conditions for their inhabitants. They also need to consider the ethical ramifications of biomedical advances that can prolong life beyond the natural capacity of a traumatized body. [Evolution, Systems and Interactions]

Human beings have complex social organizations and behaviors that have allowed them to adapt to a wide variety of environments. Unlike other organisms, humans have done this largely through cultural evolution, without changing important basic physical characteristics. Through thought, reasoning, and toolmaking, humans have manipulated their environment to the point where they can change the genetic constitution of species (e.g., through selective breeding and genetic engineering). They have learned to use the products of other organisms to build houses, gain food, and fight disease, among other things.

Because of their evolutionary success, humans have developed far-reaching interactions with most habi-

Percy L. Julian (1899–1975)

A world-renowned organic chemist, Percy L. Julian, continued the tradition of black scientists in science, medicine, and technology into twentieth-century America. He gained international acclaim for synthesizing physostigmine, a drug which prevented the blinding effects of glaucoma. Known as "the soybean chemist," he was the first to use soybean oil to manufacture economically the synthetic male and female hormones, progesterone and estrogen. But perhaps his most significant contribution to medicine was the mass production of cortisone from soybeans at a much reduced cost, thereby bringing affordable relief to millions of arthritis sufferers.

tats of the biosphere; these interactions are causing great changes in both the physical and biological environments. (See Section C, Ecosystems.) The diversity of life is threatened by some human agricultural, industrial, political, and recreational practices. Humans have a responsibility and a vested interest in maintaining natural ecosystems. [Evolution]

Section B   Cells, Genetics, and Evolution[1]

THE unifying theory of biology is evolution; as Theodosius Dobzhansky said, nothing in biology makes sense without it. It is accepted scientific fact, and has been since the mid-1800s, that organisms are descended with modification from other organisms. The patterns, processes, and mechanisms of this descent make up the theory of evolution. Such processes include (but are not limited to) genetic mutation and recombination of genetic material; populational processes of natural selection, genetic drift, migration in and out of the population; and larger-scale processes of speciation, extinction, and adaptive radiation.

[1] In this section, the term *cells* includes the general areas of cellular and molecular biology, as well as biochemical topics covered in high school biology. Cells also includes general histological and structural features of tissue and organ systems, as well as cellular parts and components in one-celled and multicelled organisms. *Genetics* includes genetic structure and developmental processes. *Evolution* includes population genetics, evolutionary biology, and paleontology.

Evolution is studied through many independent lines of evidence, including the fossil record; comparative anatomy, development, and biochemistry; and genetic structure and change. Evolution explains why similar structures in different organisms are similar and is a highly predictive and (for past events) retrodictive theory. The classification of organisms—indeed all of comparative biology—is based on evolution. Curricula must reflect this centrality of evolution in the biological sciences.

The molecular theory of the gene explains the structure of genetic material and integrates a vast amount of evidence from biochemistry, genetics, and development. In the curriculum for kindergarten through grade twelve, the simpler elements and strands of this theory should be stressed as central to molecular biology and genetics because they give us the chemical and physical bases of how the genetic material changes. This theory is also the basis for agricultural and other technological developments that depend on an understanding of molecular and cellular biology, genetics, and evolution. [Scale and Structure, Evolution, Systems and Interactions]

B-1 **What are cells? What are their component structures and their functions? How do they grow? What is the biochemical basis of life and of metabolism?**

B-2 **How are the characteristics of living things passed on through generations? How does heredity determine the development of individual organisms?**

B-3   How has life changed and diversified through time? What processes and patterns characterize the evolution of life?

B-1

What are cells? What are their component structures and their functions? How do they grow? What is the biochemical basis of life and of metabolism?

Kindergarten Through Grade Three

All living things are made of smaller structures, such as tissues and organs. (See Section A, Living Things.) These structures perform the vital functions of life and help the organism to interact with the environment and survive. [Scale and Structure, Systems and Interactions]

B-1   What are cells? What are their component structures and their functions? How do they grow? What is the biochemical basis of life and of metabolism?

Grades Three Through Six

There are many different kinds of cells in animals and plants, and different kinds of cells (e.g., muscle, blood, bone, skin, wood, and guard cells) perform different functions in the bodies of their whole organisms. The different functions of cells all contribute to the well-being of the organism. [Scale and Structure, Systems and Interactions]

Living organisms have tissues and cells that can be examined to reveal their component parts and functions. The component parts of most cells (e.g., membranes, nucleus, and other small organelles) have different functions, including the conversion and use of energy, protection, and reproduction. Some organisms are one-celled or unicellular, and even these have component parts. Organisms that are very different (e.g., sponges, humans, oak trees, ferns) nonetheless have parts that perform the same kinds of functions for their organisms. [Scale and Structure, Systems and Interactions, Energy]

There is a hierarchy in the organization of living systems, from cells and their components to tissues, organs, organ systems, and whole organisms. At each step in the hierarchy, these component parts contribute to the overall maintenance of the organism.

B-1   What are cells? What are their component structures and their functions? How do they grow? What is the biochemical basis of life and of metabolism?

Grades Six Through Nine

An organism is an individual with parts that are organized into a functional whole. The parts (cells, tissues, organs) cannot survive apart from the whole; and at every level of organization, these parts have structures that perform specific life functions. The major kingdoms of living things are characterized by differences in how cells are organized and differences in the structure of organs and tissues. [Evolution, Scale and Structure, Systems and Interactions]

Living organisms combine atoms and molecules into particular structural and functional compounds. Through the conversion and use of energy, different cell organelles perform the functions of life at the cellular level. [Energy, Scale and Structure]

The content and nutritional value of foods can be understood in terms of calories (or kilojoules) and nutrients. Food that is digested and absorbed may then be oxidized by the cells to release energy necessary to maintain cellular functions and produce new cells. Some food sources carry levels of fats, cholesterol, or other substances that can be unhealthy in excess quantities. [Energy, Scale and Structure]

In order for growth and maintenance of the body to occur, cells must divide to form new cells. Old cells are constantly dying off and being replaced by new ones. Mitosis is one phase of the repeating cycle of cell division that occurs constantly in the body. The cell cycle is governed by environmental factors inside and outside the cell that signal the appropriate time for division (in the case of cancer cells, this signal is not observed). Normally, the newly produced cells are identical to the parent cell or one-celled organism. [Patterns of Change, Stability, Energy]

B-1   What are cells? What are their component structures and their functions? How do they grow? What is the biochemical basis of life and of metabolism?

Grades Nine Through Twelve

Cytoplasm and cell organelles have specific structures and compositions, and they perform specific cellular functions, such as the production of enzymes, the metabolism of food, mitosis, and the removal of wastes. These functions are common to the cells of all living things, even though they are performed by different structures in different kinds of organisms. [Systems and Interactions, Scale and Structure]

Initially, most cells have the ability to become any kind of cell because they contain the same genetic information. Through the process of their growth and development, they differentiate and specialize in structure and function (e.g., to become blood or leaf cells), but they retain the basic information that also allows them to reproduce themselves mitotically. [Systems and Interactions, Scale and Structure]

The chemical and physical bases of metabolism, including photosynthesis and the Krebs cycle, are fundamental cellular processes. These cycles describe the release and use of energy by the organism. Enzymes serve as catalysts to promote essential chemical reactions in cells. Cellular processes that sustain and renew life can be understood by studying the interactions of molecules, atoms, and electrons. Large molecules (macromolecules: e.g., fats, polysaccharides, nucleic acids, and lipids) govern life functions by playing parts in the structure and regulation of the cell's metabolism. [Scale and Structure, Systems and Interactions, Energy]

Regulatory mechanisms in all organisms control the flow of energy and maintain homeostasis of biochemical reactions and metabolic rates. Although the normal activities of life (e.g., feeding, locomotion) cause departures from equilibrium, regulatory systems restore this balance and maintain the organism in working condition. (Disease often results from failures in these systems.) [Energy, Stability]

B-2

How are the characteristics of living things passed on through generations? How does heredity determine the development of individual organisms?

Kindergarten Through Grade Three

Living things resemble their parents because all parents pass on their physical characteristics to their offspring. In organisms with two parents, the offspring normally inherit characteristics of both. Usually, closer relationships mean more similarities: brothers and sisters tend to resemble each other more

closely than cousins or distant relatives do. [Scale and Structure, Systems and Interactions]

B-2   How are the characteristics of living things passed on through generations? How does heredity determine the development of individual organisms?

Grades Three Through Six

Within a species there is usually considerable variation in characteristics. In humans, hair color, eye color, and many other physical features are largely determined by heredity. The variation can be in the organism's appearance or in its genetic makeup (or both). Inheritance is coded by the genetic material found in the nuclei of cells. Some of this material, normally in equal amounts, comes from both parents of multicelled organisms. Variation in this material determines some of the variation in the characteristics of individuals. Although many characteristics are inherited from parents, nutrition and other environmental factors during the growing period contribute vitally to adult form and health. [Scale and Structure, Systems and Interactions]

Living organisms progress through a life cycle that is characteristic of their species. This cycle begins with the combination of genetic material in the new cell and continues through all the phases of growth and development to the adult form through reproduction and death. [Patterns of Change]

Students should understand that "mutants" and "mutations" are not terms laden with negative connotations. Mutations themselves are not helpful, harmful, or neutral, but their effects are, in given situations. Mutations are the agents of genetic change in evolution, affecting nearly all structural and developmental processes. Each human carries dozens of mutations in the chromosomal material; thus, we could all be considered "mutants" (a term that should probably be avoided because of its connotations). Many embryonic deaths, on the other hand, arise from lethal mutations.

Until the 1960s, most mutations were thought to be harmful in their effects, and wild populations were thought to have generally low levels of genetic variability. The discovery of neutral evolution in the 1960s changed this understanding. Molecular and genetic studies revealed that there was far more variation in organisms than had ever been suspected. Yet organisms seem to have no trouble surviving in spite of all this variation. Therefore, most mutations could not be deleterious in their effects but rather seem to have no strong effects at all.

B-2　How are the characteristics of living things passed on through generations? How does heredity determine the development of individual organisms?

Grades Six Through Nine

The genetic material DNA makes up the genes, which determine heredity. Genes are segments of chromosomes in the nuclei of cells. The genetic system is organized so that variations and changes can occur in several major ways, including (1) mutations; (2) errors in copying genetic material when cells divide; and (3) recombination of genetic material. Not all genes are equally expressed; some have more influence on physical form and development than others. In some cases, one gene may influence several characteristics; in other cases, several genes contribute to the same characteristic. Genetic factors contribute to individual variation, and such variations are the raw material of evolution. [Scale and Structure, Systems and Interactions, Evolution]

Mutations are changes in the DNA that may be caused by errors in replicating genetic material. Most causes of mutation (heat and cold, radiation, chemical compounds in the environment) are natural; a few result from active or accidental human interference, such as those from chemicals or X rays. Most mutations are neutral in their effects on the individual organism, though many are harmful, and some are helpful in their effects. The same mutation may have

harmful, neutral, or helpful effects in different genetic and external environments (e.g., mutations for dark or light coat color in arctic mammals may be advantageous or not, depending on the season and the surroundings). [Evolution, Patterns of Change, Systems and Interactions]

All living things follow the patterns of various cycles (e.g., life cycle, respiration and energy release, reproductive cycle, Krebs cycle) and cyclical rhythms (e.g., daily, seasonal, annual). Other patterns of change may be directional (e.g., growth, development, and maturation). [Patterns of Change]

B-2　How are the characteristics of living things passed on through generations? How does heredity determine the development of individual organisms?

Grades Nine Through Twelve

DNA, the genetic material, is universal to all organisms (except some viruses which have only RNA or DNA). DNA is read and transcribed by RNA polymerase to produce a complementary strand of RNA. DNA codes the production of proteins, which are composed of 20 different amino acids, most of which serve as catalysts for cellular functions of growth and development. The sequence of these amino acids is determined by the genetic code, read as codon triplets of the four RNA bases. Sixty-one of the 64 triplets code for the production of a specific amino acid, and the other three are stop signals.

There is great repetition in the genome, probably because this material has been duplicated and additional material has been incorporated many times through evolutionary history. There are active and inactive sections of DNA molecules, and not all parts code for characteristics. In fact, few sites appear to code for specific features, and we know very little as yet about what function most DNA serves, although the main purpose seems to be to code for specific proteins and to regulate growth.

If the sequences of DNA molecules are compared in different organisms, the evolutionary relationships of the molecules can be determined; the degree to which DNA sequences correspond in different organisms provides data about their evolutionary relationships. (See Figure 4, page 115.) DNA molecules can also be artificially modified by the addition or deletion of genetic material to promote desirable characteristics (such as frost resistance in plants) or to eliminate undesirable ones (such as virulency in an infective microorganism). [Scale and Structure, Systems and Interactions, Evolution]

The relationship between genotype and phenotype is complex: normally, there is not a one-to-one correspondence between genes and external characteristics of the organism. There is an explicit and inseparable relationship between genetics and evolution. Darwin used the methods and benefits of selective animal and plant breeding to convey the idea of natural selection by comparison to artificial selection. [Evolution, Systems and Interactions]

The genetic code instructs the production of enzymes and other proteins in the cells. The relationship between the genetic code and the fully developed adult organism is not completely understood. Most genes do not appear to code for specific structures (e.g., fingers) or functions (e.g., hearing ability). Rather, most genes appear to regulate processes of cell growth and enzyme production that function in development. The need for insight into just how genes contribute to development is one of the most exciting frontiers in biology.

Developmental programs may be continuous, as in vertebrates and many plants, or they may result in a series of very different looking, independent, free-living developmental stages. Examples include the caterpillar-pupa-butterfly transition of lepidopteran insects and the nauplius and veliger stages of many marine invertebrates, as well as in the dual life cycle of sporophyte and gametophyte seen in vascular plants. [Patterns of Change, Systems and Interactions, Evolution]

B-3

How has life changed and diversified through time? What processes and patterns characterize the evolution of life?

Kindergarten Through Grade Three

Today, there are a great many kinds of living things, including plants, animals, fungi, and many one-celled organisms. The fossil record indicates that at one time there were only very simple, one-celled forms; but through time, the larger (many-celled) plants and animals evolved from these simple forms.

As climates have changed through time, the variety of life has changed accordingly and increased tremendously. Life has been on earth for a very long time. Fossils tell us about past life, most forms of which are now extinct. [Evolution]

All living things have features that they inherit from their parents. All life forms are related to each other because they share common features. Living things are grouped together on the basis of these features, which they have inherited from common ancestors. [Evolution]

In evolution, the selective value of traits depends on the environment. The peppered moth (Biston betularia) is a famous example of natural selection under conditions of environmental change. Before the industrial revolution, both dark and light moths were present in the population. As industrial pollution increased, light-colored trees darkened, and the light-colored moths were more conspicuous to the birds that fed on them. Hence, the proportion of light-colored moths in the population decreased. However, as industrial pollution declined, the tree trunks lightened again, and lighter-colored moths were favored.

Students should understand that this is not an example of evolutionary change from light-colored to dark-colored to light-colored moths, because both kinds were already in the population. This is an example of natural selection, but in two senses. First, temporary conditions in the environment encouraged selection against dark-colored moths and then against light-colored moths. But second, and just as important, is the selection to maintain a balance of both black and white forms, which are adaptable to a variety of environmental circumstances. This balanced selection increases the chances for survival of the species. This is in many ways the most interesting feature of the evolution of the peppered moth but one that is often misrepresented in textbooks.

B-3 How has life changed and diversified through time? What processes and patterns characterize the evolution of life?

Grades Three Through Six

Organisms resemble their parents because they inherit features from them. New combinations and changes in the genetic material cause variations in offspring. Over geologic time, life has evolved and differentiated into the forms that live today. Only a very small proportion of all life forms that are known to have existed survive today. Many forms no longer living are seen in the fossil record. The sequence of these forms in the fossil record helps us to see the order in which life evolved.

The algae found in stromatolites (hardened mud layers) are more complex than are many other bacteria and microbes; therefore, the first life must have appeared somewhat earlier than 3.5 billion years ago. Many forms of life are known from rocks older than 600 million years, but they are mostly tiny and one-celled. During the Cambrian period (ca. 500–570 million years ago), nearly all the present groups of multicelled animals first appeared in the fossil record, but not all at once.

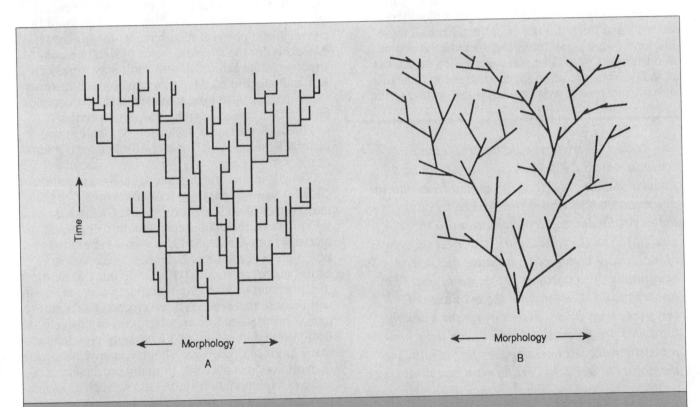

Figure 6. Punctuational evolution (left) contrasted with gradual evolution (right). In the gradual model, change is more or less regular and continuous, although rates of evolution may vary. In the punctuational model, most morphological change is concentrated at the speciation event, when new lineages split from existing ones. Species generally do not change much during their individual histories, compared to what happens at speciation. Note that the time scale has been greatly compressed; changes that seem instantaneous actually take thousands of years. Both punctuational and gradual models are consistent with Darwinian evolution, and each may fit different groups of organisms; their main difference is in the pace of evolutionary change.

Evolution is an ongoing process. There are many direct examples of quite recent natural selection (e.g., rapid evolution of genetic resistance to antibiotics by pathogenic bacteria, to insecticides by insects, and to herbicides by weeds), evolution of new species (Hawaiian moths and fruit flies), and new adaptations (e.g., British titmice have learned to pry the lids off milk bottles so that they can drink the cream).

B-3 How has life changed and diversified through time? What processes and patterns characterize the evolution of life?

Grades Six Through Nine

The earth is about 4.6 billion years old; the oldest rocks are some 4 billion years old; and life on earth is first known from rocks 3.5 billion years old. Plants, animals, and fungi did not exist then. Instead, these life forms were small, multichambered cells and tiny, thin filaments much like some one-celled organisms of today. They are often found arranged in thin beds of hardened mud layers (stromatolites) similar to the

The evolution of life should be presented to students not as a disconnected series but as a pattern of changing diversity united by evolutionary relationships and distinguished by changes in the environment and by adaptations to those changes. Nor is evolutionary history a sequence of increasing complexity, because this does not adequately or accurately define evolution. The history of life is not merely the evolution of complex forms from simpler ones; for example, parasites are generally simpler than their nonparasitic relatives because they frequently lose the ability to perform certain vital functions (such as digestion and locomotion) that their hosts now provide for them. One-celled and other simple organisms persist because they fit viable evolutionary niches. Although multicellular organisms evolved from simple one-celled ones, it is misleading to portray evolutionary history as a drive toward increasing complexity.

subtidal algal mats of today. (See Chapter 4, Section B, Geology and Natural Resources.) [Evolution]

Scientific theories about the origin of life are based on an understanding of what conditions were like on earth billions of years ago. The earliest rocks tell us what the earth, its waters, and its atmosphere were like at that time, as far as can be known. Scientists combine this information with what is known of the chemical and physical requirements for life today, especially for the simplest forms of life, to reconstruct what the earliest life on earth may have been like and how life may have first evolved. Experimental evidence is also used to understand how complex biochemical molecules may have first been assembled. (See Chapter 4, Section B, Geology and Natural Resources.) [Evolution, Systems and Interactions]

Changes in the genetic material DNA are responsible for new variations in individual organisms that may be passed on to their offspring. Changes occur in several ways, including recombination of genetic material from parents and mutations. Natural selection is an explanation of how these variations may contribute to the survival of an individual to the age of reproduction. Attaining reproductive age is important because that is when these characteristics can be passed on. Natural selection has been extensively demonstrated in natural and laboratory populations of many kinds of organisms. Though an important factor in evolution, it is only one of many processes contributing to evolutionary history. Others, such as adaptation, speciation, extinction, and chance events, are also of primary importance.

Natural selection and adaptation are different concepts. Natural selection refers to the process by which organisms whose biological characteristics better fit them to their environment are better represented genetically in future generations. With time, those that are more poorly fitted would normally become less well represented. Adaptation is the process by which organisms respond to the challenges of their environments through natural selection with changes and variations in their form and behavior. [Evolution, Patterns of Change, Systems and Interactions]

Evolution, defined as "descent with modification," is the central organizing principle in life science. It gives us a basis of comparison when we study anatomy, structure, adaptation, and ecology. Homology provides the vehicle of comparison. Homologous features are those that are inherited from the common ancestors of organisms (e.g., the forelimbs of fishes, birds, horses, and humans are homologous, because they have been inherited from a common ancestor, even though they are very different in their structure and function). Thus, homologies are defined by ancestry; the criteria used to recognize homologies of structure include the position of the structure (topology), its composition (histology), its development from the initial cell stages, and its biochemical makeup. Independent lines of evidence from anatomical, molecular, and genetic material; development; and the fossil record enable us to establish homologies, which we use to reconstruct the relationships of organisms. Classification is based on evolutionary relationships, not on any arbitrary criteria or on vague notions of similarity. (See Section A, Living Things.) [Evolution, Patterns of Change, Systems and Interactions, Scale and Structure]

Although most changes in organisms occur in small steps over a long period of time, some major biological changes have taken place during relatively short intervals and at certain points in the earth's history. These include the evolution, diversification, and extinction of much fossil life. [Evolution]

Extinction has been an inevitable biological process since life began. Over 99 percent of all the organisms that ever lived are now extinct. Extinction, therefore, is a natural process. But humans have also caused or contributed to the extinction of many forms of life and continue to contribute to a rate that is much higher than at any previous time in human history. Extinction can stimulate further evolution by opening resource space. (See Section C, Ecosystems.)

B-3   How has life changed and diversified through time? What processes and patterns characterize the evolution of life?

Grades Nine Through Twelve

The earliest known organisms on earth are known from coccoid and filamentous structures similar to those of living cyanobacteria. They are associated with lithified algal mats known as stromatolites, preserved in rocks 3.5 billion years old in South Africa and Australia. Because cyanobacteria are metabolically more complex than other microbes (e.g., they photosynthesize), it is presumed that life originated on earth at a somewhat earlier time. (See Chapter 4, Section B, Geology and Natural Resources.) [Evolution]

Conditions on earth when life first evolved are inferred from the geochemistry of the earliest rocks. Earth's earliest oceans and atmosphere were much

Homology should be kept distinct from similarity. Homology implies descent from a common ancestor. Cytochrome C molecules in humans and horses are homologous. They are also similar; their sequences differ by only 11 percent. Consider two chains of ten nucleotides, with the sequences G-C-A-T-G-C-A-T-G-C and T-A-C-G-T-A-C-G-C-G. In each, there are two As, two Ts, three Gs, and three Cs, so the two sequences are identical in composition. But there is no similarity between them because none of the sites match when the two chains are laid end to end. By contrast, two other chains, C-A-T-G-C-A-T-G-C-A and C-A-T-G-C-A-T-G-T-G, have identical nucleotides in their first eight positions, but different ones in the last two. So they are 80 percent similar. If the two sequences had a common evolutionary origin, they would also be homologous in addition to being similar. If, however, they did not have a common origin, they would be similar but not homologous.

Evolution is both a pattern and a process. It is also both a fact and a theory. It is a scientific fact that organisms have evolved through time. The mechanisms, patterns, and processes by which this evolution has occurred constitute the theory of evolution. Like gravitation and electricity, evolution explains a large range of observations and hypotheses about the natural world. (See Chapter 1, "The Nature of Science.") As more detailed understanding increases, the theory of evolution itself evolves.

different from what they are today. Available evidence does not clearly favor a single theory of how life first evolved. Current theories explore several possible mechanisms, but knowledge of these is very incomplete. Experiments attempting to synthesize complex biochemical molecules have provided considerable insight into what conditions were necessary for the earliest life to evolve. (See Chapter 4, Section B, Geology and Natural Resources.) [Evolution]

Chemical evolution refers to the assembly of more complex organic molecules from simpler ones, given

Structural constraints, inherited by organisms from their ancestors, are surmounted in interesting ways as new adaptations evolve. One example is the "thumb" that the giant panda uses to strip bamboo leaves (this is not a thumb at all, but a modified wrist bone). Unknown adaptive or developmental constraints prevented the modification of the true thumb, perhaps; but even more interesting, the panda's foot has grown a similar "thumb" from an ankle bone, even though the foot is not used to strip bamboo leaves. Evidently the same genetic mechanism controls the development of the first digit on both the hand and foot, even though natural selection is working only on the function of the panda's thumb. This shows the interaction of genetics with development that contributes to the evolutionary process. (This and other interesting evolutionary examples are explained in The Panda's Thumb *by Stephen Jay Gould.)*

appropriate materials, environmental conditions, and input energy. These complex molecules are part of biotic compounds. Chemical evolution differs from organic evolution, which is change in life forms by self-replication (or as Darwin put it, "descent with modification"). Chemical evolution entails no self-replication and no inheritance.

Evolution explains why biological patterns in structure, function, biochemistry, and genetics show the same recurring themes of relationship. It also forms the basis for the establishment of homology, which is studied through the criteria of topology, histology, ontogeny, and so forth. Evolution unites genetics and molecular biology with earth history and the physical sciences by showing the continuity of change and the records of these changes in the rocks and in the structural and biochemical compositions of all organisms. [Evolution, Patterns of Change, Systems and Interactions, Scale and Structure]

The sequence established from cladograms (see Section A, Living Things) can be compared with the independent sequences of appearance of organisms and their characteristics in the fossil record. It can also be compared to the patterns of many biochemical compounds, including the genetic material, DNA and RNA. Evolutionary relationships are thus understood through a combination of independent lines of evidence, including anatomical, genetic, and biochemical data, ontogeny, and the fossil record. Organisms are classified according to these evolutionary relationships. [Evolution, Patterns of Change, Systems and Interactions]

Genetic mutations and recombinations are two of the most important causes of the variations that form the raw material for evolutionary change. Others include errors in copying DNA, duplication and rearrangement of chromosomes, and addition and deletion of genetic material. These variations are expressed in the phenotype as evolutionary novelties, and they provide the material on which natural selection can act. Natural selection can work on variations in any characteristics at any time in an individual's development. Through geologic time, adaptation to environmental factors has been a central theme in the evolution of life. Many fossil lineages show the evolution of adaptations for feeding, locomotion, reproduction, and coping with environmental conditions. Because environmental conditions change over geologic time, populations of organisms must have sufficient variation and plasticity to meet these challenges or become extinct. Few evolutionary strategies are guaranteed success, and these cannot be predicted in advance. [Evolution]

Not all evolution is adaptive, and organisms cannot simply invent the characteristics that would serve them well in particular circumstances. Evolution is limited by the possibilities for genetic and behavioral change because organisms can use only the genetic and structural tools handed down by their ancestors. Even so, living things have great potential to be modified by natural selection to meet environmental needs (e.g., the evolution of beak shapes in the small group of Darwin's finches). [Evolution, Systems and Interactions, Scale and Structure]

The fossil record documents the appearance, diversification, and extinction of many life forms in relation to environmental regimes and changes through earth history. (See Section C, Ecosystems, and Chapter 4, Section B, Geology and Natural Resources.) The sequence of life through time is known from the geologic ranges of major groups of living things. Tectonic events, including mountain building and continental drift, and climatic patterns that result from these processes contribute to the separation and diversification of species over time, such as the present geographic restriction of the Coast redwood.

Evolution, both a pattern and a process, has many component patterns and processes, such as speciation, natural selection, adaptation, and so forth. The processes of evolution are studied at the species, population, genetic, and molecular levels; all contribute information that explains the diversity and unity of life. Rates of evolution vary, both among different groups of organisms and through geologic time.

Extinction is a natural part of life that has played an important role in evolutionary history. Extinction consists of two modes: (1) a background of ordinary extinctions of species; and (2) occasional events of

Understanding the history of life requires a knowledge of the geologic timetable (see Chapter 3, Section B, Geology and Natural Resources), including the ranges of some major groups of organisms and significant events in the history of life. These events include the emergence of important adaptations and groups of organisms, as well as evolutionary radiations and mass extinctions. The evolutionary and fossil histories of a few representative groups should be presented in life science curricula in detail, so that students can have a concrete appreciation for the data of the fossil record, the geologic column, and the methodology of phylogenetic reconstruction.

mass extinction caused by some kind of biotic or physical crisis. In earth history, mass extinctions have often been caused by regressions and transgressions of oceans, continental drift, and other geologic processes; and perhaps by external agents such as extraterrestrial objects and processes. Explanations of extinction must take into account both the extinct and the survivors. (For example, any explanation of dinosaur extinction at the end of the Cretaceous period must explain why other forms of life survived; see Chapter 4, Section B, Geology and Natural Resources.) Extinctions from the end of the Pleistocene Ice Age are still occurring, while others are caused or hastened by the activities of humans. [Evolution, Patterns of Change]

The science of biology has made great progress in the last ten years and has uncovered fundamental new concepts. Molecular biology has become one of biology's major themes; molecular biologists are exploring new horizons not dreamed of a decade ago. Accompanying these new insights is an expanding biotechnology which is raising scientific and ethical questions in medicine, agriculture, and law while at the same time forecasting far-reaching social and economic benefits for the state, the nation, and the world.

These new scientific and ethical questions are forcing a reevaluation of public policy in science and technology, the health care industry, medical research, agriculture, and, most important, in public education. Unfortunately, high school classrooms have not similarly expanded their horizons in science and its ethical concerns and are falling further and further behind the times.

As a consequence of the rapid development in molecular biology and its technologies, the gulf between scientific advance and public understanding is widening. In a 1986 study for the National Science Foundation, Jon D. Miller found that 57 percent of the American people had little or no understanding of DNA, the molecular biologists' lamp of knowledge and target of technological manipulation.[1]

For a participating democracy to succeed and flourish, an informed public in which citizens make knowledgeable decisions on technological issues is necessary. Students and teachers must have both a firm understanding of the sciences and an ethical framework for applying these ideas in a technological society. Failure to emphasize both science and ethics in the biology curriculum means, in the final analysis, failure to fulfill teaching's most important function: to prepare citizens capable of informed decision making in both the personal and public arenas.

For example, genetic engineering of bacterial DNA enabled medical researchers to mass-produce the chemical interferon, which is produced by human cells as a natural defense to viral pathogens. Prior to this biotechnological breakthrough, the interferon supply was extremely limited and very costly, over $10,000 per milligram. Mass production decreased costs, allowing widespread distribution to many more cancer patients. Although interferon's overall effectiveness was less than hoped for, many thousands of cancer patients went into remission after taking it.

Section C   Ecosystems

Ecological theory is concerned with the study of natural systems. The balance of nature is in fact a shifting balance in which nothing is constant but change. A human lifetime sees only glimpses of the vast scale of this change. There are many patterns: seasonal, reproductive, and populational cycles; migrations in and out of populations (which themselves wink in and out of existence); and extinctions.

The study of ecosystems has a dual purpose: (1) to achieve a basic understanding of natural ecosystems and how they work; and (2) to apply this understanding to making practical and ethical decisions about ecosystems, often referred to as the science of conservation. Conservation of resources does not assume that ecosystems do not change; the object is to ensure that human intervention in ecosystems does not change them so rapidly or radically that their species and ecological interactions are destroyed. Our children face a global crisis in conservation of natural resources. We are only beginning to understand its depth and ramifications for the earth's food supply, atmosphere, water cycle, and biological diversity. Communicating this awareness to students involves both the fundamental aspects of ecological theory and the applied theory of conservation biology in both ethical and practical aspects.

C-1 **What are ecosystems, and how do organisms interact in ecosystems?**

C-2 **How does energy flow within an ecosystem?**

C-3 **How do ecosystems change?**

C-4 **What are the responsibilities of humans toward ecosystems?**

C-1

What are ecosystems, and how do organisms interact in ecosystems?

Kindergarten Through Grade Three

Living things need resources from their environments in order to sustain life and help them grow. They need food, water, and space to live and grow. Living things live in particular kinds of environments, because these are where they find the things and the conditions that they need to survive. Cycles, such as the water cycle, are characteristics of environments that support life. [Scale and Structure, Systems and Interactions, Patterns of Change]

[1]Jon D. Miller, "Scientific Literacy Among American Adults." Address given at the Forum on Scientific Literacy held by the American Association for the Advancement of Science, Arlington, Virginia, October 6-7, 1989.

Some living things, such as algae and plants, produce their own food. Most others, including all animals, get food by eating or ingesting other living things. [Systems and Interactions, Energy]

Living things interact with other living things in many ways, depending on each other for food, shelter, and mutually advantageous purposes such as social groupings. The same kinds of living things often live together in groups. Usually, several different groups of interdependent living things live with or near each other. [Systems and Interactions]

C-1   What are ecosystems, and how do organisms interact in ecosystems?

Grades Three Through Six

All living things interact with each other and with the physical environment. All organisms are part of their environments; they need things from their environments that enable them to survive and grow. All organisms are influenced by environmental forces, and each organism also influences its environment to some extent. Interactions among organisms may have helpful, harmful, or neutral effects on the organisms involved. [Systems and Interactions]

All organisms have roles in their environments. They eat other species, often serve as food for other species, and may shelter (trees) or decompose (fungi) other species. Some organisms fill more than one role. [Systems and Interactions]

C-1   What are ecosystems, and how do organisms interact in ecosystems?

Grades Six Through Nine

Populations are groups of the same kind of organism (species) living together because they share common environmental needs. A population is also a natural reproductive unit. [Systems and Interactions]

Species are groups of populations of the same kind of organism, reproductively isolated from other species in their natural environments. (This definition has some exceptions, notably for many plant species, which hybridize freely in nature.) Each species has its own niche, which is the sum of its interactions with other species and with its physical environment. [Systems and Interactions, Scale and Structure]

A community is a system of species that share an environment and interact with each other. Ecosystems vary according to the physical characteristics of their environments and also by the presence or absence of particular species. Each species has particular needs and interacts in particular ways with other species in the environment. [Systems and Interactions]

Predation and competition are important regulators of populations within ecosystems, and their effects have been demonstrated in living ecosystems. However, the ability to survive within the physical environment may be the most difficult task faced by most organisms and may be the prime factor underlying both adaptation and extinction. [Systems and Interactions, Energy]

The environment of a species consists of both physical and organic resources that can be exploited and used by it and other species. There are many kinds of adaptive zones in biomes (e.g., carnivorous or herbivorous, flying or swimming, moth-pollinated or wind-pollinated). Organisms have adaptations for coping with their environments and surviving to reproduce. Some animal species live in social groups, which enhances their ability to survive. Many biological processes, such as mating and food gathering, depend for their success on a certain population size or size range. [Evolution, Systems and Interactions]

The earth supports an incredible diversity of habitats that have different kinds of physical properties and different associations of organisms. In each habitat the interaction of predation, competition, and so forth and the flow of energy through organisms in the system can be studied and compared with those of other ecosystems. [Energy, Scale and Structure, Systems and Interactions]

C-1   What are ecosystems, and how do organisms interact in ecosystems?

Grades Nine Through Twelve

The physicochemical conditions (temperature, moisture, chemical cycles) of an environment limit the biomes that can exist there. Among the biotic factors contributing to the structure of biomes, interactions relating to the acquisition of food (predation, photosynthesis, and so forth) and competition for available resources are important. Many different organisms may exploit resource zones (e.g., the coral reef environment) and may occupy the same adaptive zones (e.g., flight and insectivory in birds and bats), but the niche is a characteristic peculiar to individual species.

Ecosystems are frequently described by ecologists as systems in which organisms compete for finite resources in the environment. In many cases, resources used by one species are not available for use by other species (e.g., sunlight intercepted by upper canopy trees in a forest). In other cases, resources may appear to be incompletely exploited for reasons not connected with competition (e.g., despite the vast potential for exploitation of grasslands by herbivorous mammals and insects, plant life flourishes and appears to be undergrazed). A change in one part of an ecosystem may have far-reaching consequences for other parts of the ecosystem. [Systems and Interactions]

C-2

How does energy flow within an ecosystem?

Kindergarten Through Grade Three

Living things must gain energy from their environment, either by converting it from sunlight (algae and plants) or by eating other organisms or organic matter. Animals may eat plants, other animals, or decomposing organic material in order to gain energy.

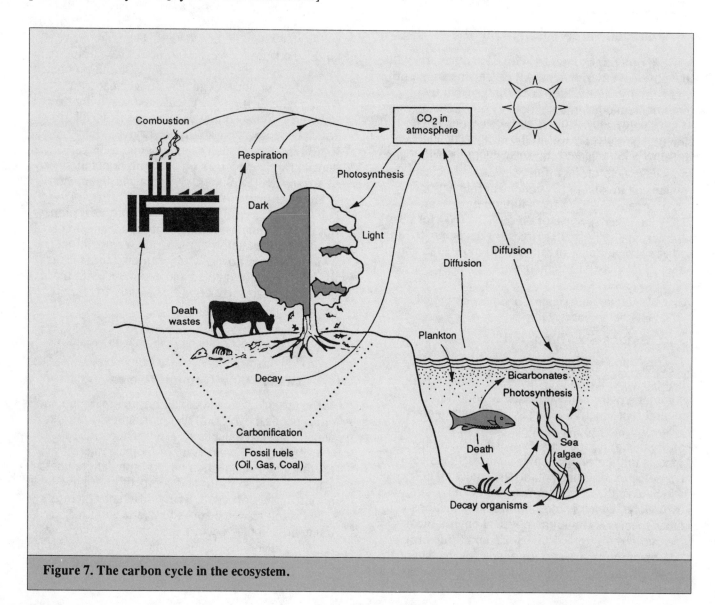

Figure 7. The carbon cycle in the ecosystem.

C-2　How does energy flow within an ecosystem?

Grades Three Through Six

Green plants are the foundation of the energy flow in most ecosystems because they produce their own food, using sunlight, water, air, and minerals from their environments. Animals eat the plants and in turn are often eaten by other animals. Food chains and food webs describe the systems of energy flow through ecosystems. Energy is transferred upward by predation through the levels of food chains and food webs and back down to the base of the food chain when organisms die and are decomposed. Nutrients are recycled as living things die and decompose.

C-2　How does energy flow within an ecosystem?

Grades Six Through Nine

Energy and matter are transferred among organisms within each ecosystem. Matter needed to sustain life is cycled and recycled within ecosystems; however, energy is eventually lost to the ecosystem and must constantly be renewed. Because energy is either used by the consumer or lost to the environment as heat energy, its flow through a food chain can be represented as a pyramid. The efficiency of energy transfer decreases upward through food chains and food webs. [Patterns of Change, Systems and Interactions]

The structure of ecosystems varies, as food chains and food webs differ in complexity. Not all biomes have secondary carnivores or even any carnivores at all. Decomposers use organic material from producers, herbivores, and carnivores, and themselves decompose. Matter and energy are thus partly recycled in the environment. [Energy, Scale and Structure, Systems and Interactions]

C-2　How does energy flow within an ecosystem?

Grades Nine Through Twelve

Organisms are adaptable, dynamic systems that continually exchange energy with their environments. Matter needed to sustain life in an ecosystem is cycled and reused. Some of the cycles are the carbon cycle, the nitrogen cycle, the water cycle, and various mineral cycles. The presence of various species in ecosystems is largely limited by these cycles. [Patterns of Change]

The biomass production of ecosystems is generally higher nearer the equator than it is toward the poles. This is because more sunlight allows greater plant productivity, which in turn permits more complex food chains and food webs. [Energy, Systems and Interactions]

Through the absence or extinction of species, food chains and webs may become simpler, and energy flow may change through an ecosystem. The proliferation of species makes food webs more complex and also affects the flow of energy. [Energy, Systems and Interactions]

Ecosystems are often characterized as being in equilibrium. This concept is invalid with respect to the flow of energy, which is only inefficiently used by consuming organisms. It is valid with respect to the cyclical flow of nutrients through trophic levels of an ecosystem, because there is a more or less constant amount of matter available for cycling through ecosystems. [Energy, Stability, Systems and Interactions]

C-3

How do ecosystems change?

Kindergarten Through Grade Three

As seasons change, living things also change. Each species has its own life cycle. Events in its life cycle are matched with particular events in its surroundings (e.g., winter dormancy, the fall of leaves, the daily cycle of opening and closing of many flowers, mating seasons). [Patterns of Change]

Ecosystems have changed through time as the living things in them have also changed. New kinds of organisms have appeared, and others have become extinct. In this way ecosystems have changed through time. Recently, changes in ecosystems have been caused or accelerated by human intervention. Some of these changes have been destructive to ecosystems, causing the extinction of species and the disappearance of their natural habitats. [Systems and Interactions]

C-3　How do ecosystems change?

Grades Three Through Six

Ecosystems and the organisms in them change with daily, seasonal, and annual cycles of environmental

Global change has also occurred in the past. Humans, for example, have caused extensive waves of habitat simplification and deterioration in Europe, the Middle East, and the Mediterranean and have caused massive extinctions of species in New Zealand, Hawaii, and other places.

change. Organisms have their own cycles of life, from birth to death, and also cycles of growth, feeding, and reproduction. [Patterns of Change]

Changes in one part of an ecosystem (such as the introduction of a new predator or the extinction of a producer species) affect other parts of the ecosystem. Populations naturally increase and decrease according to changes in the food chain, particularly changes related to available resources. [Systems and Interactions, Patterns of Change]

Changes in the physical environment of an ecosystem, such as moisture and temperature, can drastically affect the entire system. Some of these changes, such as El Niño, are a natural part of the environment; other changes, such as depletion of the ozone layer, are caused or accelerated by humans. These changes are frequently detrimental and have far-reaching consequences.

In an ecosystem species move in and out, die, and evolve to adapt to changing conditions. Change through time is a natural process of ecosystems, but in the recent past humans have quickened this change by overfarming, overhunting, and clear-cutting habitats for human use. As a result, many species have been wiped out, and others are threatened. [Evolution]

The diversity of species at the lower levels of food pyramids generally determines the diversity and complexity of interactions at higher levels. For example, an ecosystem with few green plants may have a limited number of herbivorous predators.

C-3   How do ecosystems change?

Grades Six Through Nine

The cycles of matter, such as oxygen, nitrogen, water, and minerals, are crucial to sustaining ecosystems. [Patterns of Change, Energy, Systems and Interactions]

Relationships among species also change through time. Examples are the evolution of parasitic systems (parasite and host), mutualistic systems, and com-

mensal systems. Habits such as browsing, grazing, carnivory, and herbivory have evolved many times over. For example, herbivorous dinosaurs evolved from carnivorous ones, and the diet of bears ranges from entirely carnivorous (polar bear) to omnivorous (black bear) to herbivorous (giant pandas).

Populations may stabilize over a period of time in a balanced ecosystem, where relationships among species are in a dynamic stability. Ecosystems are dynamic, and they change through time as climate and species compositions change. Speciation, extinction, immigration, and emigration are four ways in which the species composition of ecosystems can change. These changes affect the availability of sources of food and other resources (e.g., trees for shelter), and they also affect the flow of energy through ecosystems. Ecosystems have changed through time as new species and adaptations have evolved and others have disappeared. (For example, dinosaurs and giant horsetaillike trees once were the dominant land plant and animal species, but now hoofed mammals and flowering plants occupy the similar environments of today.) Recently, humans have accelerated the rates of extinction of species and also the rates of emigration of species from their natural habitats, but the rates of speciation have not increased to keep up with the very high rate of destruction of species due largely to human intervention. [Evolution]

Natural catastrophic changes in ecosystems (e.g., fire, hurricanes) can wipe out many species in an area and reset natural cycles of succession (e.g., from grasslands to shrublands to low forest to high-canopy forest; or underwater storms that can bury sedentary organisms and open an area to new colonization). Not all ecosystems have a single inevitable sequence of succession. Fire and other catastrophic agents are a natural part of most ecosystems. [Patterns of Change, Evolution, Stability]

Changes in the environment can affect the size of a population, which may lead to its local or global extinction. Species must be sufficiently adaptable to absorb these changes and respond to them. Optimal population size helps to ensure variations in the organisms necessary for the population to survive. [Systems and Interactions; Stability]

C-3   How do ecosystems change?

Grades Nine Through Twelve

Because of the intricate relationships that exist among species in a community and because of abiotic features of the biome, a change in one part of the ecosystem may have far-reaching consequences to the system. These changes are difficult to predict and to control. For example, the introduction of a pike into a South American lake or of rabbits into the Australian outback may have very detrimental consequences on the local natural flora and fauna. [Systems and Interactions, Evolution]

Various periodic cycles of organisms in an ecosystem, as well as cycles of nutrients and other necessary materials, are important controls on the diversity of ecosystems through time. Quite frequently, ecosystems have a carrying capacity for each species that they can sustain. When these conditions are exceeded, overpopulation can lead to depletion of resources, and local extinction can result. [Patterns of Change, Systems and Interactions]

Species diversity (the number of species in an ecosystem) and species richness (relative numbers of individuals of various species) are both important components of diversity and how it changes through time. Organisms tend to be dispersed through their environment according to the availability of crucial resources, which fluctuate seasonally and annually. [Evolution]

Succession is a predominant but not universal pattern of ecosystems; the dynamic stability of species composition in ecosystems is maintained by local biotic and abiotic conditions. Fire, disease, storms, and prolonged extremes in weather conditions are all natural features of ecosystems that constantly reset ecological conditions and contribute to the dynamic flux of biomes. [Evolution, Stability, Patterns of Change]

Ecological relationships among species change through time, as species evolve, become extinct, immigrate, and emigrate. This affects the flow of energy and of nutrients through the ecosystem. Some important ecological changes (such as the evolution of grasslands) open new resource zones (e.g., food for herbivorous mammals), promote the evolution of new

adaptations (e.g., grazing dentition from browsing), and create opportunities for the diversification of species (e.g., horses and other herbivores that moved from wooded to open environments in the early Tertiary period). The introduction of predators or competitors, long-term and short-term changes in climate, and environmental catastrophes are all chance factors that shape the history of ecosystems. [Energy, Evolution]

C-4

What are the responsibilities of humans toward ecosystems?

Kindergarten Through Grade Three

Human practices can often affect the well-being of other species in the environment. Humans should respect living things and foster their survival. Because we depend on other species for food, clothing, shelter, and other needs and will continue to do so, it is important for humans to respect nature and conserve natural habitats, resources, and species.

C-4   What are the responsibilities of humans toward ecosystems?

Grades Three Through Six

Waste disposal, the use of land (particularly the elimination of feeding and breeding grounds of many species), imprudent collecting, pest control, hunting

---

The current attention to tropical deforestation, acid rain, ozone layer depletion, and the greenhouse effect is not a mere fad; these processes are evidence of the stresses that human activities place on the global ecosystem. Such problems will increase in number and degree well into the next century. Instructional materials in science must address these issues in an integrated way— not as isolated symptoms but as facets of the same overarching issue. In some areas, humans have surpassed the carrying capacity of their regions, which has caused widespread famine and further deterioration of atmospheric, oceanic, and ecological systems.

---

practices, and the destruction of natural habitats through human-caused disasters have contributed to the extinction of species and to the loss of their natural geographic and ecological ranges and have threatened or destroyed ecosystems.

C-4   What are the responsibilities of humans toward ecosystems?

Grades Six Through Nine

Ecosystems often exist in a fragile balance. The extinction of a species by human contribution often affects the well-being of the ecosystem. Pollution, which can be defined as an unnatural excess of (usually) abnormal materials in an ecosystem, is a primary human cause of local extinction. The destruction of natural habitats, such as the tropical rain forest, and the elimination of necessary resources, such as breeding grounds turned into areas for recreation, agriculture, or housing, are the primary contributions by humans to the destruction of other species. With careful planning, humans can manage ecosystems to preserve their diversity and natural beauty, while allowing human use.

C-4   What are the responsibilities of humans toward ecosystems?

Grades Nine Through Twelve

Land use, pollution, energy use, and application of technology all involve ethical considerations for individuals and society. Conservation is not simply an ethical question; it is in the vested self-interest of humans to conserve and respect nature. Understanding life cycles, predator-prey relationships, metabolism of organisms, and other biotic and abiotic interactions makes it possible for humans to contribute to the well-being of species in natural ecosystems. The control or eradication of populations of destructive or disease-causing organisms is also made possible. Such activity always has some effects on the rest of the ecosystem. (See further discussion in Chapter 1, The Nature of Science.)

Humans are unique among the earth's organisms in their intelligence and adaptability. Humans can choose to change their behavior and plan to provide for the needs of future generations. These considerations extend beyond those of energy sources, minerals, and agriculture to areas of natural beauty and recreation and diverse floras and faunas of the world. [Systems and Interactions, Evolution]

Pollution comes in many forms: the introduction of unnatural substances into an ecosystem; an excess of natural substances; or the acceleration of nutrient flow through an ecosystem, bypassing natural processes and patterns (e.g., eutrophication of ponds and lakes). In addition, visual, auditory, and thermal pollution not only detract from human appreciation of natural ecosystems but also affect adversely other organisms living in them.

The environmental impacts of unregulated deforestation have serious global consequences and are often devastatingly irreversible. Deforestation is the permanent removal of forest and undergrowth. In the late 1980s, thousands of acres of virgin tropical rain forest were burned every day in order to clear land for grazing and crop production. Forest acreage equivalent to the entire state of Maine was destroyed every year. This massive combustion of carbonaceous material released enormous amounts of carbon dioxide into the atmosphere, thus exacerbating the greenhouse effect already created by petroleum-consuming countries.

Given the rate of deforestation in Third World countries to obtain lumber and food, the forests in the southern hemisphere could all but disappear within the next few decades. In a study of the effects of deforestation on species diversity, coordinated by former President Jimmy Carter, scientists predicted that 20 to 30 percent of the world's species were in jeopardy. In Colombia devegetation rendered a hydroelectric generating plant completely useless because its reservoir filled with debris. To slow these disturbing trends of erosion, forest devastation, and species annihilation, American corporations have purchased acreage in the threatened forests of the Amazon basin and elsewhere. But additional intervention is vitally needed to prevent what might be an imminent global disaster.

Part III

Achieving the Desired Science Curriculum

Chapter 6

Science Processes and the Teaching of Science

THIS chapter explains the processes of science that form the core of science pedagogy: observing, communicating, comparing, ordering, categorizing, relating, inferring, and applying. As scientists use these processes in their everyday work, so science teaching should center instruction, particularly hands-on instruction, on these fundamental processes. Expository instructional materials should show how scientists actually use these processes in their work. This chapter also considers the values and ethics of science that should be taught to students, the role of science and technology in society, and guidelines for constructing the best possible science curricula in elementary, middle, and secondary schools. Of particular importance are the efforts necessary to reach the historically underrepresented or disenfranchised students, including those for whom considerations of gender, ethnic and cultural backgrounds, and physical disabilities are of primary importance.

This chapter opens with a recapitulation and elaboration of the thinking processes formalized in the 1984 *Science Framework Addendum*. These mental functions are referred to as processes, not skills. This convention helps to avoid the educational connotation that skills imply routine, low-level procedures. The term *thinking skills* has unfortunately become an oxymoron; however, the term *processes* suggests the dynamic, higher-level effort required in thinking scientifically.

Much of Section A is devoted to building thinking processes based on prior experience; Section C tells how to develop science concepts for students. Sec-

tions D and E consider hands-on science learning and the role of ethics and values in science classes. Section E treats the need for showing the interrelationships of science and technology to society.

This chapter is oriented toward helping students build their understanding of the natural world and helping them understand its connection to our technologically advanced society. It also advocates a student-centered science program created by teachers who are free to design the types of experience that best fit their students.

Section A	Scientific Thinking Processes

SCIENCE is an active enterprise, made so by our human capacity to think. Scientific knowledge grows as scientists think about the natural world, act on that knowledge in planned ways, and then develop thoughtful explanations of the results. The knowledge of science is its *content*. There is continual dynamic interaction between the content of science and the *thinking processes* that characterize the scientific enterprise.

The content of science consists of a highly structured, complex set of facts, hypotheses, and theories in a context where many observations have meaning. Theory development is progressive; theory suggests further observations that often make possible further elaboration and testing of the theory.

Scientists use their senses and extensions of their senses to see, touch, and otherwise view the world, *observing* its characteristics and behaviors as objectively as possible. Scientists describe and picture what they observe in various ways, thus *communicating* their ideas to others so that they can exchange views and interpretations and pass along information. They test what they know against what they do not yet know, *comparing* features and behaviors for similarities and differences. Scientists organize their understandings, *ordering* and *categorizing* them into broader, more general groupings and classifications. They study the interactions among objects and describe the events, *relating* factors that reveal deeper insights into causes and effects. Scientists hypothesize and predict what will happen based on accumulated knowledge and on the events they expect to take place, *inferring* something that they have not seen because it has not yet happened or because it cannot be observed directly. And as knowledge grows through the use of these scientific thinking processes, scientists develop expertise, *applying* both knowledge and processes for useful purposes, to make still further extensions of the explanatory power of theory and to perceive fresh possibilities.

OBSERVING

The scientific thinking process from which fundamental patterns of the world are constructed

The most fundamental of the scientific thinking processes is that of observing. Only through this process can we acquire information from our environment. Given objects to play with, the young child observes them by looking, touching, tasting, smelling,

Teacher's statements and questions that facilitate the process of **observing**:

- "Tell us what you see."
- "What does this feel like?"
- "Give us information about its shape and size."
- "What do you hear?"
- "Point out the properties that you observe."
- "What characteristics seem to be predominant?"
- "What properties can you find?"

and listening to them. These senses enable the child to construct a view of the world and how it works. In a similar but more structured manner, adults place a space probe on the surface of Mars to measure and record data. A mechanical hand touches the surface and crumbles the soil. Automated chemical "laboratories" analyze the material. Sensors "smell" the atmosphere. With each of these actions—the youngster's firsthand, sensory experiences and the adult's informed, inventive extensions of the senses—humans gather information as raw material for constructing fundamental knowledge.

Sometimes when we observe, we do not see very much. If we do not know how to look, we will not see anything of importance. Knowledge from prior observations enables us to extract more useful information from a new situation. For example, we might hear the songs of birds and recognize only that some

The capacity for deriving patterns is more highly developed in humans than in any other animal that we know about. Most organisms exist in a stimulus-response relationship with their environment. Birds respond to danger by acting in ways that have a high probability of helping them escape. Frogs sit motionless and unseeing until an insect passes by; then the frog thrusts its tongue toward the insect to take it in as food. Plant growth is stimulated by sunlight or inhibited by the lack of it. Humans learn about environments by realizing patterns within them and then act on the environment to adjust or change it to suit their purposes. They are playful pattern seekers when they daydream, doodle, or just enjoy an observation; and sometimes they are purposeful pattern seekers as when they try to complete a puzzle, make sense out of something, or resolve problems. Because of this pattern-seeking capability, humans can live successfully in virtually any environment on earth. No other species is able to do so. Although all of us by nature are pattern seekers, the scientist is an expert, well-practiced pattern seeker.

> *"The whole thinking process is still rather mysterious to us, but I believe that the attempt to make a thinking machine will help us greatly in finding out how we think ourselves."*
>
> —*Alan Turing*

birds are singing. Knowing more about the characteristics of bird sounds, another person might recognize three different types of birds singing—a sparrow, a robin, and a blue jay. Even without seeing the birds, this person has a richer view of the event. Still another person might recognize that one bird is giving a warning signal and another is giving an aggressive territorial call. This expert, using both hearing and prior knowledge, "observes" something much deeper about the event than the other two listeners.

The scientist, as observer, systematically gathers information of the world through direct and creative indirect use of the human senses. With an initial body of data, the scientist refines information by using other scientific thinking processes such as comparing, categorizing, and inferring, all in an attempt to understand and explain what was observed.

As much as possible, the scientist adds a practical, trained objectivity to the process of observing. A fallen leaf is described in terms of its observable, verifiable properties—size, shape, tip, base, venation, serration, and so on. It is not described as diseased unless there is some evidential basis for doing so. Because of the importance of objectivity in the sciences, there has arisen, over the years, a myth that scientists are completely objective individuals who can remain independent of the information being gathered. The scientist is every bit as human as other people and is influenced by factors similar to those that influence anyone's objectivity. But prior experience and training are crucial factors. As noted, knowledge gained from prior experience can enable a person to "see" more in a situation. In schools, students bring with them a variety of previous experiences. Teachers can expect students to exhibit a wide range of observing behaviors, depending on the cultural background and values that each brings to, and imposes on, the objects and events that they are asked to observe. Teachers should encourage students to share their differing perspectives and welcome the diversity of the students' background.

Some students are highly influenced by what they anticipate the teacher wants them to observe. Other students may be influenced by what they feel are the expectations of their peer group. Being objective is difficult, yet scientists try to observe as objectively as is humanly possible.

Science activities that involve students in the process of observing provide them with a repertoire of concepts about size, shape, color, texture, and other observable properties of objects. As it grows, this repertoire enriches the student's ability to observe and apply concepts. This development is essential for the understanding of more complex and more abstract ideas in the sciences.

COMMUNICATING

The scientific thinking process that conveys ideas through social interchanges

Most animals are able to communicate in some way with other members of their own species, but humans, more than any other organism, are unique in the ability to create and use language and symbols that convey ideas in the present and preserve those ideas in order to communicate with others in the future.

Scientists communicate through published works, lectures, and conferences. The community of scientists in a given field, reading and studying each other's works, provides a check on the objectivity and accuracy of a scientist's work. Published research is replicated or extended by others interested in the

---

Teacher's statements and questions that facilitate the process of **communicating**:

- "What do you see?"
- "Draw a picture of what you see through the microscope."
- "Plot the data you gathered on a graph."
- "Make a histogram of the number of raisins in slices of raisin bread."
- "Write up your experiment so it can be replicated by someone else."
- "Summarize your findings and present them to the class."

---

topic. Inaccuracy or error in the work is quickly discovered.

A histogram, for example, communicates a distribution along a continuum, as in tallying the heights of youngsters in a classroom. A Cartesian graph communicates information that relates one factor to another, as in using the height of a burning candle as a function of time.

Language arts activities and mathematics, with their ways of depicting data, should not be separated from science instruction. The communication skills of one content area enhance the skills of the other.

COMPARING

The scientific thinking process that deals with concepts of similarities and differences

The process of comparing builds on the process of observing. Unfortunately, some people confuse the two: "Observe the similarities and differences between these two animals." What they mean to say is: "Compare the similarities and differences."

We can learn about the shape (or color, size, texture) of an object by comparing its shape to those of other objects. Objects are separated or put together on the basis of comparable differences or similarities. When we do this, we develop more complex concepts than with simple observations of these objects. For example, youngsters can conceptualize two distinct types of measurement involving length: (1) length as a property of an object; and (2) length as a linear distance between two objects or points.

To find out more about an unfamiliar natural phenomenon, scientists often compare it to something they know well. They learn more about the unknown—the ways in which it is similar and the ways in which it is different—from the known. All scientific measures (*length*, using rulers; *mass*, using balances; *temperature*, using thermometers; *volume*, using containers; *time*, using a stopwatch; and so forth) rely on the process of comparing an unknown to a known. Thus, when scientists use a ruler to measure an object, they are comparing the known length of the ruler to the unknown dimensions of the object. When they are finished, they know something about the object that was not known before (e.g., its length and width).

The scientist adds a dimension of objectivity to this process of comparing. While people often make

Teacher's statements and questions that facilitate the process of **comparing**:

- "How are these alike?"
- "How are these different?"
- "Compare these on the basis of similarities and differences."
- "Which is larger/smaller (softer/louder, smoother/rougher, wetter/drier)?"

broad, sweeping comparisons, scientists attempt to be exact in their comparisons. The reason is that theories and experiments have reached high levels of precision, and old standards of measures may be inadequate. For this reason the standard meter bar, kept in a temperature-controlled room in France and used until 1983 to calibrate secondary standards all over the world, was replaced by a combination of the exact known speed of light in vacuum and a very precise atomic clock. Today, one meter is the distance that a pulse of light travels (in a vacuum) in a specified time interval. Secondary standard bars are calibrated in terms of this fundamental distance. According to the theory of relativity, the speed of light in a vacuum is known to be exactly the same for all observers. Time is now measured by atoms rather than by the less uniform revolution of the earth.

ORDERING

The scientific thinking process that deals with patterns of sequence and seriation

Ordering is the process of putting objects or events in a linear format. As such, there are two kinds of ordering: *seriation* and *sequencing*.

When scientists use seriate objects or phenomena, they place them in order along a continuum—from small to large, rough to smooth, soft to loud, light to heavy, sharp to dull, dim to bright, and so on. The extremes are determined and ranges are established. Examining frequencies within ranges often reveals patterns that could not be seen by casual observations. For example, counting the number of peas in each pod in a sampling of pods is a way of determining the range of the number of seeds produced by pea plants. With a range established and appropriate units placed between them on a histogram, tallies for all the sample pods provide a frequency distribution within the range of the seeds produced. Looking at the distribution reveals information that could not be known by simply looking at peas in pods (e.g., the natural distribution curve indicates the most and least likely number of peas in pea pods).

Seriating objects can involve an almost limitless number of properties. Many are evident in scientific scales: windspeed scales (e.g., Beaufort's windspeed scale); temperature scales (Celsius, kelvin, Fahrenheit); elevation scales (below or above sea level); brightness scales (star magnitudes); tensile strength scales; decibel scales; and the electromagnetic spectrum. All of these scales were derived by serially ordering information along a continuum.

When events are ordered, they provide a sequence that tells a logical story. When scientists sequence events, they order them along a continuum of time—from earliest action to latest action, from the first moment to the last moment. Sequences often tell stories, usually of two types—either linear or cyclical.

Linear stories tell us about the growth and decay of a plant or animal, the motion of an object, or the cause and effect of an event. The ordered layers of sediments containing fossils tell a story of the history and evolution of life on earth. The order through which an insect passes through stages tells the story of the life cycle of an insect.

Cyclical stories tell us about recurring events. The water cycle is the story of how water comes to the earth as rain, snow, and so forth; rises into the atmosphere; and is returned again to the earth. A description of the seasons and the changes which occur through them is a cyclical story. The motions of the planets around the sun are repeating cyclical sequences.

CATEGORIZING

The scientific thinking process that deals with patterns of groups and classes

Categorizing is the process of putting objects or events together using a logical rationale. There are two kinds of categorizing: *grouping* and *classifying*.

When scientists categorize objects or ideas, they do so in order to compare and communicate information about them. Leaves, for example, can be grouped together on the basis of some commonality, such as type of venation, serration, tip, base, and so forth. A useful grouping is one that increases understanding of the individual items by recognizing a common characteristic among different items. Yellow flowers with five petals, for example, can be placed with all yellow flowers, regardless of the number of petals on them; they can be placed with different colored flowers that have only five petals, or they can be classified only with other yellow, five-petaled flowers. Through comparing different systems of classifications, scientists can recognize those that are most logically consistent, best reflect the history and pattern of nature, or best explain natural properties and relationships.

Conceptualization of principles and laws almost always follows a systematic compiling, ordering, and categorizing of data. Bodies of knowledge grow from long-term organizing processes. The botanist, for example, works with identified characteristics that have been compiled by many botanists for more than a century. By observing many different leaves, comparing them, and describing their characteristics, botanists have identified groupings useful in the identification and study of leaves.

Scientists in all fields—from chemistry, to physics, to astronomy, and so forth—use the categorizing process to group and classify the objects in their domain of work.

Young children generally develop in their ability to categorize by first sorting and grouping; that is, by putting items together on the basis of a single property (e.g., color: blues in one pile, reds in another, and yellows in a third pile). Experience is necessary for them to be able to put objects together on any given characteristic (e.g., the leaves pictured can be grouped on any one of the listed characteristics). As they grow older, gain experience, and develop more advanced cognitive capacities, youngsters begin to classify items, by putting them together on the basis of more than a single property at a time (e.g., rocks that contain iron and are volcanic might be grouped together on these two common characteristics and separated from rocks that contain iron but are sedimentary in origin, and rocks that are volcanic but do not contain iron).

RELATING

The scientific thinking process that deals with principles concerning interactions

Seeing relationships between and among things in our environment is quite different from comparing or categorizing objects on the basis of their characteristics. Relationships involve interactions, dependencies, and cause-and-effect events.

A zoologist might study lions and learn something about the characteristics of the animal, the environment in which it lives, and the animals it eats. But zoologists go beyond the characteristics by determining relationships among them. The lioness is the main food gatherer in a pride of lions (a characteristic of a pride). She sees only shades of gray, no colors (a characteristic of the carnivorous mammals). She sits in the tall grasses of the savannah, and through the grasses she watches her prey, the zebra, and decides when to make her move (a characteristic behavior of stalking carnivores). Zebras have black and white stripes (a characteristic of the zebra). The zoologist asks, "Is there a relationship between what the lioness sees through tall grasses and the zebra's coloration and stripe configuration?" The zebras travel in herds, placing sentinels at appropriate places in the herd to give warning of danger (characteristic behaviors of

Teacher's statements and questions that facilitate the process of **relating**:

- "What factors caused the event to take place?"
- "Explain why this is a good or inadequate experimental design."
- "State a hypothesis so that it is testable."
- "What is the relationship between the coloration of an animal, its environment, and its predators?"
- "Using this line graph, tell the relationship between distance and time."
- "Design a study to compare the evaporation rates of different liquids (e.g., alcohol and water)."

zebras). The zoologist wonders, "Is there a relationship between the coloration and its configuration and the behavior of traveling in herds?" To bring down a zebra, the lioness must pounce on its back near the shoulders, sink her fangs into its neck, then roll off, snapping the neck as she falls (a characteristic behavior of the lioness). The zoologist finds that the lioness accomplishes her task about once in every five tries. If she does not land properly near the shoulders, she is thrown from the zebra. The zoologist wonders, "Is there a relationship between her success rate and the behavior and coloration pattern of the zebras?" Clearly, the principles derived from this setting come about by using one's ability to recognize and comprehend relationships among several things—in this case, the behaviors and coloration of the predator and prey, and factors inherent in the environment. Scientists look for relationships among characteristics and behaviors in order to understand events that take place.

A physics student has a metal ball and a long, inclined grooved track. Having a way to measure the speed with which the ball reaches the bottom end of the track, the student wants to investigate the factors that influence the speed. First, fixing the angle of incline of the track and varying the starting point of the ball, the student fixes the starting point and varies the incline angle. The speed is measured each time. The student finds that the speed depends on both the starting point and the incline angle. But then the student discovers that a long roll along a gentle slope gives the same terminal speed as a shorter roll along a steeper slope, as long as the starting point has the same height in both cases. What really counts, then, is

We cannot experiment directly with galaxies, black holes, quasars, or quarks, but we still know a great deal about them. Scientific descriptions of relationships are always based on the logical arguments that encompass all the data on hand.

the height of the starting point. The direct dependence of speed on height and the less direct relationship between starting point or incline angle and speed establish a basis for understanding conservation of energy.

In the sciences, information about relationships can be descriptive (as in the lioness/zebra example) or experimental (as in the inclined plane example). Many ideas in astronomy are based on description. We cannot experiment directly with galaxies, black holes, quasars, or quarks, but we still know a great deal about them. Scientific descriptions of relationships are always based on the logical arguments that encompass all the data on hand.

Knowledge derived from experimentation requires that the scientist use the relating process through hypothesizing and controlling and manipulating variables. For example, a scientist might determine the factors that influence the rate of swing of a pendulum by isolating possible factors and testing them one at a time while holding all others constant. The scientist might consider only the variables of: (1) the weight attached to the pendulum, heavy and light; and (2) the length of the pendulum, long and short. The scientist might then set out the four combinations of possible variables: (1) heavy and long; (2) light and long; (3) heavy and short; and (4) light and short.

The ability to separate variables by exclusion (the systematic testing of each variable individually while all others are held constant in order to determine which are relevant and which have no effect) is very powerful. Instead of being closely bound to the immediate experience, the scientist thinks, "Maybe if I changed this, such and such would happen," and then performs the necessary actions to confirm or reject the supposition. What the scientist tests is a hypothesis—a reasoned description of relationships, stated so that it can be tested. The test is the scientist's deliberate and systematic manipulation of variables.

INFERRING

The scientific thinking process that deals with ideas that are remote in time and space

Inferences deal with matters that are often beyond the here and now. They are not experienced directly. The events of interest are distant in either time (such as the inferences paleontologists make about life on earth in the Paleozoic era), or space (such as are the inferences astronomers make about the origin of the universe), or scale (such as how electrons behave in atomic systems). They are established through inferential reasoning—logical conclusions made from a chain of reasoning or answers derived through reasoning from evidence and premises.

Long before we sent a probe to Mars, scientists made inferences about the planet. A century ago, the only data from which inferences could be made came from telescopic observations. Mars was described as the red planet with markings that some observers thought looked like canals. Because of the perceived canals, some inferences were made about life on Mars. More recent technology led to the detection of an atmosphere and the presence of water. And, among other things, it was inferred that Mars has or once had life on it. Today, our descriptions of Mars have become more complex and still more extensive inferences about the planet have been made. The inference about life on Mars has not yet been confirmed or rejected.

The establishment of preliminary inferences in a new context (e.g., Mars) from knowledge already obtained in another context (e.g., Earth), is one of the basic reasoning patterns humans use to understand remote places and events.

Teacher's statements and questions that facilitate the process of **inferring**:

- "What can you infer from these data?"
- "What arguments can you give to support your prediction?"
- "Explain how we know about quasars."
- "Under what conditions are we able to extrapolate or interpolate from data?"
- "How would you determine how many frogs live in a pond?"

Grade level	Science processes	Descriptions of content	Principles/Examples
K-3	1. Observing 2. Communicating 3. Comparing 4. Ordering 5. Categorizing	Focuses on one-word descriptions, discreet ideas	**Static-organizational principles** • Sea water is salty. Water in most lakes and rivers is not salty (definition by class). • Flowers produce seeds that grow into new plants (definition by function). • Machines are devices that make some tasks easier (definition by function).
3-6	1-5 above, plus 6. Relating	Focuses on principles, generalizations, laws	**Active-relational, interactive principles** • A force is a push or pull (relational). • Poikilothermic (cold-blooded) animals have body temperatures that vary with surrounding temperatures (relational). • Heat changes water from liquid into gas (interactive).
6-9	1-6 above, plus 7. Inferring	Focuses on ideas that are not directly observable	**Explanatory-predictive, theoretical principles** • Matter is composed of tiny particles that are in constant motion. In many substances these are called molecules (inference). • The characteristics of mineral crystals are the result of the way their atoms are bonded together in geometric patterns (inference). • When male and female sex cells combine in sexual reproduction, equal numbers of chromosomes from each parent determine the characteristics, including the sex, of the offspring (prediction).
9-12	1-7 above, plus 8. Applying	Focuses on inventions and technology; concepts, generalizations, principles, laws rephrased to suggest use and application	**Usable-applicational principles** • Selective breeding of plants and animals with desirable characteristics results in offspring which display these characteristics more frequently (application). • Use of the oceans and ocean resources is a focus of international conflict as well as international cooperation (application). • The development and use of more efficient lighting sources—fluorescent instead of incandescent, for example—is one way of conserving energy (invention; use).

Table 1 Matching Science Processes and Content with Children's Cognitive Development, Kindergarten Through Grade Twelve

Through evidence and reasoning, we can make inferences about the movement of continents. With those inferences and other inferences from observed phenomena, such as magnetic anomalies, we can develop a theory of plate tectonics. From inferences about events in the universe comes a big bang theory. We can make inferences about the shared characteristics of animals and plants and establish a hierarchical classification scheme that gives evidence of evolutionary relationships—a classification scheme of a higher conceptual order than one created only from observation. But inferences, no matter how orderly in their derivation, are never final; they must be tested to determine whether they are true. A valid test involves observations independent of those used to generate the inference.

Educators must be concerned with implications and valid inferences in science because inferences involve orderly, connected thinking. Using the inferring process, students learn that the conclusion of an argument is an explicit statement of something that is implicit in the premises. Its validity or consistency can be certified by logical considerations alone. To think well, students need experience in tracing their thoughts to the sources and then determining the truth of the source in order to judge its validity.

APPLYING

The scientific thinking process by which we use knowledge

The building of the Golden Gate Bridge in the San Francisco Bay Area was a spectacular accomplishment. It required hundreds of experts working cooperatively to put the bridge in place. Structural engineers who knew about expansion and contraction of metals planned how to construct components so that they would not warp during the heat of the day nor buckle during the cold of the night; the bridge needed to move by expansion and contraction without disrupting the movement of travelers. Geologists who knew about the local land formations and the placement of bedrock planned where and how to place the pilings on which the weight of the bridge was supported. Meteorologists who knew about the extremes of local weather conditions contributed the data needed to accommodate the sway of the bridge from winds in any direction. Building the bridge was a cooperative effort among experts who applied their knowledge to the task.

Teacher's statements and questions that facilitate the process of **applying**:

- "See who can invent a glider that will stay aloft the longest time."
- "Design a way to keep an ice cube on your desk all day without melting."
- "What political points of view must be considered if we are to protect the migration flight paths of birds over several countries?"
- "What factors must be weighed if experimentation on animals is to take place?"
- "How did different lines of evidence confirm a theory of continental drift?"

Applying is a process that puts extensive scientific knowledge to use. Sometimes that knowledge is used in a practical sense as in the building of a bridge. Sometimes it is used to tie together very complex data into a comprehensive framework or theory. And sometimes, the goal is to elaborate and extend the theory.

Each scientific field of endeavor produces new knowledge and understanding. Darwin organized many observations and formulated a theory that explained how living organisms change through time. Einstein showed how the physical world could be understood on the basis of relativity theory. Mendeleev logically ordered the more than 50 different elements known in his day. His first *Periodic Table of the Elements* clearly implied the existence of elements not yet identified, and he predicted their atomic weights and other important properties.

Section B   The Processes in the Context of Child Development

ALL the scientific thinking processes can be used to some extent by individuals of all ages. However, there are periods in child development in which particular processes have a higher payoff for learning, and there are periods when some processes seem to contribute little. For example, elementary school youngsters are superb at observing, communicating, comparing, ordering, and categorizing. However, although they can make simple inferences (If the ground is wet everywhere, it must have rained last night), major inferential ideas (structure of atoms, movements of planets and stars) and comprehensive theories (evolution, relativity) elude many of them. The major inferential ideas are best taught at the onset of adolescence or beyond. In view of these developmental stages, the parts of the scientific thinking processes are best introduced in a particular sequence, as Table 1 illustrates.

Kindergarten Through Grade Three

The most valuable processes for these grades are *observing, communicating, comparing, ordering,* and *categorizing.* Young students are still building a basic mental picture of the world in which they live, and they are quite adept at identifying the characteristics of objects, determining similarities and differences among objects and events, grouping items together that belong together on some rationale, and communicating to others about what they have done. Students readily recognize characteristics inherent in objects. This fundamental content matter becomes the basis for more advanced ideas. In general, the characteristics of objects in any scientific field of endeavor can be learned quickly and easily by youngsters at this age. Thus, the curriculum in kindergarten and grades one through three should emphasize the development of descriptive language through the first four scientific thinking processes across all fields of science.

Examples of content derived by using the processes for kindergarten through grade three:

- Insects have three body parts and six legs as adults.
- Leaves have identifiable characteristics: tips, bases, margins, veins, and shapes.
- Sounds can be classified on the basis of their characteristics: volume, pitch, quality.
- Light travels in all directions from a source.
- Motion can be a source of electricity.

Grades Three Through Six

In addition to the processes at which they are so adept in the earlier grades, youngsters begin to develop the process of *relating.* Using this process and building on the facts learned earlier, youngsters will derive many principles of science.

Examples of content derived by using the processes for grades three through six:

- Some plants have been naturally selected and retain camouflagic characteristics.
- Heat causes solids to expand.
- The motion of a particle is in a straight line unless acted on by external forces.
- Light can be diffracted or refracted.
- Current electricity travels through some materials better than others.
- Physical weathering can break rocks into smaller pieces.

Grades Six Through Nine

As youngsters move into adolescence, they become more able to make *inferences.* They think more about the future and understand more about the past. They can comprehend concepts that are not represented by objects and materials. If their earlier activities have provided them with appropriate experiences, they can hypothesize, design experiments, predict, and conceptualize the laws of science.

Examples of content derived by using the processes for grades six through nine:

- Evolution has been going on so long that it has produced all the groups and kinds of plants and animals now living, as well as others that have become extinct.
- Momentum is directly proportional to both mass and speed.
- Sound energy is thought of as vibrations that transfer energy in wavelike patterns through molecules.
- All matter is made up of atoms containing tiny particles that carry electric charge.

Grades Nine Through Twelve

As students reach the end of their basic schooling, the knowledge they have gained can be *applied* in various ways. They are able to read about and understand new development in the sciences; they comprehend the essence of theories, such as evolution, relativity, kinetic/molecular theory, and so on; they understand the issues related to scientific decision making; and they appreciate the value of scientific and technological endeavors and, depending on the endeavors, can build a reasoned case for supporting or not supporting them. As adults they can vote wisely on scientific issues, and they are flexible enough to adapt to new technologies and new ideas that take place in their lifetime. As future voters and members of an informed, literate public, they can apply their knowledge in making wise decisions.

Examples of content derived by using the processes for grades nine through twelve:

- Decision making about scientific endeavors (e.g., animal experimentation, expensive research endeavors, DNA alterations, genetic engineering) must be viewed from several perspectives at the same time (e.g., economic, political, ethical, environmental).
- Science alone cannot resolve the problems inherent in modern society (e.g., conservation, waste man-

agement, and pollution control), but it is an essential component of any such resolutions.
- Worldwide dialogue is needed concerning preservation of resources, wildlife, and so forth for the welfare of all humankind.

With the scientific thinking processes in place, appropriate content can follow. This arrangement provides an important way for content to progress through the grades. Repetitious instruction—topics taught in essentially the same way with the same purpose and content every few years—can be eliminated, and a foundation for advanced knowledge built which, in turn, provides the basis for still more advanced knowledge. The progressive introduction of processes and content through the grades moves students toward adult understanding of the important themes and content inherent in the sciences.

Example of a theme progressing through the grades:

EVOLUTION

Kindergarten Through Grade Three

The Processes: Observing, Communicating, Comparing, Ordering, Categorizing

Sample Content: Living things have identifiable characteristics; there is great diversity among living things.

Grades Three Through Six

The Processes: Observing, Communicating, Comparing, Ordering, Categorizing, plus Relating

Sample Content: Living things are adapted to their environment for survival; various structures of living things operate in ways that keep them alive and growing.

Grades Six Through Nine

The Processes: Observing, Communicating, Comparing, Ordering, Categorizing, Relating, plus Inferring

Sample Content: Evolution includes a process whereby living things are naturally selected from generation to generation, producing descendants with different characteristics; through geologic time, evolutionary processes have shaped the forms and adaptations of all the species of plants and animals now living, as well as others that have become extinct.

Grades Nine Through Twelve

The Processes: Observing, Communicating, Comparing, Ordering, Categorizing, Relating, Inferring, plus Applying

Sample Content: Worldwide agreements must be made for the preservation of resources and species. The characteristics of living things can be altered through manipulation of the DNA structure.

Section C Developing Science Concepts

CHILDREN create meaning for themselves; conceptualization is promoted and made more useful when presented in the context of an appropriate theoretical structure. Students construct representations of many types of knowledge, but these mental maps are especially powerful in the ways students learn (or fail to learn) science concepts. Teachers should consider what concepts students hold about science for at least three major reasons: (1) to ensure that all students learn science, they must have conceptually rich ideas with which to build new knowledge; (2) conceptions (and misconceptions) about the natural world are resistant to casual challenges unless new models are built; and (3) ultimately, students will be using whatever conceptual models they have to make sense of the world around them. The following recommendations will help teachers use students' background information as a springboard for learning new concepts:

1. **Pose questions to determine what ideas students hold about a topic before beginning instruction.**

   As a first priority, teachers are encouraged to elicit from students their prior knowledge about the subject of study. This procedure will give valuable information about students' readiness for a given idea, and it will also reveal what conceptions they have about the way things are or how things work. It is important for teachers to probe deeply for students' understandings, as well as misconceptions, as their first responses are usually intended to get the answer right.

2. **Be sensitive to and capitalize on students' conceptions about science.**

   In all science classes, but especially in those at the elementary grades, teachers can count on students to hold diverse world views about nature. Students from a variety of cultural backgrounds will bring different experiences and explanations for natural phenomena to the classroom. Their ideas should be elicited, discussed, and respected. Some students will think that the earth is round, some will have observed that the earth is flat with occasional hills, and some will not have thought too much about the character of the planet's shape at all. For a teacher to reach all the students in the class, a unit on the shape and structure of planet earth might be started with an activity that brings all the students to a conceptual understanding of planetary shape. For example, students could be shown NASA's video clips of the earth from space twice: before learning about the observations and competing hypotheses of sixteenth-century seamen and astronomers, and again afterwards. In the long run, grounding students' conceptions through activity-based science lessons will work well for all children, including the historically underrepresented.

3. **Employ a variety of instructional techniques to help students achieve conceptual understanding.**

   The resistance of students' subtle misconceptions or naive theory, as some have referred to it, about the natural world to educational intervention is becoming better documented and understood. Generally, students' misconceptions need to be challenged through direct experience with situations that the existing misconception cannot readily accommodate. Students who do not think deeply about the evidence before them often ignore or discount results that do not conform to their existing model.

   Small-group work, direct-learning activities, and sophisticated questioning strategies are shown to be effective tools for replacing the misconception; traditional science classes consisting of lectures and reading are likely to be ineffective, especially for the historically underserved student populations. For example, students with an incomplete view of how gases behave under certain conditions are likely to maintain those misconceptions if the only instruction they receive is reading several pages about the tendency of hot air to rise. On the other hand, if students raise questions they have about air and help design and perform investigations that address the relationship of temperature and pressure, the teacher can use this opportunity to ensure that all students not only learn more about air as a gas but also learn something about meteorology and space science.

4. Include all students in discussions and cooperative learning situations.

Because there are many ways to represent the workings of the natural world, the teacher must see that all students are free to express their conceptions in different ways. Discussions among small groups should be closely monitored so that a dominant voice does not take the opportunity of another student to express a similar (correct) understanding in another manner. Students should be encouraged to challenge and reformulate observations and statements that are made about the subject at hand. The open, honest exchange of ideas must be as readily acceptable to the teacher as to the students (and their parents).

Section D The Role of Direct Experience in Science Learning[1]

MUCH has been written about the need for students to conduct hands-on investigations in learning science. The reasons are many, but they essentially fall into three major categories: (1) many students will not truly understand the science they are supposed to learn if the exposure is solely verbal; (2) students learn the processes and techniques of science through the replication of experiments; and (3) students will enjoy and retain the science they learn from a laboratory activity more than from a textbook. These reasons underscore the educational maxim that learning by doing is the most effective instructional paradigm. However, our best science teachers know that experiential lessons must be planned more carefully than passive modes of instruction.

1. Engage students in science activities by placing them in a position of responsibility for the learning task.

Many teachers describe their best hands-on activities as "minds-on." Minds-on lessons grip students in a way that makes them truly engaged in the action. Students actively process the information revealed to them in direct experiences, and they demonstrate their new understandings in discussions with other students. The most directly observable clue that students are engaged in the task is that they control the learning episode. Whether the minds-on activity is hands-on or a simulation presented through electronic (or some other medium of) learning, the engaged student has the power to manipulate some aspect of what is happening. The test for an engaging hands-on experience is whether the student is controlling the situation or vice versa.

For example, upper elementary grade students might be asked to build a model house from paper, including windows made of clear cellophane. With some of the windows covered and others open, students place their houses in direct sunlight to determine which students' houses heat most rapidly. The task itself requires manipulation of scientific instruments (thermometers), control of variables, data collection and interpretation, and small-group discussion. Students' engagement in the task can be assessed by providing one or more open-ended investigations into the effect of other variables. Students can be asked to identify those variables, then given the opportunity to design and conduct independent investigations to test the various factors involved in the process of passive solar energy.

2. Provide students with experimental problem solving when the result has direct meaning for them.

Along with the issue of student activity comes the necessity for students to care about the hands-on

---

[1]Two excellent references are available to help teachers involve all students in activity-based science. The California Department of Education publishes an *Enrichment Opportunities Guide: A Resource for Teachers of Students in Math and Science (1988)*. This guide lists activities for students (and teachers) interested in participatory science learning. Copies of the guide are available from the Bureau of Publications, Sales Unit, California Department of Education, P.O. Box 271, Sacramento, CA 95802-0271. The National Science Resource Center, a collaborative effort of the Smithsonian Institution, and the National Academy of Science have recently published *Science for Children: Resources for Teachers*. This anthology of curriculum materials, supplementary resources, and information sources is available through National Academy Press, 2101 Constitution Avenue, NW, Washington, DC 20418.

activity in which they participate. Students who are working to solve problems in which they have some investment are more likely to learn and retain important concepts. Science education has an enormous opportunity to invite students to learn about their world so that students can come to understand what is important for them to learn and why.

Section E   Values and Ethics²

As a human endeavor, science has a profound impact on society. Values and ethics are important components of science teaching and must be considered by teachers, textbook authors, and curriculum writers. Students can become scientifically literate citizens responsible for themselves and the world's future only if they are well prepared to assume that responsibility. In a scientific and technological context, their ethical judgments will result in responsible decisions using sound values and scientific knowledge to make those decisions. In a personal and societal context, their ethical judgments will follow the search for knowledge demonstrated repeatedly through the history of science. The State Board of Education avers in *Moral and Civic Education and Teaching About Religion:*

> Telling the truth and expecting to be told the truth are essential to the development of (1) personal self-esteem and basic friendships; and (2) genuine understanding of our society, its history, and the democratic process. A commitment to telling the truth embraces the conscientious pursuit and scrutiny of evidence. Students must learn to respect the processes involved in the search for truth. They should learn to identify and assess facts; distinguish substantial from insubstantial evidence; separate the process of searching for truth from the acceptance of propaganda; and examine in a constructive and unbiased manner controversial subjects such as politics, ethics, and religion. School personnel should

²In dealing with issues of values and ethics in the science classroom, teachers and other readers are referred to the State Board of Education's publication *Moral and Civic Education and Teaching About Religion*. This document examines the legal and educational responsibilities for addressing moral values (and related topics) in the classroom and is available from the Bureau of Publications, Sales Unit, California Department of Education, P.O. Box 271, Sacramento, CA 95802-0271.

assist students to develop their abilities to communicate effectively as they accumulate knowledge and reach conclusions.

For these beliefs and actions to be developed, values and ethics must be an integral part of the science curriculum. Science teachers should be supported with instructional materials and curriculum that help students:

1. **Identify the commonly shared values of the scientific community.**

   The disciplines of science constitute a community of individuals sharing a general set of common values. The research geneticist, the chemist, and the oceanographer all practice science, using the same generally shared scientific values. The set of shared values is likely to include the scientific values of curiosity, open-mindedness, objectivity, and skepticism.

   For example, the value of objectivity often arises when immature students (regardless of grade level) find it easier to ignore data they have collected if they conflict with those collected by the majority of other students, especially if, in so ignoring, they are able to arrive at the "correct" answer to a problem. If students are expected to roll marbles down an inclined plane covered with different materials, one can expect a certain regularity in reported results. One student, however, might observe and record discrepant data. If the student misrepresents the data (or ignores them in reporting) in order to conform with classmates, not only has that student missed the point of honest scientific reporting, but perhaps the entire class has missed the opportunity to investigate the effect of differing angles of inclination, differing effects of applied force, or whatever other variable might account for the discrepant results. Students must be encouraged to report all data they collect in an activity and to explain them in an honest and ethical manner (even if it means admitting to procedural error).

2. **Promote scientific values in the classroom.**

   Students best understand a scientific value and how it is applied when they recognize and apply it themselves. For example, it would be hypocriti-

Students must learn to respect the processes involved in the search for truth. They should learn to identify and assess facts; distinguish substantial from insubstantial evidence; separate the process of searching for truth from the acceptance of propaganda; and examine in a constructive and unbiased manner controversial subjects such as politics, ethics, and religion.

cal for teachers to laud efforts to protect native habitats and then use rare wild specimens in the classrooms. Science teachers should not create a market for animals that are collected from the wild; rather, they should insist that supply houses certify that dissection specimens are raised explicitly for that purpose. In class, teachers should take time to present their position on this issue and other sensitive issues related to the humane treatment of all living things.

3. Develop rational decision-making skills applicable to major issues of personal and public concern.

Any thorough learning experience regarding values and ethical considerations makes use of rational decision-making skills. Students need to analyze issues by resolving ambiguities, taking into account the most relevant values of the decision makers, balancing the advantages and drawbacks of alternative solutions, and projecting the likely consequences of a particular choice. By combining such a decision-making procedure with pertinent scientific and technological information, students move toward achieving scientific literacy.

A major purpose of experiences in decision making is to stimulate students to become not only lifelong learners but also scientifically literate citizens, seriously concerned with the interrelationships of science, technology, and society. For example, the topic of heart transplants could challenge students to research a variety of issues, including the latest surgical techniques, host rejection and other technical complications, trends in patient prognosis, and

economic and societal constraints in caring for patients. The central issue could be how an individual and society make decisions about going forward with heart transplants.

Section F Science, Technology, and Society

SCIENCE is directed toward a progressively greater understanding of the natural world. Technology is related to science as a human endeavor, but the direction is toward using accumulated human knowledge from science and other fields in order to control and alter the way things work. Technology is a means by which society develops and advances. Teaching with a Science, Technology, and Society (STS) approach is invariably interdisciplinary, with strong connections to history–social science, mathematics, literature, and the arts.

Just as the thematic approach (see Chapter 2) brings together disciplines within the sciences, an STS approach unites larger fields of study. Students who learn with peers and teachers about the inextricable connections among science, technology, and society have a very different experience from those who learn out of context. Imagine the English class that teaches rules of syntax and never sees them applied in literature or journalism; a mathematics class where algorithms are drilled outside meaningful problem-solving situations; or a history class filled with events, but without the cultures and characters that make them come alive. These subjects would be little more than skill-driven shells of the rich disciplines that are their heritage. Teaching science in the context of STS helps reveal the situations in which science has meaning. Science teachers should:

1. Demonstrate how the enterprise of science operates in the United States and elsewhere in the world.

The scientific enterprise embodies societal concern for advances in understanding the natural world. Highly technological nations, like Japan, place a high priority on scientific and technological advancement. This priority is evident in both the private and public sectors, where huge investments are made to ensure the expansion and refinement of scientific and technological developments. Much can be learned about the values of a society by investigating the relative priorities and tradeoffs in these large-scale investments.

Students can experience how society makes decisions among competing alternatives by simulating complex decisions involving space exploration. Students can form groups representing diverse constituencies for and against expanding funding for the development of space technologies. By rehearsing their group's own point of view, as well as those of competing groups, they can learn the interrelationships and tradeoffs for future investments in space exploration.

2. **Examine the array of job prospects and interest areas within the science and technology arena.**

Science and technology will have an increasingly significant impact on careers and avocations in science-related fields. Every major projection of employment markets predicts the need for scientifically literate job seekers. The Department of Labor estimates that 50 to 60 percent of the new job opportunities will be in information and science/technology (sci/tech) fields.

Because California has about 12 percent of the U.S. population and employs over 20 percent of the science and technology labor force, well over 60 percent of our students need to be educated to participate in that job market. The diversity of California's science and technology economy ensures a range of opportunities for students who graduate with the interest and appropriate background. In fact, for California it is imperative that all students be given an opportunity to compete for the types of jobs that are and will be available. In addition, there are many hobbies, avocations, and interests that relate to studies in science and technology. Regardless of our students' backgrounds, there is likely to be some outlet for creativity, aesthetics, and enjoyment that appeals to each of them. Such interests should be highlighted and nurtured as part of the comprehensive science curriculum.

Using civil engineering as an activity base, students could form design teams that would simulate the planning of some large (or significant) construction project. It could be construction of a local dam (where they would do an environmental impact study); a bridge (where they would investigate span designs); or a multi-purpose sports stadium (where they would consider seating options, traffic patterns, and so forth).

3. **Describe how the products of science and technology change society.**

The products of scientific endeavors are readily available to people in our culture, and students should understand the origins and implications of these products. Developments in agriculture, transportation, allied health fields, and design and

"Science and technology spring from two different but equally important activities. One is the search for knowledge and understanding, the second is the application of knowledge to satisfy human needs."
—*Albert Baez*

"Aviation and space technologies have unlimited potential, not only for meeting industrial, commercial, and leisure needs, but also for offering insights and solutions to scientific problems and challenges. By expanding our knowledge and understanding, aerospace and aviation education can extend our reach and inspire our young people, the builders and inventors of the future."

—*President Ronald Reagan, July 8, 1983,*
in a statement to the Third Biennial World Congress on Aerospace Education

The waterproof properties of the sap extracted from the rubber tree was known for centuries by the Quechua Indians of South America. While heating the sap, the Indians added sulphur to make the rubber stronger and more resilient and remove its stickiness and foul odor. This same process of vulcanization was accidentally rediscovered by Charles Goodyear in 1839, and a multiplicity of new inventions and practical applications followed.

manufacturing are all part of the sci/tech landscape. The benefits and costs of these fields are important areas of investigation for the science student. The standard of living we currently enjoy is a direct product of science and technology. The tradeoffs for such a highly consumption-oriented culture must be understood and appreciated for all those who live in this society. Failure to understand science results in the type of illiteracy that leads to educational, economic, and political disenfranchisement.

Section G   Elementary School Science

THE elementary school science curriculum holds great potential for exploring natural phenomena and technological applications in science. At a time when children are most curious about the world, teachers can capitalize on this joy of learning in ways that make science enjoyable, interesting, and meaningful. Elementary science programs, as far as possible, must:

1. **Provide a balanced curriculum in the physical, earth, and life sciences.**

   All three disciplines should have laboratory activities that involve students in "doing science." Each subject should receive roughly one-third of the total class time for any given year.

2. **Show students that science is enjoyable.**

   If the joy of learning permeates science classes, students will be eager to learn. The motivation process begins with teachers modeling a fascination with science and its dynamic presence in our daily lives. The motivation process continues and expands as students are given more and more opportunities to explore the natural and technological world.

3. **Reinforce conceptual understanding rather than rote learning.**

   Conceptual understanding requires higher-level thinking processes than lower-level recall and thus requires more in-depth experience and reinforcement in the classroom. Larger science concepts can be embedded in longer-term instructional events (two- and three-week units) where daily lessons include experiential learning and continually reinforce the overarching theme(s) and related science concept(s). Conceptual understanding is strengthened when students draw connections from concepts being studied to daily experience, novel situations, and previously learned ideas.

4. **Organize an articulated scope and sequence at the school level.**

   Principals, other school site leaders, teachers, and parents should jointly plan a sequence of science units according to which each grade level treats some significant portion of the total science curriculum for kindergarten through grade six. Once the curriculum has been divided among grade levels, and teachers are clear on their curricular expectations, adequate planning ensures that teachers have the professional development, instructional materials, and class time to teach the agreed-on science curriculum. Of the total time spent learning science, at least 40 percent should be involved in activity-based lessons.

5. **Arrange the classroom setting and student grouping to optimize positive attitudes for learning science.**

   There are many accommodations that can transform the usual classroom setting into one that encourages curiosity and motivates students to learn more science. Classroom tables can be arranged to facilitate small-group work on direct science experiences. Science equipment and materials, as well as reference books and periodicals, should be visible and within easy reach of the students. Bulletin boards can display the results of the most current unit of study, from student work to related articles, including science careers and technology. A number of study areas in the room can be devoted to science learning, making it clearly evident that this is an environment that encourages questioning and inquiry. Students should have opportunities to work in cooperative groups, perform investigations, manipulate science equipment, and follow safety precautions. These groups can be organized to assume responsibility for their learning.

6. **Integrate science with other subjects.**

Scientific literacy could receive a considerable boost if science were used as a vehicle to enhance reading, mathematics, and the arts. The use of science to teach other fields has been shown to be quite successful in many exemplary elementary science programs. Science reading should be encouraged and integrated in the overall curriculum. During these integrated lessons featuring two or more subjects, it is essential that science maintain its rigor and uniqueness as a field of study. For example, students who sketch for the dual purposes of refining their artistic skills and furthering their botanical knowledge need to observe (and perhaps classify) several types of leaves carefully before rendering them in an aesthetic manner that is also botanically correct.

7. **Make full use of community resources.**

Community resources should be enlisted to participate in elementary science lessons. Students who may have less outside experience to draw on are enriched by community resource agencies and their personnel. The local grocer, fire fighter, florist, or farmer can add a real-world dimension to a science experience. Field trips to local parks, gardens, streams, or other science-related settings can illustrate concepts or ideas introduced in science lessons. As with other types of science study, students should be

encouraged to ask volunteers questions that build on what the students already know or have learned in classroom science activities. California offers an array of science museums and other informal science education settings where students can revel in the many areas of inquiry and examination. Outdoor schools offer a wonderful resource for science instruction; all upper elementary students should have the opportunity to spend a week in these outdoor settings.

Section H Middle School Science

THE most effective middle school science program is composed of five semesters of science coursework (during grades six through eight). There should also be another semester of health and other important adolescent topics as well as electives for interested students. According to the most common middle-school configurations now in use, there should be: (1) four semesters in traditional seventh and eighth grade junior high schools; (2) six semesters in a sixth, seventh, and eighth grade pattern; and (3) six semesters for schools using a seventh, eighth, and ninth grade pattern. In short, all middle grades students should be taking science each year.

In most curricular areas, middle school programs are seen as transitions from a sound basis provided during elementary grades to the specialization of the high school years. Articulation through regular discussions among staff and administrators from elementary and middle schools is strongly recommended. Middle school science programs, as far as possible, must:

1. **Introduce students to the connections among the disciplines of the physical, earth, and life sciences.**

During the middle school years, students should have the cognitive ability to understand that developments in one field can have major implications for another. Nowhere is this more true than in the natural sciences. For example, if a local business causes a toxic spill in a nearby creek, students can examine what effects toxic chemicals will have on the soil, plants, and animals of the area.

Often, the physical sciences are not well developed in middle school science programs. It is especially timely to introduce basic concepts in chemistry and physics to these students. Instructional materials can provide helpful hints to the middle school science teacher on how to address a more integrated science program in both lecture and laboratory activities.

2. Expand the role of the science processes.

As students mature during this period of adolescence, they become ready to tackle more sophisticated thinking processes than was possible earlier in their education. Activities should raise students' expectations for the level of thinking of which they are capable. Students should be able to appreciate the connections among disciplines and to apply higher-level thinking processes in their study of science.

3. Motivate students to take and learn more science.

A major goal of middle school science is to maximize students' exposure to high-interest science topics so that they will be eager to enroll in a variety of science classes in high school. These students, more than those in any other age group, need to see a direct relationship between science education and their daily life. Courses designed to help students learn about themselves (adolescence in human biology) and their world (environmental/earth science) are highly motivating to these students. Science lessons should be highly experiential, manipulative, and laboratory oriented. Students should be working in small groups, cooperating on peer-group projects, and solving laboratory-oriented problems.

4. Create long-term projects with students.

Consistent with the recommendations from *Caught in the Middle*,[3] students in the middle grades are ready to assume responsibility for a larger share of their learning. Middle grade science teachers can offer students the opportunity to select projects that are consistent with the curriculum for the course and involve consider-

---

[3]The California Department of Education published *Caught in the Middle*, a description of the middle grades reform initiative. It is available from the Bureau of Publications, Sales Unit, California Department of Education, P.O. Box 271, Sacramento, CA 95802-0271.

able out-of-class work. Science projects increase the possibility that students will take responsibility for what they learn. As they develop this growing sense of responsibility for learning, they should be encouraged to seek assistance from peers, parents, teachers, and others in the community. Whether schools adopt a project orientation to their science program or not, at least 40 percent of the class time should be spent on activity-based lessons.

5. Make full use of community resources.

Middle grade students are also capable of creating their own field trips. From the physics of skateboarding to the design and manufacture of new devices or inventions or to the study of local fauna in a natural environment, these students can and should be challenged to learn what they want on their own, as extensions of material learned in class. They should be encouraged to visit the high school they will attend and sit in on laboratory activities to get a sense of what type of science study lies ahead. And, of course, these students should be given responsibility for selecting and inviting guest lecturers on topics of interest. Many community agencies are open to participating in classes where adolescents care about what they learn. As students take initiative in learning science, they will learn more about their community and possible future vocations.

6. Establish the relevance of science lessons outside the school context.

Middle grade students often challenge teachers about the relevance of a particular topic or concept. These challenges ought to be seen as requests for the relevancy of science to students' daily lives, and students should not be put off with an answer like, "You will need to know this in order to do well in high school."

If students are to take responsibility for their learning, they ought to be given reasonable justification for what they are learning. Fortunately, the middle school science curriculum abounds with material of high interest. It may prove useful to entreat these students to develop the rationale themselves. In this way, they can begin to model the self-sufficiency towards learning they will use throughout their adult lives.

THE secondary science curriculum is less subject to mandate than that of the elementary school. Many students take a minimum of science courses in high school, and no textbook adoption process, beyond legal compliance criteria, is used beyond the grade eight. Strong traditions exist regarding what high school biology, chemistry, and physics courses should be like. Regardless, many excellent options for teachers and students have been developed. Science teachers, with support from administrators, must reexamine all portions of the program in the light of modern trends and needs.

An effective science program is more than a curriculum or a textbook or a set of laboratory exercises. It is science as experienced and understood by the students and taken by them beyond the classroom. The science department should be concerned, of course, with the curriculum offerings and the pathways that individual students follow through secondary school, but also with the effectiveness of the instruction and the degree to which attempts to integrate within and beyond the discipline of science become part of the student's life and experience.

The process of science as an aesthetic pursuit and an effective tool with the power to both create and solve problems must be apparent to graduates from high school. At each school, science teachers (and other faculty) must ask for the leadership, time, and budgetary resources to perform ongoing review and improvement of the program. A secondary school science program will accomplish the following:

1. **Build on a solid foundation of science instruction in kindergarten through grade eight.**

In an exemplary school, science teachers work together within the department with school administrators and with district curriculum committees and administrators, to create articulated science programs. Secondary science instruction and what precedes it are seen to be working in harmony to create a steady accumulation of science knowledge, science processes, and conceptual understanding. Such a curriculum is designed to revisit all the concepts and provide further experience with processes introduced in the elementary schools. At the higher grade levels, a much greater degree of understanding, performance, and descriptive ability is expected, as well as a far greater emphasis on quantitative reasoning. For example, secondary students study the melting of ice, which they saw first in the early grades, by investigating how water purity affects the freezing point, how energy changes may be measured, how different forms of ice may exist at different temperatures, and what effects are caused by trapped gases.

2. **Lead in a coherent fashion to greater opportunities for all students.**

All science courses should encourage students to understand that there are yet more exciting things to discover and important concepts to learn. Both college- and employment-bound students should take courses beyond the state-mandated two years because all courses have been designed to encourage students to become involved in more advanced science. Technology-based programs are part of the advanced curriculum and have been designed to reinforce basic science understanding as well as to explore specific technological areas.

The science department should work closely with those responsible for special groups of students to be sure that all students have the opportunity to experience a challenging and developmentally significant science curriculum. Possible organization plans for science programs in high school are presented in the chart that follows. Courses in the high school science program should be designed specifically to allow students to shift from one sequence to another. For this to happen, science departments must be more detailed in the relationship of one course to another. For too long only students in the four-year mathematics sequence met prerequisites for physics enrollment. As a consequence, physics enrollment in California in the 1987-88 school year lagged behind the national physics enrollment pattern by about 33 percent. Nationally, about 20 percent of graduating seniors have taken physics, while in California only 13 percent have taken physics.

Science departments are encouraged to develop pathways for all students to be able to take physics and chemistry, even if the pathways are nonquantitative. In fact, many science educators at the secondary and college levels prefer conceptual physics and chemistry courses over the more quantitative courses. The following chart demonstrates connections among pathways for students with differing entry points. (Of course, there are many other possible combinations within and beyond the current tradition of single-subject, five-hours-per-week science classes.)

Grade	General sequence	Quantitative sequence	Conceptual sequence
9	Physical science	Earth science or elective*	Earth science or elective*
10	Life science	Biology	Conceptual physics
11	Conceptual chemistry	Quantitative chemistry	Conceptual chemistry
12	Conceptual physics	Quantitative physics	Biology

*Science electives might include oceanography, astronomy, ecology, and so forth.

An even broader reform of the high school curriculum has been proposed by the National Science Teachers Association. In "Essential Changes in Secondary School Science: Scope, Sequence, and Coordination," NSTA Executive Director Bill Aldridge writes:

> The fundamental problem with high school biology, chemistry, and physics courses is that they are not coordinated, are highly abstract and theoretical, do not spend enough time on each subject, and do not use correct pedagogy. In short, we never give students the chance to *understand* science. . . .
>
> By contrast, consider the secondary school level science courses offered in the USSR and the People's Republic of China. In both countries, all—yes *all* students take several years of biology, chemistry, and physics. And essentially all children learn these subjects successfully. . . .
>
> As you can see in [the accompanying table], the average student in the USSR and China [PRC] spends almost twice as much time studying

biology and chemistry and more than three times as much time studying physics as his or her American counterpart. Notice that the ratios are even higher when you compare years spent on each subject:

Time Spent on Biology, Chemistry, and Physics			
	US	USSR	PRC
Biology	180 hrs. 1 year	321 hrs. 6 years	256 hrs. 4 years
Chemistry	180 hrs. 1 year	323 hrs. 4 years	372 hrs. 4 years
Physics	180 hrs. 1 year	492 hrs. 5 years	500 hrs. 5 years

In accordance with the NSTA proposal, a possible scenario for redesigning the California secondary school science curriculum is illustrated in the table on the following page. This table outlines just one of many possible designs for changing secondary school science. Coordination is essential if these components are to be learned properly. And, of course, any such broad changes in curricula would pose significant staffing, scheduling, and other problems. But change can come only from exploring what is ideal and possible and working from there to what is practicable.

Science faculty should integrate the science curriculum so that students fully understand the interconnectedness and interdependence of the traditional disciplines. Less discipline-oriented courses help students to understand that basic principles of physics, chemistry, and biology have a common foundation, and that applications of these principles constitute most of modern-day science and technology. For example, a biology class examines the physics of motion and the concept of work and machines when discussing bones and muscles; a chemistry class reviews digestion and blood chemistry when discussing acids and bases; a physics class investigates the structure of the human and other animal eyes when discussing refraction, light, and color theory.

3. **Help students understand the nature of science—in particular, its experimental, nondogmatic nature and the methods by which progress is made.**

Students should practice an ethical understanding of the responsibilities of science in their own laboratory and other investigations. Honest and clear observation and reporting are rewarded. Inadequate recording, misrepresentations, or clear dishonesty are actively discouraged and are considered unacceptable in science. Dilemmas existing in modern science are examined and debated in the classroom. Students understand the limitations of measurements and observations and learn how to communicate clearly the true meaning and limits of investigatory activities.

4. **Develop in students a strong sense of the interrelationship between science and technology and an understanding of the responsibility of scientists and scientifically literate individuals to both present and future societies.**

In the exemplary school, teachers assist students to appreciate the implications of the power and limitations of science in addressing societal issues as they learn how to use their scientific knowledge and skills to make decisions and judgments about important matters for present society and the future of the planet earth.

Science and social science teachers work together to make science relevant for students by considering the social impacts of science and technology and the need for all citizens to be responsible world inhabitants. Major issues, such as the impact of human population growth on other species and on world resources and environmental deterioration, are to be discussed in an open manner by all students, not just those choosing science careers.

The science curriculum in all science courses, without exception, provides opportunities for interaction; students participate in model debates and forums on such public issues as water use, air pollution, gene splicing, and biological species conservation. These exercises employ proper data, gathering from both science experiments and surveys. Teachers from various disciplines work together to help students learn valid methods for data acquisition, analysis, and reporting.

A Proposed Science Curriculum for Grades Seven Through Twelve in California							
	Hours per week, by grade level						Total hours spent on science
Subject	7	8	9	10	11	12	
Biology	2	2	1	1	1	1	288
Chemistry	1	1	2	2	1	1	288
Physics	1	1	1	1	2	2	288
Earth science	1	1	1	1	1	1	216
Total hours per week	5	5	5	5	5	5	
Emphasis	Descriptive, phenomenological		Empirical, semi-quantitative		Theoretical, abstract		

5. **Foster each student's ability to act as an independent investigator and thinker rather than a "recipe follower."**

High school students should be responsible for their own science education. Students should leave class with questions as often as with answers and learn to obtain answers from a variety of sources—library books and journals, videotapes, computer data bases, parents, community members, and other students. They should learn to work effectively alone and as members of cooperative learning groups, where they have had opportunities to play different roles. In the laboratory they can organize work in groups, are motivated to complete experiments, create professional-looking records of what happens, and are responsible for their own safety, understanding the need for personal protection and mature behavior. Students should spend at least 40 percent of their time on practical activities designed to foster manipulative skill development as well as higher-order thinking.

6. **Reinforce basic tools of language and mathematical communication.**

Science faculty within schools must work closely with their colleagues in other disciplines to help students see the overall plan in the high school curriculum. Communication tools should be emphasized by having English teachers read and grade science reports for grammar and style, while science teachers suggest topics for English class assignments. Science and language arts teachers could create avenues for students to read and discuss literature relevant to science. Drama classes offer opportunities for students to explore historical figures in science: Galileo or Marie Curie, for example. In this way students learn about the importance of environment and personality in science as well as the brilliance of discovery.

Lessons in algebra and science can be co-taught so students see mathematics in action; at the advanced levels, probability, statistics, trigonometry, and calculus are presented in the context of science experiments. No student is expected to use mathematics beyond his or her level of understanding, but science is used to motivate the presentation of more advanced mathematics, and the lack of specific mathematical power is not seen as an excuse or barrier to avoid exploring science concepts.

Computers are used in a variety of ways in the exemplary science classroom. Mainly, they are perceived as a useful tool for students in expanding their ability to gather and organize information. Simulations and modeling programs are used just as they are in science investigations. Science classrooms have access to data bases by computer network and a laser disk system that allows students to observe experiments that cannot be done in the classroom.

7. **Provide an expanded view of science-related careers.**

Students should understand what science-related careers are available to them and what courses they need to prepare for these careers. Science, English, and mathematics teachers, as well as counselors, need to work together to inform and place students in science classes and to see that female and minority students are equitably represented, especially in more advanced science classes. The importance of education beyond high school is emphasized for all students, whether at a community college, technical college, or four-year university. Students recognize that being a teacher of science is a worthwhile and rewarding experience. To show students the wide range of opportunities in science, teachers have found ways to visit businesses, industries, and research laboratories and to arrange for visits to the classroom by scientists from academia, government, medicine, business, and industry. Students experience the enthusiasm of males and females of all ethnic backgrounds working in careers at all levels, from the technician to the laboratory director.

Teachers should recognize that reading about scientists in books in itself may not generate much interest or connection. Hearing only about science superstars may give too unrealistic a picture and imply that all persons working in science are geniuses. Teachers can emphasize that many individuals, now and in the future, will make their living in science or science-related employment. Students in all science classes should have such opportunities explained to them, not just those who major in science.

Section J   Teaching All Students

THE demographic trend of the California school population is on a collision course with the scientific illiteracy rate. The populations of minority and at-risk youth are increasing, along with the number of dropouts and graduates without solid backgrounds in science and technology. This state cannot afford a citizenry or work force composed of individuals lacking the scientific literacy to compete in a technologically sophisticated economy. While the economic incentives for scientific literacy are compelling, they are not the only force driving public schools toward a greater emphasis on science learning. More than ever, voters are asked to make difficult choices between development and environmental issues. Consumers are besieged by advertisements and counterclaims about energy efficiency, competing technologies, and other aspects of the process of product selection.

In a technologically advanced culture, the scientifically illiterate are disallowed entry into educational, economic, and political arenas. As women and minorities become larger segments of the California work force, they are less well represented in the fields of science and technology. Science teachers are now assuming greater responsibility for helping females and minorities learn to succeed in these fields (as well as in mathematics). With concerns of domestic equity and international competitiveness, science educators must help ensure that all students have an equal opportunity to succeed in science-related endeavors.

The two sections that follow show how science teachers can help overcome societal and cultural factors that mitigate against success of the historically underrepresented. In the first section, there are general strategies for working with females and minorities (especially blacks, Hispanics, and American Indians). The second section presents strategies for working with linguistic minorities.

With concerns of domestic equity and international competitiveness, science educators must help ensure that all students have an equal opportunity to succeed in science-related endeavors.

Teaching Science to the Historically Underrepresented

By all reports and analyses, females, minority groups (with the exception of some Asian ethnic groups), and persons with disabilities are underrepresented in undergraduate and graduate study, research, industry, and other scientific enterprises. The many reports addressing this situation document the shortcomings of the system but do little to treat the problem or its causes. Fortunately, there are individuals and pilot programs working to help youngsters overcome barriers that keep them from succeeding. The successes of dedicated professionals who believe and regularly demonstrate that all children can achieve lead to the recommendation that teachers should:

1. **Model positive attitudes about all students' successes in mathematics and science.**

   The most powerful force in helping the underrepresented to achieve is the consistent belief that they can succeed. Teachers are especially effective in promoting positive attitudes about students' abilities and achievements. From the start, teachers must demonstrate that every child in the classroom can make a significant contribution to a lesson, and the conscientious classroom teacher draws out students who may be reticent. Meaningful recognition from a caring teacher can spark interest and enthusiasm and reveal students' natural abilities.

   The use of role models in science instruction cannot be underestimated. While teachers and in-class speakers provide the most impact on students, videotapes and other supplemental learning materials can readily demonstrate the expanding presence of females, minorities, and persons with disabilities in science careers and avocations. Role models who speak of their early motivation and preparation are very effective in translating personal experience into touchstones for students with interest in science and technology. Above all, role models prove that historically underrepresented students can succeed in highly technological fields.

2. **Prepare students well in the mathematics and language arts.**

Comprehensive programs in English-language arts and mathematics are much broader and deeper than reading and computation tools, but at some level students need to manipulate text and numeric symbol systems in order for them to succeed in science. The development of such tools should not be seen as prerequisite to science, any more than they are prerequisite to literary appreciation or problem solving. Learning science can occur simultaneously with such tool development. And, in fact, science is often a source for this development because it capitalizes on students' innate curiosity about the natural world and how things work. Females, minority students, and students with disabilities should be given frequent opportunities to learn science in the context of developing other skills. History–social science and the arts bring special skills and understandings that further these students' general and science education.

3. **Provide enrichment opportunities in mathematics and science for females, minority students, and students with disabilities.**

Often, students who could benefit the most from extracurricular activities do not get a chance to participate. And, often they are not aware of or are precluded from participating in the extra programs available to others. Some special programs like science fairs, Invent America!, and the Science Olympiad allow students to demonstrate their creativity and interest in science-related areas during regular school hours. Opportunities such as the Mathematics, Engineering, and Science Achievement (MESA) program provide extended assistance for students who demonstrate an early interest in and motivation for technical careers. Other programs require some involvement from home or community in order for students to participate fully. Before students can actualize their interest in science enrichment activities, they must be made aware of the opportunities, they must be encouraged to participate, and they need to achieve success. No student succeeds without awareness and participation.

4. **Build parent involvement and peer recognition programs.**

The same sociocultural forces that create barriers to the interest in science of females, minorities, and students with disabilities can be turned around to help them succeed in scientific and technical fields. Perhaps the most persuasive influences for and against learning science are the normative mores and values about science and technology. Homes and neighborhoods that are disenfranchised from the world of science and technology pass along this indifference and ignorance to children. This trap is especially destructive to the opportunities of females who, if there were no cultural stereotypes about science-related fields, might follow their own interests and abilities and pursue more science education. When parents and peers show an interest in and acceptance of science endeavors, there is more room for these students to participate and succeed. Local PTAs and PTOs, other community action groups, university incentive programs, and afterschool clubs and enrichment programs all work to build more healthy attitudes about acceptance and success in scientific and technical fields.

5. **Capitalize on students' prior knowledge.**

In the section on concept learning, we saw that students learn more effectively in all areas (but especially mathematics and science) if new material is incorporated within the existing knowledge base. For the historically underrepresented populations, this presents two challenges: (1) the prior experience students bring to school may be fundamentally different from the mainstream culture; and (2) the prior knowledge students have may be incomplete, especially in the physical and earth sciences. The first challenge can be mitigated through large-group discussions or background information for all children in the classroom. To do so is more difficult than might be thought because discussing or passively viewing and listening (in the case of video background information) alone may not develop rich experiences for all students. Here again, direct experience with concrete materials may be needed to further enrich students' world view. The second challenge is best overcome by working in smaller, heterogeneous groups.

All students with limited-English proficiency, regardless of their primary language, should have rigorous English-as-a-second-language (ESL) lessons. A strong ESL component is necessary to build a foundation in English for access and success in content instruction that will later be taught solely in English. ESL classes, especially for intermediate level speakers of English, might integrate science vocabulary and science concepts as part of language development activities.

Cooperative learning offers the possibility that direct experience of working with others allows all students to develop an understanding of the concepts of science. Care must be taken in these situations to ensure that historically underrepresented students are not dominated in discussions by students who claim to know more or have broader experience. The diversity of experiences that students bring to the classroom should be accepted and respected; teachers should make every effort to encourage students to share their perspectives. Both these challenges require close observation by the classroom teacher and other instructional staff; both the process and substance of learning need to be watched closely to ensure that all students have similar cognitive constructs before new concepts are introduced.

6. **Maintain the same standards for all students.**

Learning any subject deeply requires hard work. In fact, the root of the word *tuition* comes from the effort (not the money) required to learn. It is essential that females, minorities, and students with disabilities experience the challenge and hard work it takes to master mathematics, science, and technology. With positive attitudes about their abilities to succeed, they can and will. It does no good (and may do irreparable harm) to inflate the grades or successes of one group relative to others. The standards for success must be equivalent so that a common metric is understood and appreciated by all students.

Teaching Science to Limited-English-Proficient Students

The rapid changes in California's population are directly reflected in our schools. More and more students come to class with primary languages other than English. Limited-English-proficient (LEP) students lack the English language skills to benefit from instruction which is designed for native English speakers.

While providing comprehensible science instruction for students who are not fluent in English has implications for instruction, so does the amount of prior schooling these children have had. Some of the same students new to English have never been to school in their homeland, coming from rural backgrounds in countries with educational systems that are less developed than ours. Many of these youngsters come to our schools preliterate. Other children, while not proficient in English, have had schooling in advanced educational systems and are highly literate in their own language. Students proficient in languages other than English can learn the science content appropriate for their grade level as outlined in this framework. The problem is not one of cognitive capability; it is a problem of delivery.

All students with limited-English proficiency, regardless of their primary language, should have rigorous English-as-a-second-language (ESL) lessons. A strong ESL component is necessary to build a foundation in English for access and success in content instruction that will later be conducted solely in English. ESL classes, especially for intermediate level speakers of English, might integrate science vocabulary and science concepts as part of language development activities. The critical variable here is second-language acquisition (English) and not science per se. Experiences in advanced-level ESL classes may also include readings from the basic science program textbook.

When the ESL teacher and science teacher work together to develop vocabulary and assign readings in science, students come to science classes with enough English language skills to make science instruction successful. This is not to say that students must be as fluent in English as they are in their primary language. In addition to providing support in the primary language for limited-English-proficient (LEP) students, science instruction can be meaningful for LEP students if appropriate techniques are used to make that instruction comprehensible—techniques which are based on good teaching in general and good science teaching in particular.

All children in California, including those whose primary language is other than English, should have access to high-level science instruction. These students who are limited-English proficient can have immediate access into science via their primary language while acquiring English. As students reach intermediate fluency, they depend less on primary language support. Intermediate speakers ought to be able to string sentences together, even though their sentences may be grammatically incorrect. These students can gain comprehension skills when the content is delivered orally with context clues. Context clues help to lower the linguistic barriers to high-level science instruction.

The important task of modifying science instruction to remove barriers to comprehension will have to be met by all teachers of science, not only those trained for ESL or bilingual programs. These teachers have within their teaching repertoire strategies that can be used to lower the linguistic barriers preventing access to their disciplines. The following strategies are not to imply a simplification of science; rather, they are used with the same content as for English-proficient students. We are not to create two science curricula. Perhaps the most powerful teaching tool is the expectation that all students can and will succeed. Using techniques founded in sound teaching practices, teachers should:

1. **Simplify the input.**

   Use a slower but natural speech rate with clear enunciation. A modified, controlled vocabulary may be appropriate. Science teachers should resist the temptation to make science a vocabulary development course. Use proper science terms when necessary, but avoid obfuscation. Do make attempts to restate, redefine, provide familiar examples, and draw on students' prior backgrounds. Define words with multiple meanings and avoid the use of idiomatic speech.

2. **Provide context clues.**

   Be animated, use gestures, and when possible act out the meaning. Use props, graphs, visuals, and real objects. Hold up the mortar and pestle and demonstrate how to grind leaves in preparation for extracting chlorophyll. Make frequent visual and word associations. Show students the finished product when possible.

3. **Draw on prior background.**

   Have students brainstorm, list things they already know about the topic at hand, and be prepared for and accept single word or limited responses. Categorize their responses to show associations and relationships. Use graphic organizers, such as chapter or concept maps. Provide multisensory activities and ask open-ended questions to elicit a variety of responses and record the students' responses when possible.

4. **Work to ensure understanding.**

   Repeat ideas or concepts frequently. Expand, restate, and reinforce important points. Do regular comprehension checks to confirm that students really understand the concept under investigation. Frequent interaction between teachers and students and among students are strategies, along with others, for formative evaluation.

5. **Make sure instruction is content-driven.**

   Identify a few key concepts. Attempt to ensure understanding of fewer, larger ideas rather than many factoids, those isolated facts and definitions that have long dominated science instruction. Make sure those few concepts are learned well rather than many ideas developed superficially. Select essential vocabulary, about five to seven words, but certainly not 20 or 30 per chapter. Teach the selected vocabulary through a variety of interactive ways (avoid simply assigning them to be defined). Explain textual features such as bold print, italics, and chapter summaries in order to build comprehension. Show students how to use context clues in the text, such as pictures, graphs, tables, flow charts, and similar graphic materials.

6. **Ensure that instruction is student-centered.**

   Use a variety of grouping strategies, such as small-group, large-group, and cooperative learning. Provide instruction with direct experiences—about 40 percent of instructional time—

which are appropriate to various learning modes. As much as possible, put materials in students' hands; demonstrations are not as effective as manipulation. Provide opportunities for students to *use* concepts rather than merely reiterate the concept label and definition.

7. **Use science text effectively.**

When using text materials, begin by establishing students' prior background and be prepared to add background when necessary. Select the essential vocabulary and teach it through a variety of interactive and contextual ways that capitalize on prior experience. Begin a chapter with an activity; try starting with the first laboratory activity even if it is located three or four pages into the chapter.

All students in California deserve access to high-quality science instruction. Using techniques to reduce linguistic barriers will ensure access for students with limited-English proficiency. Rather than trying merely to *cover* the content, we should *uncover* science content.

Chapter 7

Implementing a Strong Science Program

THIS chapter deals with the implementation of strong science programs at the school district and site levels. It includes considerations of organization, selection, and administration of curricula; the use of educational technology in science classrooms; the physical resources of the school and the community resources of the district; and guidelines for staff development, using resources available from state agencies and other sources.

Section A Introduction

A WELL-FORMULATED districtwide plan for science education provides the basic design for the establishment of an effective science program. The most effective programs result when administrators and specialists provide leadership and support to teachers with a collaborative spirit; and teachers who will be implementing the plan need to be involved at every step of the process. One goal of an implementation plan must be the development of expertise among teachers at *all* levels; only then will the planned curriculum be taught. The definition of programs and the adoption of textbooks provide some of the elements needed to put that plan into practice. However, unless learners experience conceptual, sequential, and integrated science in the classroom, all the best made policies, plans, and intentions become poor substitutes for success. Proof of the establishment of a good science program lies in student growth in understanding and enthusiasm for science.

Implementation entails more than the dissemination of information, materials, and programs. If an adopted science curriculum is to result in knowledge, experience, and understanding for students, the program must be challenging, stimulating, and useful. Students should be doing science in their classrooms, not merely reading about it. Teachers need opportunities to increase their understanding of science by trying out the activities or lessons they will use in instruction. In order to be in a position to support teachers, administrators need to gain experience by attending staff development workshops with high-quality science instruction, and the community needs to know enough about the science curriculum so that its many members can contribute their expertise and support.

The design of a district science implementation plan is a process that should involve all of the people identified above over a sustained period of time. To begin, planners need to have a broad view of the entire implementation process in order to understand how all the parts fit together. Once the process is understood as a whole, planners can concentrate on key elements of implementation—planning, staff development, assessment, and resources (including learning environment, technology, and community). Planners need to be aware of the relationship between this framework and those in other subject areas in order to facilitate the integration among subject areas that are increasingly seen as essential. The material in this chapter follows the sequence described for planners.

TIME, people, and resources are the main factors to be considered when planning the implementation of the curriculum.

Time for Implementation

It is not enough to focus on science for the one adoption year out of every seven. The adoption of materials should be preceded by extensive planning and staff development and followed by more staff development and assessment. The changes suggested by this framework build on the preceding *Science Framework* and *Science Framework Addendum* and strengthen the position that students should actively experience science rather than passively read about it. The changes in practice that are required to implement this framework faithfully, however, are more radical—the shift from instruction that emphasizes accumulation of knowledge to a program that develops concepts and the understanding of the connections among them. Teachers and administrators need to experience the changes themselves and have the time to plan, to experiment, to revise their plans, and to implement the changes at a pace that allows for adequate reflection and internalization.

The California Department of Education issues each year a new framework in a different discipline, a schedule which may present districts, and elementary grade teachers especially, with an overwhelming task: improving three or four curricula at once without pause. The changes called for in the various frameworks, as profound as they are, are harmonic with one another. For example, the move to use cooperative groups to develop the ability to communicate mathematical thinking has made ready the way for the same kind of group work called for in this framework. The need to focus on the connections between ideas, rather than on isolated facts, is emphasized in the *History–Social Science Framework*. An important benefit of this interdisciplinary harmony in the frameworks is that teachers and districts can, to a significant extent, accomplish critical improvements in several curricular areas at the same time. A later section of this chapter delineates the relationships between this framework and each of the other subject areas.

People for Implementation

Effective implementation involves administrators, school faculty at all grade levels and students, parents, and other members of the community in a continuous, cyclical process that has evaluation elements throughout. The steps in this process are detailed in Figure 8. A comprehensive needs assessment, as outlined in the first column, enables the development of a detailed plan, characterized in the second column, with a high potential for successful implementation, described in the third column.

Effective implementation incorporates both a districtwide plan and plans for individual schools. A communication plan must ensure articulation among various levels (e.g., state, county, board, district office, school site, and classroom); within and among elementary, middle, and high schools; and between and among teachers at different grade levels within schools. A comprehensive communication structure, with teachers representing each school in planning and implementing committees, is a prerequisite to integration and articulation across grade levels within the district. Such a structure should also identify locally available resources, together with their appropriate contribution to the total program. These resources include mentor teachers and science education specialists; educators trained in technological applications; local college or university scientists and science educators; community experts in science, medicine, and technology; and parents.

A whole range of people should participate throughout the implementation process—principals, governing boards, district and county personnel, and local college and university representatives. They should be familiar with the goals of the framework and with implementation strategies so that they can lead and assist the process effectively, build enthusiasm in the staff, and model informed, committed support. Knowledgeable administrators are effective managers of time, money, and supplies. They should be selected in part for their ability to offer creative suggestions for the use of existing funds, but they should also be well informed about special grants and moneys that might become available. They should enhance their effectiveness by identifying individuals with science leadership responsibility and by providing necessary support to them.

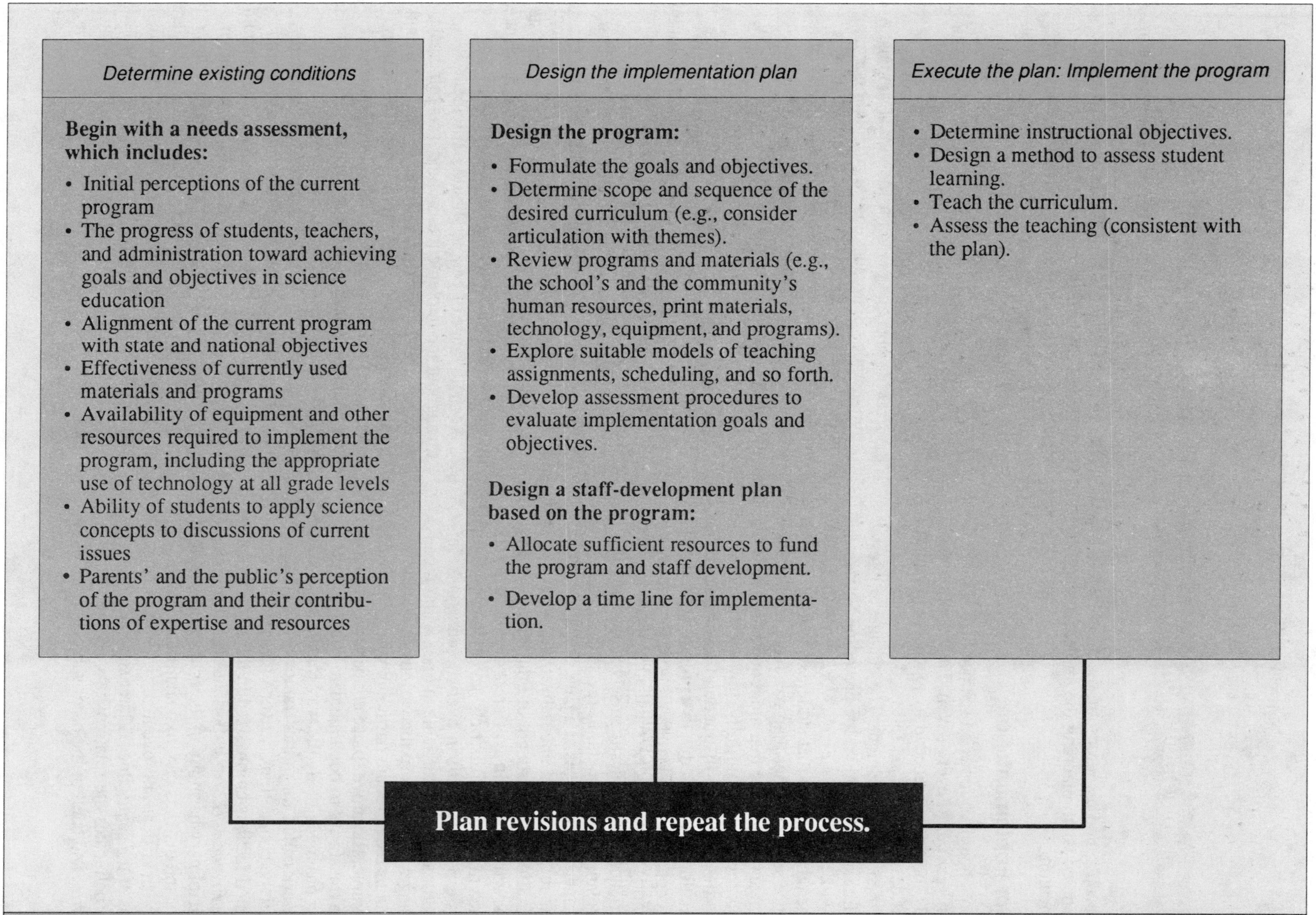

Determine existing conditions

Begin with a needs assessment, which includes:

- Initial perceptions of the current program
- The progress of students, teachers, and administration toward achieving goals and objectives in science education
- Alignment of the current program with state and national objectives
- Effectiveness of currently used materials and programs
- Availability of equipment and other resources required to implement the program, including the appropriate use of technology at all grade levels
- Ability of students to apply science concepts to discussions of current issues
- Parents' and the public's perception of the program and their contributions of expertise and resources

Design the implementation plan

Design the program:

- Formulate the goals and objectives.
- Determine scope and sequence of the desired curriculum (e.g., consider articulation with themes).
- Review programs and materials (e.g., the school's and the community's human resources, print materials, technology, equipment, and programs).
- Explore suitable models of teaching assignments, scheduling, and so forth.
- Develop assessment procedures to evaluate implementation goals and objectives.

Design a staff-development plan based on the program:

- Allocate sufficient resources to fund the program and staff development.
- Develop a time line for implementation.

Execute the plan: Implement the program

- Determine instructional objectives.
- Design a method to assess student learning.
- Teach the curriculum.
- Assess the teaching (consistent with the plan).

Plan revisions and repeat the process.

Figure 8. The Implementation Process

Resources for Implementation

Resources are available to assist the implementation planning process. See, for example:

- *Science Education for the 1980s* (includes advice and an extensive checklist for conducting a self-evaluation at the local level) (California Department of Education, 1982)
- *Quality Criteria* for elementary schools, middle grades, and high schools (California Department of Education, revised annually to reflect new frameworks)
- Recommendations of the California Science Teachers Association (Lawrence Hall of Science, Berkeley, CA 94720), the National Science Teachers Association (1972 Connecticut Ave., Washington, DC 20009), and other professional organizations

Section C   Staff Development

An effective science program depends primarily on teachers who are enthusiastic, informed, and provided with adequate resources. We hope that teacher preparation programs will be able to educate new teachers in the kind of science education called for by this framework. Yet, teaching is a profession that requires ongoing professional development, and teachers need the opportunity to experience the kind of instruction they are being asked to provide. A good staff development program should:

- Be ongoing, comprehensive, and based on the implementation plan.
- Involve teachers in planning, conducting, and evaluating workshops.
- Provide appropriate science content and scientific thinking and illustrate that scientific knowledge is a product of the scientific process.
- Provide opportunities to practice new activities—hands-on, laboratory, investigative, and field activities—in low-risk environments.
- Provide formal and informal opportunities for peer coaching and feedback.
- Allocate additional released time for teachers to reflect, discuss, solve problems, and exchange ideas.

While generic workshops on teaching techniques and classroom management strategies are of benefit to science teachers, it is important that substantial time and resources be devoted to strategies for incorporating these techniques most effectively in the teaching of science. Cooperative learning is a technique of great value to science teachers; cooperation in laboratory work and student projects needs to be emphasized to achieve the most from this technique.

To encourage an articulated program, those responsible for staff development must ensure that some portion of the training of district and school level take place across the grade levels. It is important for elementary teachers to anticipate where the curriculum is going and for secondary teachers to gain firsthand knowledge of where the students have been. In a collegial setting, the elementary teachers' expertise in a variety of teaching methods is as instructive to secondary teachers as the secondary teachers' subject matter expertise and enthusiasm are to the elementary teachers. As the content is specified by grade level, differentiated experiences are necessary at some point for teachers at different grade levels to receive enough specificity to carry out the program at their level. At every point, however, participants should have an active role, experiencing the processes

---

A favorite problem for workshops is the following: "You have two glasses of liquid, one white and one red, each initially containing the same amount. You take a teaspoon of white liquid out of the white glass and put it into the glass of red liquid. After stirring thoroughly, you take a teaspoon of slightly diluted red liquid from the red glass and put it into the glass of white liquid. After you stir it again, which glass is more contaminated, the red with the white or the white with the red? Or, are they equal?" This is a favorite problem because it elicits heated discussion and because it is easier to solve with a real model than with an algebraic one.

If an evaluator comes into a science classroom to observe and finds that all of the students are working in groups on projects of their own design and decides to return when the teacher is teaching, he or she devalues this mode of instruction and discourages teachers from using it. Certain features of the clinical supervision paradigm, particularly a conference before the observation to discuss the teacher's goals and a conference after the observation to compare the observer's and the teacher's perceptions of the success of achieving those goals, are valuable features that should be part of any assessment of instruction. Other features, such as the requirement that all lessons should include considerable time for practice, as if complex new ideas can be mastered through practice, are at odds with the idea of students' constructing their knowledge through investigation.

of science, as leaders model better ways to teach for conceptual understanding.

Section D Assessment

A TRUISM in education is, "What you test is what you get." Students will focus their attention on the activities that determine their grades, placement, and career opportunities. Similarly, teachers will guide their instructional decision making toward the criteria by which they and their students are evaluated. Principals will provide instructional leadership that is consistent with the basis on which their schools are judged. The superintendent will emphasize the school board's and state's criteria for success in his or her interactions with the principals and the district's curricular leaders. Of course, each level must be accountable to the next, yet it is essential that each level be held accountable for the right things. In this context, the right things are the agreed-on goals for the science program. If the goals of the science program are scientific literacy and the ability to make sense of the world, then tests of vocabulary and factual knowledge will not measure their attainment. The design of an assessment program requires as much care and consideration as the design of the instructional program itself.

Before an administrator can design and implement an effective assessment of science teaching at a given school, he or she must be familiar with the goals and methods of the science curriculum. Adequate assessment of teaching must reflect the same range of

teacher behavior as adequate assessment of student outcomes reflects the wide range of desired student outcomes. There is a temptation to limit assessment of teachers to what can be most easily observed: direct instruction. This is as much to be avoided as limiting student assessment to what can be most easily measured: factual recall. While direct instruction—the teacher addressing the whole class from the front of the classroom—has a role in science instruction and has a well-described paradigm for assessment, its effectiveness is limited as a mechanism for giving students direct experience with doing science. The assessment of instruction must meet the challenge of the wide range of instructional strategies proposed in this framework in the same way as the teacher meets these challenges in making decisions about instruction.

Administrators should begin the process of teacher assessment by asking teachers to assess themselves, using the following questions. At the same time, administrators need to ask themselves whether they have provided the teachers with opportunities to develop positive responses to each question.

- Am I using a variety of teaching methods? Are they appropriate for the subject and the learners? Am I moving toward hands-on, active learning of science and away from passive, text-only learning?
- Have I made adjustments in addressing the needs, strengths, and interests of my students when direct observation and evaluation indicate that particular methods are not succeeding?
- Am I acquainted with and employing specific instructional strategies designed for students in

categorical programs such as bilingual education, compensatory education, special education, and gifted education?

- Am I aware of each student's perception of what is being taught? Am I using a range of assessment techniques to determine student understanding, including performance assessment, portfolio review, and the safe manipulation of scientific apparatus?
- How do I handle controversial issues, and do I model positive attitudes toward important issues in science and society?
- Does my classroom promote inquiry, ethical values, and respect for others' opinions?
- Do my classroom and school provide a variety of materials supplemental to the core program, resources for independent student work, and an emphasis on safety and humane treatment of animals?
- Am I involved in the school's and district's overall science program? In addition to serving on committees, do I take advantage of the opportunity to work on program development with teachers at other schools and with teachers of different courses at my own school?
- Am I continuing my professional development through participation in professional organizations, attendance at conferences, and active participation in staff development activities?

Assessment of school science programs at the district, county, and state levels should incorporate the following additional considerations:

- Alignment with the framework and other curriculum documents such as the *Science Model Curriculum Guide, K–8*, the *Model Curriculum Standards, Grades 9–12*, the *Statement on Preparation in Natural Science Expected of Entering Freshmen*, and the *Quality Criteria* (for elementary schools, middle grades, and high

schools). All major concepts and processes in the framework should be assessed. Local variations in curriculum should be intentional and explicit; they should be reflected in local assessments.
- Modeling good instruction. Assessment criteria that reward poor or unimaginative instructional methods should not be used. Because instruction is greatly influenced by the methods and criteria of its assessment, only assessment criteria that model good classroom practices should be used at each level of assessment. In particular, assessment should be performance-based wherever possible; students should demonstrate understanding and skill in situations that parallel prior classroom experience.
- Design and administration of assessment by practicing teachers who have been given special preparation to do so. Teacher involvement gives teachers a sense of ownership, improves teaching methods, and helps to ensure the practicality of the assessments. Knowing what to observe and the various strategies for administering performance tasks will require special preparation, particularly to ensure consistency among assessors.
- Coordination with the assessment of other disciplines as appropriate. Skills and concepts in mathematics, English–language arts, history–social science, and the visual and performing arts should be included in science performance tasks if they are integral parts of the tasks.
- Consistency with the developmental levels of children.
- Inclusion of periodic surveys of students' attitudes towards science.
- Provision of timely feedback to teachers. Results of assessment programs should be available soon after the assessment is conducted so that teachers can make appropriate adjustments in the program.
- Provision of well-explained qualitative and quantitative information to the public.

If an evaluator comes into a science classroom to observe and finds that all of the students are working on hands-on activities, he or she should not assume that everything is fine. Questions that the evaluator should ask include, "Are students following a recipe or investigating?" "Do they know why they are following the procedures they are using, what they are looking for, what the data mean?"

Section E Resources

THE preceding sections have emphasized the human resources of implementation—staff development and assessment efforts—yet their success depends on adequate investment in physical resources that support excellence in science teaching. Instructional materials play a key role in defining and supporting the science curriculum and are explicitly described in Chapter 8, "Instructional Materials Criteria." The classroom environment, the availability of equipment (particularly new technologies), considerations of safety, and the incorporation of community resources, including parents, are discussed in this section.

The Classroom Environment

The physical resources of the entire school plant and the community should be taken into consideration in planning the science instructional program. Optimal school facilities for science will provide flexibility to accommodate large- and small-group instruction, laboratory activities, outdoor experiences, demonstrations, audiovisual presentations, activities enhanced by educational technology, seminars, and individual or small-group projects. Teaching a laboratory or activity-oriented program in the elementary school does not necessarily require sophisticated laboratory facilities, but it requires at least tables and sinks. Adequate floor and storage space, lighting, ventilation, and chalkboard space must be provided. The availability of bulletin boards to permit display of colorful posters and examples of student work enhances the classroom. Secondary science programs generally require more elaborate facilities, including laboratory stations equipped with running water, gas, electricity, and storage space for student equipment. Safe storage for volatile, flammable, or corrosive chemicals is mandatory. The number of students in the laboratory classroom should be determined by factors such as safety, number of stations, and total classroom square footage, rather than school scheduling needs.

Equipment and materials must be made available to all teachers—elementary and secondary. It is as important for a first grader to be able to manipulate a hand lens, a magnet, or other materials through hands-on activities as it is for the high school student to be able to use chemistry equipment. A substantial yearly science budget must be available to teachers so that they can replenish the consumables and purchase the essential additions that encourage the expansion of an effective program and experimentation with new ways to present concepts.

When adopting instructional materials, district staff must consider the cost of equipment and consumable materials along with the cost of textbooks, software, videotapes, videodisks, and so forth. Evaluators at the local level should decide what program is best for their students, determine the cost of implementing that program, and present their recommendations to the administration or governing board. While it may not be possible to purchase and equip the optimal program, decision makers need to know what is considered best, next best, and so forth.

Safety is a particularly important component of the learning environment in science. A safety policy must delineate the roles and responsibilities of students, teachers, site administrators, and district administrators. The *Education Code* places responsibility for certain safety practices, such as the provision of eye-protection devices, on the local governing board and responsibility for the implementation of these practices on teachers. Districts need to develop procedures so that each person is aware of his or her responsibility and is given the resources needed to enact it. The California Department of Education has developed a handbook, *Science Safety Handbook for California High Schools,* to assist districts in carrying out this aspect of the implementation of an effective science program. Safety concerns should be addressed directly and not used as a rationale for the elimination of activity-based science.

Teaching Technologies

As indicated in the preceding section, equipment and materials are essential components of science programs at all levels. Traditional equipment, such as test tubes, scales, meter sticks, and microscopes, have always had a prominent role in effective science programs. As newer technological devices, such as scientific calculators, computers, videotapes, and videodisks, become less expensive and more significant as mechanisms for teaching and learning, their role should be constantly evaluated for their contribution to an effective science program. These technologies can support teachers in administrative tasks and can be used in obtaining new information and ideas. The effectiveness of the newer technological devices, of course, depends on teachers receiving adequate preparation in their use and time to incorporate them in their work. This section considers the rationale for using newer technologies in teaching, the mechanisms for incorporating them in the curriculum, and some criteria for evaluating the use of technology in the science curriculum.

Technology can provide conduits to new information, new experiences, and an opportunity to experiment and fail in a supportive environment. The storage and computational capacities of computers can help to eliminate the misconception that science is merely a collection of facts to be memorized and data to be manipulated. Used properly, they serve as a bridge that permits students to concentrate their attention on making connections among the facts and making sense of the results of numerical computations. While computers can be deployed as electronic textbooks and programmed to provide drill and practice, their most important contributions are to simulate simple and complex systems, assist in the collecting and interpreting of laboratory data, and serve as adaptable reference stations. Computers can also be used as part of a telecommunications network in which students and teachers share data and ideas with one another, comparing the pH of rain across the nation, for example, or the results of a classroom survey of genetic traits. For the teacher, they are also an invaluable relief from administrative burdens, such as maintaining student records and preparing exams.

Videotapes and videodisks extend the range of experiences available to students and teachers. Experiments that are too dangerous or costly to conduct in the classroom, historical or one-time events, and activities at a distance can all come into the classroom environment. Use of a video camera is also a way for students and teachers to bring their own projects and experiences outside the classroom into the arena for discussion. The ability to preview, review, and stop and discuss that is offered by a videocassette recorder increases the range of this teaching technology; the ability to program the interface with a videodisk offers even greater potential for the individualization of materials to the teacher who has the time to take advantage of this technology.

In each of these cases—computer and video—the person who benefits most from the experience is the person who designs it. Therefore, as far as possible, students should be involved in the control of this experience. They can be involved in selecting the technology for the instructional purpose, previewing it, explaining it to other students, predicting what will happen next, forming generalizations, and summarizing the experience. This mode of using technologies is analogous to the use of laboratory experiences; it must be thoroughly integrated in the instructional environment in order to contribute to it. Passive uses, such as watching an hour-long video, should be made active through preparation, discussion during watching, and expectations for follow-up activities.

A likely result of the increased use of technology in the classroom is the evolution of the role of the teacher from disseminator of information to facilitator of the students' learning. As individual students go in different directions with a wide array of information and resources, it is not possible, nor desirable, for the teacher to anticipate every path taken by every student. Teachers need to gain sufficient experience with this style of learning themselves that they feel comfortable with the perceived lack of disciplined control. They will soon discover that the technology frees them from the management of information and allows them to devote more time to one-on-one interactions with the students. From these discussions, the student acquires an understanding and appreciation for the fact that science results from making sense of information rather than from the information itself.

Mechanisms for changing the way teachers teach will have to incorporate this view of technology's role in instruction. Just as mechanics must learn how to use a tool in the context of their work, teachers must learn to how to use technology as a pedagogical tool in the context of their classroom. The application of technology to teaching is more than a skill; it is an art that requires practice. The introduction and continued use of technology requires:

- Support for people at all levels of the educational structure, from the teacher through the academic administration, including opportunities for sustained experience

- Support from the administration and the community for long-term investments in staff development and acquisition and maintenance of equipment and instructional materials

- Reevaluation of educational goals and methods as teachers evolve new teaching strategies using technology
- Consideration of technology-based educational materials in the curriculum planning, adoption, and implementation cycles

Criteria for evaluating materials in science have been presented in the *Technology in the Curriculum: Science Resource Guide*, distributed by the California Department of Education to all public schools in California in 1986. Instructional technology programs should be used to (1) provide experiences that cannot be provided better through other means; (2) promote active involvement by relating content to appropriate science processes; (3) contribute to the development of a positive attitude toward science; (4) overcome bias and singular points of view; and (5) support and be integrated into the science curriculum.

Other Valuable Resources

Parents and the community offer tremendous potential for supporting and enhancing the school's science program. Parents should be regularly informed about the science program, teachers' expectations, homework policies, and the student's progress. Active parent involvement can be encouraged as a means of supplementing classroom science instruction. The teacher can:

- Encourage parents to visit the classroom to observe and discuss the student's interest, assignments, and skills in science.
- Provide a listing to encourage family visits to science resources in the community—museums, planetariums, libraries, research labs, zoos, and other locations with interesting ecological features.
- Provide information regarding science-related television programs, books, magazines, and newspaper articles. Encourage parents to view or read and discuss the content with the student.
- Invite parents to become volunteers in the classroom or resource persons to share information regarding their science-related careers or hobbies.
- Extend the science classroom to the home by designing homework involving experiments or surveys to be carried out with family involvement.

The community also provides a rich resource for extending the science program. In addition to visits to facilities where science is practiced and exemplified, the people in the community who work in science-related occupations are frequently interested in public education and willing to visit classrooms to discuss their work with students. Role models motivate student interest in science careers. It is especially important that such role models include representatives of groups traditionally underrepresented in science, such as women and minorities. Scientists and others who use science in their jobs should be encouraged to bring slides, photographs, and the tools they use so that students can better envision the experience and excitement of being a scientist.

Section F   An Implementation Model

THE California Science Implementation Network has developed a school-based model that many teachers and principals have found useful. The planning process, which involves the entire school staff, has three steps: (1) complete a matrix for program elements and one for content; (2) conduct indicated staff development; and (3) monitor individual teacher progress.

Program Elements Matrix

Filling in the program elements matrix is a whole-staff activity. The staff should decide what elements are important to put in the first column of the matrix; the list in Table 2 is simply a starting point. The other columns represent steps in the continuum from where the staff is to where they would like to be.

The columns in Table 2 are to be filled in with a three-year perspective. The bare minimum of science instruction in grade one might be 60 minutes per week, and the goal might be 120 minutes per week, with entries in the first and third columns. The midpoint, a reasonable transition goal, would be 90 minutes per week. Similarly, the values for grade five might range from a starting point of 120 minutes per week, transition of 150 minutes per week, and a goal of 200 minutes per week. The amount of content covered might range from three units per year at the start to five units per year as the goal. The way in

Table 2	A Matrix for Program Elements in Science Education		
Element	Starting point	Transition	Attainable goal
Time			
Content			
Instructional strategies			
Integration			
Materials			
Resources			
Assemblies			
Science fairs			
Family science			

which teachers present information might range from teacher demonstrations to teacher-led activities to student investigations. Once the entries are agreed on, teachers can locate their current programs on the chart and set personal goals for moving over one column each year. Thus, if a teacher is already teaching science 90 minutes per week, he or she would aim for 120 minutes per week the following year and 150 minutes per week the third year, even though it is off the chart.

Content Matrix

A goal in designing a schoolwide articulated content matrix following the mandates of this framework is to balance the three science disciplines (physical, earth, and life) so that the curriculum spirals through the grades and is united through the use of the themes of science.

There are many approaches for developing such a matrix; some are more effective than others in reaching the goals of the framework. Themes might be included in the curriculum on an awareness level. Although this is better than no attempt at conceptualization, it does not incorporate the thrust of the framework. Themes can also be introduced in the curriculum. This is a more sophisticated goal toward which the matrix might be directed. A third approach to building the matrix involves theme induction. This

process uses known content to build discipline-specific strands that are organized around unifying concepts. The content of the strands is then analyzed for themes that emerge as commonalties in the disciplines. This method is presented in detail in this section.

One must remember that building a content matrix is like playing with a Rubik's Cube. All of the pieces eventually fit together, but they may need to be juggled or fine-tuned to create the best fit of ideas. The fluidity of the matrix allows for many different examples to be developed using the same content. The amount of variety depends on the emphasis of the component parts of the matrix (i.e., unifying concepts, grade-level concepts, subconcepts, themes). Planners are encouraged to design their own planning model. (Two examples are presented later in this section [tables 4 and 7]. They are not mandates for how a curriculum should look, but rather a process by which a curriculum is designed.)

General Structure of the Matrix

Table 3 represents a pattern for a content matrix that is to be filled in with conceptual and thematic ideas. It is used by the staff to design the scope and sequence of the curriculum over a three-year period. Implementation of the matrix can then be done in "little steps":

3 units ✕ 7 grade levels = 21 units for year one
4 units ✕ 7 grade levels = 28 units for year two
5 units ✕ 7 grade levels = 35 units for year three

Schools that include grades seven and eight would expand the matrix to include the additional grades.

The matrix in Table 3 consists of five columns and seven rows (for grade levels kindergarten through grade six). Grade-level themes are to be inserted in the second column. The third, fourth, and fifth columns represent the traditional disciplines of science and might be considered by some districts as the core science curriculum. The next two columns take into consideration the diversity found in California's school system and are purposely left open for decision making at the district and school site levels. We suggest that these columns be filled with units of study that either complete the core curriculum or enrich it and that they be organized to be consistent with the themes driving the other units found in that row (grade level). Columns are organized through unifying concepts that are discipline-specific and tie the grade levels together. The rows of the matrix represent curricula at successive grade levels, kindergarten through grade six. Units in a row are united by the themes of science and interrelated content.

Building the Vertical Columns of the Matrix

Unifying concept(s) and grade-level concepts and subconcepts are developed for each discipline: physical, earth, and life science. (Subconcepts are illustrated in more detail in tables 5, 6, 8, and 9.) Steps for defining and identifying these components in each discipline follow:

Unifying concepts. The unifying concepts help teachers answer the question: "What do you want your students to know after they leave grade six (grade eight) in _____ science?" These concepts:

- Are broad enough that students at each grade level can learn from them.
- Are discipline-specific; i.e., they explain the nature of the discipline and help to organize and understand it.
- Provide a framework for the developmental sequence of traditional content.

Process for identifying unifying concepts. The process for identifying unifying concepts includes four steps:

1. Brainstorm about the most important things for a student to know and experience in a given discipline. A resource for doing this is the content section of the *Framework*, which is arranged by central organizing principles and organizing questions.
2. From the brainstorm session, cluster topics of ideas and activities that seem to fit into bigger ideas. It is very likely that traditional topics can be categorized several ways. For example, rocks can be included as products of the changing earth or can be discussed from the perspective of the structure of the earth; body systems can be included in a structure/function relationship, but also to explain the diversity of life; and matter can be described from the energy required to change it or from the relationship of microscopic to macroscopic interactions.
3. From the cluster, select a unifying concept or concepts broad enough to be developed for kindergarten through grade eight by the use of grade-level concepts.
4. Express the unifying concept in a sentence to clarify its meaning. Here are some examples:

> The earth, within its universe, is changing.
> Life is diverse.
> Matter and energy can be changed but cannot be created or destroyed.

Grade-level concepts. The grade-level concepts are characterized as:

- Supporting the unifying concepts (similar to developing a topic sentence and its supporting details).
- Describing content from a conceptual basis, rather than presenting isolated facts. For example, if the unifying concept is that the earth is changing, then the traditional subject of oceanography would be addressed from the standpoint of how oceans affect or are affected by the changing earth, rather than presented as unrelated bits and pieces.
- Being arranged in a developmentally appropriate sequence.

Process for selecting grade-level concepts. We suggest two methods for developing and selecting grade-level concepts: (1) brainstorm supporting concepts for unifying concepts, or use content de-

Table 3   A Pattern for a Content Matrix in Science Education—Kindergarten Through Grade Six

	Physical science	Earth science	Life science	Local options
		Unifying concepts		
Grade	Theme(s)	Grade-level concepts and subconcepts		
K				
1				
2				
3				
4				
5				
6				

scribed in the appropriate grade-level span of the *Framework*; or (2) brainstorm the content that is currently taught at each grade level and rephrase it in the focus of the unifying concept. For example, traditional content for grade two might include the ideas that plants have roots, stems, and leaves and animals have body systems. If the unifying concept is that life is diverse, then this content can be refocused as a grade-level concept to read: Living things have similar needs but diverse structure to meet their needs. If the content that is brainstormed does not seem appropriate to the unifying concept, set it aside for consideration in other areas.

After completing method (1) or (2) for selecting grade-level concepts, place the sentence describing each grade-level concept in sequence so that the sequence is developmentally appropriate.

Subconcepts. Subconcepts exhibit the following characteristics:

* They support the grade-level concepts by identifying the content to be taught at each grade level.
* They describe the how and why as well as the what of the content. For example, if the unifying concept for earth science has been identified as "The earth, within its universe, is changing," and the concept for grade five has been identified as "Forces that work on the earth are responsible for the changes that we observe," then traditional topics such as erosion deposition, rocks, tectonics, layers of the earth, and so forth can be organized by three subconcepts: (1) forces change the earth; (2) products result from these changes; and (3) change occurs over time.

Process for selecting subconcepts. (Treatment of subconcepts in the process is illustrated in tables 5, 6, 8, and 9.)

1. Brainstorm the *stuff* that is taught. Sources include the *Framework*'s content section, previous experience, textbooks, and other reference materials.
2. Combine similar subconcepts, eliminate those that do not address the grade-level concept, and select three to five that meet the above characteristics for subconcepts.

After completing the process for identifying the unifying concepts for physical science, repeat the process for earth science and life science. We suggest building each strand with reference to the other strands. In this way, one can start to look for thematic connections from the subconcepts across a grade level.

Building the Horizontal Rows of the Matrix

The goal in constructing a horizontal row is to make the subconcepts of the units match and relate to each other and be unified by the themes of science. This can be done using the following steps:

1. Analyze the subconcepts of each column to identify which themes seem to be expressed.
2. Identify commonalities of themes across a row (some literally *pop out* at you).
3. Correct for mismatches of themes by making alterations, including slight rephrasing of subconcepts, modification of focus, movement of grade-level concepts to another row, or identification of additional themes.
4. Review the entire matrix to ensure that all themes have been presented in the curriculum for kindergarten through grade six or eight. We recommend two to three themes per year and that the themes be repeated.

Sample Matrices

Tables 4 and 7 illustrate two models of matrices that have been developed using the aforementioned processes. Each of the models is different in the sense that each develops a proposed curriculum at one grade level and for one discipline: Example A (Table 4) for grade four in the earth sciences; Example B (Table 7) for grade one in the physical sciences. The grade-level choices are a slice of what the curriculum might look like for primary and upper elementary grades. The matrices are also different in the selection of unifying concepts and the emphasis on different themes. Both, however, use traditional content knowledge as a basis for the matrix.

Note that two units, grade one "Water in the World" and grade four "Energy Transformations," are presented in both models. These units are organized under different unifying concepts in the two models so that planners can see how the same topics can be approached from different points of view. When referring to the matrix, notice that the grade-level concepts (which were identified using the aforementioned process) are listed, followed by a unit title in italics. In order to avoid repetition, the grade-level concepts are referenced in this section by the unit title. The themes are italicized in the narrative.

Example A. Explication. This example (Table 4) looks at the earth science strand and the grade-four slice of a curriculum. Consider first the earth science column. In the development of this strand, it is desired that students first experience and describe the world immediately around them, expand their horizons to talk about the larger world, and then consider their place within the universe. They will do so within the context of the unifying concept "The earth, within its universe, is changing."

Kindergarten students need to explore the immediate. They can talk about observable changes in their world (day and night, seasons, the weather, and so forth), the landforms with which they are familiar, and the world of their community (which integrates nicely with the *History–Social Science Framework*).

In "Water in the World," students in grade one are prepared to take on slightly more challenging investigations. This unit addresses several themes that appear in all grade-one units in this matrix. Students can be introduced to several related concepts: (1) that there is *stability* in the forms and content of the earth's water by looking at oceans and other bodies of water; (2) that *energy* from the sun warms the earth and its water, driving the water cycle; (3) that water changes its state; (4) that clouds are a part of the water cycle; and (5) that this water cycle is a major factor in the creation of local weather. *Patterns of change* in the local weather can be experienced as students collect and report daily weather data.

In "Changing Earth," students in grade two can investigate the macroscopic products that come from the earth (rocks and soils, for example). They can also come to an understanding that certain forms of *energy* are at work in the earth, creating and reshaping those products. *Patterns of change* in the earth involve processes that occur over long periods of time.

A broader background with geologic processes enables grade three students to examine "Changes in the Ocean." Landforms and ocean basins can be described and defined and shown to have changed over geologic time. [*Evolution*] The *energy* of wave patterns can be investigated, and their relation to changing landforms studied. The mechanics of wave motion itself can be introduced or reinforced at this level. Connections to other disciplines can also be made as students examine the influence of oceans on weather and climate and the effect these have on living organisms and ecosystems. [*Systems and Interactions*]

These discoveries prepare students to revisit "Meteorology" in grade four. A review of the water cycle prepares them to understand how the *energy* of

heat transfer interacts with and affects atmospheric pressure, wind patterns, and precipitation. The effect of weather and climate on ecosystems can also be studied. [*Systems* and *Interactions*]

In grade five, students return to a study of "Changing Earth," but at a more sophisticated level. They are prepared to begin a deeper investigation of geologic time and the changes it has brought. [*Evolution*] They are ready to look at the various *patterns of change* that can be observed in river systems, crystals, and rock formations. They might also examine the effect those changes have had on both landforms and organisms. [*Systems* and *Interactions*]

Having concentrated on the earth, students are prepared in grade six to look at the universe from the perspective of the earth. In "Astronomy," they can investigate the changes wrought by the sun and moon and examine the earth's place in the solar system. [*Systems* and *Interactions*] They can also begin to understand the clues provided by the stars of the *evolution* of the universe. This study, in turn, prepares students for a more sophisticated look at similar topics in the middle school years. For a more detailed look at the subconcepts that make up each of these grade-level units, see Table 5.

Table 6 is the grade-four row of this matrix. It is detailed to show the relationships among the unifying concepts, grade-level concepts, subconcepts, and themes. Analysis of the subconcepts reveals the content of each unit, suggests connections among the three disciplines, and forms the basis for the identification of the themes. Notice that the themes are keyed to the subconcepts.

Two optional units for grade four are "Food and Nutrition" and "California Landforms." (See Table 4.) They are presented as possible choices to complete the thematic approach. In the first unit, focus should be directed toward clarifying the energy needs of the human body and how adequate diet, caloric intake, and balanced nutrition meet those needs. Students can also investigate the role of humans in the food chain. The second unit might fulfill a "local options" need and provide an integration with the topics of California history and geography that is mandated by the *History–Social Science Framework* for grade four. This unit might be a multidisciplinary study that looks at the interrelationships among energy transformation, meteorology, and geology on the specific landforms in our state and the ecosystems that have developed as a result of that interaction.

Table 4   Content Matrix: Example A—Kindergarten Through Grade Six

Grade	Theme(s)	Physical science	Earth science	Life science	Ecology, technology, health aviation/space science	Local options
		Unifying concepts				*Local options*
		Energy causes changes in matter.	The earth, within its universe, is constantly changing.	Living things and systems demonstrate a structure-function relationship.	A healthy individual understands and interacts with the environment.	Understanding in science helps to explain phenomena in other fields.
		Grade-level concepts (with unit titles)				
K	Me in My World		There are observable changes on the earth. "Me in My World"			
1	Stability, Energy, Patterns of Change		Water is an important element of change on the earth. "Water in the World"			
2	Scale and Structure, Patterns of Change		Different forms of energy reshape products of the earth. "Changing Earth"			
3	Systems and Interactions, Energy		Oceans affect or are affected by the changing earth. "Changes in the Ocean"			
4	Energy, Systems and Interactions	Energy can be transmitted and converted from one form to another. "Energy Transformations"	Changes in the atmosphere affect and are affected by changes in the earth. "Meteorology"	Structures of an ecosystem are related to the flow of energy through it. "Interrelationships"	Energy derived from food is necessary for all living things. "Food and Nutrition"	The climate and geography of California affect landforms and ecosystems. "California Landforms"
5	Evolution, Patterns of Change, Systems and Interactions		Forces that work on the earth cause the changes we observe. "Changing Earth"			
6	Evolution, Systems and Interactions		The changing earth is part of a changing universe. "Astronomy"			

		Table 5 Content Matrix: Example A—Earth Science Sample Grade-Level Concepts and Subconcepts
		Unifying Concept: The earth, within its universe, is constantly changing.
Grade	*Theme(s)*	*Grade-level concepts and subconcepts*
K	*Me in My World*	There are observable changes on the earth. • I see changes in the world around me. —Weather —Day and night —Seasons • I see different landforms (mountains, valleys, plains, hills, deserts, oceans, and so forth). • The world of my community is made of different things (living and nonliving; integrated with history–social science).
1	*Stability* *Energy* *Patterns of Change*	Water is an important element of change on the earth. • Most of the earth's water is found in the oceans and is salty. Fresh water is found in lakes, river systems, streams, creeks, and other drainage systems. • Water undergoes changes. • The sun warms the earth and the sea and drives the water cycle. Clouds can be observed and are part of the water cycle. • The water cycle, in conjunction with other factors, creates the earth's weather. • Weather data can be collected and reported, and the patterns can be described.
2	*Patterns of Change* *Scale and Structure*	Different forms of energy reshape products of the earth. • Forces at work in the earth create and reshape it. • The earth (and its forces) work change over long periods of time.
3	*Energy* *Evolution* *Systems and Interactions*	Oceans affect or are affected by the changing earth. • Landforms and ocean basins can be described and defined. • The energy of wave patterns in the ocean changes landforms. Wave patterns can be studied as mechanical motions. • The oceans have a profound influence on weather and climate, which, in turn, affect living organisms. • Diverse life forms are found in the ocean habitat.
4	*Systems and Interactions* *Energy*	Changes in the atmosphere affect and are affected by changes in the earth. • The sun warms the earth, sea, and air and drives the water cycle. • Uneven heating of the earth affects air pressure and gives rise to wind patterns that move locally and around the globe. • Moving air masses of different temperature and different moisture content come in contact, resulting in precipitation and other identifiable weather phenomena. • Weather data can be collected and reported. • Weather has profound effects on climate and life forms.

Table 5 (continued)		
Grade	Theme(s)	Grade-level concepts and subconcepts
5	*Evolution* *Patterns of Change* *Systems and Interactions*	Forces that work on the earth cause the changes we observe. • The earth is very old and has changed over geologic time. • Forces arising from heat flow in the earth have caused it to change. • The changing earth has had a profound effect on landforms and living organisms
6	*Evolution* *Systems and Interactions*	The changing earth is part of a changing universe. • Both the sun and the moon, bodies within our solar system, have observable and identifiable effects on the earth: —The sun is the source of all energy. —The moon and the sun are responsible for tidal movement. —Seasons are related to the earth's orientation to the sun. • The earth is a part of the solar system; it is both like and unlike other planets. • Stars provide information about the history of the universe. The earth is but a small part of the universe.

Table 6 Content Matrix: Example A—Subconcepts in the Grade Four Core Curriculum Keyed to Themes

Grade	Theme(s)		Physical science	Earth science	Life science
4	* Energy • Systems and Interactions	**Unifying concepts**	Energy causes changes in matter.	The earth, within its universe, is constantly changing.	Living things and systems demonstrate a structure-function relationship.
		Grade-level concepts *(with unit titles)*	Energy can be transmitted and converted from one form to another. "Energy Transformation"	Changes in the atmosphere affect and are affected by changes in the earth. "Meteorology"	Structures of an ecosystem are related to the flow of energy. "Interrelationships"
		Subconcepts	• The ultimate source of most of the energy we use is the sun. *• Energy can be converted from one form to another; there are many forms of energy. • In food chains the sun's radiant energy is converted through photosynthesis to chemical energy which, in turn, is transformed into mechanical energy. Some of this energy is lost as heat energy. *• In physical systems energy from a number of sources is used to do work. Heat energy is often a by-product of this transformation. • Heat energy moves through the environment from warmer to cooler regions by processes called conduction, convection, and radiation. This movement has an effect on meteorologic and geologic processes and on ecosystems.	* The sun warms the earth and air and drives the water cycle. • Uneven heating of the earth affects pressure and temperature, creating wind patterns that move locally and around the globe. *• Moving air masses of different temperature and different moisture content come in contact, resulting in precipitation and other forms of weather phenomena; weather data can be collected and used to make predictions. • Different kinds of weather have profound effects on climate and on living organisms and contribute to the structure of ecosystems.	• There are structures of and identifiable relationships within an ecosystem. These include: biotic/abiotic, niche/community habitats; producer/consumer/decomposer. *• Energy is transferred through an ecosystem from the nonliving to the living (food chains, food webs, and food pyramids). • Components of ecosystems interact and are interdependent. • Human beings (people) affect the ecosystem.

Example B. Explication. In this example (Table 7), the physical science strand is organized around the unifying concept, "Matter and energy can be changed but not created or destroyed." In the development of this strand, it is desired that students first experience and describe the world immediately around them. Doing so will allow them to explore the macroscopic properties of matter, energy, and motion. Understanding these observable properties prepares students to begin investigations into ever more discrete concepts related to energy transfer and the structure of matter itself.

Kindergarten students need to explore the immediate. In "Matter Around Me," they can observe and discuss the properties of the *stuff* around them (color, size, texture, shape; whether it sinks or floats in water; the state in which it is found; and so forth). They can also examine things to observe that everything is made of smaller structures. The things that they observe can, in part, be drawn from materials in the other two core units of this grade level.

In "Kinds of Energy," grade one students observe, classify, and describe the unique properties of different forms of energy as observed at differing levels of observation. [*Scale and Structure*] Students investigate such important concepts as transmission, reflection, and absorption of energy. In addition, they can explore the idea that energy can be used to do work and make changes in matter. [*Systems and Interactions*]

"Matter," in grade two of this model, continues to deal with the properties of macroscopic things, but students can approach their study in a more formalized manner. They can review previous learnings about phase changes and sinking/floating and can be introduced to the concepts of matter occupying space and having weight and substance. In addition, grade two students can begin to use tools of measurement and observation to examine the differing *scale and structure* of all matter. They can also conduct investigations into simple physical and chemical changes [*Systems and Interactions*], with an emphasis on understanding that changes in matter sometimes require energy and sometimes release energy.

In grade three, students examine forces that act on matter and affect its motion. After investigating those forces, students measure and observe the *patterns of change* in moving objects in terms of distance, time, and weight. They can apply force to objects in order to move them through a distance, and they can construct simple machines to do work and to create change in their environments. [*Systems and Interactions*] These simple energy transformations form the basis for understanding the concepts of mechanical energy.

The grade-four unit, "Energy Transformation," is organized around the major themes of *systems and interactions* and *energy*. Students will investigate a variety of conversions from one form of energy to another, recognizing that the total energy in the system is conserved. They will expand their studies of mechanical energy in an understanding that energy conversions from a number of sources are used to do mechanical work, often with heat energy as a by-product of the transformation. Processes that transfer this heat energy will conclude the unit of study.

"Waves, Light, and Sound" provides grade five students with a look at some of the microscopic properties of matter and energy transfer. [*Scale and Structure*] They can investigate the similarities and differences between electromagnetic and mechanical waves. They can also explore the unique properties of light and sound *energy*. This unit has a variety of topics suitable for integration with other science disciplines, as well: infrared radiation and heat transfer (geology and meteorology), photosynthesis (ecosystems and food chains), sight and hearing (anatomy and health), and the effect of concussive waves (earthquakes), to name a few.

The grade-six unit, "Matter," looks at the *scale and structure* of atoms and demonstrates how chemistry is devoted to understanding the properties and interactions of atoms and groups of atoms. [*Systems and Interactions*] Students can investigate such concepts as mass, displacement, and density. They can explore physical changes in matter and chemical reactions. They can also come to a fuller understanding of various energy transformations involved in chemical reactions. As such, this is a fitting summarizing unit for the learning that has gone before and a challenging introduction to the concepts needed for a rich middle school experience.

For a more detailed look at the subconcepts that make up each of these grade-level units, see Table 8.

Table 9 is the grade one row of Example B. As with Example A, the subconcepts for this row are detailed, and the themes are keyed to the subconcepts.

The fourth and fifth columns in the grade-one row on Table 7 identify an outdoor education strand and a

Table 7 Content Matrix: Example B—Kindergarten Through Grade Six

Grade	Theme(s)	Physical science	Earth science	Life science	Local options	
					Ecology, technology, health aviation/space science	
		Unifying concepts				
		Matter and energy can be changed but not created or destroyed.	Earth systems interact in cyclical patterns.	Life is diverse.	Respect for nature develops from understanding how nature works.	The application of scientific knowledge changes the world.
		Grade-level concepts (with unit titles)				
K	*Me in My World*	Matter can be observed and classified. "Matter Around Me"				
1	*Systems and Interactions Scale and Structure*	Energy comes in different forms. "Kinds of Energy"	Water affects life on earth. "Water in the World"	There are similarities and differences in living things. "Diversity of Life"	Human beings affect the environment. "Conservation"	Resources are limited; some can be recycled. "Recycling"
2	*Scale and Structure Energy*	Matter has properties and can be changed. "Matter"				
3	*Systems and Interactions Patterns of Change*	Forces act on matter and cause motion. "Changes in Motion; Simple Machines"				
4	*Energy Systems and Interactions Scale and Structure*	Energy can be converted from one form to another. "Energy Transformation"				
5	*Energy Scale and Structure Systems and Interactions*	Matter and energy interact at a microscopic level. "Waves, Light, Sound"				
6	*Energy Systems and Interactions Scale and Structure*	The structure of matter at a microscopic level affects chemical reactions. "Matter"				

Table 8 Content Matrix: Example B—Physical Science Sample Grade-Level Concepts and Subconcepts

Unifying Concept: Matter and energy can be changed but not created or destroyed.

Grade	Theme(s)	Grade-level concepts and subconcepts
K	*Me in My World*	Matter can be observed and classified. • Everything around me is made of "stuff." The stuff can be described and classified by many characteristics: —Color, texture, shape —Hardness, flexibility —Taste, odor —Sound or light that might be emitted or reflected —State (solid, liquid, or gas) —Tendency to float or sink in water • All things are made of similar structures.
1	*Systems and Interactions* *Scale and Structure*	Energy comes in different forms. • At the macroscopic level, each of the various forms of energy has unique characteristics. Observe and compare the properties of different manifestations of energy (light, sound, static electricity, magnetism, heat, wave motions, and so forth) in order to classify and describe. • Energy can be transmitted, reflected, and absorbed. • Energy can be used to do work and to make changes in matter. Changes in matter sometimes require energy and sometimes release energy.
2	*Energy* *Scale and Structure*	Matter has properties and can be changed. • Matter has definable properties that can be described and reported: —It occupies space. —It has weight and substance. —It sinks and floats. —It exists in three states. • Matter is made of smaller structures. We use tools to measure, perceive, and better understand these structures when they exist at a scale too small, too fast, or too far away for normal perception (telescopes, microscopes, thermometers, scales, clocks, and so forth). The more we understand the structure and function of matter, the better we understand living organisms and how they interact with their environment and the better we understand the changing earth. • Matter undergoes physical and chemical changes.
3	*Patterns of Change* *Systems and Interactions*	Forces act on matter and cause motion. • Forces act on matter. Forces include: —Pushes and pulls by direct contact —Gravity —Friction —Magnetism These forces can affect the motion of matter. • Motion can be measured in terms of distance, time, and weight. —Speed is the distance covered divided by the elapsed time.

Table 8 *(Continued)*

Grade	Theme(s)	Grade-level concepts and subconcepts
3 *(Continued)*	*Patterns of Change* *Systems and Interactions*	—The weight of an object is related to the amount of force necessary to change its motion. • Work is done when a force is applied to an object that moves it through a distance. • Simple machines help people do work and change their environment.
4	*Systems and Interactions* *Scale and Structure*	Energy can be converted from one form to another. • The ultimate source of most of the energy we use is the sun. • Energy can be converted from one form to another. In the process the total energy in the system is conserved but not necessarily in the same form. We use energy from a number of sources (the sun, water, heat within the earth, nuclear reactions, and so forth) to do mechanical work. • Heat energy moves through the environment from warmer to cooler regions by processes called conduction, convection, and radiation. This movement affects meteorologic and geologic processes and ecosystems.
5	*Scale and Structure* *Energy* *Systems and Interactions*	Matter and energy interact at a microscopic level. • Light and sound energy are similar in many ways, but they are not the same thing: —Both travel as waves and can be reflected, refracted, and absorbed. Both have frequencies and wavelengths. —Light is an electromagnetic form of energy. —Sound is a mechanical wave arising from vibrating objects. • Infrared radiation is an electromagnetic form of energy. Light carries heat in the form of infrared radiation. When infrared radiation is absorbed by matter, it releases heat energy. • As a mechanical wave, energy can be a force that can do severe damage (earthquakes). • Animals perceive their environment by means of light and sound energy: —Electrochemical impulses arise from light striking the retina and are processed by the central nervous system. —Electromechanical impulses arise from sound in the middle ear and are processed by the central nervous system. • Plants use electrochemical processes in photosynthesis to manufacture food from sunlight.
6	*Systems and Interactions* *Scale and Structure* *Energy*	The structure of matter at a microscopic level affects chemical reactions. • All matter has unique properties that can be observed and measured: —It has weight and mass. —It occupies space and displaces other matter from the same space. —It has density. • The properties of matter depend very much on the scale at which we look at them. Properties of matter at the large scale (macroscopic) depend on its properties at the small scale (microscopic). • Chemistry is the study of the properties and interactions of atoms and the study of groups of atoms as they combine to form compounds and mixtures.

Table 9 Content Matrix: Example B—Subconcepts in the Grade One Core Curriculum Keyed to Themes

Grade	Theme(s)	Physical science	Earth science	Life science
		Unifying concepts		
		Energy transformations bring about many changes in the physical world, but, overall, energy is conserved.	Cycles are repeatable patterns in nature.	Diversity is the concept that represents the panoramic variability in the natural world.
		Grade-level concepts (with unit titles)		
1	• Systems and Interactions • Scale and Structure	Energy comes in different forms, each with its own characteristics. "Kinds of Energy"	The water cycle governs much of the environmental conditions on earth. "Water in the World"	The diversity of life arises from the intersection of evolutionary mechanisms with environmental conditions. "Diversity of Life"
		Subconcepts		
		• At the macroscopic level each of the various forms of energy has unique characteristics that can be observed, described, and classified. • Energy can be transmitted, reflected, and classified. • Energy can be used to do work and to make changes in matter. Changes in matter sometimes require energy and sometimes release energy.	• Water is essential for life on this planet. • Water undergoes changes when heat energy is added or removed. • The sun warms the earth and drives the water cycle. Clouds can be observed and are part of the water cycle. • The water cycle, in conjunction with other factors, creates the earth's weather. • Weather affects the earth and living organisms.	• Living things need food, water, shelter, and space. Living things share characteristics, including growth, reproduction, response to environmental stimuli, and so forth. • There is tremendous diversity in living organisms and between them. • There is great diversity in the homes and habitats of living things. • Within diverse habitats, plants and animals secure their needs in different ways but often depend on one another.

technology strand as optional topics to be developed. In this row, the first unit is entitled "Conservation" and deals with the primary ideas of conserving things and littering. "Recycling" takes these ideas a step further, illustrates what we can do with the things we cannot conserve, and helps to awaken student concern over social issues.

Section G   Relationship with Other Frameworks

THE reforms in science education that are reflected in this *Framework* are part of an overall reform strategy to transform education for all students so that it promotes thinking and reasoning. As described by Lauren Resnick in her monograph, *Education and Learning to Think,* there is nothing new in a curriculum that promotes thinking; there has always been the tradition of the academy in which students were challenged to read demanding texts, to write critical essays, and to understand the basic tenets of scientific and mathematical reasoning. What is new about the promotion of higher-order thinking skills in the reform of the 1980s is the expectation that *all* students can and must be involved in such a demanding curriculum. As Resnick points out, the definition of "higher-order thinking skills" is elusive, but we can recognize it when it occurs. It is nonalgorithmic and complex, it involves multiple solutions and judgment, and it often involves uncertainty. The thinker must examine his or her thinking and must impose meaning on the situation. Such thinking is required by all of our citizens, not just the elite, and must be the outcome of schooling.

The manifestation of the attempt to cultivate higher-order thinking takes different forms in different subject areas. Mathematics educators are inclined to talk in terms of *problem solving*; history and social science educators speak of *critical thinking*; science educators talk about *the nature of science*, as illustrated in Chapter 1. In each case, the details and mechanics of the discipline are being subordinated to the goal of a meaning-centered curriculum with the aim of increasing the thinking and reasoning in which students are engaged.

The focus of the *Mathematics Framework,* approved by the State Board of Education and published in 1985, is "mathematical power, which involves the ability to discern mathematical relationships, reason logically, and use mathematical techniques effectively. . . ." It emphasizes teaching for understanding, instead of teaching rules and procedures for their own sake. The consistent call to relate mathematical techniques to the solution of problems that are meaningful and accessible to students makes the bridge to science instruction a natural alliance. The practice of computational, measurement, and graphing skills makes obvious connections between mathematics and science. Science educators should be particularly conscious of the *Mathematics Framework*'s emphasis on selection of the appropriate method for achieving numerical results—estimation, mental arithmetic, paper-and-pencil, or calculator—depending on the nature of the problem and the numerical information involved. Students should learn to select the method and the appropriate level of accuracy of the result. They should be making their own selections, both on class assignments and on tests, by the end of grade six. Use of scientific calculators, advocated in mathematics for secondary students, should also be incorporated in secondary science programs.

Beyond computation, however, the mathematics curriculum also includes the important strands of statistics and probability, patterns and functions, and logic. The statistics and probability strand includes the formulation of questions, collection and organization of data in a variety of representations, and comparison of empirical results with theoretical probabilities. The patterns and functions strand includes the search for patterns in data and the representation of these patterns in verbal, visual, numerical, graphical, and algebraic forms. The logic strand includes the organization of ideas with an accurate use of terms such as *all, some, and, or, if . . . then,* and *not,* and making valid inferences. These skills are both required by and developed in the science curriculum, so coordination with the mathematics curriculum is essential for science and mathematics.

The theme of *scale and structure* is particularly well suited to integration of mathematics with science; developing the number sense for very large and very small numbers and the scientific notation to express them, ratio and proportion, and even the idea of scale itself are central concepts for both disciplines. *Patterns of change* is another important bridge, as quantitative analysis is often the method used to differentiate among cycles, trends, and random changes.

The *English–Language Arts Framework* was approved by the State Board of Education in 1986 and published in 1987. Also centered on the construction of meaning, its focus is an integrated curriculum in which the language arts of reading, writing, speaking, and listening are treated together in meaningful contexts rather than treated separately, apart from context. With an emphasis on a literature base, it exposes students to significant literary works, rather than brief narratives constructed to teach skills. This approach is particularly well suited to coordination with science instruction, as science investigations provide meaningful contexts for reading, writing, speaking, and listening and help students to develop their language arts skills related to nonfiction. Of course, science fiction and literature about science themes are additional avenues for coordination of the science and English–language arts curricula.

The *History–Social Science Framework* was approved by the State Board of Education in 1987 and published in 1988. One of its themes is the importance of "history as a story well told." It emphasizes depth over breadth, using the opportunity to examine in depth the connections among history, geography, and culture, particularly the literature of and about a period. The notion that science is a human activity and that it takes place in certain places and certain times due to the conditions that have gone before as well as current circumstances is certainly in accord with such study. In fact, the role of science and technology in societal development is an important component of history, particularly as it relates to contemporary issues and events. Incorporating the achievements of people from diverse cultures in the history of science, whether it be discussed in history or science or both, is a particularly appropriate approach. Care should be taken to ensure the accuracy of the portrayals of historical figures. The

History–Social Science Framework also makes clear that controversial topics and discussion of values are to be embraced rather than avoided. As discussed in Chapter 1 of the *Science Framework*, "The Nature of Science," controversy and values are not the province of history–social science alone and must be handled as legitimate concerns of the science curriculum as well. Finally, the themes of *evolution*, which is directional change, and *patterns of change*, which includes cyclical change, are important bridges between history–social science and natural science. The ideas of *systems and interactions* and *stability* are further links between these fields.

The *Foreign Language Framework* is the most recently developed framework, approved in 1988 and published in 1989. Its emphasis is on communication, again subordinating skills to the meaning that is necessary for the development of understanding. While particular connections with the science curriculum are few, the general trend toward meaning and away from vocabulary for its own sake is certainly as valid in science as it is in foreign language. It has been estimated that some high school science textbooks introduce more new vocabulary words than a typical first-year foreign language textbook. Such practices should be compared with exemplary practice in foreign language instruction and abandoned.

The *Visual and Performing Arts Framework*, aproved in 1981, published in 1982, and reissued in 1989, is constructed around four components of arts education: aesthetic perception, creative expression, arts heritage, and aesthetic valuing. The relationship between science and the arts should not be limited to an "arts and crafts" approach but should extend to the common intellectual processes and content of these fields. The critical-thinking processes associated with science are paralleled in the arts, as students use all of their senses to observe, analyze, and synthesize the sights, sounds, and movements in the world around them. The work of both scientists and artists includes communicating their impressions, evaluating their own work and the work of others, and making thoughtful and informed judgments. Certain scientific topics, such as light, sound, and perception, are particularly appropriate areas of integration between science and the arts. Certain arts skills, such as observing, drawing, and acting, can also enhance the study of science. Most of the major themes of science find their representation in the visual and performing arts curriculum, but certainly *scale and structure*, *systems and interaction*, and *energy* are likely vehicles for connecting the arts and the sciences.

The next framework to be revised, with a committee established in 1989 and a product anticipated in 1990, is the *Health Framework*, the current edition of which was approved by the State Board of Education in 1977 and published in 1978. The old document explicitly avoided any commentary about relationships with other subject areas, deferring to "the prerogative of local school districts." The new health framework will reflect the thrust of the "Healthy Kids, Healthy California" comprehensive health education initiative in which the various aspects of school life that promote health—including health education, nutrition, health and psychological services, and physical education—are coordinated with each other and with the total school program. While health education will maintain its distinctive role in the curriculum, consistent with *Education Code* requirements to offer health education at elementary and secondary levels, it is likely that connections with other subject areas, including science, will be defined and encouraged.

In addition to the conceptual connections among the frameworks, certain pedagogical techniques, such as cooperative learning and writing across the curriculum, are appearing with increasing frequency. Broader notions of assessment—away from multiple choice and towards student-generated work, projects, and portfolios—are also becoming increasingly prominent. These teaching and assessment strategies are required by the attention to higher-order thinking, as it is necessary to develop one's ideas by discussing them with others and by writing about them, and it is necessary to assess a student's progress by using conditions similar to the learning.

When the curricula emphasized mastery of narrow skills, such as long division, spelling, historical dates, and science vocabulary, individual students practicing isolated exercises in quiet rows of desks may have been an efficient and effective strategy. The curricula are moving toward attention to skills in order to make more meaningful activity possible—division for the purpose of solving a complex problem, perhaps using a calculator; spelling for the purpose of publishing an essay, possibly using a computer spell-checking program; dates for the purpose of a historical argument, maybe using a reference book; and vocabulary for the purpose of communicating about a scientific investigation.

These meaningful activities are characterized by communication about thinking with others, enriched by interaction with other students, and less likely to proceed effectively in quiet rows of isolated students. The groups of four that are assembled for mathematical problem solving become the peer response groups for revising writing, the debate team for enacting a historical argument, and the research group for investigating a scientific question. This is not to say that there are not some things that need to be learned individually or quietly; merely that the movement toward meaning-centered curriculum is coming in all subject areas and that some of the changes in teaching and assessment that support one subject will prove to be valuable in others.

Chapter 8

Instructional Materials Criteria

THIS chapter summarizes the criteria that California will apply to the adoption of science instructional materials in 1992, based on the philosophy, content, and guidelines of the foregoing chapters. Of particular importance are (1) the shift of emphasis on content, away from inclusion of topics and toward covering fewer topics in depth and thematically; (2) the emphasis on representing science accurately and honestly, particularly the nature of science, its philosophies and methods, and its language; and (3) the forsaking of disconnected, vocabulary-driven chapters and units that merely pile facts on definitions, in favor of a considerate narrative prose that cares less about readability formulas and more about readable text.

Section A   Introduction

CALIFORNIA is one of 22 states in the United States that conducts state level review and adoption of educational materials. According to procedures set forth in the *Education Code*, the State Board of Education selects from five to 15 programs for each subject area at each level, kindergarten through grade eight, that can be purchased with money in the Instructional Materials Fund (IMF). Each year, school districts are financed from the IMF on the basis of the number of students they serve. Currently, 70% of the IMF funds for materials for students in kindergarten through grade eight are restricted to programs[1] that

---

[1] By "program" is meant the sum of instructional materials purchased for use in the classroom, including but not limited to textbooks, software, charts, maps, equipment, and supplies. Also included in a good curriculum are features such as field trips, extramural visits and speakers, and other audiovisual aids.

are listed on the adoption list (often called "the matrix") for the particular subject area, unless the district completes a waiver process demonstrating that different materials are necessary to meet the district's needs. (The remaining 30% of the funds may be spent on any materials that meet the state's legal compliance requirements. Districts are also permitted to use their own funds to purchase any materials that they select.)

The purpose of state adoption is to ensure that state funds are used for materials that are consistent with the state's curriculum guidelines, as set out in the frameworks for the subject areas. Critics have pointed out that some of the problems with current instructional materials can be traced to the adoption process. The fact that 22 different states develop different criteria for acceptance, including specifications of the content to be covered, has forced publishers to include ever-increasing numbers of topics and considerations. This has led to the practice of *mentioning*, treating many topics superficially rather than a smaller number of the most important topics in depth, and has resulted in textbooks that are encyclopedic collections of vocabulary that correspond to the content on every state's list. Local selection agencies have often exacerbated the situation by applying readability formulas that judge the reading level of the text by characteristics such as sentence length and vocabulary used, regardless of the actual readability of the material. The stress on readability formulas in content areas has favored choppy sentences and the evasion of appropriate vocabulary, especially in elementary science textbooks.

Most educators, including authors and editors, agree that *mentioning* and the use of readability formulas make it very difficult to produce good educational materials. These practices, however, are not inherent in the adoption process, and it may even be possible to use the adoption process to discourage such practices. California's State Board of Education has begun to use the adoption process as a way of supporting the curriculum reform reflected in its recent frameworks and standards. In 1985 the Board required science textbooks before they were accepted to be strengthened in certain topics that had been treated too superficially. In 1986 the Board required more substantial rewriting of mathematics books to align them better with the *Mathematics Framework.*

With recent English–language arts and history–social science instructional material criteria, the Board has also taken a leadership position; instead of selecting the best of what has been available, the Board has asked for improvements in what the publishers have offered.

These more stringent criteria place additional demands on publishers and teachers alike. In one situation the materials requested will be appropriate for the best prepared teachers in the state but will provide too great a challenge to the teachers who are

Table 10   Weighting of Criteria for Adoption of Instructional Materials

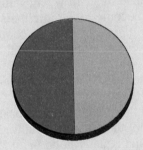

Content (50%)

1. Material discussed in Content sections is present (5%).
2. Material is treated accurately and correctly (15%).
3. Material is treated thematically (15%).
4. Depth of treatment is adequate (10%).
5. Emphasis is placed on how scientific knowledge is gained (5%).

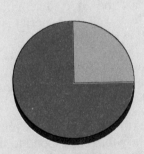

Presentation (25%)

6. Language is made accessible to students (5%).
7. Prose is considerate and engaging; scientific language is respected (10%).
8. Science is open to inquiry and controversy and is presented non-dogmatically (5%).
9. Science is shown as an enterprise connected to society (5%).

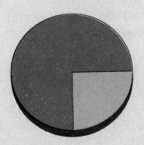

Pedagogy (25%)

10. Hands-on experience is emphasized; there is an explicit connection with real experience and problem-solving; textbooks and other materials are not the sole source of information (15%).
11. Instructional materials recognize cultural diversity (5%).
12. Assessment reflects experience, integration, and creativity (5%).

not so familiar with the content and instructional strategies advocated in the new frameworks. Almost everyone would agree that more staff development is necessary and that we may never have adequate resources to do the job. Clearly, staff development and instructional materials are intimately related, and staff development programs are essential to support the entire science program, as indicated in Chapter 7, Section C. Yet we feel that fine instructional materials can themselves instruct teachers while they support student learning. Further, improvement in instructional materials cannot afford to wait until such time as all of the teachers who will be using them are optimally prepared. With the view that improvements in science education must proceed on all fronts, including both staff development and instructional materials, we present the criteria in this chapter.

The instructional materials criteria that follow are different from past criteria in a number of ways. As Table 9 summarizes, the list is short and to the point.

Content is treated dynamically, including a thematic approach that makes connections among ideas and that values depth over breadth of coverage. These ideas are consistent with the national calls for change in science education, exemplified by the American Association for the Advancement of Science (AAAS) report, *Science for All Americans*, which suggests that we should teach less material, teach it better, and spend more time on it. The presentation of material should be open and engaging, with vocabulary used to facilitate understanding rather than as an end in itself. Finally, students must experience science as it is connected with real experience and problem solving, and the materials that support these experiences must be considered part of the basic program (i.e., in the 70 percent category).

Many of the criteria that follow address the particular issues of text. To some this will imply a text-based program. Although it is likely that many science programs will have a variety of print materials, including a basic textbook, this in no way is meant to discourage the use of other media such as film, videotape, and videodisk; software and other computer tools; specimens, equipment, and other objects; reference books, readers, glossaries, and other print material. In fact, criterion 10 explicitly calls for hands-on experiences to be integral (40 percent) to the science program.

Following the criteria, which will be used to guide the adoption process for kindergarten through grade eight materials at the state level, suggestions are offered to guide the local selection process.

The following three sections—on content, presentation, and pedagogy—develop the 12 criteria listed in Table 10.

Section B Content

CONTENT refers to the subject matter—how well it represents what is currently known of science; whether it uses themes to integrate information; whether it provides deep discussion of topics, integrating ideas and facts, instead of shallow, encyclopedic coverage of topics that become little more than defined terms; and whether it stresses how we come to know what we know in science and how scientists do their work.

In examining adopted materials for local selection, committees should assume that the state-adopted materials have satisfied minimal requirements for the quality of content. This is not the same as assuming that the content is optimal and equally good in all adopted materials. Local selectors are urged to read and examine printed materials and directed activities with an eye toward seeing how well the material is treated. One good approach is for an evaluator to choose a unit or several units with which he or she is most familiar and judge how well these materials meet the criteria explained here, as well as the needs of the students in a given district.

1

The topics discussed in Part II of this framework are treated in the instructional materials under consideration.

The three chapters on physical, earth, and life sciences give the broad outlines of a content curriculum in natural science. Not all possible topics are mentioned by name, nor does the vocabulary in these sections necessarily correspond to the vocabulary that appears in instructional materials of the corresponding grade level. However, the concepts given at particular grade levels in this framework should be treated at those levels in the instructional materials under consideration. For example, the concept of lithification (how rocks are formed) should be introduced in materials intended to discuss earth science in grades six through nine, and not earlier or later; but it is not necessary to use the term *lithification* in these grades.

Experienced educators and producers of instructional materials will note our relative deemphasis on the *presence* of content (5 percent). This is because we emphasize that it is more important to treat certain topics well and to integrate them with other concepts and ideas than it is to provide encyclopedic coverage. Consequently, we strongly recommend deemphasizing or eliminating checklists in selecting materials for local use. Rather than enumerating whether every topic is covered, it is more important to consider whether what is included is considered well, in detail, and accurately. We urge the use of qualitative rather than quantitative criteria when considering instructional materials for local adoption.

2

Content is treated accurately and correctly.

By accurately and correctly we mean that instructional material should present what is currently understood in science, not simply rehash traditionally covered materials. Content should also be presented as what is understood in science, not qualified with modifiers ("many scientists believe") when dealing with robust scientific conclusions.

Considerable improvement is needed in the validity of scientific content presented in instructional materials. In general, there are three classes of problems with the content in typical science materials. First, there are simple errors of fact (such as "most mutations are harmful," when it should state that the *effect* of most mutations on organisms is, in fact, neutral). These are generally easy to correct, but remain nagging problems if not corrected. Local selection committees are encouraged to contact the Mathematics, Science, and Environmental Education Unit of the Department of Education if they have questions about content presented in instructional materials under consideration.

Second, there are errors in interpretation. For example, the principle of uniformitarianism in earth science should not be presented as the "Law of Uniform Change" and interpreted as a doctrine that says that things now happen pretty much as they always have. (Uniformitarianism is nothing more than the operating principle that the laws of the universe have not changed since the beginning of time; but that differs from inferring constant rates of erosion, sedimentation, and so forth.)

Third, there are failures to integrate obviously related concepts, such as continental drift, changes in the fossil record of continents through time, and the genetic mechanisms that underlie changes in species through evolutionary history. It is as important to correct these kinds of errors as it is to correct the simplest error. The reason for this is explained in the next criterion.

3

Instructional programs should be organized around themes, not around facts.

The big ideas of science are what hold it together as a discipline, united in its methods and in the continuity of its evidence. Science programs no longer can be compilations of disjointed trivia, even if such compilations achieve high success in training students to pass standardized tests. Concepts and ideas should be integrated, and their connections made explicit, within and among chapters and units. Instructional programs should not be written or marketed as if the units in them could be presented in any order. That is unrealistic. Material in the later units of science programs should refer to material learned in previous units, because that is how science builds on itself— just as a person's education builds on itself. Statements like "Remember this concept from Chapter 4?" and "You will see how this fits into earth science in Chapter 11" are to be encouraged.

As one example, consider the parts of a flower: the sepals, petals, anthers, stamens, pistil, and so on. These can be taught in a perfectly straightforward and dry fashion, as a series of boldfaced terms to be memorized and labeled on a diagram. But in the context of a theme such as *structure and function*, or *evolution*, the student is able to realize that the facts fit into a larger picture; there is a reason for learning them, and the larger picture may even be interesting. Sepals and petals, for instance, look very similar and may arise from the same kinds of tissues. But sepals often support the flower, whereas petals often attract visually oriented pollinators such as bees and moths. The larger picture of *structure and function*, of *systems and interactions*, integrates the facts and makes them relevant.

As another example, consider the vital interrelationship of genetics, evolutionary biology, and the fossil record. In most science programs, there are separate units on these three topics. And in many such programs, no connection is made among the three. But the genetic code determines the development of the individual, which must survive to reproduce its genes in the next generation. As it does so, its genetic material combines with the genes of its mate to determine the composition of the next generation. Natural selection plays a vital part in the differential survival of these individuals, and it fosters the change in composition of populations that is the raw material of evolution. The track of evolution is seen not only in the living world but also through more than 600 million years of the fossil record. The succession of rock beds that encase these fossils and the geochemical means of determining their ages bring physics and chemistry back into the process of understanding the history of life, just as physics and chemistry form the basis of molecular biology of the gene.

No instructional program can be acceptable if it fails to treat these topics or fails to show their necessary interrelationship. The theme of evolution links all the disciplines necessary to the study of life. Even if genetics, evolutionary biology, and the fossil record are accorded separate units, their connection must be explicitly shown and cross-referenced in each supporting unit.

An important implication for the use of themes in instructional materials and curricula is that the component units of scientific curricula should be taught in a meaningful order, and this criterion will be of prime importance in evaluating instructional materials. Interconnections among ideas and concepts that span several subfields require knowledge of some concrete facts and some abstract concepts before others can be covered in a meaningful way. In designing curricula, attention must be paid to thematic development as facts and concepts are introduced, and this means that the order in which material

is presented is important. In the physical sciences, energy must be taught before the concepts of electricity, magnetism, and gravity are introduced. In the biological sciences, evolution must be explained before classification, because classification is based on evolutionary relationships. Then the diversity of life and its phylogenetic interrelationships can be treated.

It is stressed at several places in this framework, notably in Chapter 2, that the themes suggested and developed here are not to be regarded as rigid. There are many other possible configurations of thematic ideas besides those suggested here. What is important is that some thematic strands be selected and incorporated in the presentation of science in all curricula.

4

Instructional materials in science should emphasize depth of understanding, not encyclopedic breadth of coverage.

Textbooks should not be encyclopedic. No textbook can cover the entire discipline and do it well. Instead, instructional materials should take a major theme or several major themes or strands and interweave them into a logical and coherent exposition of the discipline under study. This criterion has some direct implications for the adoption of instructional materials and for the assessment of student performance.

It is dismaying that checklists are often the principal way in which content is assessed. The coverage of concepts, terms, and subjects, when measured by checklists, produces instructional objectives connected in prose. *Mentioning* or defining a topic does not *cover* it, and even covering it, regardless of the length at which it is covered, does not ensure meaningful or readable prose. Often, it ensures only an opportunity to insert more definitions and mentions. These counterproductive criteria of the adoption process drive the engine of mediocrity and make dictionaries of textbooks. We urge local selection agencies to eliminate quantitative criteria for the assessment of instructional materials and to focus on qualitative evaluation of the coverage of key issues, fundamental concepts, and integration of ideas.

Clearly, a thematic orientation of textual material requires shortening or eliminating some material currently found in most instructional programs if textbooks are not to grow excessively large. But educators can be confident that a great deal of material in current curricula can be scrutinized and abridged or eliminated without detriment to the science program. This is discussed further in Chapter 2, The Major Themes of Science. Submitted instructional materials will not be penalized for omitting breadth of coverage in favor of depth and good integration of thematic lines.

5

Explanations should embroider the accumulation of knowledge, with a detailed description of how it is that we come to know these facts and why this information is important.

This approach is preferable to a recitation of trivia that is not particularly worth knowing outside any context. For example, in discussing the features of the seafloor, the author of a textbook might state:

> The land on the continents is primarily flat. There are also mountains and valleys. These features provide variability in the land. Similarly, the seafloor is like the surface of the land. Most of the seafloor is flat. Near the middle of the oceans, there are mountains and canyons. Here is where the seafloor is said to be spreading.

The author could have presented the information much better in this way:

> After World War I, scientists developed sonar, so that they could *see* objects under water by bouncing sound waves off them and picking up the echo. It had been assumed that the ocean bottom was largely flat, but when sound waves were bounced off the floor in the mid-Atlantic Ocean, they showed great mountains and chasms. This is where the seafloor is spreading.

The relief features of the surface of the continents, described in the first passage, should be fairly obvious to most students. Teachers are eminently capable of filling in the context by contrasting the familiar (surface features on land) with the unfamiliar (surface features of the ocean floor). It makes more sense to use available space to tell them what they do not already know and to motivate them by showing them how discoveries are made.

Section C Presentation

PRESENTATION means how science is described, organized, written, and illustrated.

6

Language must be made accessible to students.

As discussed in Chapter 6, Section J, students with limited proficiency in English must not be excluded from the study of science until such time as they are proficient in English. Teachers' editions and reference materials must suggest ways that instruction for limited-English-proficient (LEP) students can be made comprehensible to them, age appropriate, and at a level commensurate with their academic ability and training. Providing editions in the primary language of the LEP students is one way of giving them access to the curriculum. Providing glossaries and summaries of key concepts in the primary language of these students is another way. The five largest language groups among LEP students in California, in rank order, are Spanish, Vietnamese, Chinese, Cambodian, and Pilipino.

7

The prose style of instructional materials should be considerate and engaging, and the language and vocabulary of science should be respected.

Too often, the selection of instructional materials is subjugated to constricting, destructive readability formulas, with no consideration for student interest or the liveliness of prose. Just as important, the way in which scientific terms are used, particularly those that relate to science as a method of inquiry, are distorted. Consequently, students never really learn what science is, or how it differs from other kinds of inquiry, and how its terminology reflects this.

(a) *Lively, Engaging Style.* Instructional materials should be written in a lively, engaging style (referred to as *considerate text*), rather than in choppy prose driven by readability formulas, or in a passive voice that talks down to the reader in a manner that creates passivity and boredom. It is dismaying that readability indices, some of which use vocabulary lists outmoded decades ago, are still dominating determinations of grade-level suitability. For many years it was popular to argue that content-area materials should be written one or two grade levels below ordinary reading levels to avoid frustration. This is particularly disabling in content subjects, because usually some number of new and unfamiliar words must be learned in order to manipulate concepts and ideas easily, and many of these words are polysyllabic. But if a readability computation on a typical issue of *Spiderman Comics* yields a twelfth grade reading level, are we to assume that the nine-year-old who sits enthralled with the book is not understanding it?

Readability formulas are injurious to publishers and, by extension, to students. Formulas force publishers into what can be called a maximum-minimum bind; that is, they are obliged to use technical terms and so must compensate for their effect on readability formulas by using only very simple words and short sentences in the rest of their prose. No one benefits from this situation. Children, like adults, are motivated to read what interests them. If the prose is sufficiently interesting and the illustrations effective and appropriate, we need not underestimate the potential interest of students. An engaging narrative prose style can overcome the stultifying effect of readability formulas.

If text does not read well, it will probably not engage its readers. Try this exercise: read passages from a textbook aloud to yourself, to colleagues, and to students. You will know from their expressions whether this book is effective in its prose style. If, as in one recent junior high life science book, the authors require five sentences to convey to the student that trilobites, mammoths, and sabertooth cats are extinct, the prose is probably not particularly engaging. Students who are old enough to be taught science are old enough to appreciate good narrative style and probably prefer Nancy Drew and the Hardy Boys to *The Cat in the Hat*. Therefore, textbooks should be written as explanations of discovery, not as primers.

(b) *Respect for Language and Students*. Instructional materials should respect the language of

science and should respect the intelligence of students. Modifiers such as "Some scientists believe" and "Many scientists agree" present science as a consensus activity. Rather, textbooks should emphasize the fact that scientists base their conclusions on data, which are valid at a given point. We have taken up this issue in Section B of this chapter and in Chapter 1. We restate it here in a form that applies to the construction of vocabulary in science materials.

(c) *Vocabulary*. Vocabulary should not be a main focus of text. Books that contain an inordinate number of boldfaced or italicized words may be more intent on defining these words than on explaining and relating the concepts to which they are germane. More than likely, such textbooks emphasize the memorization of terms at the expense of understanding and integrating ideas. Textbooks should emphasize vocabulary development only when the terms introduced add to the abilities of students to understand concepts and communicate about the subject. Vocabulary loads should not occupy space better devoted to other, more meaningful scientific inquiry. It is less important to know the names of the three kinds of rocks than it is to understand how rocks are formed and how this came to be understood.

Consider, for example, the following sample passage on levers:

> A bar that is used for a lever always turns on a fixed point called a fulcrum. The fulcrum is the spot where the lever is held in place as it moves. The fulcrum placement determines exactly how the lever works. When a bar, used as a lever, has the fulcrum between the effort exerted and the object to be moved, it is called a first-class lever. A second-class lever has the object between the effort and the fulcrum. A nutcracker is a second-class lever. When the lever action is between the resistance and the fulcrum, it is referred to as a third-class lever. A shovel is considered a third-class lever.

The terms *lever, fulcrum, effort,* and *object* are arguably necessary terms to communicating ideas about the transmission of force. But what is the purpose of this passage other than to taxonomize various forms of a simple tool? When are various classes of levers useful or necessary? Why are some nutcrackers second-class levers while others are first-class levers? Is a shovel always a third-class lever, or can it also be a first-class lever? Which class of lever requires the most force, and why would anyone want to use a third-class lever, anyway?

(d) *Glossaries.* The glossaries of instructional materials often misuse scientific vocabulary. Often, nouns are defined as if they were verbs; and verbs, as if they were adjectives; and the phonetic pronunciations supplied are both incorrect and phonically inconsistent with the standard practices of diction. These deficiencies are signs of a slipshod text. More important, however, definitions of terms given in glossaries should not merely paraphrase the sentences in the text in which these terms appear. (That is what an index is for.) A student will not be enlightened by finding an unfamiliar term with an inadequate description in the text, then by looking it up in the glossary find the same words but rearranged. Those who select instructional materials will find it instructive to spend some time with the glossaries of materials under review.

(e) *SI Metric System.* The metric system is used by scientists for units of measurement because of its simplicity in calculations and its international acceptance. Traditional units of measure, however, may be more familiar to many students and thus easier for them to use and understand. Although students should gradually become familiar with the metric system, it is more important for them to understand concepts of measurement than to memorize unfamiliar terms primarily because they are more accepted in the scientific community. Thus, instructional materials should reflect the use of measurement units that will be likely to be understood by students. At the appropriate pedagogical levels, students should be introduced to scientific practices and conventions of measurement as well as to the reasons why these practices and conventions are favored (e.g., ease of calculating in a decimal system; international acceptance).

(f) *Corruptive Euphemism.* One of the most disturbing features of current instructional materials is the practice of what could be called *corruptive euphemism.* This is the use of one word, usually a weaker pseudosynonym or a word with more neutral value in a social context, as a substitute for the genuine scientific term or concept.

Some corruptive euphemisms are used to accommodate readability formulas. The law of uniformitari-anism, already mentioned as an example, is frequently garbled as "the law of uniformity" or, worse yet, "the law of uniform change," which is precisely *not* what uniformitarianism is about. (Uniformitarianism is a statement that the natural laws of the universe have always been in effect, not that rates and processes have always been the same.) In this example, the corruptive euphemism distorts and confuses the science that it is supposed to present in the service of inappropriate prescriptions of grade-level suitability.

Other corruptive euphemisms occur in the context of historically sensitive terms. For example, some textbooks use the term *development*, which refers specifically to an individual's growth from one-celled stage to adult, as a false synonym for *evolution* in an effort to avoid the social repercussions that the word evolution evokes from some individuals. This practice is reprehensible. The only way that publishers will be freed of this practice is for the correct terms to be specified in frameworks, and for the use of weak or invalid alternative terms to be discouraged.

A third kind of corruptive euphemism involves what might be called *special* science. Frequently, one encounters a passage in a textbook such as, "Desalination of seawater is done with special equipment," with no further explanation. What does the word *special* mean in that sentence? It means, perhaps, the same as *magic*, a word that may as well have been substituted for it. It means, perhaps, "You're not smart enough to understand this," and so the intelligence of the student is insulted. Why, then, include the concept of desalination at all? Or perhaps the use of the term *special* in that sentence means that the author of the text could not find a way to explain it to the audience, could not explain it with terms that would fit readability formulas, or did not have the necessary space in the text to do so. The word *special* has no particular scientific meaning, and it should never be used in a text to substitute for an explanation.

Teachers and other selectors of instructional materials at the local level are encouraged to monitor closely the materials submitted for their consideration. We have provided here only a sample of the faults of presentation frequently encountered in textbooks and other materials. We suggest that a close critical reading of submitted materials, with these ideas in mind, may help to discriminate among possible choices. We also suggest asking students themselves how the books *read* to them.

8

The character of science must be represented faithfully. This means that it must be shown as open to inquiry, open to controversy, and nondogmatic by its nature.

These particulars are explained in the paragraphs that follow.

(a) *The Nature of Science.* Instructional materials should explain and exemplify the nature of science as a form of inquiry and understanding. For a full explanation and examples of what this means, see Chapter 1, The Nature of Science. We stress here that this understanding is not to be roped off in an introductory chapter but is to be integrated thoroughly in the narrative of the text. The scientific method is not a monolithic formula that can be reduced to hypothesis-materials-methods-observations-conclusions. Instead, examples of how scientists investigate problems—examples that delineate the processes, successes, and limitations of science—should appear in every chapter.

(b) *Controversy in Science.* Instructional materials should encourage responsible, science-based discussion of controversial or contentious issues. Science should be portrayed as a vital, changing endeavor with controversy and competing lines of intellectual discussion—not as a sterile, dogmatic discipline in which facts are known and approaches are agreed on. The historical growth of science should be reflected in controversy.

This desideratum must be explained carefully. History is usually written by the winners, but science that survives does so because ideas and findings have withstood constant further inquiry. In science, it is not the struggle of individuals against individuals that matters, but of ideas and evidence against competing ideas and evidence. Controversies in science should be presented as matters of evidence, not of personalities. Historical figures are not to be trotted out simply to show the faults and quaintness of earlier workers. An example of this is Lamarck, whose theory of evolution predated and was challenged by Darwin's. Students are often presented with simplified explanations of Lamarck's ideas but are seldom shown what work was done to falsify them. This is a disservice. It presents not the resolution of controversy but the supplanting of apparently archaic ideas. That is not how science works.

Above all, in discussing scientific controversies, attention should be focused on the weight of evidence. There are nearly always certain facts and observations that can be interpreted in a light different from prevailing theories. The evidence of our human senses, for example, would suggest that the simplest explanation of the patterns of night and day is that the sun, like the moon, goes around the earth. And indeed, it is difficult for the average person to refute this inference. But the weight of evidence does not accord with it, and undue significance should not be given to isolated facts or inferences in responsible classroom instruction and instructional materials. Specific examples of controversial issues in science and how they should be treated are given in Chapter 1, Section E, Social Issues in Science.

(c) *Understanding, Not Dogmatism.* Instructional materials should not be dogmatic or selectively dogmatic. The thrust of the text should direct the student toward inquiry rather than conclusions. Science should not be presented as a corpus of settled dogma or authoritarian statements. It should be shown to be authoritative, but not authoritarian, and constantly self-correcting (again, see Chapter 1, Section C, Teaching "What Science Is").

Moreover, sensitive issues in science, that is, those with some social relevance or controversy, should not be roped off as conjectural or as matters of opinion. Certainly, some issues connected with science are controversial, but that does not mean that the science itself is controversial. The implications of issues on which science bears are complex matters of public policy and cultural interpretation, but this has no bearing on the science itself. Furthermore, no instructional materials should ever convey the impression that science itself is a matter of guesswork, belief, or opinion.

We repeat here the fundamental conviction of this framework: Education does not compel belief; it seeks to encourage understanding. Nothing in science, or in any other field, should be taught dogmatically. But teaching about something does not constitute advancing it as truth. In science, there is no truth. There is only knowledge that tests itself and builds on itself constantly. This is the message that students should take away with them.

9

Science should not be presented as an enterprise operating in isolation from society and technology or from other fields of knowledge.

Technological advances are based on fundamental science, including a proper appreciation of the philosophy and methods of science. Integration of science and technology, where appropriate, is part of any good science program.

As a corollary, emphasis on recent advances in science should be mandatory in every science program. For example, discoveries of Mendel and Darwin are important to explain, but the sciences of genetics and evolution have made considerable progress since the mid-1800s. Students should be presented with these advances so that they can understand the intellectual vibrance of these fields and the ways in which science progresses, always testing and building on what has gone before with new ideas, new techniques, and new evidence.

In the same way, science should be explicitly integrated with other disciplines, especially the linguistic, historical, and mathematical fields. It should not be seen as an isolated discipline estranged from other fields of inquiry, such as the arts and health. The etymology of scientific words, the accounts made by scientists of their own discoveries and of their times, and the applications of mathematics and of numerical organization of information to scientific investigations are all examples of vitally important features of a good science curriculum.

Section D Pedagogy

PEDAGOGY refers to the instructional methods that are employed. We stress several goals here. First, hands-on experience should be emphasized, and both printed materials and activities should be related to real experiences. Second, the textbooks and other instructional materials should not be the sole sources of information for the students. Third, assessment of learning should go beyond the level of recall and paraphrased recall to include assessment of how students can use the concepts learned and relate them

to other concepts. Assessment should also take a variety of forms, including activities, journals, recorded observations, problem solving, and portfolios of accomplished work.

10

Instructional programs must be connected with experience.

There are four major features by which instructional materials should be evaluated in the context of this criterion.

(a) *Student Involvement.* Instructional materials should involve students in science through problem solving and decision making. Programs should encourage active learning on the part of students in which they are actively engaged in the *doing* of science, rather than treating students as passive learners, the empty vessels into which accumulated knowledge is poured. Part of this approach is to use hands-on, manipulative experimental materials to solve problems. This approach is canonical in most science curricula at the present time, so we do not expect this criterion to be regarded as revolutionary. We do support the goal of increasing hands-on time in science classes to at least 40 percent of the total devoted to teaching science, and instructional programs should reflect this goal.

There is considerable pedagogical benefit in having students repeat experiments or investigations that have become part of the basic understanding of science—such as manipulating the conditions of water, soil, and light under which bean plants grow. Most students could understand the conditions that produce the best growth in plants simply by having them explained verbally. But actually performing the manipulations validates and internalizes these ideas and makes them vivid to the student.

Experiment can also stimulate further inquiry of a more open-ended sort. (What happens if I plant marigolds and beans together?) Instructional materials should suggest further investigations that can be carried out in order to take the basic questions a step further, not just to perform variations on a theme. In addition, instructional materials can show students how the kinds of experiments they are carrying out have led to advances in science and technology. (For example, farmers rotate certain crops so as not to deplete minerals in the soil; some plants used in this way, such as clover, actually return vital nitrogenous compounds to the soil.) Instructional materials should encourage students to explore the "what if?" questions that lead to creative, integrated, and applied learning.

The teacher's edition of instructional materials is often the best place to suggest open-ended, hands-on inquiries and activities that can motivate student interest and learning. Districts should encourage science supervisors and curriculum developers to emphasize hands-on units and activities in working with classroom teachers. Administrators should provide and encourage the use of release time for teachers to attend in-service training designed to familiarize teachers with hands-on approaches to science teaching. Elementary and middle school teachers should be encouraged in this effort as much as junior and senior high specialist teachers.

(b) *Interdisciplinary Approach*. Scientific discoveries should be presented in the social, political, and historical contexts in which they took place, much as they are treated in the *History–Social Science Framework*. Vaccines and medical advances have historically been developed in the context of a dire social need for them at a particular time and place. Darwin worked out his theory of natural selection because, although the fact of evolution was generally accepted by scientists of his time, a mechanism for change in the species of organisms through time was still needed. Kepler worked out an elliptical model of the orbits of the planets around the sun because he could not make any circular model fit the observations available to him. The understanding of mechanics of the solar system was central to the natural philosophy of Renaissance knowledge on which so much intellectual, political, and cultural philosophy depended. The agricultural research that resulted in the Green Revolution of the 1970s was stimulated by an impending crisis in the world's supply of food—just as a tragically misguided effort, headed by Lysenko in the USSR from the 1930s through the 1950s, was designed to meet increasingly ominous food shortages in the Soviet Union at that time. Nearly every technological tool has an important historical and social context that was vital to its development. Even the familiar microwave ovens of our kitchens today are the by-products of the need to develop better radar facilities during World War II.

By bringing out these historical, cultural, and social aspects as the context of scientific discoveries, the writers of instructional materials can show students that science is put to work for people, that research is stimulated because of real needs of real people, and that discoveries in science help us to make informed decisions about the critical problems that face humanity.

For example, many instructional programs on the environment have units in which conservation of natural resources is encouraged and waste is deplored. These are commendable. However, to be comprehensive with respect to the scientific side of conservation issues, instructional materials should provide students with tables of estimates of representative nonrenewable natural resources (coal, oil, aluminum, and so forth), together with estimated rates of depletion. Students should also understand how long it takes typical waste materials, such as glass, paper, styrofoam, and aluminum and steel cans, to degrade in the environment. For a hands-on component, they should be encouraged to measure the use of nonrenewable resources and energy sources by themselves, their families, and their schools. They should calculate the amount of yearly use by their community or region and compare this to the use of such resources by other communities or cultures, and to the estimates of remaining stores of these nonrenewable resources. Only then will students be able to make informed decisions as adult citizens about some of the scientifically based issues that will face them in their daily lives. Instructional materials should encourage and suggest to teachers the possibilities of including people from the community to provide information, insight, and bases for discussion of "real-world" problems connected with scientific knowledge.

(c) *Meaningful Activities*. Activities must be meaningful and integrative, not simply based on recall. Activities in science textbooks and supplemental materials frequently do not help teachers and students to internalize and manipulate the concepts and evidence presented in the units. Role-playing games and arts and crafts projects may be fun and are intrinsic to some kinds of learning, but in the context of most of the ideas in which they are commonly employed in textbooks, they are irrelevant. "Make a model of the Grand Canyon," suggested one textbook to eighth graders. And how many years would that take? More significantly, what is a student supposed to learn from this exercise? The textbook provided no clue.

Rather than have students make casts and molds of leaves and shells each year from the third through the eighth grade, it would be more useful to explore the preservation of fossil remains by leaving chicken bones in different kinds of local environments and checking on them every few days until differential deterioration becomes noticeable. Rather than have students imagine how many carnivores and herbivores can coexist in an imaginary ecosystem, teachers should bring well-done films on actual ecosystems into class, thereby increasing motivation, experience, and basis for discussion. Such resources are readily available, and publishers need to find and list them in their teachers' resources, instead of the repetitious, unimaginative works that often constitute such recommendations. (For suggestions, contact the Mathematics, Science, and Environmental Education Unit of the Department of Education.)

As an underpinning to this recommendation, the materials and supplies (apart from expendable materials that need periodic replacement) necessary to instructional programs should be considered part of the basic program eligible for expenditure under the 70 percent criterion of the State Board of Education. Basic instructional materials are those parts of a program without which the program could not be carried out effectively. In a program devoted in large part to hands-on activities, which is the goal of this criterion of the framework, such materials would include experimental and other equipment and supplies used in student participation and teacher demonstrations, in addition to print and electronic media that are fundamental parts of the curriculum. If a concept or unit cannot be taught in the program under consideration without a given piece of equipment (whether printed, electronic, or manipulable), it is considered necessary to the instructional program and should qualify for the 70 percent funds.

(d) *Variety of Resources.* Textbooks and other provided instructional materials should not be the sole sources of information for the student. As stated above, instructional materials should not be encyclopedic in their coverage, nor can they possibly be expected to satisfy all of a student's curiosity. Part of good education is to teach and encourage students to seek supplementary resources. Instructional programs will be most useful when they do this conscientiously and effectively. This means that reading lists, activities, and chapter reviews should be more creative, appropriate, and conscientiously constructed.

Great improvement is needed in the suggestions for further reading at the end of a chapter or unit in most current instructional programs. Typical suggestions in current instructional materials frequently list outdated, nonauthoritative, or relatively inaccessible sources. These features of instructional programs appear to promise much, but generally are not very helpful to teachers. Publishers and adoption committees should work with content area experts to find better treatments that explain and expand topics in the chapters and that are engaging in their prose style to students and (for teachers' editions) teachers alike. These would also be of great use to school librarians.

Instructional materials could be greatly improved by the inclusion of first-person accounts of scientific discoveries and the excitement of science. There are many classic examples ranging from Beaumont's study of the stomach processes of a wounded trapper; to Darwin's account of his discoveries on board the H.M.S. *Beagle*; to Richard Feynman's stories of building a crystal radio set as a child, picking the locks at Los Alamos National Laboratories, and discovering how a flaw in construction of the O-rings destroyed the Challenger spacecraft. Such accounts could be framed in a few paragraphs in a "box" typical of features now present in all textbooks. Original source materials are vital to conveying the understanding and excitement of science. And, as noted in *Eyeopeners!* reading levels should not be assumed to be a problem; good books are ageless.[2]

11

Instructional materials must recognize cultural diversity and reflect strategies that research and practice have shown to be successful in meeting the needs of *all* students.

Many of the suggestions in Chapter 6 that are designed for all students are especially important for students from groups historically underrepresented in advanced science courses. Because it is imperative that culturally different students succeed in science education, this criterion emphasizes the pedagogical techniques that enable them to be successful:

(a) *Current Research.* Instructional practices based on current research on cultural learning styles should

---

[2]Beverly Kobrin, *Eyeopeners!* New York: Penguin Books, 1988.

be included in the content of teachers' manuals and integrated in the design of the students' materials.

(b) *Learning Goals.* The full range of learning goals, including the processes of science and applied problem solving, must be part of the program for every student.

(c) *Relevance.* Connections with student experience are made in several ways. First, teachers must be given suggestions of ways to bring the students' environment and experience into the classroom so that it connects in a meaningful way with the activities that take place there. Second, the program should provide activities in the classroom so that all students have a common experiential base. The more that the knowledge and processes are relevant in the students' everyday life, the more likely they will be able to learn them.

(d) *Successful Instructional Practices.* Successful instructional practices are incorporated. Active endeavors are more successful than passive ones. Thus, hands-on experiences are particularly important for students from diverse backgrounds. Heterogeneous, cooperative groups are particularly effective with students of varied language backgrounds and achievement levels who are working toward a common instructional goal. Other successful practices include an integrated curriculum that emphasizes depth over breadth and a multidimensional program that uses a variety of teaching methods.

(e) *Reasoning, Not Drill.* Certain practices have been shown to discourage students and to distance them from school. These include excessive drill and practice and pressure to get one right answer. Programs that allow for reflective thinking value a student's reasoning more than a single and quick right answer and provide for informal group work; such programs are to be encouraged.

12

Assessment should be integrative and oriented toward solving problems, not simply recall-based.

Reviews of chapters should expand on the text's presentation, not just repeat its lessons and drill students in its minutiae. These failings characterize textbooks that are little more than dictionaries; a real textbook with good narrative prose and true exposition of ideas and concepts should elicit much more creative and intellectually fruitful exercises at the conclusions of units. Questions at the ends of chapters should be less regurgitative and more integrative, pulling together the themes that should be woven into the chapters. The standard response in a teachers' edition, "Answers may vary," is not particularly helpful for teachers.

There are many ways to assess student performance. Objective tests measure recall and some integration of facts, ideas, and concepts. In a largely hands-on curriculum, other more creative tools of assessment are necessary. Problem solving, particularly solving real-world problems, involve not only recall but also integration of ideas and creativity of solutions. These means may be more appropriate for activity-oriented curricula. For example, in learning the basic methods of designing scientific experiments, students may want to test rival claims of laundry detergent manufacturers. A real-world test would have to take into consideration variables such as type of clothing, amount of detergent, water temperature, and so forth. Organizing students in pairs or teams can add to the creativity and stimulate much animated intergroup discussion.

Written work, particularly when not limited by the time and response constraints of a classroom test situation, can provide deeper insights in the creative processes and integrated understanding of students. Projects and essays integrate writing skills and language arts concepts in the science curriculum and may be used to interface with those disciplines where nonfiction literature is encouraged. Students should be encouraged to assemble portfolios of their work in a science class, including class exercises, team work, reports on activities, creative projects, designs for experiments, and observational accounts of their results. By varying the format of assessment, teachers can assess and appreciate the varied abilities of all students, and they can better plan how to help individual students improve their abilities in a variety of contexts.

It is dismaying that curricula in science are so largely driven by student performance on standardized tests. Teachers are thus forced to *teach to* the end-of-year evaluations or institutionalized examinations. There is no doubt that these tests measure something, but what? Too often, the memorization of minutiae can ensure at least above average performance of a student population profile. It is arguable that an ineffective teacher can remain undetected without such monitors. But standardized tests can only poorly evaluate philosophical understanding, creativity, originality, and competence in approaching problems—to say nothing of the individual's ability to express himself or herself on subjects. Publishers are forced by these criteria to cram into their textbooks and other materials even more trivia, boldfaced terms, and jargon useful only for their own sake. We suggest that if standardized tests are to be used at all, that their results be scrutinized with care and put into perspective against other indicators of learning and teaching effectiveness.

Section E Local Considerations

THE criteria in the preceding section will guide the Instructional Materials Evaluation Panel (IMEP), a group of approximately 40 teachers, curriculum specialists, and scientists who will review the materials submitted for adoption and submit their recommendations to the Curriculum Development and Supplemental Materials Commission (CDSMC), that will in turn make recommendations to the State Board of Education. Once the State Board has adopted the materials for science, local districts and schools are faced with the challenge of making selections from that adopted list. Local reviewers should have the following things in mind as they evaluate materials:

1. Be aware of the criteria used in and the results of the state-level adoption process. Reports from the IMEP's review are displayed at the Instructional Materials Display Centers (IMDC) in conjunction with the adopted materials, and a report from the CDSMC is sent to every district. Those reports may allow reviewers to see the characteristics of materials that were judged similar and the ones that differed among programs. This will save time for the local panel, which can focus its attention on the reported differences.

2. Do not turn the content evaluation into a checklist. The thematic approach advocated in this framework should make the use of a checklist a frustrating experience, because ideas and topics are meant to be interwoven and connected, not necessarily listed under conventional chapter headings. Vocabulary should be hard to find in boldfaced definitions, because it should be used and defined in context. Indices to books make no distinction between a *mention* and an in-depth treatment of a concept, so to check the number of entries is a misleading exercise. Finally, a checklist is likely to penalize the authors who took a genuinely thematic approach and to reward those who presented material in a bulleted, point-by-point fashion.

3. Do not apply a readability formula to the text. As indicated in the introduction to this chapter, such formulas reward choppy sentences and frustrate communication. If reading level is an issue in the district or school, the suitability of the text should be determined by reading it aloud, or having a student of the appropriate grade level read it aloud or silently and answer questions. The textbook should not be the sole source of instruction; students should have a variety of hands-on and other experiences. Thus, the challenge posed by the reading level of the text should be put in the context of the rest of the curriculum and the proportion of time that students are actually expected to be reading.

4. Provide for students whose English is not yet proficient enough to understand instruction in English. This is a concern to an increasing number of California school districts. Provision of glossaries and summaries of key concepts for students whose knowledge of English is limited should be given extra weight in the local adoption process.

Section F Conclusion: Putting Criteria into Practice

WE conclude with some examples of what is and is not to be desired in science writing.

The first example is the type that might come from a passage that could appear at the end of a section on the "four main groups of reptiles." Crocodiles, turtles, lizards, and snakes would be presented, even though snakes are, in a phylogenetic sense, merely specialized lizards. No indication of the relationships of these reptile groups is given, and another living group, the sphenodontids, is omitted:

> Most life scientists believe that many reptile groups existed long ago. Their fossil remains indicate that these large dinosaurs that once existed were reptiles. Other reptile groups could have included species that dwelt in the oceans or flew. Science has still left undetermined why these organisms became extinct.

Of course, there is no reasonable doubt among scientists that "many reptile groups existed long ago," and fossil remains do more than "indicate" that dinosaurs were reptiles. Nor is it merely that other reptiles "could have" lived in the oceans or flown through the air. Yet, weasel-wording aside, the sterile text above has just managed to maul one of the scientific topics that excites children most: dinosaurs and other fossil reptiles. That passage could be greatly improved in many ways, including this one:

> The living groups of reptiles are only a shadow of the many groups of reptiles that have lived on the earth. Most of these are now extinct, but they reached the climax of their evolutionary history during the Age of Dinosaurs, which began over 200 million years ago. But fossil reptiles also include many swimming and flying species that were not dinosaurs. In fact, the earliest members of the living groups of reptiles arose at about the same time that the first dinosaurs appeared. What does that suggest to you about the extinction of the dinosaurs?

If the last two sentences are omitted, the length of the text is as long as the original passage. But the additional sentences could easily have fit on the original page in question. The new text was written, incorporating some of the ideas in criteria 2, 3, 4, 5, 7, and 8 discussed in this chapter.

A second example might appear in a junior high general science textbook:

> Fault zones can also be at a distance from the ends of crustal plates. Most geologists believe that the fault formation is related to plate motion. Movement of plates places stress on the rocks of the plate. When the stress has enough force, the rock breaks at the weakest spots. These cracks are considered faults.

This example, apart from the objectionable phrase, "Most geologists believe," is mainly deficient by virtue of its choppy sentence construction. Consider the following possible text:

> Not all faults are found at the edges of crustal plates. But maybe this should not be surprising. If you put a frozen chocolate bar in a vise and squeezed it, the chocolate might snap at many places along its length. Crustal plates are a bit like that chocolate bar: they receive stress on their edges, but they often release the energy of that stress in faults well away from their edges.

This rewritten version attempts to incorporate some of the ideas given in criteria 6, 7, and 10.

The third example describes the simultaneous discovery by Darwin and Wallace of the theory of natural selection (often erroneously equated with the theory of evolution). Here is how one text sample might explain the process of science:

> Alfred Wallace, a British biologist, was doing research in Malaya in 1858. He sent Charles Darwin a scientific article he was planning to publish. Darwin was astonished to see his ideas represented in Wallace's article. Wallace arrived at the identical conclusions as Darwin did. This occurs in science quite often where two scientists, working alone, make similar conclusions or discoveries.
>
> Both scientists reached the conclusion that different species of plants and animals were related. They found new species appearing and other species disappearing. New species came from old. However, new species exhibited different characteristics.
>
> Wallace and Darwin decided to present their findings to the world. Neither man had to have major credit. Both wanted to make their findings known everywhere. Their theory is referred to as the theory of evolution by natural selection. The theory demonstrates how slow, gradual changes in organisms occur over a period of years. Changes result from selection of those organisms best adapted to their surroundings.

The following rewrite avoids some of the misrepresentation of the case, as well as preserves the narrative style of the original text:

In 1858, Alfred Wallace, a British biologist, was studying the tropical fauna and flora of Malaya. Sick in his tent from malaria, Wallace thought about the amazing diversity of plants and animals he had seen. What processes could lead to such a range of different forms and adaptations? Wallace knew from his observations of tropical life that there was great variation in natural populations of plants and animals. He also knew that many more organisms are born than can survive to give birth to the next generation. The ones that survive, he concluded, must do so because they are better adapted to their environments. Only they will live to pass on their characteristics to the next generation.

Wallace wrote to Darwin about his discovery because he learned from a mutual friend that Darwin was exploring the same ideas. Darwin later reported in his autobiography how shocked he was at seeing his own ideas, on which he had been working for decades, presented to him by Wallace's distant hand. Darwin had been deliberately waiting to bring his ideas to the public until he could accumulate what he felt would be an undeniable mountain of evidence in favor of them. But now, he decided that he must publish his ideas immediately, and that the fairest thing to do would be to publish them together with Wallace. He did so, and their theory came to be known as natural selection.

The rewrite is a little longer, but it contains approximately twice as much information and presents events as we now understand them to have happened. There are also some differences corrected with respect to the facts of the case and the theory that was actually developed. It was written attempting to incorporate some of the ideas described above in criteria 2, 3, 4, 5, 6, 7, and 8.

These examples should not be considered in any way exceptional. The rewrites should in no way be regarded as definitive. They merely point out how much room there is for improvement on any typical page of any typical science textbook. Whether adoption agencies encourage publishers to make such improvements is a matter of future history, but without such improvements science education can be consigned to the oblivion of lists of trivia, memorization, and disjointed facts with no common thread.

In summary, the most important points made in this section are:

1. The desirability of thematic orientation in science curricula
2. The motivation and learning that can be generated by hands-on, experience-oriented activities and curricula
3. The importance of *considerate prose* and the elimination of readability formulas as determiners of grade-level appropriateness of curricular materials
4. The fundamental respect for scientific methods of inquiry and for the language and philosophy of science that is absolutely necessary to any adequate science program

Improvement in instructional materials, support for more in-service training for teachers, and the reevaluation and change in criteria commonly used in the adoption and selection of instructional materials are the principal means by which the current system of developing, adopting, and using instructional materials can meet the challenges of educating students about what science really is and how it can matter to their lives.

Significant Court Decisions Regarding Evolution/Creation Issues

1. *Edwards* v. *Aguillard* (1987) 482 U.S. 578, 55 U.S. Law Week 4860, 107 S. Ct. 2573, 96 L. Ed 2d 510. The U.S. Supreme Court invalidated as unconstitutional Louisiana's "Creationism Act," which prohibited the teaching of the theory of evolution in a public school unless accompanied by instruction in the theory of "creation science." The Court found that the Act impermissibly endorses religion by advancing the religious belief that a supernatural being created humankind. The term *creation science* embraces this religious teaching. Forbidding the teaching of evolution when creation science is not also taught undermines the provision of a comprehensive scientific education.

2. *Epperson* v. *Arkansas* (1968) 393 U.S. 97, 37 U.S. Law Week 4017, 89 S. Ct. 266, 21 L. Ed 228. The U.S. Supreme Court invalidated as unconstitutional an Arkansas statute that prohibited the teaching of evolution. The First Amendment to the U.S. Constitution does not permit a state to require that teaching and learning must be tailored to the principles or prohibitions of any religious sect or dogma.

3. *McLean* v. *Arkansas Board of Education* (1982) 529 F. Supp. 1255, 50 U.S. Law Week 2412. In this case the federal court held a balanced treatment statute to be in violation of the Establishment Clause of the U.S. Constitution. The Arkansas statute required public schools to give balanced treatment to creation-science and to evolution-science. The court found that the statute did not have a secular purpose. The court also found that the emphasis on origins of life as an aspect of the theory of evolution is peculiar to creationist literature. Although the subject of origins of life is within the province of biology, the scientific community does not consider origins of life part of evolutionary theory. The theory of evolution assumes the existence of life and is directed to an explanation of how life evolved. Evolution does not presuppose the absence of a creator or God.

4. *Segraves* v. *State of California* (1981) Sacramento Superior Court #278978. In this case Mr. Segraves contended that the California State Board of Education's *Science Framework* was dogmatic in its discussion of evolution and thus prohibited the free exercise of religion by himself and his children. The court found that the *Science Framework*, as written and as qualified by the antidogmatism policy of the State Board of Education, provided sufficient accommodation for the religious views of Mr. Segraves. That policy provided that, in a discussion of origins in science texts and classes, dogmatism be changed to conditional statements where speculation is offered as explanation for origins and that science emphasizes "how" and not "ultimate cause" for origins. The court directed the Board to make a widespread dissemination of the policy. In 1989 the policy was expanded to include all areas of science, not just those addressing issues of origins.

Education Code Sections of Special Relevance to Science Educators

Education Code sections that are of special significance to science educators appear below. Included are regulations pertaining to devices designed to protect the eyes, instruction in personal health and public safety, treatment of animals, requirements for graduation, and sex education courses.

32030. Duties Regarding Eye Protective Devices

It shall be the duty of the governing board of every school district, and of every county superintendent of schools, and of every person, firm, or organization maintaining any private school, in this state, to equip schools with eye protective devices as defined in Section 32032, for the use of all students, teachers, and visitors when participating in the courses which are included in Section 32031. It shall be the duty of the superintendents, principals, teachers or instructors charged with the supervision of any class in which any such course is conducted, to require such eye protective devices to be worn by students, teachers, or instructors and visitors under the circumstances prescribed in Section 32031.

32031. Courses in Which Devices to Be Used; Substances and Activities Dangerous to Eyes

The eye protective devices shall be worn in courses including, but not limited to, vocational or industrial arts shops or laboratories, and chemistry, physics or combined chemistry-physics laboratories, at any time at which the individual is engaged in, or observing, an activity or the use of hazardous substances likely to cause injury to the eyes.

Hazardous substances likely to cause physical injury to the eyes include materials which are flammable, toxic, corrosive to living tissues, irritating, strongly sensitizing, radioactive, or which generate pressure through heat, decomposition or other means as defined in the California Hazardous Substances Labeling Act.[1]

Activity or the use of hazardous substances likely to cause injury to the eyes includes, but is not necessarily limited to, the following:

1. Working with hot molten metal.
2. Milling, sawing, turning, shaping, cutting, grinding, and stamping of any solid materials.
3. Heat treating, tempering, or kiln firing of any metal or other materials.
4. Gas or electric arc welding.
5. Repairing or servicing of any vehicles, or other machinery or equipment.
6. Working with hot liquids or solids or with chemicals which are flammable, toxic, corrosive to living tissues, irritating, strongly sensitizing, radioactive, or which generate pressure through heat, decomposition, or other means.

32032. Standards for Devices

For purposes of this article the eye protective devices utilized shall be industrial quality eye protective devices which meet the standards of the American National Standards Institute for "Practice for Occupational and Educational Eye and Face Protection" (Z87.1—1968), and subsequent standards that are adopted by the American National Standards

---

[1] *Health and Safety Code* sections 28740 et seq.

Institute for "Practice for Occupational and Educational Eye and Face Protection."

32033.   Sale of Devices at Cost to Pupils and Teachers

The eye protective devices may be sold to the pupils and teachers or instructors at a price which shall not exceed the actual cost of the eye protective devices to the school or governing board.

32255.1.   Pupil with Moral Objection to Dissection or Otherwise Harming or Destroying Animals; Notice; Alternative Educational Project

(a) Except as otherwise provided in Section 32255.6, any pupil with a moral objection to dissecting or otherwise harming or destroying animals, or any parts thereof, shall notify his or her teacher regarding this objection, upon notification by the school of his or her rights.

(b) If the pupil chooses to refrain from participation in an education project involving the harmful or destructive use of animals, and if the teacher believes that an adequate alternative education project is possible, then the teacher may work with the pupil to develop and agree upon an alternate education project for the purpose of providing the pupil an alternate avenue for obtaining the knowledge, information, or experience required by the course of study in question.

(c) The alternative education project shall require a comparable time and effort investment by the pupil. It shall not, as a means of penalizing the pupil be more arduous than the original education project.

(d) The pupil shall not be discriminated against based upon his or her decision to exercise his or her rights pursuant to this chapter.

(e) Pupils choosing an alternative educational project shall pass all examinations of the respective course of study in order to receive credit for that course of study. However, if tests require the harmful or destructive use of animals, a pupil may, similarly, seek alternative tests pursuant to this chapter.

(f) A pupil's objection to participating in an educational project pursuant to this section shall be substantiated by a note from his or her parent or guardian. (*Enacted* 1988.)

51202.   Instruction in Personal and Public Health and Safety

The adopted course of study shall provide instruction at the appropriate elementary and secondary grade levels and subject areas in personal and public safety and accident prevention, including emergency first-aid instruction, instruction in hemorrhage control, treatment for poisoning, resuscitation techniques, and cardiopulmonary resuscitation when appropriate equipment is available; fire prevention; the protection and conservation of resources, including the necessity for the protection of our environment; and health, including venereal disease and the effects of alcohol, narcotics, drugs, and tobacco upon the human body.

51540.   Treatment of Animals

In the public elementary and high schools or in public elementary and high school school-sponsored activities and classes held elsewhere than on school premises, live vertebrate animals shall not, as part of a scientific experiment or any purpose whatever:

(a) Be experimentally medicated or drugged in a manner to cause painful reactions or induce painful or lethal pathological conditions.

(b) Be injured through any other treatments, including, but not limited to, anesthetization or electric shock.

Live animals on the premises of a public elementary or high school shall be housed and cared for in a humane and safe manner.

The provisions of this section are not intended to prohibit or constrain vocational instruction in the normal practices of animal husbandry.

51225.3.   Requirements for Graduation Commencing with the 1986-87 School Year

(a) Commencing with the 1986-87 school year, no pupil shall receive a diploma of graduation from high school who, while in grades 9 through 12, has not completed:

(1) At least the following numbers of courses in the subjects specified, each course having a duration of one year.

(A) Three courses in English.

(B) Two courses in mathematics.

(C) Two courses in science, including biological and physical sciences.

(D) Three courses in social studies, including United States history and geography; world history, culture, and geography; and American government, civics, and economics.

(E) One course in fine arts or foreign language.

(F) Two courses in physical education unless the pupil has been exempted pursuant to the provisions of this code.

(2) Such other coursework as the governing board of the school district may by rule specify.

(b) The governing board, with the active involvement of parents, administrators, teachers, and pupils, shall adopt alternative means for students to complete the prescribed course of study which may include practical demonstration of skills and competencies, supervised work experience or other outside school experience, interdisciplinary study, independent study, and credit earned at a postsecondary institution. Requirements for graduation and specified alternative modes for completing the prescribed course of study shall be made available to pupils, parents, and the public.

51550.   Sex Education Courses[1]

No governing board of a public elementary or secondary school may require pupils to attend any class in which human reproductive organs and their functions and processes are described, illustrated or discussed, whether such class be part of a course designated "sex education" or "family life education" or by some similar term, or part of any other course which pupils are required to attend.

If classes are offered in public elementary and secondary schools in which human reproductive organs and their functions and processes are described, illustrated or discussed, the parent or guardian of each pupil enrolled in such class shall first be notified in writing of the class. Sending the required

[1] References to related sections from the *Education Code* appear in the *Health Instruction Framework for California Public Schools*. Sacramento: California Department of Education, 1978, p. 68.

notice through the regular United States mail, or any other method which such local school district commonly uses to communicate individually in writing to all parents, meets the notification requirements of this paragraph.

Opportunity shall be provided to each parent or guardian to request in writing that his child not attend the class. Such requests shall be valid for the school year in which they are submitted but may be withdrawn by the parent or guardian at any time. No child may attend a class if a request that he not attend the class has been received by the school.

Any written or audiovisual material to be used in a class in which human reproductive organs and their functions and processes are described, illustrated, or discussed shall be available for inspection by the parent or guardian at reasonable times and places prior to the holding of a course which includes such classes. The parent or guardian shall be notified in writing of his opportunity to inspect and review such materials.

This section shall not apply to description or illustration of human reproductive organs which may appear in a textbook, adopted pursuant to law, on physiology, biology, zoology, general science, personal hygiene, or health.

Nothing in this section shall be construed as encouraging the description, illustration, or discussion of human reproductive organs and their functions and processes in the public elementary and secondary schools.

The certification document of any person charged with the responsibility of making any instructional material available for inspection under this section or who is charged with the responsibility of notifying a parent or guardian of any class conducted within the purview of this section, and who knowingly and willfully fails to make such instructional material available for inspection or to notify such parent or guardian, may be revoked or suspended because of such act. The certification document of any person who knowingly and willfully requires a pupil to attend a class within the purview of this section when a request that the pupil not attend has been received from the parent or guardian may be revoked or suspended because of such act.

Selected References

Aldridge, Bill G. "Essential Changes in Secondary Science: Scope, Sequence, and Coordination," *NSTA Reports!* (January, 1989) 66–74.

Burke, James. *Connections.* Boston: Little, Brown & Co., 1980.

Caught in the Middle: Educational Reform for Young Adolescents in California Public Schools. Sacramento: California Department of Education, 1987.

English–Language Arts Framework for California Public Schools. Sacramento: California Department of Education, 1987.

Enrichment Opportunities Guide: A Resource for Teachers of Students in Math and Science. Sacramento: California Department of Education, 1988.

Feynman, Richard P. *Surely You're Joking, Mr. Feynman!* New York: Bantam Books, 1986.

Feynman, Richard P., and Ralph Leighton. *What Do You Care What Other People Think? Further Adventures of a Curious Character.* New York: W.W. Norton, 1988.

Foreign Language Framework for California Public Schools. Sacramento: California Department of Education, 1989.

Gould, Stephen Jay. *The Panda's Thumb: More Reflections in Natural History.* New York: W.W. Norton, 1980.

Hammond Barnhart Dictionary of Science. Edited by Robert K. Barnhart. Maplewood, N.J.: Hammond, Inc., 1986.

Health Instruction Framework for California Public Schools. Sacramento: California Department of Education, 1978.

History–Social Science Framework for California Public Schools. Sacramento: California Department of Education, 1988.

Instructional Materials and Framework Adoption: Policies and Procedures. Sacramento: California Department of Education, Office of Curriculum Framework and Textbook Development, 1988.

Kobrin, Beverly. *Eyeopeners! How to Choose and Use Children's Books About Real People, Places, and Things.* New York: Penguin Books, 1988.

Mathematics Framework for California Public Schools. Sacramento: California Department of Education, 1985.

Miller, Jon D. "Who Is Scientifically Literate?" Paper presented to the 1990 Science Education Forum, American Association for the Advancement of Science.

Model Curriculum Standards, Grades Nine Through Twelve Sacramento: California Department of Education, 1985.

Moral and Civic Education and Teaching About Religion. Sacramento: California State Board of Education, 1988.

A Nation at Risk: The Imperative for Educational Reform. Washington, D.C.: U.S. Government Printing Office, 1983.

Quality Criteria for Elementary Schools: Planning, Implementing, Self-Study, and Program Quality Review. Sacramento: California Department of Education, 1990.

Quality Criteria for Middle Grades: Planning, Implementing, Self-Study, and Program Quality Review. Sacramento: California Department of Education, 1990.

Quality Criteria for High Schools: Planning, Implementing, Self-Study, and Program Quality Review. Sacramento: California Department of Education, 1990.

Resnick, Lauren. *Education and Learning to Think.* Washington, D.C.: National Academy Press, 1987 monograph.

Science Education for the 1980s. Sacramento: California Department of Education, 1985.

Science for All Americans. Washington, D.C.: American Association for the Advancement of Science, Inc., 1989.

Science for Children, Resources for Teaching. Washington, D.C.: National Academy Press, 1988.

Science Model Curriculum Guide, K–8. Sacramento: California Department of Education, 1988.

The Science Report Card. National Assessment of Educational Progress. Princeton: Educational Testing Service, 1988.

Science Safety Handbook for California High Schools. Sacramento: California Department of Education, 1987.

Statement on Preparation in Natural Science Expected of Entering Freshmen. Sacramento: The Academic Senates of the California Community Colleges, The California State University, and the University of California, 1986.

Technology in the Curriculum: Science Resource Guide (included in full package of six subject areas, diskettes, and updates). Sacramento: California Department of Education, 1986, 1987, 1988.

Temple, Robert. *The Genius of China: 3,000 Years of Science, Discovery and Invention.* New York: Simon & Schuster, 1986.

Visual and Performing Arts Framework for California Public Schools. Sacramento: California Department of Education, 1989.

Publications Available from the Department of Education

This publication is one of over 650 that are available from the California Department of Education. Some of the more recent publications or those most widely used are the following:

ISBN	Title (Date of publication)	Price
0-8011-0890-x	Bilingual Education Handbook: A Handbook for Designing Instruction for LEP Students (1990)	$4.25
0-8011-0862-4	California Education Summit: Background and Final Report (a set) (1990)	5.00
0-8011-0889-6	California Private School Directory, 1990	14.00
0-8011-0853-5	California Public School Directory, 1990	14.00
0-8011-0874-8	The Changing History–Social Science Curriculum: A Booklet for Parents (1990)*	5.00/10
0-8011-0867-5	The Changing Language Arts Curriculum: A Booklet for Parents (1990)*	5.00/10
0-8011-0777-6	The Changing Mathematics Curriculum: A Booklet for Parents (1989)*	5.00/10
0-8011-0856-x	English as a Second Language Handbook for Adult Education Instructors (1990)	4.50
0-8011-0041-0	English–Language Arts Framework for California Public Schools (1987)	3.00
0-8011-0849-7	Food Sanitation and Safety Self-Assessment Instrument for Child Care Centers (1990)	3.75
0-8011-0850-0	Food Sanitation and Safety Self-Assessment Instrument for Family Day Care Homes (1990)	3.75
0-8011-0851-9	Food Sanitation and Safety Self-Assessment Instrument for School Nutrition Programs (1990)	3.75
0-8011-0804-7	Foreign Language Framework for California Public Schools (1989)	5.50
0-8011-0824-1	Handbook for Teaching Cantonese-Speaking Students (1989)†	4.50
0-8011-0250-2	Handbook on California Education for Language Minority Parents-Chinese/English Edition (1986)**	3.25
0-8011-0712-1	History–Social Science Framework for California Public Schools (1988)	6.00
0-8011-0782-2	Images: A Workbook for Enhancing Self-esteem and Promoting Career Preparation, Especially for Black Girls (1988)	6.00
0-8011-0358-4	Mathematics Framework for California Public Schools (1985)	3.00
0-8011-0840-3	Price List and Order Form for Science Instructional Materials, 1990–1992 (1990)	2.50
0-8011-0368-1	Program Descriptions for Science Instructional Materials (1986)	2.50
0-8011-0886-1	Program Guidelines for Individuals Who Are Deaf-Blind (1990)	6.00
0-8011-0817-9	Program Guidelines for Language, Speech, and Hearing Specialists Providing Designated Instruction and Services (1989)	6.00
0-8011-0899-3	Quality Criteria for Elementary Schools: Planning, Implementing, Self-Study, and Program Quality Review (1990)	4.50
0-8011-0906-x	Quality Criteria for High Schools: Planning, Implementing Self-Study, and Program Quality Review (1990)	4.50
0-8011-0905-1	Quality Criteria for Middle Grades: Planning, Implementing Self-Study, and Program Quality Review (1990)	4.50
0-8011-0858-6	Readings for Teachers of United States History and Government (1990)	3.25
0-8011-0831-4	Recommended Literature, Grades 9—12 (1990)	4.50
0-8011-0863-2	Recommended Readings in Literature: Kindergarten Through Grade Eight, Addendum (1990)	2.25
0-8011-0745-8	Recommended Readings in Literature, Kindergarten Through Grade Eight, Annotated Edition (1988)††	4.50
0-8011-0870-5	Science Framework for California Public Schools (1990)	6.50
0-8011-0669-9	Science Safety Handbook for California High Schools (1987) (without binder)	5.75
0-8011-0668-0	Science Safety Handbook for California High Schools (1987) (with binder)	8.75
0-8011-0665-6	Science Model Curriculum Guide, K—8 (1988)	3.25
0-8011-0855-1	Strengthening the Arts in California Schools: A Design for the Future (1990)	4.75
0-8011-0846-2	Toward a State of Esteem: The Final Report of the California Task Force to Promote Self-Esteem and Personal and Social Responsibility (1990)	4.00
0-8011-0854-3	Toward a State of Esteem, Appendixes to (1990)	4.00
0-8011-0805-5	Visual and Performing Arts Framework for California Public Schools (1989)	6.00

Orders should be directed to:

California Department of Education
P.O. Box 271
Sacramento, CA 95802-0271

Please include the International Standard Book Number (ISBN) for each title ordered.

Remittance or purchase order must accompany order. Purchase orders without checks are accepted only from governmental agencies. Sales tax should be added to all orders from California purchasers.

A complete list of publications available from the Department, including apprenticeship instructional materials, may be obtained by writing to the address listed above or by calling (916) 445-1260.

*The price for 100 booklets is $30.00; the price for 1,000 booklets is $230.00.
†Also available at the same price, for students who speak Japanese, Pilipino, and Portuguese.
**The following editions are also available, at the same price: Armenian/English, Cambodian/English, Hmong/English, Japanese/English, Korean/English, Laotian/English, Pilipino/English, Spanish/English, and Vietnamese/English.
††Includes complimentary copy of *Addendum*, (ISBN 0-8011-0863-2).

88 78089

87-174 (03-0326) 78089 300 8-90